Collected Papers

I

PHAENOMENOLOGICA

COLLECTION PUBLIÉE SOUS LE PATRONAGE DES CENTRES
D'ARCHIVES-HUSSERL

11

ALFRED SCHUTZ

Collected Papers

I

Comité de rédaction de la collection:
Président: H. L. Van Breda (Louvain);
Membres: M. Farber (Buffalo), E. Fink (Fribourg en Brisgau),
J. Hyppolite † (Paris), L. Landgrebe (Cologne), M. Merleau-Ponty † (Paris),
P. Ricœur (Paris), K. H. Volkmann-Schluck (Cologne), J. Wahl (Paris);
Secrétaire: J. Taminiaux (Louvain).

ALFRED SCHUTZ

ALFRED SCHUTZ

Collected Papers

I

The Problem of Social Reality

EDITED AND INTRODUCED BY

MAURICE NATANSON

WITH A PREFACE BY

H. L. VAN BREDA

MARTINUS NIJHOFF / THE HAGUE / 1971

Third unchanged edition

**UNIVERSITY LIBRARY
GOVERNORS STATE UNIVERSITY**

ISBN 90 247 5089 x

© *1971 by Martinus Nijhoff, The Hague, Netherlands*
All rights reserved, including the right to translate or to
reproduce this book or parts thereof in any form

PRINTED IN THE NETHERLANDS

H
61
.S44
c.1
v.1

PREFACE

(ENGLISH TRANSLATION)

This volume brings together a series of studies that Alfred Schutz devoted to various questions centering around a major philosophical problem: the problem of sociality. Most of these studies have already been published elsewhere, but they have not always been easily accessible. In this volume we present the first part of what the author had intended to be a collection of the many essays he wrote after coming to the United States at the beginning of the last war. His disciple and friend Maurice Natanson was to be the editor of this volume. Death overtook Alfred Schutz before he saw his project realized. The successive publication of the collected essays, faithfully following the author's plans, is surely the most appropriate homage which we could offer to this scholar who was our friend and who, without the slightest doubt, deserves to occupy such an important rank in phenomenological thought – a rank which the dramatic circumstances of his life and his extreme personal modesty prevented him from occupying during his life-time.

I would like to speak of the man, to evoke the acumen of his mind, his penetrating irony, his serenity and courage in exile, the wide range of his interests, the gift of youthfulness and sympathetic understanding which enabled him to assimilate successfully a new culture at the age of forty and to become accomplished in it. Fearing to say too little and to say it inaptly, I limit myself to recalling his unceasing passion to understand man. Schutz was a philosopher, a psychologist, a sociologist, a musicologist: all of these approaches served that passion.

Born in Vienna in 1899, he studied law and the social sciences there under such famous scholars as Ludwig von Mises, Othmar Spann, Hans Kelsen, Friedrich von Wieser. In German academic

PRÉFACE

Le présent volume rassemble plusieurs études qu'Alfred Schutz avait consacrées à diverses questions qui gravitent autour d'un problème philosophique majeur: celui de la socialité. La plupart de ces études ont été publiées ailleurs, mais elles étaient dispersées et d'un accès parfois difficile. Tel quel, l'ouvrage que nous présentons n'est que la première partie d'un ensemble dans lequel l'auteur se proposait de faire réunir par son disciple et ami Maurice Natanson les nombreux essais qu'il avait écrits depuis son arrivée aux États-Unis au début de la dernière guerre. La mort l'empêcha de voir réaliser ce projet. Il nous a semblé que la publication successive de cet ensemble, dans la fidélité aux indications laissées par l'auteur, était le plus bel hommage que nous pussions rendre à ce penseur qui fut notre ami et méritait sans nul doute de tenir dans le courant phénoménologique une place de premier plan que faillirent lui refuser les circonstances dramatiques de sa vie, jointes à sa trop grande modestie personnelle.

Il me faudrait ici parler de l'homme, évoquer sa finesse d'esprit, son ironie pénétrante, sa sérénité et son courage dans l'exil, l'éventail très vaste de ses préoccupations, le don de jeunesse et de sympathie grâce auquel il entreprit à quarante ans d'assimiler avec bonheur une culture nouvelle, pour y exceller bientôt. Dans la crainte de dire trop peu et de le dire mal, je me borne à rappeler sa passion sans cesse renouvelée pour la connaissance de l'humain: philosophe, psychologue, sociologue, musicologue, Schutz était tout cela à la fois et toutes ces démarches en lui s'alimentaient à cette même passion.

Né à Vienne en 1899, il y avait fait des études de droit et de sciences sociales, sous la conduite de maîtres illustres, tels Ludwig

circles this was the period of methodological controversy concerning the *Naturwissenschaften* and *Geisteswissenschaften*. Dilthey, whose influence on German philosophy and sociology was profound, had shown that the knowledge of the human world and of historical cultures presupposes an understanding of certain significations immanent in life and that the apprehension of such significations differs radically from the causal explanations practiced in the physical sciences. Rickert followed with detailed analyses of this methodological difference. Then Max Weber developed the notion of sociology as a discipline which tries to unravel social and historical phenomena through the use of ideal types, that is, of essences pure in some way and actively created by the human mind. The methodological aspects of the sciences of man which were familiar to Schutz were thus circumscribed by the critique of naturalism, the reflection of conscious life on itself, the understanding of significations, ideation. Soon it became his aim to establish a rigorous philosophical foundation for these aspects and he pursued this ideal throughout his life. In the course of his investigation he was destined to encounter the phenomenology of Husserl. To found philosophically the understanding of meaning as actually employed and understood by social sciences, is to find its source in the life of consciousness itself. Schutz does not fail to observe the significance of Bergson and the return to the immediate data of consciousness and to the experience of inner time. But it was Husserl's theory of intentionality and his notions of intersubjectivity and of the *Lebenswelt* which were to guide Schutz's thought and to give it its specific character.

After twelve years of research he published his main work in 1932: *Der sinnhafte Aufbau der sozialen Welt: Eine Einleitung in die verstehende Soziologie*. In this work, fortunately republished recently, he undertook to trace the origin of categories peculiar to the social sciences in the fundamental facts of the life of consciousness, thus establishing a connection between Weber's *verstehende Soziologie* and Husserl's transcendental phenomenology.

Schutz dedicated a copy of his book to Husserl whom he had not yet met at that time. Husserl thanked him with words of

von Mises, Othmar Spann, Hans Kelsen, Friedrich von Wieser. C'était, dans les milieux universitaires germaniques, l'époque de la controverse méthodologique au sujet des *Naturwissenschaften* et des *Geisteswissenschaften*. Dilthey dont l'influence fut si grande sur la philosophie et la sociologie allemandes avait montré que l'intelligence du monde humain et des cultures historiques suppose la compréhension de certaines significations immanentes à la vie et que cette lecture immédiate du sens est radicalement différente de l'explication causale pratiquée par les sciences de la nature. Après lui Rickert avait analysé et précisé cette différence méthodologique. Enfin Max Weber avait imposé l'idée d'une sociologie compréhensive s'efforçant de déchiffrer les phénomènes sociaux et historiques à la lumière de certains types idéaux, ou d'essences en quelque sorte pures et activement forgées par l'esprit. Critique du naturalisme, réflexion de la vie sur elle-même, compréhension des significations, idéation, telles étaient les dimensions méthodologiques des sciences humaines auxquelles Schutz s'était familiarisé. Très vite et pour toute sa vie pensante son seul idéal fut de fonder ces dimensions philosophiquement et en toute rigueur. Dans cette recherche Schutz se devait de rencontrer la phénoménologie de Husserl. Fonder philosophiquement la compréhension du sens telle qu'elle est exercée et visée par les sciences sociales, c'est en retrouver la source dans la vie même de la conscience. Sur ce point Schutz ne manqua pas de saluer la pensée de Bergson, et le retour aux données immédiates de la conscience et à la durée vécue. Mais ce sont les notions husserliennes d'intentionnalité, d'intersubjectivité, et de *Lebenswelt*, qui allaient guider sa réflexion et lui conférer son allure propre.

Après douze ans de recherches, il publia en 1932 son maître ouvrage: *Der sinnhafte Aufbau der sozialen Welt. Eine Einleitung in die verstehende Soziologie*. Cet ouvrage, fort heureusement réédité aujourd'hui, visait à retrouver l'origine des catégories propres aux sciences sociales dans les faits fondamentaux de la vie de la conscience, et reliait en ce sens la sociologie compréhensive de Weber à la phénoménologie transcendantale de Husserl.

Schutz fit hommage d'un exemplaire de ce livre à Husserl, que jusqu'alors il n'avait pas encore rencontré. Celui-ci l'en remercia par de vifs éloges. Il lui écrivit notamment en date du 3 mai 1932:

praise. In a letter of May 3, 1932, Husserl wrote: "Ich bin begierig einen so ernsten und gründlichen Phänomenologen kennen zu lernen, einen der ganz Wenigen, die bis zum tiefsten und leider so schwer zugänglichen Sinn meiner Lebensarbeit vorgedrungen sind und die ich als hoffnungsvolle Fortsetzer derselben, als Repräsentanten der echten *Philosophia perennis*, der allein zukunftsträchtigen Philosophie ansehen darf." [1] On Husserl's invitation, Schutz went to Freiburg to join in investigations with a group of phenomenologists in whose work the founder of phenomenology placed much hope. Husserl appreciated the collaboration of the young philosopher and asked him to become his assistant. For personal reasons Schutz had to decline this offer, yet he continued to pay frequent visits to Freiburg and corresponded with Husserl until the latter's death.

The dialogue with Husserl's phenomenology remained at the center of Schutz's thought. The coming occupation by Nazi Germany forced him to leave Austria. He stayed in Paris for over a year, and then decided to emigrate to the United States, arriving there in July, 1939. Through the initiative of Marvin Farber he was asked to join in the establishment of the *International Phenomenological Society* and to become a member of the editorial board of *Philosophy and Phenomenological Research*, the journal published by the Society. He was appointed lecturer and later professor in the Graduate Faculty of Political and Social Science of the *New School for Social Research* in New York, where he found colleagues and friends who had also studied with Husserl, especially Dorion Cairns and Aron Gurwitsch. In this favorable environment he took up his investigations again and pursued them in a dialogue with American philosophy and sociology. His horizons had changed, the new culture provided him with new perspectives, yet the mainstream of his thought followed the same direction. It was always a matter of retracing the original constitution of the fundamental skeleton of the life-world which man takes for granted in the natural attitude and which the social scientist rarely makes thematic. In his last studies Schutz ap-

---

[1] "I am anxious to meet such a serious and thorough phenomenologist, one of the few who have penetrated to the core of the meaning of my life's work, access to which is unfortunately so difficult, and who promises to continue it as representative of the genuine *Philosophia perennis* which alone can be the future of philosophy."

"Ich bin begierig einen so ernsten und gründlichen Phänomenologen kennen zu lernen, einen der ganz Wenigen, die bis zum tiefsten und leider so schwer zugänglichen Sinn meiner Lebensarbeit vorgedrungen sind und die ich als hoffnungsvolle Fortsetzer derselben, als Repräsentanten der echten *Philosophia perennis*, der allein zukunftsträchtigen Philosophie ansehen darf." Sur l'invitation de Husserl, Schutz se rendit bientôt à Fribourg pour y participer à ce travail d'équipe dans lequel l'initiateur de la phénoménologie mettait tant d'espoir. Husserl apprécia la collaboration du jeune philosophe et lui proposa même de devenir son assistant. Pour des raisons personnelles, l'intéressé devait décliner cette offre, mais il fit de fréquents séjours à Fribourg et entretint avec Husserl une correspondance qui ne s'arrêta qu'à la mort du maître.

Mais le dialogue avec la phénoménologie husserlienne était au coeur de la pensée de Schutz et il allait demeurer la tâche centrale de sa méditation. Obligé de quitter l'Autriche qui allait être envahie par l'Allemagne nazie, Schutz s'installa pour plus d'un an à Paris, mais il prit bientôt la décision d'émigrer aux États-Unis où il arriva en juillet 1939. A l'initiative de Marvin Farber, il fut appelé à participer à la fondation de l'*International Phenomenological Society* et à siéger au comité de rédaction de la revue éditée par cette société : *Philosophy and Phenomenological Research*. Nommé conférencier, puis professeur à la *Graduate Faculty of Political and Social Science* de la *New School for Social Research* à New York, il y retrouva des collègues et des amis qui avaient été comme lui élèves de Husserl, notamment Dorion Cairns et Aron Gurwitsch. C'est dans ce milieu favorable qu'il reprit ses recherches, et les développa en les confrontant avec la philosophie et la sociologie américaines. Son horizon culturel avait changé, l'avait enrichi de vues nouvelles, mais le foyer de sa réflexion restait identique. Il s'agissait toujours de retracer la constitution originaire des articulations fondamentales du monde de la vie, que l'homme de l'attitude naturelle suppose acquises et que le savant aux prises avec la réalité sociale ne thématise guère. Peut-être à ce problème, qui est celui de la constitution, ses derniers travaux apportent-ils une réponse qui n'est plus celle de son premier ouvrage ? Après avoir tenté de dériver l'intersubjectivité à partir de l'Ego transcendantal, Schutz semble avoir

pears to have approached a new solution to this problem of constitution, and shifted the perspective of his first book. Having tried, at first, to derive intersubjectivity from the transcendental Ego, Schutz seems to have recognized the limitations of the egological perspective in encountering intersubjectivity as a primordial fact. But one may ask whether on this point, too, Schutz's thinking did not come very close to the final position of Husserl himself.

These are open questions. They speak for the relevance of Schutz's work to contemporary thought and they testify to his unwavering devotion to the ideals which shaped his life under the inspiration of Husserl.

May I express my profound gratitude to Mrs. Alfred Schutz for her decision to entrust to us the *Collected Papers* of her late husband, thereby enabling us to publish them in the *Phaenomenologica* series.

H. L. VAN BREDA

reconnu les limites de ce point de vue égologique en se heurtant à l'intersubjectivité comme à une sorte de facticité primordiale. Mais peut-être aussi sur ce point Schutz rencontre-t-il la dernière pensée de Husserl lui-même?

Ces questions sont ouvertes, elles témoignent en tout cas de la signification toute contemporaine des travaux de Schutz et de son inlassable fidélité au sens profond qu'à l'instar de Husserl il avait voulu donner au labeur de sa vie.

Daigne Madame Alfred Schutz trouver ici l'expression de toute la reconnaissance que je lui porte pour avoir bien voulu nous confier les *Collected Papers* de son mari et nous permettre d'en assurer l'édition dans les *Phaenomenologica*.

H. L. van Breda

CONTENTS

Preface by H. L. VAN BREDA ... VI
Editor's Note ... XXIII
Introduction by MAURICE NATANSON ... XXV

Part I / On the Methodology of the Social Sciences

COMMON-SENSE AND SCIENTIFIC INTERPRETATION OF HUMAN
    ACTION ... 3
  I. Introduction: Content of Experience and Thought
      Objects ... 3
    1. The constructs of common-sense and of scientific
       thinking ... 3
    2. Particular structure of the constructs of the social
       sciences ... 5
  II. Constructs of Thought Objects in Common-Sense
      Thinking ... 7
    1. The individual's common-sense knowledge of the
       world is a system of constructs of its typicality ... 7
    2. The intersubjective character of common-sense
       knowledge and its implication ... 10
      a. The reciprocity of perspectives ... 11
      b. The social origin of knowledge ... 13
      c. The social distribution of knowledge ... 14
    3. The structure of the social world and its typification
       by common-sense constructs ... 15

4.	Course-of-action types and personal types	19
	a. Action, project, motive	19
	b. Social interaction	22
	c. The observer	26
III.	Rational Action within Common-Sense Experience	27
IV.	Constructs of Thought Objects by the Social Sciences	34
	1. The postulate of subjective interpretation	34
	2. The social scientist as disinterested observer	36
	3. Differences between common-sense and scientific constructs of action patterns	38
	4. The scientific model of the social world	40
	5. Postulates for scientific model constructs of the social world	43
	a. The postulate of logical consistency	43
	b. The postulate of subjective interpretation	43
	c. The postulate of adequacy	44
V.	Scientific Model Constructs of Rational Action Patterns	44
VI.	Concluding Remarks	47

CONCEPT AND THEORY FORMATION IN THE SOCIAL SCIENCES 48

CHOOSING AMONG PROJECTS OF ACTION 67

I.	The Concept of Action	67
II.	The Time Structure of the Project	68
III.	In-Order-To and Because Motive	69
IV.	Fancying and Projecting	72
V.	The Foundation of Practicability	74
	a. The world as taken for granted	74
	b. The biographically determined situation	76
VI.	Doubting and Questioning	77
VII.	Problematic and Open Possibilities According to Husserl	79
VIII.	Choosing Among Objects within Reach	83

CONTENTS

IX.	Choosing Among Projects	84
X.	Bergson's Theory of Choice	85
XI.	Leibniz's Theory of Volition	88
XII.	The Problem of Weight	93
XIII.	Summary and Conclusion	94

Part II / Phenomenology and the Social Sciences

SOME LEADING CONCEPTS OF PHENOMENOLOGY	99
PHENOMENOLOGY AND THE SOCIAL SCIENCES	118
HUSSERL'S IMPORTANCE FOR THE SOCIAL SCIENCES	140
SCHELER'S THEORY OF INTERSUBJECTIVITY AND THE GENERAL THESIS OF THE ALTER EGO	150
I. Scheler's Concept of Man	150
II. Scheler's Concept of Person	153
III. Scheler's Theory of Intersubjectivity	156
a. The problems involved	156
b. Inference and empathy	159
c. Scheler's perceptional theory of the alter ego	162
IV. Critical Observations	164
a. Intersubjectivity as a transcendental problem	164
b. Intersubjectivity as a mundane problem	167
V. The General Thesis of the Alter Ego and its Time Structure	172
VI. The Perception of the Alter Ego	176
VII. The Problem of Perspectives Related to Intersubjectivity	177
SARTRE'S THEORY OF THE ALTER EGO	180
I. Sartre's Criticism of the Realistic and the Idealistic Approach to the Problem of Intersubjectivity	180

II.	Sartre's Criticism of Husserl, Hegel, and Heidegger	183
	a. Husserl	183
	b. Hegel	185
	c. Heidegger	186
III.	Sartre's Own Theory of the Other's Existence	187
IV.	Sartre's Theory of the Body	191
V.	On Husserl's Theory of the Other	194
VI.	Critical Observations Concerning Sartre's own Theory	197

Part III / Symbol, Reality and Society

ON MULTIPLE REALITIES — 207

I. The Reality of the World of Daily Life — 208
  1. The natural attitude of daily life and its pragmatic motive — 208
  2. The manifestations of man's spontaneous life in the outer world and some of its forms — 209
  3. The tensions of consciousness and the attention to life — 212
  4. The time perspectives of the "ego agens" and their unification — 214
  5. The social structure of the world of daily life — 218
  6. The strata of reality in the everyday world of working — 222
  7. The world of working as paramount reality; the fundamental anxiety; the epoché of the natural attitude — 226

II. The Many Realities and their Constitution — 229
III. The Various Worlds of Phantasms — 234
IV. The World of Dreams — 240
V. The World of Scientific Theory — 245

CONTENTS

LANGUAGE, LANGUAGE DISTURBANCES, AND THE TEXTURE OF CONSCIOUSNESS — 260

   I. Goldstein's Theory of Language — 261

   II. Philosophical Interpretations of Language Disturbances — 269

   III. Relevance and Typification — 283

SYMBOL, REALITY AND SOCIETY — 287

   I. Introductory Remarks — 287
     1. Some controversial points in the present discussion of signs and symbols — 287
     2. Plan of the following investigation — 292

   II. Appresentation as the General Form of Significative and Symbolic Relations — 294
     1. Husserl's concept of appresentation — 294
     2. The various orders involved in the appresentational situation — 297
     3. Bergson's theory of concurring orders — 300
     4. Application of Bergson's theory to some controversial opinions concerning signs and symbols — 301
     5. The principles governing structural changes of appresentational relations — 303
        a. The principle of the relative irrelevance of the vehicle — 303
        b. The principle of variability of the appresentational meaning — 304
        c. The principle of figurative transference — 305

   III. The World within my Reach and its Dimensions, Marks, and Indications — 306
     1. The World within my actual and potential reach and the manipulatory sphere — 306
     2. Marks — 308
     3. Indications — 310

CONTENTS

- IV. The Intersubjective World and its Appresentational Relations: Signs ... 312
  1. The World of everyday life is from the outset an intersubjective one ... 312
  2. Our knowledge of the other mind is itself based on appresentational references ... 313
  3. The general thesis of the reciprocity of perspectives ... 315
     a. The idealization of the interchangeability of standpoints ... 315
     b. The idealization of the congruency of the systems of relevances ... 316
  4. The transcendence of the Other's world ... 316
  5. Comprehension, manifestation, signs, communication ... 319
     a. Comprehension ... 319
     b. Manifestation ... 320
     c. Types of signs ... 320
     d. Communication proper ... 321
     e. Language, pictorial, expressive, and mimetic presentation ... 324
  6. World within reach and world of everyday life ... 326

- V. The Transcendence of Nature and Society: Symbols ... 329
  1. The experience of this transcendence ... 329
  2. Symbolization ... 331
     a. Definition ... 331
     b. Genesis of the symbolic appresentation ... 332
     c. The particularities of the symbolic appresentation ... 337

- VI. On Multiple Realities ... 340
  1. William James's subuniverses; finite provinces of meaning ... 340
  2. The paramount reality ... 341
  3. The definition of symbol restated ... 343
  4. The transition from the paramount reality to other finite provinces of meaning, experienced through a shock ... 343
  5. The concept of finite provinces of meaning illustrated by symbols in science and poetry ... 345

CONTENTS

VII. Symbol and Society   347
  1. The dependence of appresentational references on the social environment   347
  2. The symbolic appresentation of society   352

VIII. Concluding Remarks   356

Index   357

EDITOR'S NOTE

Not long before his death in 1959, Alfred Schutz asked me to undertake the editing of the present volume. Since the papers that comprise this volume were originally published as articles in journals or as chapters in books, some repetition was inevitable. "Your editorial work would consist first of all," Dr. Schutz wrote to me, "in eliminating repetitions which were unavoidable when presenting the papers in various journals, but which would be only confusing in a volume containing collected papers. For example, various of these papers contain definitions of Conduct, Action, etc., frequently in different versions. The best statement should be selected and incorporated in the first paper, whereas cross references should be made in the other papers, where the repetitious parts would have to be eliminated ... Finally, I would be only too happy if you were willing to write the general introduction and if so advisable the special introductions to each of the parts." When I originally agreed to edit this volume, I assumed that the author would oversee and approve of the changes to be made. Since Dr. Schutz died before he could review my work, it was decided that it would be best to restrict changes to stylistic and grammatical matters and to let stand, as far as possible, the original wording of the author. Hence, a number of repetitious passages have been retained, and no effort has been made to rewrite those sentences or paragraphs whose stylistic quality could be improved upon. When stylistic changes have been made – and they have throughout the work – the decision was dictated by the fact that the intellectual content at issue was obscured by the language. As much editorial effort has gone into decisions to retain the original wording of certain problematic passages as in devising alternative formulations for parts that were changed. Although it has not been feasible to attempt to indicate stylistic changes in the text, page by page, I have added my initials (M.N.) whenever I have altered Dr. Schutz's footnotes or added to them. In the Introduction I have said all I thought necessary to guide the reader who might be coming to Dr. Schutz's work for the first time. I found it unnecessary to add special introductions to each of the parts of the book.

The essays were originally published in the following form: "Common-Sense and Scientific Interpretation of Human Action," *Philosophy and Phenomenological Research* (hereafter referred to as PPR), Vol. XIV, September 1953; "Concept and Theory Formation in the Social Sciences," *Journal of Philosophy*, Vol. LI, April 1954; "Choosing Among Projects of Action," PPR, Vol. XII, December 1951; "Some Leading Concepts of Phenomenology," *Social Research*, Vol. XII, No. 1, 1945; "Phenomenology and the Social Sciences," in *Philosophical Essays in Memory of Edmund Husserl* (edited by Marvin Farber), Harvard University Press, Cambridge, 1940; "Husserl's Importance for the Social Sciences," in *Edmund Husserl 1859–1959*, (Phaenomenologica 4), Martinus Nijhoff, The Hague, 1959; "Scheler's Theory of Intersubjectivity and the General Thesis of the Alter Ego," PPR, Vol. II, March 1942; "Sartre's Theory of the Alter Ego," PPR, Vol. IX, December 1948; "On Multiple Realities," PPR, Vol. V, June 1945; "Language, Language Disturbances, and the Texture of Consciousness," *Social Research*, Vol. XVII, No. 3, 1950; "Symbol, Reality and Society," in *Symbols and Society:* Fourteenth Symposium of the Conference on Science, Philosophy and Religion (edited by Lyman Bryson, Louis Finkelstein, Hudson Hoagland, and R. M. MacIver), Harper, New York, 1955. Grateful acknowledgment is made to the editors and publishers of these journals and books for permission to republish these papers. I wish to express my thanks to Professors Dorion Cairns and Aron Gurwitsch, Father Van Breda, Drs. J. Taminiaux and Rudolf Boehm, and, finally, Mrs. Alfred Schutz. In different ways they have all helped in the preparation of this book.

INTRODUCTION

by

MAURICE NATANSON

Department of Philosophy, University of North Carolina

I

According to Bergson, a true philosopher says only one thing in his lifetime, because he enjoys but one point of contact with the real. Understood in its proper sense, this means that whatever variegation and richness a philosophical mind may possess, however extensive its interests and research, there is ultimately but one cardinal insight into reality that it achieves, one decisive illumination on which everything else turns and which is the philosopher's claim to truth. In this sense, it might be said that the philosophy of Alfred Schutz articulates a single intuition, the discovery in full depth of the presuppositions, structure, and signification of the common-sense world. Although he possessed prodigious learning in and a profound appreciation of philosophy, sociology, and social psychology, although his studies and writings covered a truly remarkable range of problems in all of these fields, and although he had a very deep grasp of literature and the arts (music in particular), the *fil conducteur* of his intellectual life was a concern for the meaningful structure of the world of daily life, the everyday working world into which each of us is born, within whose limits our existence unfolds, and which we transcend completely only in death. To see this world in its massive complexity, to outline and explore its essential features, and to trace out its manifold relationships were the composite parts of his central task, the realization of a philosophy of mundane reality, or, in more formal language, of a phenomenology of the natural attitude. The understanding of the paramount reality of common-sense life is the clue to the understanding of the work of Alfred Schutz.

Whatever other allegiances an individual has, he is first of all a citizen of the republic of daily life. Each one of us is part of an on-going world of everyday affairs which is, for the most part, taken for granted in its essential being. Although we have special concerns and interests in our various roles, we are forever rooted in a primordial range of experience out of which these concerns and interests arise and to which they remain connected. The taken for granted everyday world of living and working is the nuclear presupposition of all other strata of man's reality, and it is this ground of social reality to which Dr. Schutz turned and which he took as a point of departure for analysis. The central and most cunning feature of the taken for granted everyday world is that it *is* taken for granted. As common-sense men living in the mundane world, we tacitly assume that, of course, there *is* this world all of us share as the public domain within which we communicate, work, and live our lives. Moreover, we naively assume that this world has a history, a past, that it has a future, and that the rough present in which we find ourselves is epistemically given to all normal men in much the same way. In the simplest terms, we are all born into the same world, grow up as children guided by parents and other adults, learn a language, come into contact with others, receive an education, move into some phase of the business of life, and go through the infinitely detailed catalogue of human activity: we play, love, create, suffer, and die. But throughout all of the routine elements and forms of existence, we simply assume, presuppose, take it for granted that the daily world in which all of these activities go on is *there;* it is only on special occasions, if at all, that a serious doubt arises as to the veridical character or philosophical signification of our everyday world. Thus, the essential foundation of mundane existence remains unrecognized by common-sense men whose lives are nevertheless structured by and built upon the matrix of daily life. The philosopher's privilege is to render the taken for granted the object of his critical inspection, and this indeed was the procedure of Dr. Schutz. His problem was to achieve a rationale of the essential structure of daily life through an examination of its manifold typifications. What follows now is an outline of the results of his analysis.

II

1. THE COMMON-SENSE WORLD

"The common-sense world," "world of daily life," "every-day world" are variant expressions for the intersubjective world experienced by man within what Husserl terms the "natural attitude." This world existed, we believe, before our birth, has its history, and is given to us in an organized fashion. It is primarily the scene of our actions and the locus of resistance to action: we act not only within but upon the world. And our initial purpose is not so much the interpretation or understanding of the world but the effecting of changes within it; we seek to dominate before we endeavour to comprehend. The common-sense world, then, is the arena of social action; within it men come into relationship with each other and try to come to terms with each other as well as with themselves. All of this, however, is typically taken for granted, and this means that these structures of daily life are not themselves recognized or appreciated formally by common sense. Rather, common sense sees the world, acts in the world, and interprets the world through these implicit typifications. That there is a social world, that there are fellow men, that we can communicate meaningfully with others, that there are very broad and general principles true for daily life – these prime facts are inwoven in the texture of the natural attitude. Their explication depends on a detailed examination of the conditions *a priori* for the possibility of the common-sense world.

a) Biographical situation

Although the common-sense reality forms the matrix for all social action, each individual locates himself in daily life in a particular manner, in the light of what Dr. Schutz has called his "biographical situation." To be born into the world means first of all to be born of parents who are unique to us, to be raised by adults who constitute the guiding elements of *our* segment of experience. And since, as Dr. Schutz puts it, human beings are born of mothers and not concocted in retorts, the formative period of each life is realized in a unique way. Moreover, each person continues throughout his life to interpret what he encounters in the world in the perspective of his special interests, motives, desires, aspirations, religious and ideological commitments. Thus, common-sense reality is given to us all in historical and cultural forms of universal validity, but the way in which these forms are translated in an individual life depends on the totality of the experience a person builds up in the course of his concrete existence. Among the conditions I find circumscribing my life, I come to recognize two types of elements: those either within my control or capable of being brought into control and those outside of or beyond the possibility of control. Acting in the world, I seek to change and alter it, to modify the scene of my activities. My biographical situation defines the way in which I locate the arena of action, interpret its possibilities, and engage its challenges. Even the determination of what the individual can modify or not modify is affected by his unique situation. The funded experience of a life, what a phenomenologist would call the "sedimented" structure of the individual's experience, is the condition for the subsequent interpretation of all new events and activities. "The" world becomes transposed into "my" world in accordance with the relevant elements of my biographical situation. Thus, the individual as an actor in the social world defines the reality he encounters. As Dr. Schutz writes, "The actor's actual situation has its history; it is the sedimentation of all his previous subjective experiences. They are not experienced by the actor as being anonymous but as unique and subjectively given to him and to him alone."

b) Stock of Knowledge at Hand

The biographical situation has as its cardinal feature the fact that at any moment in his life the individual has what Dr. Schutz terms a "stock of knowledge at hand." This stock is made up of typifications of the common-sense world. Each of us accepts this world as not only existing but existing before our birth, as not only inhabited by fellow men but as interpreted by them in typical ways, as not only having a future but as having a future that is only at best partially determinate. Still further, we know that our world includes animate beings as well as inert objects. These beings and objects are from the outset perceived typically and within a horizon of familiarity. What is new and different is recognized as unusual because it arises against a background of the ordinary. But no one has to teach us that the ordinary *is* ordinary, that the familiar *is* familiar; the very texture of common-sense life includes these typifications which indeed make further predications possible. This "stockpiling" of typifications is endemic to common-sense life. From childhood on, the individual continues to amass a vast number of "recipes" which then serve as techniques for understanding or at least controlling aspects of his experience. The thousands of concrete problematic situations that arise in the course of daily affairs and have to be handled in some form are perceived and even initially formulated in terms of the individual's stock of knowledge at hand. The fund of his experience typically apprehended and interpreted is then the basis for his subsequent action. It is clear that for certain problems a person's stock of knowledge is more than adequate and that for other situations he must improvise and extrapolate, but even improvisation proceeds along typically possible lines and is restricted to the individual's imaginative possibilities. Those possibilities, in turn, are grounded in the stock of knowledge at hand. Finally, the typifications which comprise the stock of knowledge are generated out of a social structure. Here as everywhere, knowledge is socially rooted, socially distributed, and socially informed. Yet its individuated expression depends on the unique placement of the individual in the social world.

c) *The Co-ordinates of the Social Matrix*

A cartographer's description of a geographical area would be quite distant from my personal awareness or remembrance of the same region. The co-ordinates he must use in mapping the terrain are objectively necessary for his professional task, but they are certainly far removed from my concerns. First of all, the cartographer plots his map in terms of a universally recognized system of longitudes and latitudes; *his* geographical position at the time of mapping is necessarily irrelevant. Similarly, the actual position of the reader of the map is irrelevant to understanding what is mapped, although it may be relevant for other purposes. But in my appreciation of a certain landscape, it is precisely *my* position in space and time which is the primary consideration. The elements of the scene are *before* me, the aspects I consider marginal are marginal with regard to what I deem central, and the knowledge I possess of the surroundings is dependent on my physical placement in the world. Fore and aft, to the side of, near and far, above and below, here and there – these are all rendered intelligible by my placement in the world. Furthermore, the temporal perspectives of now and then, earlier and later, soon or not so soon, hinge upon my placement in time. In addition, then, to the co-ordinates of mathematics and natural science there are the co-ordinates of immediate personal experience, and it is these personal co-ordinates which are of fundamental importance to common-sense reality. Dr. Schutz maintains that "the place which my body occupies within the world, my actual Here, is the starting point from which I take my bearing in space. It is, so to speak, the center O of my system of coordinates ... And in a similar way my actual Now is the origin of all the time perspectives under which I organize the events within the world ..." To say, as we have, that "the" world is transposed in common-sense experience into "my" world would mean here that the standardized space and time of natural science is not the basis for the typifications of spatial and temporal location utilized by men in daily life. Indeed, the reverse is the case: the primary grounding of our being in the world is in subjective space and time. Once again, as with the biographical situation and the stock of knowledge at hand, the definition of the individual's world arises out of his uniquely sedimented and structured subjectivity. But, as Dr. Schutz would say, this is only half the story. Although the individual defines his world from his own perspective, he is nevertheless a social being, rooted in an intersubjective reality. "The world of daily life into which we are born is from the outset an intersubjective world." The philosophical problem of intersubjectivity is the clue to social reality.

2. INTERSUBJECTIVITY

It is a characteristic of daily life that the philosophical question of how knowledge of other minds is possible never arises as a formal problem for common-sense men. Instead, intersubjectivity is taken for granted as an obvious quality of our world – *our* world is the underlying typification of common sense. But a philosophy of what common sense takes for granted must necessarily raise and face the question of intersubjectivity if it is to come to terms with the formative features underlying human experience. Recognizing that it is a decisive feature of daily life that the problem of intersubjectivity does not arise as a formal issue, we may still say that it is part of the task of philosophy to account for this state of affairs as well as to go on to develop the methodological principles underlying relationships between persons. The first question to be asked here is that of how knowledge of other selves is possible at all. Setting aside considerations of transcendental phenomenology with which Dr. Schutz was deeply concerned, his approach to the nature of intersubjectivity is by way of a descriptive analysis of the typifications of the common-sense world.

a) The "Here" and "There" of the Ego

Taking my body as the center point for the co-ordinates which map *my* world, I may say that the position of my body constitutes my Here in relationship to which the body of a fellow man is There. I find that it is possible to alter my position and move from Here to There. Having moved, the There then becomes a Here. But the body of my fellow man remains There for me as it remains still a Here for him. Although I cannot in fact stand directly in the perspective of the other's Here, I can subjunctively attribute to him a reciprocity of perspectives. Thus the objects and events of the world are common to both of us because I can perceive from There the same things I perceive from Here, despite the change in perspective. Within the common-sense world it is simply taken for granted that the reciprocity of perspectives holds, that the objects and events of human experience are intersubjectively available and more or less the same for all "normal" perceivers. The concept of normalcy itself, it might be suggested, is derivative from the implicit assumptions common sense makes about the structure of sensory perception. The interchangeability of Here and There between egos is the necessary condition for a shared reality. But the problem goes much further, for in addition to spatial co-ordinates there are the temporal relationships founded on the null point of my Now. A reciprocity of temporal perspectives forms the analogue of the dialectic of Here and There.

b) The Alter Ego

Among the elements of my experience of the outer world are not only physical objects but fellow men, alter egos. Encountering the body of another human being is qualitatively different from the experience of inert bodies, bodies as things. First of all, the body of a fellow man is experienced as part of a psycho-physical unity, and this means that coeval with the recognition of the body is the awareness and appreciation of the ego who possesses, in addition to a body, a world of cognitive and conative awareness similar in general to mine. This ego is indeed an alter ego, a being for whom there is a world. Although I know infinitely more about myself than I do about the other, there is a crucial respect in which the knowledge I have of the other transcends my self-knowledge. In reflection I can grasp myself only in my past acts. The very act of reflection is possible only if the object of reflection is part of the past, even if it is the immediate past. This implies, as Dr. Schutz points out, that "the whole present ... and also the vivid present of our Self, is inaccessible for the reflective attitude. We can only turn to the stream of our thought as if it had stopped with the last grasped experience. In other words, self-consciousness can only be experienced *modo preterito*, in the past tense." Our knowledge of the other, however, is possible in an immediate present. "We catch the other's thought in its vivid presence and not *modo preterito;* that is, we catch it as a 'Now' and not as a 'Just now.' The other's speech and our listening are experienced as a vivid simultaneity." This simultaneity is the essence of intersubjectivity, for it means that I grasp the subjectivity of the alter ego at the same time as I live in my own stream of consciousness. In these terms, it is possible to define the alter ego as "that subjective stream of thought which can be experienced in its vivid present." And this grasp in simultaneity of the other as well as his reciprocal grasp of me makes possible *our* being in the world together.

c) *Predecessors, Contemporaries, Consociates, and Successors*

The designation "fellow men" really covers a broad range of alter egos possessing strata with different characteristics. My fellow man may be a predecessor, one who lived before my time and who is known to me only through the reports of others, a contemporary, one who is now alive and with whom I share a temporal reality (we are alive in the same age), a consociate, a contemporary with whom I share also a face to face relationship (we live in the same spatial segment of the world), or a successor, one who will live after I die and who remains during my lifetime necessarily anonymous. The social structures relevant to all of these types are radically different. The knowledge I have of my predecessors is always in the mode of the past; their lives and ideas may influence my acts but they remain beyond the boundary of my influence. They influence but cannot be influenced. And, of course, I may not know them but only *about* them in varying degrees of clarity and detail. Successors occupy a more ghostly perspective. Toward them I may orient my actions, but they remain, in principle, unknowable. It is with contemporaries and consociates that most of my social traffic occurs. And here again they are known by way of the typifications of the common-sense world. The "face to face" relationship is fundamental for all other structures of social relatedness. In my face to face encounter with consociates I share a community of space within our reach in which I interpret the other's acts, but I share a temporal community as well. Consociates are involved in an on-going temporal flow, bounded by common spatial limits. Thus, Dr. Schutz writes, "each partner participates in the onrolling life of the other, can grasp in a vivid present the other's thoughts as they are built up step by step. They may ... share one another's anticipations of the future as plans, or hopes or anxieties. In brief, consociates grow older together; they live, as we may call it, in a pure We-relationship." It is only in the life of consociates that the individual identity, the uniqueness of the person, may be grasped. Though even here, it is merely a facet of individuality which is available to the understanding of the other. As with all social relationships, predecessors, contemporaries, consociates, and successors are, in variant ways, located and interpreted through the typifications of common-sense life.

3. ACTION

Dr. Schutz defines "action" as human conduct self-consciously projected by the actor. "Act," on the other hand, designates accomplished action. The difference between action and mere phantasying is that a voluntative fiat is involved in the former which establishes the action as purposive. Action is either overt or covert. By definition, all overt action is both projected and purposive. Purposive phantasying would be termed a "performance," not an action. But overt action is only part of the total complex of action. Refraining from action – what may be termed negative action – is also a type of action, indeed an especially interesting and important phenomenon. "Covert" action, then, covers all forms of negative decision in which the actor purposively chooses to refrain from certain overt conduct. The surgeon's decision not to operate, the statesman's decision not to compromise, the businessman's decision not to sell, the politician's decision not to run for office are all examples of covert action. But the list should be extended radically to include the infinite range of situations which men in daily life confront and define in their own way, often through negative action. The crucial feature of action in every case is its purposive and projective character. Action has its source in the consciousness of the actor.

a) The Subjective Interpretation of Meaning

Taking as his point of departure Max Weber's postulate of the subjective interpretation of meaning, Dr. Schutz is predominantly concerned with the understanding of social action as the meaning which the actor bestows upon his action, i.e., the meaning his action has for him. Rather than treat Weber's postulate as a formal methodological device, Dr. Schutz thinks of the subjective interpretation of meaning as above all a typification of the common-sense world, the actual way in which men in daily life do interpret their own and each other's behavior. More strictly put, the subjective interpretation of meaning as well as the whole problem of interpretive understanding (*Verstehen*) involves three related but different issues: "*Verstehen* (1) as the experiential form of common-sense knowledge of human affairs, (2) as an epistemological problem, and (3) as a method peculiar to the social sciences." As the experiential form of common sense knowledge of human affairs *Verstehen* means simply that men in daily life interpret their world from the outset as a meaningful one. In addition to the body of the other being understood as an integral part of a psycho-physical unity, his acts are similarly treated as the conduct of a purposeful creature. Motives and goals are as inescapably part of the other's behavior as they are of our own. When I encounter a man acting in the social world, I know that I must understand him as a human being, and this means that his actions mean something to him as well as to me, relate to his world as well as to mine, and are ultimately rooted in the interpretive scheme he has created for living his life. But this knowledge is itself taken for granted by me as well as by him; its being taken for granted by *us* is precisely the typification which makes intersubjectivity possible. The philosophical problem involved here, however, transcends the scope of the common-sense world and constitutes the second meaning of *Verstehen* as an epistemological issue. Here Dr. Schutz argues that *Verstehen* in this sense is rooted in what Husserl calls the *Lebenswelt*, the Life-world that encompasses the rich totality of common-sense experience lived through by the individual in his concrete existence. And it is the *Lebenswelt* also which is the ground for understanding the meaning of *Verstehen* in the third sense, as a method peculiar to the social sciences. The objects investigated by the methods of the natural sciences are first-order constructs; they are, however complex, merely objects within the world of the observer. The social scientist, on the other hand, must face a qualitatively different situation. His objects are not only objects for his observation, they are beings who have their own pre-interpreted world, who do their own observing; they are fellow-men caught up in social reality. These "objects," then, are second-order constructs, and the method of *Verstehen* is employed in the social sciences in order to come to terms with the full subjective reality of the human beings they seek to comprehend.

b) The Definition of the Situation

If the primary concern of the social scientist should be the meaning which the actor bestows upon his own act, it follows that the actor is responsible for defining that meaning as well as the situation of which it is a part. The situation of the actor is primarily *his* problem, not that of the scientific observer. Moreover, the way in which the actor locates and interprets a given situation is a function of his subjectivity and corresponds to elements of his biographical situation. The social world is constituted by a multiplicity of actors, each of whom defines that world in related but individuated ways. Whether or not an actor defines his situation in a manner that tallies generally with what we call "objective" facts, his action is meaningful and quite relevant to the social scientist. However an actor defines his situation, his action is a datum for inquiry. That there is not only a multiplicity but a relativity in the definition of a situation by different actors or even by the same actor at different times is part of the essential structure of daily life. Understanding the social world means understanding the way in which men define their situations. Here Dr. Schutz turns to the sociology of W. I. Thomas as an American and more recent complement to Weber's subjective interpretation of meaning. "If men define situations as real," Thomas writes, "they are real in their consequences." If I define a situation as pleasant, threatening, boring, challenging, or fantastic, the way in which I have defined it establishes the status that situation has within my world, for the time being at least. Rather than treating such definition as a "response" or "reaction" to certain objective states of affairs, the social scientist, Dr. Schutz suggests, has to understand that definition means action and that interpreting the world is a prime mode of acting in it. That I may define the "same" situation in a radically different manner than does my fellow man leads philosophically to the problem of reality. Insisting as common sense does, if questioned, that there is an objective reality which is the "same" for all normal observers is not to be confused with demonstrating that this is indeed so or even understanding what is implied in such a claim. Men living in the paramount reality of everyday life are enmeshed in situations as *they* define them in the context of their lives. It is idle for the neutral observer to point out to committed actors the "objective" situation. As Sartre puts it: for the Romans, Carthage was conquered, but for the Carthagenians, Carthage was enslaved.

c) Horizons of Action

Action is never isolated, unrelated to other action, divorced from the world. Whether overt or covert, all action has its horizons of relatedness with social reality. As Dr. Schutz writes, "No object is perceived as an insulated object; it is from the outset perceived as 'an object within its horizon,' a horizon of typical familiarity and preacquaintanceship." So it is with every action. To perform or reperform the "same" action presupposes a typification deeply rooted in common-sense life, which Husserl calls the idealization of "I-can-do-it-again," that is, as Dr. Schutz puts it, "the assumption that I may under typically similar circumstances act in the typically similar way that I did before in order to bring about a typically similar state of affairs." The basic typification involved here underlies as well the structure of my biographical situation and my stock of knowledge at hand. And since action presupposes the situation of the actor, the initial constitution of "my" world is grounded in the typicality with which I handle the data of my experience. But even the idealization of "I-can-do-it-again" has its connections; it is the subjective correlate of the idealization of what Husserl calls "and so on," that is, the open horizon of determinability which attaches to any predication. Once again, these constructs reflect back on the epistemic situation of the actor. The co-ordinates of the social matrix, the Here and Now of the ego, imply the possibility of returning to or regaining perspectives once held but

4. PROJECTS AND ROLES

"All projecting," Dr. Schutz writes, "consists in an anticipation of future conduct by way of phantasying." In phantasying, I visualize in anticipation the action I am projecting as though it were already performed, completed. Recalling the distinction between "action" and "act," we may say that projecting is the phantasying of acts. Clearly, the time structure of the project is of central importance. In projecting, I anticipate the act as already having been accomplished; I place myself imaginatively in the future perfect tense. But the possibility of doing this rests on certain essential elements of the present. My biographical situation and my stock of knowledge at hand are the condition for my "as-if" projection into the future. Between the present anticipation and the fulfilled act lies the temporal "in between" which I must pass through in order to realize my project. The realization of my plans presupposes my growing older in a world of necessary "in betweens." Of course, all projects are not fulfilled, and even those which are realized are seldom achieved in the pure form in which they were projected. Disappointment is no less a characteristic of daily life than attainment; we know, if only intuitively, that in the course of realizing a project the "I" who phantasied will not be identical with the "I" who later reflects on his fulfilled act. And even the notion of a "pure" phantasying is ambiguous, for the "I" who phantasies is in reality a complex and changing ego whose knowledge of the world and of others is as fragmentary as his knowledge of himself. These considerations prove decisive for any theory of social roles.

a) "Because" and "In-Order-To" Motives

The difficulty with defining action as "motivated behavior" is the equivocation implicit in the term "motive." Dr. Schutz prefers to distinguish two different types of concepts, too often herded into one shed. Motives which involve ends to be achieved, goals sought for, are termed "in-order-to" motives; motives which are explained on the basis of the actor's background, environment, or psychic disposition are called "because" motives. The time structure of both types is different. In-order-to motives are dominated by the future tense; because motives by the past tense. As I project my action now, I am aware of my in-order-to motives; indeed, it is precisely these motives which spur my action. But the because motives which could explain certain aspects of my projecting, their causal conditions, remain obscure and marginal to my awareness. These temporal differences lead to a larger differentiation: in-order-to motives form a subjective category; because motives an objective category. The actor caught up in his action, understood as part of the on-going process of projecting, defines and interprets the meaning of his action in terms of in-order-to motives. To refer to these motives as a subjective category is consistent with the meaning of Weber's postulate of the subjective interpretation of meaning and Thomas' theory of the definition of the situation. "Subjective" here refers to the relationship action bears to the consciousness of the actor; it has nothing to do with notions of introspection, psychological conditions, or private attitudes. In exploring the subjectivity of the actor, then, Dr. Schutz is concerned with those aspects of consciousness which are accessible to phenomenological inspection and description. The analysis of the objective conditions underlying because motives is a causal affair open to the methods of natural scientific inquiry. Out of the problematic relationship between the two types of motives arises the metaphysical problem of free will and determinism.

b) Fragmentation

The ego cannot be considered simply an "I." First of all, any act of reflection involves the distance between the reflector and the reflected upon described earlier with regard to the problem of the alter ego. When I reflect upon myself, I cannot seize myself as I am in the immediate now; I can only attend to myself as an object for reflection, and this means that it is always an earlier phase of myself which I capture. George H. Mead's distinction between the "I" and the "me" aspects of the self is quite relevant here, as Dr. Schutz points out. For Mead, the "I" is always the subject of any action, the "me" the object. The relationship between the two is highly dialectical, for the self is continually involved in action in which both aspects appear. This dialectic is also a temporal one: the "I" as subject of a present action may become the "me" reflected upon in a later phase of conduct. Quite apart from the theory of the social genesis of the self which Mead develops, however, the problem of the "I" and "me" aspects of the self leads to a conception of the fragmentation of the ego. Each of us, as Simmel has shown, is not only a fragment of the social collectivity, each of us is but a fragment of his own possibilities. The individual presents himself to society, to his fellow men, with varying sides or aspects of his nature, realized in the form of social roles; but he remains in a problematic relationship with himself as well, for he sees himself in a partial way and comprehends merely a fragment of his being. All projects and roles are permeated with the underlying imperfection of self-knowledge and knowledge of other selves. Each of us is destined to play a multitude of roles in the everyday world; yet the full meaning of these roles remains latent in experience. In Simmel's formulation, as expressed by Dr. Schutz, "man ... enters any social relationship merely with a part of his self and is, at the same time, always within and outside of such a relationship." The fragmentation of the self is a metaphysical constant of the human condition.

c) *Relevance*

If the common-sense world is from the outset a pre-interpreted one, if all of the elements of this world have their horizons of typicality, and if the notions of the biographically determined situation, the stock of knowledge at hand, and the definition of the situation are reliable guides for the interpretation of social reality, there must be some underlying principle of selection which accounts for the concrete choices, attitudes, decisions, and commitments the individual expresses and makes. For Dr. Schutz, "relevance" is the rubric under which he includes the types and forms of action undertaken by the individual. I decide upon a course of action in one direction rather than another in the light of what I deem to be relevant to my deepest convictions or interests. Although I share certain general relevance systems with most of my fellow men, I recognize that I often share them for somewhat different reasons and that these reasons can be explicated only in terms of my scheme of fundamental concerns. Similarly, I know that what is interesting to me may bore another, what is sacred to me may be laughable to him, what I prize may leave him indifferent. Underlying all of these disagreements is the prime difference of variant or even contradictory systems of relevance. Just as the co-ordinates of the social matrix determine the way in which the world presents itself to me, so there is a kind of "Here and Now" of the relevance structure of my life, a null point at the very center of my axiological existence, in terms of which all evaluative predication takes on significance and direction. The ultimate grounding of the system of relevances which guides the life of the individual is in an existential theme explored by Dr. Schutz within the framework of his theory of multiple realities.

5. MULTIPLE REALITIES

Following William James, Dr. Schutz approaches the problem of reality in terms of the orders of reality which James calls "sub-universes": the world of physical things, of science, of religion, and even of "sheer madness and vagary." Although the tendency among common-sense men is to conceive of these worlds in more or less disconnected fashion, James holds that "each world whilst it is attended to is real after its own fashion; only the reality lapses with the attention." The problem now is to determine the nature of the connections or bridges which bind these worlds to each other, and to see how the individual may inhabit any of them or all of them in the course of his existence. Dr. Schutz attacks his problem by setting aside the psychologistic grounding and orientation of James' theory. Instead of speaking, then, of "sub-universes," he will refer to "finite provinces of meaning." "We speak of provinces of *meaning* and not of sub-universes," Dr. Schutz writes, "because it is the meaning of our experiences and not the ontological structure of the objects which constitutes reality." The essential features of all finite provinces of meaning are described. Each province has its own cognitive style with respect to which experiences within each world are inter-consistent. And each of the finite provinces of meaning may receive the "accent of reality," may be attended to as real. But there is no formula of transformation which enables one to pass smoothly from one province to another; it is only by a Kierkegaardian "leap" that passage is possible. Finally, these considerations require one qualification: although they extend to the world of daily life, they do so with a difference, for "the world of working in daily life," according to Dr. Schutz, "is the archetype of our experience of reality. All the other provinces of meaning may be considered as its modifications."

a) The Paramount Reality

The world of working or, in alternative language, the world of common sense and daily life, is taken as the paramount reality. Within it the individual locates himself as a body, as operating physically in the world, and as meeting the resistance of fellow men as well as of things. Working means gearing into the outer world, in Dr. Schutz' terminology, and this, in turn, means that as an actor in the common-sense world I know that my action will cause changes that will affect other states of affairs and will be noticed by other men. Reviewing my acts, I recognize their causal character as well as their productive value. Anticipating acts in the projective mood of phantasy, I imagine their consequences and their effects. Finally, it is in the world of working, the wide awake world of adult daily life, that communication has its primary locus. Gearing into the world also means communicating in it. And since communication presupposes intersubjectivity, and intersubjectivity the typifications underlying all social relatedness, the individual is born into the paramount reality in which, as Dr. Schutz has tried to show, all typifications are rooted. It is this reality which the individual takes for granted and which he believingly lives in within the natural attitude. What Husserl terms the "general thesis of the natural attitude," the doxic belief in the very being of the world, finds its primary expression in the common-sense world. All modifications of this thesis must then be treated as having their root in daily life, just as all movements from one finite province of meaning to another presuppose the bed-rock of common sense. How does it happen, then, that traffic between worlds occurs at all? Or to point to the same problem from a different perspective, how is the boundary of the paramount reality protected from invaders? These questions ultimately generate the phenomenological problem of how a philosophy of the natural attitude is possible.

b) *The Epoché of the Natural Attitude*

One of the most important insights of Dr. Schutz' theory of multiple realities is his notion of the "epoché of the natural attitude." It deserves to be quoted at length: "Phenomenology has taught us the concept of phenomenological *epoché*, the suspension of our belief in the reality of the world as a device to overcome the natural attitude by radicalizing the Cartesian method of philosophical doubt. The suggestion may be ventured that man within the natural attitude also uses a specific *epoché*, of course quite another one than the phenomenologist. He does not suspend belief in the outer world and its objects, but on the contrary, he suspends doubt in its existence. What he puts in brackets is the doubt that the world and its objects might be otherwise than it appears to him. We propose to call this *epoché the epoché of the natural attitude*." Our natural believing in the world, in its reality, its being there, its having a past and the likelihood of a future, and of its being given to us all in much the same way is the philosophical foundation of the common-sense world. The paramount reality is founded on the apparent truth of the natural attitude. The implications of Dr. Schutz' idea of an *epoché* of the natural attitude are of considerable consequence. Essentially, he is suggesting that the natural attitude itself is an achievement based on a prior suspension of doubt. To be sure, this is not a self-conscious affair any more than the natural attitude itself is self-consciously constructed. Suspension of doubt may now be considered a clue to the very concept of typification, of the taken for granted idealizations which structure daily life. If an implicit rationale underlies the *epoché* of the natural attitude, explains why it should be effected at all, the underlying reasons must be sought for in those existential themes which are the philosophical climax of Dr. Schutz' account of multiple realities. Here also we will find the constitutive roots for his theory of relevance.

c) The Fundamental Anxiety

"The whole system of relevances which govern us within the natural attitude," Dr. Schutz argues, "is founded upon the basic experience of each of us: I know that I shall die and I fear to die. This basic experience we suggest calling the *fundamental anxiety*. It is the primordial anticipation from which all the others originate. From the fundamental anxiety spring the many interrelated systems of hopes and fears, of wants and satisfactions, of chances and risks which incite man within the natural attitude to attempt the mastery of the world, to overcome obstacles, to draft projects, and to realize them." The fear of death is here the fear of my death, and it might be suggested, though Dr. Schutz does not develop this idea, that the *epoché* of the natural attitude includes within its brackets the awareness that I will die. It would be an error, however, to treat the fundamental anxiety as a version of Heidegger's conception of death, an interpretation for which Dr. Schutz had considerable understanding but little sympathy. Nor would it be proper to consider the fundamental anxiety an existential theme in the narrower sense of a topic developed in the complex movement known simply as "existentialism." Again, Dr. Schutz had a profound grasp of the problems of existential philosophy but equally profound reservations about its conclusions. Let us rather consider the fundamental anxiety as an existential theme exploited not only by existentialists but by every metaphysical mind in the entire range of philosophy. In these terms, the fear of death is a primordial datum of human existence, as inescapable in its philosophical pertinence as it is in its implications for any theory of social reality. The paramount reality of daily life is founded on the secret grasp each man has of his own mortality.

However he defines his awareness of death, he cannot avoid its conceptual and emotive impact. It is the sovereign condition of human existence that the paramount reality transcends us all.

III

It would be misleading to suggest that Dr. Schutz' concern with the structure of common-sense life and his study of its essential forms were original because other philosophers had somehow ignored this stratum of experience. Mundane existence has been an ancient and persistent theme for philosophical treatment, and Dr. Schutz' historical indebtedness is manifest in his appreciative treatment of such thinkers as Leibniz, Bergson, Whitehead, and, above all, Husserl. Instead, we should say that the striking originality of the work which follows is in the methodological perspective in terms of which the central theme is approached and in terms of which the analysis is developed. We have here a phenomenological investigation into the nature of social reality, the first fully conceived and systematically realized description of the eidetic structure of the *Lebenswelt*. But it would be equally mistaken to say that Dr. Schutz' work is merely an extension of Husserl's thought or merely an application of phenomenological method to the problems of the social sciences. Dr. Schutz was deeply involved in phenomenology, but he was also an independent philosopher for whom phenomenology was a guide, not a master. He had the rare advantage of a comprehensive grasp of the concrete problems of sociology, social psychology, economics, history, political theory, and jurisprudence as well as the philosophical apparatus capable of handling them. Phenomenology served him as the instrument for ordering these problems into a coherent unity; never did it dictate to him, *a priori*, a methodological mold to which these disciplines had to conform. His originality expressed itself, then, in the union of a phenomenological philosophy with a unique placement of the very concept of social reality. The result involves a radical reconsideration of the starting point of philosophy.

Traditionally, perception has been taken as the decisive issue for philosophical orientation and appraisal. The full impact of Dr.

Schutz' work leads to the denial of the validity of this starting point for any philosophy concerned with social reality. Instead, *action* becomes the dominant theme. The implications of this transformation for epistemology are far-reaching, but its effects on the methodology of the social sciences are of more immediate concern to us here. Fundamentally, positivistic and naturalistic philosophies of science have assumed that since perception or sensation generally is paradigmatic as a point of departure for a methodology of the natural sciences, it is necessarily the case that it has the same status for a methodology of the social sciences. The assumption is that the ideal for the social sciences would be a science of society patterned, of course, after the eminently successful models of physics and mathematics. To challenge the status of perception, in this context, is to challenge the assumption that informs so much of contemporary methodology. Dr. Schutz goes as far as to suggest that "the particular methodological devices developed by the social sciences in order to grasp social reality are better suited than those of the natural sciences to lead to the discovery of the general principles which govern all human knowledge." What emerges from this view is a particular conception of methodology but also an approach to a theory of man.

The stress upon action as the starting point for a methodology of the social sciences is not a plea for a new kind of knowledge; it is rather an insistence on the qualitative difference between the kinds of reality investigated by natural scientists and social scientists. It is a plea for appreciating the fact that men are not only elements of the scientist's field of observation but pre-interpreters of their own field of action, that their overt conduct is only a fragment of their total behavior, that the first challenge given to those who seek to understand social reality is to comprehend the subjectivity of the actor by grasping the meaning an act has for him, the axis of the social world. Finally, Dr. Schutz's emphasis on action returns us to his cardinal insight, his analysis of the typifications of the common-sense world. The social scientist's task is the reconstruction of the way in which men in daily life interpret their own world. This is Dr. Schutz' Bergsonian point of contact with the real. But the final development of his position would, as he recognized, require the working out of a philosophical anthropology, a theory of man. Hints toward such a theory are given throughout his work; now they remain seminal fragments of an extraordinary achievement. The critical evaluation of that achievement is beyond our present scope, but to attest to its brilliance may be permitted as a final privilege. Dr. Schutz was modest in his claims but certain of the truth of his endeavour. "Of my results I am not so sure," he once said, "others may do better; but of one thing I am deeply convinced. *Here* are the problems of the social sciences."

The Problem of Social Reality

PART I

On The Methodology of the Social Sciences

COMMON-SENSE AND SCIENTIFIC INTERPRETATION OF HUMAN ACTION

I. INTRODUCTION: CONTENT OF EXPERIENCE AND THOUGHT OBJECTS

1) The constructs of common-sense and of scientific thinking

"Neither common sense nor science can proceed without departing from the strict consideration of what is actual in experience." This statement by A. N. Whitehead is at the foundation of his analysis of the Organization of Thought.[1] Even the thing perceived in everyday life is more than a simple sense presentation.[2] It is a thought object, a construct of a highly complicated nature, involving not only particular forms of time-successions in order to constitute it as an object of one single sense, say of sight,[3] and of space relations in order to constitute it as a sense-object of several senses, say of sight and touch,[4] but also a contribution of imagination of hypothetical sense presentations in order to complete it.[5] According to Whitehead, it is precisely the last-named factor, the imagination of hypothetical sense presentation, "which is the rock upon which the whole structure of common-sense thought is erected"[6] and it is the effort of reflective criticism "to construe our sense presentation as actual realization of the hypothetical thought object of perceptions."[7] In other words, the so-called concrete facts of common-sense perception are not so concrete as it seems. They already involve abstractions of a highly complicated nature, and

---

[1] Alfred North Whitehead: *The Organization of Thought*, London, 1917, now partially republished in *The Aims of Education*, New York, 1929, also as "Mentor-Book," New York, 1949. The quotations refer to this edition. For the first quotation see p. 110.
[2] *Ibid.*, Chapter 9, "The Anatomy of Some Scientific Ideas, I Fact, II Objects."
[3] *Ibid.*, p. 128f. and 131.
[4] *Ibid.*, p. 131 and 136.
[5] *Ibid.*, p. 133.
[6] *Ibid.*, p. 134.
[7] *Ibid.*, p. 135.

we have to take account of this situation lest we commit the fallacy of misplaced concreteness.[8]

Science always, according to Whitehead, has a twofold aim: First, the production of a theory which agrees with experience, and second, the explanation of common-sense concepts of nature at least in their outline; this explanation consists in the preservation of these concepts in a scientific theory of harmonized thought.[9] For this purpose physical science (which, in this context, is alone of concern to Whitehead) has to develop devices by which the thought objects of common-sense perception are superseded by the thought objects of science.[10] The latter, such as molecules, atoms, and electrons have shed all qualities capable of direct sense presentation in our consciousness and are known to us only by the series of events in which they are implicated, events, to be sure, which are represented in our consciousness by sense presentations. By this device a bridge is formed between the fluid vagueness of sense and the exact definition of thought.[11]

It is not our concern to follow here step by step the ingenious method by which Whitehead uses the principle briefly outlined for his analysis of the organization of thought, starting from the "anatomy of scientific ideas" and ending with the mathematically formulated theories of modern physiscs and the procedural rules of symbolic logic.[12] We are, however, highly interested in the basic view which Whitehead shares with many other prominent thinkers of our time such as William James,[13] Dewey,[14] Bergson,[15] and Husserl.[16] This view can be, very roughly, formulated as follows:

---

[8] Alfred North Whitehead: *Science and the Modern World*, New York, 1925, reprinted as "Mentor-Book," New York, 1948, p. 52 ff.

[9] *The Aims of Education*, p. 126.

[10] *Ibid.*, p. 135.

[11] *Ibid.*, p. 136.

[12] *Ibid.*, pp. 112-123 and 136-155.

[13] William James, *Principles of Psychology*, Vol. I, Chapter IX, "The Stream of Thought," p. 224f; especially p. 289f.

[14] John Dewey, *Logic, The Theory of Inquiry*, New York, 1938, especially Chs. III, IV, VII, VIII, XII; See also the essay, "The Objectivism-Subjectivism of Modern Philosophy" (1941) now in the collection *Problems of Men*, New York, 1946, p. 316f.

[15] Henri Bergson, *Matière et mémoire*, Ch. I, "La Sélection des Images par la Représentation."

[16] See for instance Edmund Husserl, *Logische Untersuchungen*, II Bd., II, "Die ideale Einheit der Species und die neuen Abstraktions Theorien"; rendered excellently by Marvin Farber, *The Foundation of Phenomenology*, Cambridge, 1943,

All our knowledge of the world, in common-sense as well as in scientific thinking, involves constructs, i.e., a set of abstractions, generalizations, formalizations, idealizations specific to the respective level of thought organization. Strictly speaking, there are no such things as facts, pure and simple. All facts are from the outset facts selected from a universal context by the activities of our mind. They are, therefore, always interpreted facts, either facts looked at as detached from their context by an artificial abstraction or facts considered in their particular setting. In either case, they carry along their interpretational inner and outer horizon. This does not mean that, in daily life or in science, we are unable to grasp the reality of the world. It just means that we grasp merely certain aspects of it, namely those which are relevant to us either for carrying on our business of living or from the point of view of a body of accepted rules of procedure of thinking called the method of science.

2) *Particular structure of the constructs of the social sciences*

If, according to this view, all scientific constructs are designed to supersede the constructs of common-sense thought, then a principal difference between the natural and the social sciences becomes apparent. It is up to the natural scientists to determine which sector of the universe of nature, which facts and events therein, and which aspects of such facts and events are topically and interpretationally relevant to their specific purpose. These facts and events are neither preselected nor preinterpreted; they do not reveal intrinsic relevance structures. Relevance is not inherent in nature as such, it is the result of the selective and interpretative activity of man within nature or observing nature. The facts, data, and events with which the natural scientist has to deal are just facts, data, and events within his observational field but this field does not "mean" anything to the molecules, atoms, and electrons therein.

But the facts, events, and data before the social scientist are of an entirely different structure. His observational field, the social

Ch. IX, esp. p. 251f; Husserl, *Ideen zu einer reinen Phänomenologie*, English translation by Boyce Gibson, London, 1931, First Section; *Formale und transzendentale Logik*, Halle, 1929, Secs. 82–86, 94–96 (cf. Farber, l.c., p. 501ff.); *Erfahrung und Urteil*, Prague, 1939, Secs. 6–10, 16–24, 41–43, and *passim*.

world, is not essentially structureless. It has a particular meaning and relevance structure for the human beings living, thinking, and acting therein. They have preselected and preinterpreted this world by a series of common-sense constructs of the reality of daily life, and it is these thought objects which determine their behavior, define the goal of their action, the means available for attaining them – in brief, which help them to find their bearings within their natural and socio-cultural environment and to come to terms with it. The thought objects constructed by the social scientists refer to and are founded upon the thought objects constructed by the common-sense thought of man living his everyday life among his fellow-men. Thus, the constructs used by the social scientist are, so to speak, constructs of the second degree, namely constructs of the constructs made by the actors on the social scene, whose behavior the scientist observes and tries to explain in accordance with the procedural [17] rules of his science.

Modern social sciences find themselves faced with a serious dilemma. One school of thought feels that there is a basic difference in the structure of the social world and of the world of nature. This insight leads, however, to the erroneous conclusion that the social sciences are *toto coelo* different from the natural sciences, a view which disregards the fact that certain procedural rules relating to correct thought organization are common to all empirical sciences. The other school of thought tries to look at the behavior of man in the same way in which the natural scientist looks at the "behavior" of his thought objects, taking it for granted that the methods of the natural sciences (above all, mathematical physics), which have achieved such magnificent results, are the only scientific methods. On the other hand, it takes for granted that the very adoption of the methods of the natural sciences for establishing constructs will lead to reliable knowledge of social reality. Yet these two assumptions are incompatible with each other. An ideally refined and fully developed behavioristic system, for example, would lead far away from the constructs in terms of which men in the reality of daily life experience their own and their fellow-men's behavior.

---

[17] On the concept of procedural rules, see Felix Kaufmann, *Methodology of the Social Sciences*, New York, 1944, esp. Chs. III and IV; on the divergent views of the relationship between the natural and the social sciences, *ibid.*, Ch. X.

COMMON-SENSE AND SCIENTIFIC INTERPRETATION

To overcome this difficulty particular methodological devices are required, among them the constructs of patterns of rational action. For the purpose of further analysis of the specific nature of the thought objects of social sciences we have to characterize some of the common-sense constructs used by men in everyday life. It is upon the latter that the former are founded.

II. CONSTRUCTS OF THOUGHT OBJECTS IN COMMON-SENSE THINKING

1) *The individual's common-sense knowledge of the world is a system of constructs of its typicality*

Let us try to characterize the way in which the wide-awake [18] grown-up man looks at the intersubjective world of daily life within which and upon which he acts as a man amidst his fellow-men. This world existed before our birth, experienced and interpreted by others, our predecessors, as an organized world. Now it is given to our experience and interpretation. All interpretation of this world is based on a stock of previous experiences of it, our own or those handed down to us by parents or teachers; these experiences in the form of "knowledge at hand" function as a scheme of reference.

To this stock of knowledge at hand belongs our knowledge that the world we live in is a world of more or less well circumscribed objects with more or less definite qualities, objects among which we move, which resist us and upon which we may act. Yet none of these objects is perceived as insulated. From the outset it is an object within a horizon of familiarity and pre-acquaintanceship which is, as such, just taken for granted until further notice as the unquestioned, though at any time questionable stock of knowledge at hand. The unquestioned pre-experiences are, however, also from the outset, at hand as *typical*, that is, as carrying open horizons of anticipated similar experiences. For example, the outer world is not experienced as an arrangement of individual unique objects, dispersed in space and time, but as

[18] As to the precise meaning of this term, see "On Multiple Realities," p. 213. (Note: where articles are cited without further indication of source, as in this instance, the reference is to the present volume.) (M.N.)

"mountains," "trees," "animals," "fellow-men." I may have never seen an Irish setter but if I see one, I know that it is an animal and in particular a dog, showing all the familiar features and the typical behavior of a dog and not, say, of a cat. I may reasonably ask: "What kind of dog is this?" The question presupposes that the dissimilarity of this particular dog from all other kinds of dogs which I know stands out and becomes questionable merely by reference to the similarity it has to my unquestioned experiences of typical dogs. In the more technical language of Husserl, whose analysis of the typicality of the world of daily life we have tried to sum up,[19] what is experienced in the actual perception of an object is apperceptively transferred to any other similar object, perceived merely as to its type. Actual experience will or will not confirm my anticipation of the typical conformity with other objects. If confirmed, the content of the anticipated type will be enlarged; at the same time the type will be split up into sub-types; on the other hand the concrete real object will prove to have its individual characteristics, which, nevertheless, have a form of typicality.

Now, and this seems to be of special importance, I *may* take the typically apperceived object as an *exemplar* of the general type and allow myself to be led to this concept of the type, but I do not *need* by any means to think of the concrete dog as an exemplar of the general concept of "dog." "In general" my Irish setter Rover shows all the characteristics which the type "dog," according to my previous experience, implies. Yet exactly what he has in common with other dogs is of no concern to me. I look at him as my friend and companion Rover, as such distinguished from all the other Irish setters with which he shares certain typical characteristics of appearance and behavior. I am, without a special motive, not induced to look at Rover as a mammal, an animal, an object of the outer world, although I know that he is all this too.

Thus, in the natural attitude of daily life we are concerned merely with certain objects standing out over against the unquestioned field of pre-experienced other objects, and the result of the selecting activity of our mind is to determine which

---

[19] Edmund Husserl, *Erfahrung und Urteil*, Secs. 18-21 and 82-85; cf. also "Language, Language Disturbances and the Texture of Consciousness," esp. pp. 277-283.

particular characteristics of such an object are individual and which typical ones. More generally, we are merely concerned with some aspects of this particular typified object. Asserting of this object S that it has the characteristic property p, in the form "S is p," is an elliptical statement. For S, taken without any question as it appears to me, is not merely p but also q and r and many other things. The full statement should read: "S is, among many other things, such as q and r, also p." If I assert with respect to an element of the world as taken for granted: "S is p," I do so because under the prevailing circumstances I am interested in the p-being of S, disregarding as not relevant its being also q and r.[20]

The terms "interest" and "relevant" just used are, however, merely headings for a series of complicated problems which cannot be elaborated upon within the frame of the present discussion. We have to restrict ourselves to a few remarks.

Man finds himself at any moment of his daily life in a biographically determined situation, that is, in a physical and sociocultural environment as defined by him,[21] within which he has his position, not merely his position in terms of physical space and outer time or of his status and role within the social system but also his moral and ideological position.[22] To say that this definition of the situation is biographically determined is to say that it has its history; it is the sedimentation of all man's previous experiences, organized in the habitual possessions of his stock of knowledge at hand, and as such his unique possession, given to him and to him alone.* This biographically determined situation includes certain possibilities of future practical or theoretical activities which shall be briefly called the "purpose at hand." It is this purpose at hand which defines those elements among all the others contained in such a situation which are relevant for this purpose. This system of relevances in turn determines what elements have to be made a substratum of

---

[20] See literature referred to in Footnote 19.
[21] As to the concept of "Defining the Situation," see the various pertinent papers of W. I. Thomas, now collected in the volume, *Social Behavior and Personality, Contributions of W. I. Thomas to Theory and Social Research*, ed. by Edmund H. Volkart, New York, 1951. Consult index and the valuable introductory essay by the editor.
[22] Cf. Maurice Merleau-Ponty, *Phénoménologie de la perception*, Paris, 1945, p. 158.
* See "Choosing among Projects of Action", pp. 76-77. (M.N.)

generalizing typification, what traits of these elements have to be selected as characteristically typical, and what others as unique and individual, that is, how far we have to penetrate into the open horizon of typicality. To return to our previous example: A change in my purpose at hand and the system of relevances attached thereto, the shifting of the "context" within which S is interesting to me, may induce me to become concerned with the q-being of S, its being also p having become irrelevant to me.

2) *The intersubjective character of common-sense knowledge and its implication*

In analyzing the first constructs of common-sense thinking in everyday life we proceeded, however, as if the world were my private world and as if we were entitled to disregard the fact that it is from the outset an intersubjective world of culture. It is intersubjective because we live in it as men among other men, bound to them through common influence and work, understanding others and being understood by them. It is a world of culture because, from the outset, the world of everyday life is a universe of significance to us, that is, a texture of meaning which we have to interpret in order to find our bearings within it and come to terms with it. This texture of meaning, however – and this distinguishes the realm of culture from that of nature – originates in and has been instituted by human actions, our own and our fellow-men's, contemporaries and predecessors. All cultural objects – tools, symbols, language systems, works of art, social institutions, etc. – point back by their very origin and meaning to the activities of human subjects. For this reason we are always conscious of the historicity of culture which we encounter in traditions and customs. This historicity is capable of being examined in its reference to human activities of which it is the sediment. For the same reason I cannot understand a cultural object without referring it to the human activity from which it originates. For example, I do not understand a tool without knowing the purpose for which it was designed, a sign or symbol without knowing what it stands for in the mind of the person who uses it, an institution without understanding what it means for the individuals who orient their behavior with regard to its existence. Here is the origin of the so-called postulate of subjective interpretation of the social sciences which will call for our attention later on.

Our next task is, however, to examine the additional constructs which emerge in common-sense thinking if we take into account that this world is not my private world but an intersubjective one and that, therefore, my knowledge of it is not my private affair but from the outset intersubjective or socialized. For our purpose we have briefly to consider three aspects of the problem of the socialization of knowledge:
a) The reciprocity of perspectives or the structural socialization of knowledge;
b) The social origin of knowledge or the genetic socialization of knowledge;
c) The social distribution of knowledge.

a) The reciprocity of perspectives

In the natural attitude of common-sense thinking in daily life I take it for granted that intelligent fellow-men exist. This implies that the objects of the world are, as a matter of principle, accessible to their knowledge, i.e., either known to them or knowable by them. This I know and take for granted beyond question. But I know also and take for granted that, strictly speaking, the "same" object must mean something different to me and to any of my fellow-men. This is so because
i) I, being "here," am at another distance from and experience other aspects as being typical of the objects than he, who is "there." For the same reason, certain objects are out of my reach (of my seeing, hearing, my manipulatory sphere, etc.) but within his, and vice versa.
ii) My and my fellow-man's biographically determined situations, and therewith our respective purposes at hand and our respective systems of relevances originating in such purposes, must differ, at least to a certain extent.

Common-sense thinking overcomes the differences in individual perspectives resulting from these factors by two basic idealizations:
i) The idealization of the interchangeability of the standpoints:

I take it for granted – and assume my fellow-man does the same – that if I change places with him so that his "here" becomes mine, I shall be at the same distance from things and see them with the same typicality as he actually does; moreover, the same things would be in my reach which are actually in his. (The reverse is also true.)

ii) The idealization of the congruency of the system of relevances: Until counterevidence I take it for granted – and assume my fellow-man does the same – that the differences in perspectives originating in our unique biographical situations are irrelevant for the purpose at hand of either of us and that he and I, that "We" assume that both of us have selected and interpreted the actually or potentially common objects and their features in an identical manner or at least an "empirically identical" manner, i.e., one sufficient for all practical purposes.

It is obvious that both idealizations, that of the interchangeability of the standpoints and that of the congruency of relevances – together constituting the *general thesis of reciprocal perspectives* – are typifying constructs of objects of thought which supersede the thought objects of my and my fellow-man's private experience. By the operation of these constructs of common-sense thinking it is assumed that the sector of the world taken for granted by me is also taken for granted by you, my individual fellow-man, even more, that it is taken for granted by "Us." But this "We" does not merely include you and me but "everyone who is one of us," i.e., everyone whose system of relevances is substantially (sufficiently) in conformity with yours and mine. Thus, the general thesis of reciprocal perspectives leads to the apprehension of objects and their aspects actually known by me and potentially known by you as everyone's knowledge. Such knowledge is conceived to be objective and anonymous, i.e., detached from and independent of my and my fellow-man's definition of the situation, our unique biographical circumstances and the actual and potential purposes at hand involved therein.

We must interpret the terms "objects" and "aspect of objects" in the broadest possible sense as signifying objects of knowledge taken for granted. If we do so, we shall discover the importance of the constructs of intersubjective thought objects, originating

COMMON-SENSE AND SCIENTIFIC INTERPRETATION 13

in the structural socialization of knowledge just described, for many problems investigated, but not thoroughly analyzed, by eminent social scientists. What is supposed to be known in common by everyone who shares our system of relevances is the way of life considered to be the natural, the good, the right one by the members of the "in-group"; [23] as such, it is at the origin of the many recipes for handling things and men in order to come to terms with typified situations, of the folkways and mores, of "traditional behavior," in Max Weber's sense, [24] of the "of-course statements" believed to be valid by the in-group in spite of their inconsistencies,[25] briefly, of the "relative natural aspect of the world." [26] All these terms refer to constructs of a typified knowledge of a highly socialized structure which supersede the thought objects of my and my fellow-man's private knowledge of the world as taken for granted. Yet this knowledge has its history, it is a part of our "social heritage," and this brings us to the second aspect of the problem of socialization of knowledge, its genetic structure.

b) The social origin of knowledge

Only a very small part of my knowledge of the world originates within my personal experience. The greater part is socially derived, handed down to me by my friends, my parents, my teachers and the teachers of my teachers. I am taught not only how to define the environment (that is, the typical features of the relative natural aspect of the world prevailing in the in-group as the unquestioned but always questionable sum total of things taken for granted until further notice), but also how typical constructs have to be formed in accordance with the system of relevances accepted from the anonymous unified point of view of

---

[23] William Graham Sumner, *Folkways, A Study of the Sociological Importance of Manners, Customs, Mores and Morals*, New York, 1906.

[24] Max Weber, *The Theory of Social and Economic Organization*, translated by A. M. Henderson and Talcott Parsons, New York, 1947, pp. 115ff; see also Talcott Parsons, *The Structure of Social Action*, New York, 1937, Ch. XVI.

[25] Robert S. Lynd, *Middletown in Transition*, New York, 1937, Ch. XII, and *Knowledge for What?*, Princeton, 1939, pp. 38-63.

[26] Max Scheler, *Die Wissensformen und die Gesellschaft, Probleme einer Soziologie des Wissens*, Leipzig, 1926, pp. 58ff. Cf. Howard Becker and Helmut Dahlke, "Max Scheler's Sociology of Knowledge," *Philosophy and Phenomenological Research*, Vol. II, 1942, pp. 310-22, esp. 315.

the in-group. This includes ways of life, methods of coming to terms with the environment, efficient recipes for the use of typical means for bringing about typical ends in typical situations. The typifying medium *par excellence* by which socially derived knowledge is transmitted is the vocabulary and the syntax of everyday language. The vernacular of everyday life is primarily a language of named things and events, and any name includes a typification and generalization referring to the relevance system prevailing in the linguistic in-group which found the named thing significant enough to provide a separate term for it. The pre-scientific vernacular can be interpreted as a treasure house of ready made pre-constituted types and characteristics, all socially derived and carrying along an open horizon of unexplored content.[27]

c) The social distribution of knowledge

Knowledge is socially distributed. The general thesis of reciprocal perspectives, to be sure, overcomes the difficulty that my actual knowledge is merely the potential knowledge of my fellow-men and vice versa. But the stock of *actual* knowledge at hand differs from individual to individual, and common-sense thinking takes this fact into account. Not only *what* an individual knows differs from what his neighbor knows, but also *how* both know the "same" facts. Knowledge has manifold degrees of clarity, distinctness, precision, and familiarity. To take as an example William James'[28] well known distinction between "knowledge of acquaintance" and "knowledge-about," it is obvious that many things are known to me just in the dumb way of mere acquaintance, whereas *you* have knowledge "about" what makes them what they are and vice versa. I am an "expert" in a small field and "layman" in many others, and so are you.[29] Any individual's stock of knowledge at hand is at any moment of his life structured as having zones of various degrees of clarity, distinctness and precision. This structure originates in the

---

[27] See "Language, Language Disturbances, and the Texture of Consciousness", p. 285f.

[28] William James, l.c., Vol. I, p. 221f.

[29] Alfred Schutz, "The Well-Informed Citizen, an Essay on the Social Distribution of Knowledge," *Social Research*, Vol. 13, 1946, pp. 463–472.

system of prevailing relevances and is thus biographically determined. The knowledge of these individual differences is itself an element of common-sense experience: I know whom and under what typical circumstances I have to consult as a "competent" doctor or lawyer. In other words, in daily life I construct types of the Other's field of acquaintance and of the scope and texture of his knowledge. In doing so, I assume that he will be guided by certain relevance structures, expressing themselves in a set of constant motives leading to a particular pattern of action and even co-determining his personality. But this statement anticipates the analysis of the common-sense constructs related to the understanding of our fellow-men, which is our next task.[29a]

3) *The structure of the social world and its typification by common-sense constructs*

I, the human being, born into the social world, and living my daily life in it, experience it as built around my place in it, as open to my interpretation and action, but always referring to my actual biographically determined situation. Only in reference to me does a certain kind of my relations with others obtain the specific meaning which I designate with the word "We"; only with reference to "Us," whose center I am, do others stand out as "You," and in reference to "You," who refer back to me, third parties stand out as "They." In the dimension of time there are with reference to me in my actual biographical moment "contemporaries," with whom a mutual interplay of action and reaction can be established; "predecessors," upon whom I cannot act, but whose past actions and their outcome are open to my interpretation and may influence my own actions; and

---

[29a] With the exception of some economists (e.g., F. A. Hayek, "Economics and Knowledge", *Economica*, February 1937, now reprinted in *Individualism and Economic Order*, Chicago 1948) the problem of the social distribution of knowledge has not attracted the attention of the social scientists it merits. It opens a new field for theoretical and empirical research which would truly deserve the name of a sociology of knowledge, now reserved for an ill-defined discipline which just takes for granted the social distribution of knowledge, upon which it is founded. It may be hoped that the systematic investigation of this field will yield significant contributions to many problems of the social sciences such as those of social role, of social stratification, of institutional or organizational behavior, of the sociology of occupations and professions, of prestige and status, etc.

"successors," of whom no experience is possible but toward whom I may orient my actions in a more or less empty anticipation. All these relations show the most manifold forms of intimacy and anonymity, of familiarity and strangeness, of intensity and extensity.[30]

In the present context we are restricting ourselves to the interrelationship prevailing among contemporaries. Still dealing with common-sense experience we may just take for granted that man can understand his fellow-man and his actions and that he can communicate with others because he assumes they understand his actions; also, that this mutual understanding has certain limits but is sufficient for many practical purposes.

Among my contemporaries are some with whom I share, as long as the relation lasts, not only a community of time but also of space. We shall, for the sake of terminological convenience, call such contemporaries "consociates" and the relationship prevailing among them a "face-to-face" relationship, this term being understood in a sense other than that used by Cooley [31] and his successors; we designate by it merely a purely formal aspect of social relationship equally applicable to an intimate talk between friends and the co-presence of strangers in a railroad car.

Sharing a community of space implies that a certain sector of the outer world is equally within the reach of each partner, and contains objects of common interest and relevance. For each partner the other's body, his gestures, his gait and facial expressions, are immediately observable, not merely as things or events of the outer world but in their physiognomical significance, that is, as symptoms of the other's thoughts. Sharing a community of time – and this means not only of outer (chronological) time, but of inner time – implies that each partner participates in the on-rolling life of the other, can grasp in a vivid present the other's thoughts as they are built up step by step. They may thus share one another's anticipations of the future as plans, or hopes or anxieties. In brief, consociates are mutually involved in one

---

[30] Alfred Schutz, *Der sinnhafte Aufbau der sozialen Welt*, Vienna, 1932, 2nd edition 1960. See also Alfred Stonier and Karl Bode, "A New Approach to the Methodology of the Social Sciences," *Economica*, Vol. V, November, 1937, pp. 406–424, esp. pp. 416ff.

[31] Charles H. Cooley, *Social Organization*, New York, 1909, Chs. III–V; and Alfred Schutz, "The Homecomer," *American Journal of Sociology*, Vol. 50, 1945, p. 371.

another's biography; they are growing older together; they live, as we may call it, in a pure We-relationship.

In such a relationship, fugitive and superficial as it may be, the Other is grasped as a unique individuality (although merely one aspect of his personality becomes apparent) in its unique biographical situation (although revealed merely fragmentarily). In all the other forms of social relationship (and even in the relationship among consociates as far as the unrevealed aspects of the Other's self are concerned) the fellow-man's self can merely be grasped by a "contribution of imagination of hypothetical meaning presentation" (to allude to Whitehead's statement quoted earlier), that is, by forming a construct of a typical way of behavior, a typical pattern of underlying motives, of typical attitudes of a personality type, of which the Other and his conduct under scrutiny, both outside of my observational reach, are just instances or exemplars. We cannot here [32] develop a full taxonomy of the structuredness of the social world and of the various forms of constructs of course-of-action types and personality types needed for grasping the Other and his behavior. Thinking of my absent friend A, I form an ideal type of his personality and behavior based on my past experience of A as my consociate. Putting a letter in the mailbox, I expect that unknown people, called postmen, will act in a typical way, not quite intelligible to me, with the result that my letter will reach the addressee within typically reasonable time. Without ever having met a Frenchman or a German, I understand "Why France fears the rearmament of Germany." Complying with a rule of English grammar, I follow a socially approved behavior pattern of contemporary English-speaking fellow-men to which I have to adjust my own behavior in order to make myself understandable. And, finally, any artifact or utensil refers to the anonymous fellow-man who produced it to be used by other anonymous fellow-men for attaining typical goals by typical means.*

These are just a few examples but they are arranged according to the degree of increasing anonymity of the relationship among contemporaries involved and therewith of the construct needed

---

[32] See footnote 30.
* See Alfred Schutz, "The Problem of Rationality in the Social World", *Economica*, Vol. X, May 1943. (M.N.).

to grasp the Other and his behavior. It becomes apparent that an increase in anonymity involves a decrease of fullness of content. The more anonymous the typifying construct is, the more detached it is from the uniqueness of the individual fellow-man involved and the fewer aspects of his personality and behavior pattern enter the typification as being relevant for the purpose at hand, for the sake of which the type has been constructed. If we distinguish between (subjective) personal types and (objective) course-of-action types, we may say that increasing anonymization of the construct leads to the superseding of the former by the latter. In complete anonymization the individuals are supposed to be interchangeable and the course-of-action type refers to the behavior of "whomsoever" acting in the way defined as typical by the construct.

Summing up, we may say that, except in the pure We-relation of consociates, we can never grasp the individual uniqueness of our fellow-man in his unique biographical situation. In the constructs of common-sense thinking the Other appears at best as a partial self, and he enters even the pure We-relation merely with a part of his personality. This insight seems to be important in several respects. It helped Simmel [33] to overcome the dilemma between individual and collective consciousness, so clearly seen by Durkheim [34]; it is at the basis of Cooley's [35] theory of the origin of the Self by a "looking glass effect"; it led George H. Mead [36] to his ingenious concept of the "generalized other"; it is, finally, decisive for the clarification of such concepts as "social functions," "social role," and, last but not least, "rational action." *

[33] Georg Simmel: "Note on the Problem: How is Society Possible?" translated by Albion W. Small, *The American Journal of Sociology*, Vol. XVI, 1910, pp. 372–391; see also, *The Sociology of Georg Simmel*, translated, edited and with an introduction by Kurt H. Wolff, Glencoe, Ill. 1950, and consult Index under "Individual and Group".
[34] An excellent presentation of Durkheim's view in Georges Gurvitch, *La Vocation Actuelle de la Sociologie*, Paris, 1950, Ch. VI, pp. 351–409; see also Talcott Parsons, *The Structure of Social Action*, Ch. X; Emile Benoit-Smullyan: "The Sociologism of Emile Durkheim and his School," in Harry Elmer Barnes: *An Introduction to the History of Sociology*, Chicago, 1948, pp. 499–537, and Robert K. Merton: *Social Theory and Social Structure*, Glencoe, Ill. 1949, Ch. IV, pp. 125–150.
[35] Charles H. Cooley, *Human Nature and the Social Order*, rev. ed., New York, 1922, p. 184.
[36] George H. Mead: *Mind, Self, and Society*, Chicago, 1934, pp. 152–163.
* For critical clarification of this concept, see "The Problem of Rationality in the Social World", *Economica*, Vol. X, May 1943. (M.N.)

But this is merely half the story. My constructing the Other as a partial self, as the performer of typical roles or functions, has a corollary in the process of self-typification which takes place if I enter into interaction with him. I am not involved in such a relationship with my total personality but merely with certain layers of it. In defining the role of the Other I am assuming a role myself. In typifying the Other's behavior I am typifying my own, which is interrelated with his, transforming myself into a passenger, consumer, taxpayer, reader, bystander, etc. It is this self-typification which is at the bottom of William James' [37] and of George H. Mead's [38] distinction between the "I" and the "Me" in relation to the social self.

We have, however, to keep in mind that the common-sense constructs used for the typification of the Other and of myself are to a considerable extent socially derived and socially approved. Within the in-group the bulk of personal types and course-of-action types is taken for granted (until counter-evidence appears) as a set of rules and recipes which have stood the test so far and are expected to stand it in the future. Even more, the pattern of typical constructs is frequently institutionalized as a standard of behavior, warranted by traditional and habitual mores and sometimes by specific means of so-called social control, such as the legal order.

4) *Course-of-action types and personal types*

We have now briefly to investigate the pattern of action and social interaction which underlies the construction of course-of-action and personal types in common-sense thinking.

a) *Action, project, motive*

The term "action" as used in this paper shall designate human conduct devised by the actor in advance, that is, conduct based upon a preconceived project. The term "act" shall designate the

---

[37] William James, *op. cit.*, Vol. I, Ch. X.
[38] George H. Mead, *op. cit.*, pp. 173–175, 196–198, 203; "The Genesis of the Self," reprinted in *The Philosophy of the Present*, Chicago, 1932, pp. 176–195; "What Social Objects Must Psychology Presuppose?" *Journal of Philosophy*, Vol. X, 1913, pp. 374–380.

outcome of this ongoing process, that is, the accomplished action. Action may be covert (for example, the attempt to solve a scientific problem mentally) or overt, gearing into the outer world; it may take place by commission or omission, purposive abstention from acting being considered an action in itself.

All projecting consists in anticipation of future conduct by way of phantasying, yet it is not the ongoing process of action but the phantasied act as having been accomplished which is the starting point of all projecting. I have to visualize the state of affairs to be brought about by my future action before I can draft the single steps of such future acting from which this state of affairs will result. Metaphorically speaking, I must have some idea of the structure to be erected before I can draft the blueprints. Thus I have to place myself in my phantasy at a future time, when this action *will* already *have been* accomplished. Only then may I reconstruct in phantasy the single steps which *will have* brought forth this future act. In the terminology suggested, it is not the future action but the future act that is anticipated in the project, and it is anticipated in the Future Perfect Tense, *modo futuri exacti*. This time perspective peculiar to the project has rather important consequences.

i) All projects of my forthcoming acts are based upon my knowledge at hand at the time of projecting. To this knowledge belongs my experience of previously performed acts which are typically similar to the projected one. Consequently all projecting involves a particular idealization, called by Husserl the idealization of "I-can-do-it-again," [39] i.e., the assumption that I may under typically similar circumstances act in a way typically similar to that in which I acted before in order to bring about a typically similar state of affairs. It is clear that this idealization involves a construction of a specific kind. My knowledge at hand at the time of projecting must, strictly speaking, be different from my knowledge at hand after having performed the projected act, if for no other reason than because I "grew older" and at least the experiences I had while carrying out my project have modified my biographical circumstances and enlarged my

[39] Edmund Husserl, *Formale und transzendentale Logik*, Halle, 1929, Sec. 74, p. 167; *Erfahrung und Urteil*, Sec. 24, Sec. 51b.

stock of experience. Thus, the "repeated" action will be something else than a mere re-performance. The first action A' started within a set of circumstances C' and indeed brought about the state of affairs S'; the repeated action A'' starts in a set of circumstances C'' and is expected to bring about the state of affairs S''. By necessity C'' will differ from C' because the experience that A' succeeded in bringing about S' belongs to my stock of knowledge, which is an element of C'', whereas to my stock of knowledge, which was an element of C', belonged merely the empty anticipation that this would be the case. Similarly S'' will differ from S' as A'' will from A'. This is so because all the terms – C', C'', A', A'', S', S'' – are as such unique and irretrievable events. Yet exactly those features which make them unique and irretrievable in the strict sense are – to my common-sense thinking – eliminated as being irrelevant for my purpose at hand. When making the idealization of "I-can-do-it-again" I am merely interested in the typicality of A, C, and S, all of them without primes. The construction consists, figuratively speaking, in the suppression of the primes as being irrelevant, and this, incidentally, is characteristic of typifications of all kinds.

This point will become especially important for the analysis of the concept of so-called rational action. It is obvious that in the habitual and routine actions of daily life we apply the construction just described in following recipes and rules of thumb which have stood the test so far and in frequently stringing together means and ends without clear knowledge "about" their real connections. Even in common-sense thinking we construct a world of supposedly interrelated facts containing exclusively elements deemed to be relevant for our purpose at hand.

ii) The particular time perspective of the project sheds some light on the relationship between project and motive. In ordinary speech the term "motive" covers two different sets of concepts which have to be distinguished.

    a) We may say that the motive of a murderer was to obtain the money of the victim. Here "motive" means the state of affairs, the end, which is to be brought about by the action undertaken. We shall call this kind of motive the "in-order-to motive." From the point of view of the actor this class of motives refers to the future. The state of affairs to be brought about by the future action, pre-phantasied in its project, is the in-order-to motive for carrying out the action.

b) We may say that the murderer has been motivated to commit his deed because he grew up in this or that environment, had these or those childhood experiences, etc. This class of motives, which we shall call "(genuine)[39a] because-motives" refers from the point of view of the actor to his past experiences which have determined him to act as he did. What is motivated in an action in the form of "because" is the project of the action itself (for instance, to satisfy his need for money by killing a man).

We cannot enter here [40] into a more detailed analysis of the theory of motives. But it should be pointed out that the actor who lives in his ongoing process of acting has merely the in-order-to motive of his ongoing action in view, that is, the projected state of affairs to be brought about. Only by turning back to his accomplished act or to the past initial phases of his still ongoing action or to the once established project which anticipates the act *modo futuri exacti* can the actor grasp retrospectively the because-motive that determined him to do what he did or what he projected to do. But then the actor is not acting any more; he is an observer of himself.

The distinction between the two kinds of motives becomes of vital importance for the analysis of human interaction to which we now turn.

b) Social interaction

Any form of social interaction is founded upon the constructs already described relating to the understanding of the Other and

---

[39a] Linguistically in-order-to motives may be expressed in modern languages also by "because"-*sentences*. Genuine because-motives, however, cannot be expressed by "in-order-to" *sentences*. This distinction between the two possibilities of linguistic expressions relating to the in-order-to motive, important as it is in another context, will be disregarded in the following and the term "because-motive" or "because-sentence" will be exclusively reserved for the genuine because-motive and its linguistic expression.

[40] See footnote 30.

the action pattern in general. Take as an example the interaction of consociates involved in questioning and answering. In projecting my question, I anticipate that the Other will understand my action (for instance my uttering an interrogative sentence) as a question and that this understanding will induce him to act in such a way that I may understand his behavior as an adequate response. (I: "Where is the ink?" The Other points at a table.) The in-order-to motive of my action is to obtain adequate information which, in this particular situation, presupposes that the understanding of my in-order-to motive will become the Other's because-motive to perform an action in-order-to furnish me this information – provided he is able and willing to do so, which I assume he is. I anticipate that he understands English, that he knows where the ink is, that he will tell me if he knows, etc. In more general terms, I anticipate that he will be guided by the same types of motives by which in the past, according to my stock of knowledge at hand, I myself and many others were guided under typically similar circumstances. Our example shows that even the simplest interaction in common life presupposes a series of common-sense constructs – in this case constructs of the Other's anticipated behavior – all of them based on the idealization that the actor's in-order-to motives will become because-motives of his partner and vice versa. We shall call this *idealization* that *of the reciprocity of motives*. It is obvious that this idealization depends upon the general thesis of the reciprocity of perspectives, since it implies that the motives imputed to the Other are typically the same as my own or that of others in typically similar circumstances; all this is in accordance with my genuine or socially derived knowledge at hand.

Suppose now that I want to find some ink in order to refill my fountain pen so that I can write this application to the fellowship committee which, if granted, will change my entire way of life. I, the actor (questioner), and I alone know of this plan of mine to obtain the fellowship which is the ultimate in-order-to motive of my actual action, the state of affairs to be brought about. Of course, this can be done merely by a series of steps (writing an application, bringing writing tools within my reach, etc.) each of them to be materialized by an "action" with its particular project and its particular in-order-to motive. Yet all these "sub-actions" are merely phases of the total action and all intermediary steps to be materialized by them are merely means for attaining my final goal as defined by my original project. It is the span of this original project which welds together the chain of sub-projects into a unit. This becomes clear if we consider that in this chain of interrelated partial actions, designed to materialize states of affairs which are merely "means" for attaining the projected end, certain links can be replaced by others or even drop out without any change in the original project. If I cannot find some ink I may turn to the typewriter in order to prepare my application.

In other words, only the actor knows "when his action starts and where it ends," that is, why it will have been performed. It is the span of his projects which determines the unit of his action. His partner has neither knowledge of the projecting preceding the actor's action nor of the context of a higher unit in which it stands. He knows merely that fragment of the actor's action which has become manifest to him, namely, the performed act observed by him or the past phases of the still ongoing action. If the addressee of my question were asked later on by a third person what I wanted from him he would answer that I wanted to know where to find some ink. That is all he knows of my projecting and its context, and he has to look at it as a selfcontained unit action. In order to "understand" what I, the actor, meant by my action he would have to start from the observed act and to construct from there my underlying in-order-to motive for the sake of which I did what he observed.

It is now clear that the meaning of an action is necessarily a different one (a) for the actor; (b) for his partner involved with him in interaction and having, thus, with him a set of relevances and purposes in common; and (c) for the observer not involved in such relationship. This fact leads to two important consequences: First, that in common-sense thinking we have merely a *chance* to understand the Other's action sufficiently for our purpose at hand; secondly that to increase this chance we have to search for the meaning the action has for the actor. Thus, the postulate of the "subjective interpretation of meaning," as the unfortunate term goes, is not a particularity of Max

Weber's [41] sociology or of the methodology of the social sciences in general but a principle of constructing course-of-action types in common-sense experience.*

But subjective interpretation of meaning is merely possible by revealing the motives which determine a given course of action. By referring a course-of-action type to the underlying typical motives of the actor we arrive at the construction of a personal type. The latter may be more or less anonymous and, therewith, more or less empty of content. In the We-relationship among consociates the Other's course of action, its motives (insofar as they become manifest) and his person (insofar as it is involved in the manifest action) can be shared in immediacy and the constructed types, just described, will show a very low degree of anonymity and a high degree of fullness. In constructing course-of-action types of contemporaries other than consociates, we impute to the more or less anonymous actors a set of supposedly invariant motives which govern their actions. This set is itself a construct of typical expectations of the Other's behavior and has been investigated frequently in terms of social role or function or institutional behavior. In common-sense thinking such a construct has a particular significance for projecting actions which are oriented upon my contemporaries' (not my consociates') behavior. Its functions can be described as follows:

1) I take it for granted that my action (say putting a stamped and duly addressed envelope in a mailbox) will induce anonymous fellow-men (postmen) to perform typical actions (handling the mail) in accordance with typical in-order-to motives (to live up to their occupational duties) with the result that the state of affairs projected by me (delivery of the letter to the addressee within reasonable time) will be achieved. 2) I also take it for granted that my construct of the Other's course-of-action type corresponds substantially to his own self-typification and that to the latter belongs a typified construct of my, his anonymous partner's, typical way of behavior based on typical and sup-

---

[41] Max Weber, *op. cit.*, pp. 9, 18, 22, 90, esp. p. 88: "In 'action' is included all human behavior when and insofar as the acting individual attaches a subjective meaning to it . . . Action is social insofar as, by virtue of the subjective meaning attached to it by the acting individual (or individuals), it takes account of the behavior of others and is thereby oriented in it course." See Talcott Parsons, *op. cit.*, esp. pp. 82ff, 345-47, and 484ff; Felix Kaufmann, *op. cit.*, pp. 166f.

* Cf. "Concept and Theory Formation in the Social Sciences," p. 56f. (M.N.)

posedly invariant motives. ("Whoever puts a duly addressed and stamped envelope in the mailbox is assumed to intend to have it delivered to the addressee in due time.") 3) Even more, in my own self-typification – that is by assuming the role of a customer of the mail service – I have to project my action in such a typical way as I suppose the typical post office employee expects a typical customer to behave. Such a construct of mutually interlocked behavior patterns reveals itself as a construct of mutually interlocked in-order-to and because motives which are supposedly invariant. The more institutionalized or standardized such a behavior pattern is, that is, the more typified it is in a socially approved way by laws, rules, regulations, customs, habits, etc., the greater is the chance that my own self-typifying behavior will bring about the state of affairs aimed at.

c) The observer

We have still to characterize the special case of the observer who is not a partner in the interaction patterns. His motives are not interlocked with those of the observed person or persons; he is "tuned in" upon them but not they upon him. In other words, the observer does not participate in the complicated mirror-reflexes involved by which in the interaction pattern among contemporaries, the actor's in-order-to motives become understandable to the partner as his own because motives and vice versa. Precisely this fact constitutes the so-called "disinterestedness" or detachment of the observer. He is not involved in the actor's hopes and fears whether or not they will understand one another and achieve their end by the interlocking of motives. Thus, his system of relevances differs from that of the interested parties and permits him to see at the same time more and less than what is seen by them. But under all circumstances, it is merely the manifested fragments of the actions of *both* partners that are accessible to his observation. In order to understand them the observer has to avail himself of his knowledge of typically similar patterns of interaction in typically similar situational settings and has to construct the motives of the actors from that sector of the course of action which is patent to his observation. The constructs of the observer are, therefore, different ones than those used by the participants in the interaction, if for no other reason than the fact that the purpose of the observer is different from that of the interactors and therewith the systems of relevances attached to such purposes are also different. There is a mere chance, although a chance sufficient for many practical purposes, that the observer in daily life can grasp the subjective meaning of the actor's acts. This chance increases with the degree of anonymity and standardization of the observed behavior. The scientific observer of human interrelation patterns, the social scientist, has to develop specific methods for the building of his constructs in order to assure their applicability for the interpretation of the subjective meaning the observed acts have for the actors. Among these devices we are here especially concerned with the constructs of models of so-called rational actions. Let us consider first the possible meaning of the term "rational action" within the common-sense experience of everyday life.

III. RATIONAL ACTION WITHIN COMMON-SENSE EXPERIENCE *

Ordinary language does not sharply distinguish among a sensible, a reasonable, and a rational way of conduct. We may say that a man acted sensibly if the motive and the course of his action is understandable to us, his partners or observers. This will be the case if his action is in accordance with a socially approved set of rules and recipes for coming to terms with typical problems by applying typical means for achieving typical ends. If I, if We, if "Anybody who is one of us" found himself in typically similar circumstances he would act in a similar way. Sensible behavior, however, does not presuppose that the actor is guided by insight into his motives and the means-ends context. A strong emotional reaction against an offender might be sensible and refraining from it foolish. If an action seems to be sensible to the observer and is, in addition, supposed to spring from a judicious choice among different courses of action, we may call it reasonable even if such action

* Cf. "The Problem of Rationality in the Social World", *Economica*, Vol. X, May, 1943. (M.N.)

follows traditional or habitual patterns just taken for granted. Rational action, however, presupposes that the actor has clear and distinct insight [41a] into the ends, the means, and the secondary results, which "involves rational consideration of alternative means to the end, of the relations of the end to other prospective results of employment of any given means and, finally, of the relative importance of different possible ends. Determination of action, either in affectual or in traditional terms, is thus incompatible with this type." [42]

[41a] This postulate of Leibniz obviously underlies the concept of rationality used by many students of this topic. Pareto, distinguishing between logical and non-logical actions, requires that the former have logically to conjoin means to ends not only from the standpoint of the subject performing the action but also from the standpoint of other persons who have a more extensive knowledge, that is, of the scientist. [Vilfredo Pareto, *Trattato de Sociologia Generale*, English translation under the title *The Mind and Society*, ed. by Arthur Livingston, New York 1935 and 1942; see especially Volume I, Secs. 150ff.] Objective and subjective purpose have to be identical. Professor Talcott Parsons (*The Structure of Social Action*, p. 58) develops a similar theory. Pareto admits, however, (l.c., sect. 150) that from the subjective point of view nearly all human actions belong to the logical class. Professor Howard Becker (*Through Values to Social Interpretation*, Durham, 1950, pp. 23–27) is of the opinion that action may be found (expediently) rational where it is completely centered upon means viewed by the actor as adequate for the attainment of ends which he conceives as unambiguous.

[42] Max Weber, *op. cit.*, p. 117. The characterization of "rational action" follows Max Weber's definition of one of the two types of rational actions distinguished by him, (*op. cit.*, p. 115) namely, the so-called *"zweckrationales Handeln"* (rendered in Parsons' translation by "rational orientation to a system of discrete ends"). We disregard here Weber's second type of rational action, the *"wertrationales Handeln"* (rendered by "rational orientation to an absolute value") since the distinction between both types can be reduced in the terms of the present discussion to a distinction between two types of "because-motives" leading to the project of an action as such. "Zweckrationales Handeln" implies that within the system of hierarchical projects, which we have called the "plans," several courses of action stand to choice and that this choice has to be a rational one; "Wertrationales Handeln" cannot choose among several projects of action equally open to the actor within the system of his plan. The project is taken for granted, but there are alternatives open for bringing about the projected state of affairs, and they have to be determined by rational selection. Parsons has rightly pointed out (l.c., p. 115, footnote 38) that it is nearly impossible to find English terms for *"Zweckrational"* and *"Wertrational,"* but the circumscription chosen by him for their translation already implies an interpretation of Weber's theory and obfuscates an important issue: Neither is, in the case of *"Zweckrationalität,"* a system of *discrete* ends presupposed nor, in the case of *"Wertrationalität,"* an absolute value. (For Parsons' own theory, see pp. 16ff. of his introduction to the Weber volume.)

Far more important for our problem than the distinction of two types of rational action is the distinction between rational actions of both types, on the one hand, and traditional and affectual actions on the other. The same holds good for the modifications suggested by Howard Becker (*op. cit.*, p. 22ff) between "four types of means" followed by the members of any society in attaining their ends: (1) expedient rationality; (2) sanctioned rationality; (3) traditional non-rationality; (4) affective non-rationality. Whereas Weber and Parsons include the ends in their concept of rationality, Becker speaks of types of means.

These very preliminary definitions for sensible, reasonable, and rational actions are stated in terms of common-sense interpretations of other people's actions in daily life but, characteristically, they refer not only to the stock of knowledge taken for granted in the in-group to which the observer of this course of action belongs but also to the subjective point of view of the actor, that is, to his stock of knowledge at hand at the time of carrying out the action. This involves several difficulties. First, it is, as we have seen, our biographical situation which determines the problem at hand and, therewith, the systems of relevances under which the various aspects of the world are constructed in the form of types. Of necessity, therefore, the actor's stock of knowledge will differ from that of the observer. Even the general thesis of the reciprocity of perspectives is not sufficient to eliminate this difficulty because it presupposes that both the observed and the observer are sharing a system of relevances sufficiently homogeneous in structure and content for the practical purpose involved. If this is not the case, then a course of action which is perfectly rational from the point of view of the actor may appear as non-rational to the partner or observer and vice versa. Both attempts, to induce rain by performing the rain-dance or by seeding clouds with silver iodine, are subjectively seen, rational actions from the point of view of the Hopi Indian or the modern meteorologist respectively, but both would have been judged as non-rational by a meteorologist twenty years ago.

Secondly, even if we restrict our investigation to the subjective point of view, we have to ascertain whether there is a difference in the meaning of the term "rational," in the sense of reasonable, if applied to my own past acts or to the determination of a future course of my actions. At first glance, it seems that the difference is considerable. What I did has been done and cannot be undone, although the state of affairs brought about by my actions might be modified or eliminated by countermoves. I do not have, with respect to past actions, the possibility of choice. Anything anticipated in an empty way in the project which had preceded my past action has been fulfilled or not by the outcome of my action. On the other hand, all future action is projected under the idealization of "I can do it again," which may or may not stand the test.

Closer analysis shows, however, that even in judging the reasonableness of our own past action we refer always to our knowledge at hand at the time of projecting such action. If we find, retrospectively, that what we had formerly projected as a reasonable course of action under the then known circumstances proved to be a failure, we may accuse ourselves of various mistakes: of an error in judgment if the then prevailing circumstances were incorrectly or incompletely ascertained; or of a lack of foresight if we failed to anticipate future developments, etc. We will, however, not say that we acted unreasonably.

Thus, in both cases, that of the past and of the future action, our judgment of reasonableness refers to the project determining the course of action and, still more precisely, to the choice among several projects of action involved. As has been shown elsewhere,[43] any projecting of future action involves a choice between at least two courses of conduct, namely, to carry out the projected action or to refrain from doing so.

Each of the alternatives standing to choice has, as Dewey says,[44] to be rehearsed in phantasy in order to make choice and decision possible. If this deliberation is to be strictly a rational one then the actor must have a clear and distinct knowledge of the following elements of each projected course-of-action standing to choice:

a) of the particular state of affairs within which his projected action has to start. This involves a sufficiently precise definition of his biographical situation in the physical and socio-cultural environment;

b) of the state of affairs to be brought about by his projected action, that is, its end. Yet since there is no such thing as an isolated project or end, (all my projects, present to my mind at a given time, being integrated into systems of projects, called my plans and all my plans being integrated into my plan of life), there are also no isolated ends. They are interconnected in a hierarchical order, and the attaining of one might have repercussions on the other. I have, therefore, to have clear and distinct knowledge of the place of my project within the hierarchical order of my plans (or the inter-

---

[43] "Choosing Among Projects of Action."
[44] John Dewey, *Human Nature and Conduct*, Modern Library edition, p. 190.

relationship of the end to be achieved with other ends), the compatibility of one with the other, and the possible repercussions of one upon another, briefly: of the secondary results of my future action, as Max Weber calls it.[45]

c) of the various means necessary for attaining the established end, of the possibility of bringing them within my reach, of the degree of the expediency of their application, of the possible employment of these same means for the attainment of other potential ends, and of the compatibility of the selected means with other means needed for the materialization of other projects.

The complication increases considerably if the actor's project of a rational action involves the rational action or reaction of a fellow-man, say of a consociate. Projecting rationally such a kind of action involves sufficiently clear and distinct knowledge of the situation of departure not only as defined by me but also as defined by the Other. Moreover, there has to be sufficient likelihood that the Other will be tuned in upon me and consider my action as relevant enough to be motivated in the way of because by my in-order-to motive. If this is the case, then there has to be a sufficient chance that the Other will understand me, and this means in the case of a rational interrelationship that he will interpret my action rationally as being a rational one and that he will react in a rational way. To assume that the Other will do so implies, however, on the one hand, that he will have sufficiently clear and distinct knowledge of my project and of its place in the hierarchy of my plans (at least as far as my overt actions makes them manifest to him) and of my system of relevances attached thereto; and, on the other hand, that the structure and scope of his stock of knowledge at hand will be in its relevant portion substantially similar to mine and that his and my system of relevances will, if not overlap, be at least partially congruent. If, furthermore, I assume in my projecting that the Other's reaction to my projected action will be a rational one, I suppose that he, in projecting his response, knows all the aforementioned elements (a), (b), (c) of his reaction in a clear and distinct way. Consequently, if I project a rational action which

---

[45] See quotation from Max Weber on p. 28.

requires an interlocking of my and the Other's motives of action to be carried out (e.g., I want the Other to do something for me), I must, by a curious mirror-effect, have sufficient knowledge of what he, the Other, knows (and knows to be relevant with respect to my purpose at hand), and this knowledge of his is supposed to include sufficient acquaintance with what I know. This is a condition of *ideally* rational interaction because without such mutual knowledge I could not "rationally" project the attainment of my goal by means of the Other's co-operation or reaction. Moreover, such mutual knowledge has to be clear and distinct; merely a more or less empty expectation of the Other's behavior is not sufficient.

It seems that under these circumstances rational social interaction becomes impracticable even among consociates. And yet we receive reasonable answers to reasonable questions, our commands are carried out, we perform in factories and laboratories and offices highly "rationalized" activities, we play chess together, briefly, we come conveniently to terms with our fellow-men. How is this possible?

Two different answers seem to offer themselves. First, if interaction among consociates is involved we may assume that the mutual participation in the consociate's onrolling life, the sharing of his anticipations so characteristic of the pure We-relation establishes the prerequisites for rational interaction just analyzed. Yet it is precisely this pure We-relation which is the irrational element of any interrelationship among consociates. The second answer refers not only to the interrelationship among consociates but among contemporaries in general. We may explain the rationality of human interaction by the fact that both actors orient their actions on certain standards which are socially approved as rules of conduct by the in-group to which they belong: norms, mores of good behavior, manners, the organizational framework provided for this particular form of division of labor, the rules of the chess game, etc. But neither the origin nor the import of the socially approved standard is "rationally" understood. Such standards might be traditionally or habitually accepted as just being taken for granted, and, within the meaning of our previous definitions, behavior of this kind will be sensible or even reasonable but not necessarily rational. At any rate, it will not be "ideally" rational, that is, meeting all the requirements worked out in the analysis of this concept.

We come, therefore, to the conclusion that "rational action" on the common-sense level is always action within an unquestioned and undetermined frame of constructs of typicalities of the setting, the motives, the means and ends, the courses of action and personalities involved and taken for granted. They are, however, not merely taken for granted by the actor but also supposed as being taken for granted by the fellow-man. From this frame of constructs, forming their undetermined horizon, merely particular sets of elements stand out which are clearly and distinctly determinable. To these elements refers the common-sense concept of rationality. Thus we may say that on this level actions are at best partially rational and that rationality has many degrees. For instance, our assumption that our fellow-man who is involved with us in a pattern of interaction knows its rational elements will never reach "empirical certainty" (certainty "until further notice" or "good until counter-evidence") [46] but will always bear the character of plausibility, that is, of subjective likelihood (in contradistinction to mathematical probability). We always have to "take chances" and to "run risks," and this situation is expressed by our hopes and fears which are merely the subjective corollaries of our basic uncertainty as to the outcome of our projected interaction.

To be sure, the more standardized the prevailing action pattern is, the more anonymous it is, the greater is the subjective chance of conformity and, therewith, of the success of intersubjective behavior. Yet – and this is the paradox of rationality on the common-sense level – the more standardized the pattern is, the less the underlying elements become analyzable for common-sense thought in terms of rational insight.

All this refers to the criterion of rationality as applicable to the thinking of everyday life and its constructs. Only on the level of models of interaction patterns constructed by the social scientist in accordance with certain particular requirements defined by the methods of his science does the concept of rationality obtain its full significance. In order to make this clear we have first to examine the basic character of such scientific constructs and

[46] Edmund Husserl, *Erfahrung und Urteil*, Sec. 77, p. 370.

their relationship to the "reality" of the social world, as such reality presents itself to the common-sense thought of everyday life.

IV. CONSTRUCTS OF THOUGHT OBJECTS BY THE SOCIAL SCIENCES

1) The postulate of subjective interpretation

There will be hardly any issue among social scientists that the object of the social sciences is human behavior, its forms, its organization, and its products. There will be, however, different opinions about whether this behavior should be studied in the same manner in which the natural scientist studies his object or whether the goal of the social sciences is the explanation of the "social reality" as experienced by man living his everyday life within the social world. The introductory section of the present discussion attempted to show that both principles are incompatible with each other. In the following pages we take the position that the social sciences have to deal with human conduct and its common-sense interpretation in the social reality, involving the analysis of the whole system of projects and motives, of relevances and constructs dealt with in the preceding sections. Such an analysis refers by necessity to the subjective point of view, namely, to the interpretation of the action and its settings in terms of the actor. Since this postulate of the subjective interpretation is, as we have seen, a general principle of constructing course-of-action types in common-sense experience, any social science aspiring to grasp "social reality" has to adopt this principle also.

Yet, at first glance, it seems that this statement is in contradiction to the well-established method of even the most advanced social sciences. Take as an example modern economics. Is it not the "behavior of prices" rather than the behavior of men in the market situation which is studied by the economist, the "shape of demand curves" rather than the anticipations of economic subjects symbolized by such curves? Does not the economist investigate successfully subject matters such as "savings," "capital," "business cycle," "wages" and "unemployment," "multipliers" and "monopoly" as if these phenomena were entirely detached from any activity of the economic subjects, even less without entering into the subjective meaning structure such activities may have for them? The achievements of modern economic theories would make it preposterous to deny that an abstract conceptual scheme can be used very successfully for the solution of many problems. And similar examples could be given from the field of almost all the other social sciences. Closer investigation, however, reveals that this abstract conceptual scheme is nothing else than a kind of intellectual shorthand and that the underlying subjective elements of human actions involved are either taken for granted or deemed to be irrelevant with respect to the scientific purpose at hand – the problem under scrutiny – and are, therefore, disregarded. Correctly understood, the postulate of subjective interpretation as applied to economics as well as to all the other social sciences means merely that we always *can* – and for certain purposes *must* – refer to the activities of the subjects within the social world and their interpretation by the actors in terms of systems of projects, available means, motives, relevances, and so on.[47]

But if this is true, two other questions have to be answered. First, we have seen from the previous analyses that the subjective meaning an action has for an actor is unique and individual because it originates in the unique and individual biographical situation of the actor. How is it then possible to grasp subjective meaning scientifically? Secondly, the meaning context of any system of scientific knowledge is objective knowledge but accessible equally to all his fellow scientists and open to their control, which means capable of being verified, invalidated, or falsified by them. How is it, then, possible to grasp by a system of objective knowledge subjective meaning structures? Is this not a paradox?

Both questions can be satisfactorily met by a few simple considerations. As to the first question, we learned from Whitehead that all sciences have to construct thought objects of their own which supersede the thought objects of common-sense

---

[47] Ludwig Von Mises rightly calls his "Treatise on Economics" *Human Action*, New Haven, 1949. See also F. A. Hayek, *The Counter-Revolution of Science*, Glencoe, 1952, pp. 25–36.

thinking.⁴⁸ The thought objects constructed by the social sciences do not refer to unique acts of unique individuals occurring within a unique situation. By particular methodological devices, to be described presently, the social scientist replaces the thought objects of common-sense thought relating to unique events and occurrences by constructing a model of a sector of the social world within which merely those typified events occur that are relevant to the scientist's particular problem under scrutiny. All the other happenings within the social world are considered as being irrelevant, as contingent "data," which have to be put beyond question by appropriate methodological techniques as, for instance, by the assumption "all other things being equal." ⁴⁹ Nevertheless, it is possible to construct a model of a sector of the social world consisting of typical human interaction and to analyze this typical interaction pattern as to the meaning it might have for the personal types of actors who presumptively originated them.

The second question has to be faced. It is indeed the particular problem of the social sciences to develop methodological devices for attaining objective and verifiable knowledge of a subjective meaning structure. In order to make this clear we have to consider very briefly the particular attitude of the scientist to the social world.

2) *The social scientist as disinterested observer*

This attitude of the social scientist is that of a mere disinterested observer of the social world. He is not involved in the observed situation, which is to him not of practical but merely of cognitive interest. It is not the theater of his activities but merely the object of his contemplation. He does not act within it, vitally interested in the outcome of his actions, hoping or fearing what their consequences might be but he looks at it with the same detached equanimity with which the natural scientist looks at the occurrences in his laboratory.

A word of caution is necessary here to prevent possible mis-

---

⁴⁸ See above, pp. 5-6.
⁴⁹ On this concept see Felix Kaufmann, *op. cit.*, p. 84ff and 213ff, on the concept "scientific situation" p. 52 and 251 n. 4.

understandings. Of course, in his daily life the social scientist remains a human being, a man living among his fellow-men, with whom he is interrelated in many ways. And, surely, scientific activity itself occurs within the tradition of socially derived knowledge, is based upon co-operation with other scientists, requires mutual corroboration and criticism and can only be communicated by social interaction. But insofar as scientific activity is socially founded, it is one among all the other activities occurring within the social world. Dealing with science and scientific matters within the social world is one thing, the specific scientific attitude which the scientist has to adopt toward his object is another, and it is the latter which we propose to study in the following.

Our analysis of the common-sense interpretation of the social world of everyday life has shown how the biographical situation of man within the natural attitude determines at any given moment his purpose at hand. The system of relevances involved selects particular objects and particular typical aspects of such objects as standing out over against an unquestioned background of things just taken for granted. Man in daily life considers himself as the center of the social world which he groups around himself in layers of various degrees of intimacy and anonymity. By resolving to adopt the disinterested attitude of a scientific observer – in our language, by establishing the life-plan for scientific work – the social scientist detaches himself from his biographical situation within the social world. What is taken for granted in the biographical situation of daily life may become questionable for the scientist, and vice versa; what seems to be of highest relevance on one level may become entirely irrelevant on the other. The center of orientation has been radically shifted and so has the hierarchy of plans and projects. By making up his mind to carry out a plan for scientific work governed by the disinterested quest for truth in accordance with preestablished rules, called the scientific method, the scientist has entered a field of pre-organized knowledge, called the corpus of his science.[50] He has either to accept what is considered by his fellow-scientist as established knowledge or to "show cause" why he cannot do so. Merely within this frame may he select his particular

[50] *Ibid.*, pp. 42 and 232.

scientific problem and make his scientific decisions. This frame constitutes his "being in a scientific situation" which supersedes his biographical situation as a human being within the world. It is henceforth the scientific problem once established which determines alone what is and what is not relevant to its solution, and thus what has to be investigated and what can be taken for granted as a "datum," and, finally, the level of research in the broadest sense, that is, the abstractions, generalizations, formalizations, idealizations, briefly, the constructs required and admissible for considering the problem as being solved. In other words, the scientific problem is the "locus" of all possible constructs relevant to its solution, and each construct carries along – to borrow a mathematical term – a subscript referring to the problem for the sake of which it has been established. It follows that any shifting of the problem under scrutiny and the level of research involves a modification of the structures of relevance and of the constructs formed for the solution of another problem or on another level; a great many misunderstandings and controversies, especially in the social sciences, originate from disregarding this fact.

3) Differences between common-sense and scientific constructs of action patterns

Let us consider very briefly (and very incompletely) some of the more important differences between common-sense constructs and scientific constructs of interaction patterns originating in the transition from the biographically determined to the scientific situation. Common-sense constructs are formed from a "Here" within the world which determines the presupposed reciprocity of perspectives. They take a stock of socially derived and socially approved knowledge for granted. The social distribution of knowledge determines the particular structure of the typifying construct, for instance, the assumed degree of anonymity of personal roles, the standardization of course-of-action patterns, and the supposed constancy of motives. Yet this social distribution itself depends upon the heterogeneous composition of the stock of knowledge at hand which itself is an element of common-sense experience. The concepts of "We," "You,"

"They," of "in-group" and "out-group," of consociates, contemporaries, predecessors, and successors, all of them with their particular structurization of familiarity and anonymity are at least implied in the common-sense typifications or even co-constitutive for them. All this holds good not only for the participants in a social interaction pattern but also for the mere observer of such interaction who still makes his observations from his biographical situation within the social world. The difference between both is merely that the participant in the interaction pattern, guided by the idealization of reciprocity of motives, assumes his own motives as being interlocked with that of his partners, whereas to the observer merely the manifest fragments of the actors' actions are accessible. Yet both, participants and observer, form their common-sense constructs relatively to their biographical situation. In either case, these constructs have a particular place within the chain of motives originating in the biographically determined hierarchy of the constructor's plans.

The constructs of human interaction patterns formed by the social scientist, however, are of an entirely different kind. The social scientist has no "Here" within the social world or, more precisely, he considers his position within it and the system of relevances attached thereto as irrelevant for his scientific undertaking. His stock of knowledge at hand is the corpus of his science, and he has to take it for granted – which means, in this context, as scientifically ascertained – unless he makes explicit why he cannot do so. To this corpus of science belong also the rules of procedure which have stood the test, namely, the methods of his science, including the methods of forming constructs in a scientifically sound way. This stock of knowledge is of quite another structure than that which man in everyday life has at hand. To be sure, it will also show manifold degrees of clarity and distinctness. But this structurization will depend upon knowledge of problems solved, of their still hidden implications and open horizons of other still not formulated problems. The scientist takes for granted what he defines to be a datum, and this is independent of the beliefs accepted by any in-group in the world of everyday life.[51] The scientific problem, once established, determines alone the structure of relevances.

---

[51] We intentionally disregard the problems of the so-called sociology of knowledge here involved.

Having no "Here" within the social world the social scientist does not organize this world in layers around himself as the center. He can never enter as a consociate in an interaction pattern with one of the actors on the social scene without abandoning, at least temporarily, his scientific attitude. The participant observer or field worker establishes contact with the group studied as a man among fellow-men; only his system of relevances which serves as the scheme of his selection and interpretation is determined by the scientific attitude, temporarily dropped in order to be resumed again.

Thus, adopting the scientific attitude, the social scientist observes human interaction patterns or their results insofar as they are accessible to his observation and open to his interpretation. These interaction patterns, however, he has to interpret in terms of their subjective meaning structure lest he abandon any hope of grasping "social reality."

In order to comply with this postulate, the scientific observer proceeds in a way similar to that of the observer of a social interaction pattern in the world of everyday life, although guided by an entirely different system of relevances.

4) *The scientific model of the social world* [52]

He begins to construct typical course-of-action patterns corresponding to the observed events. Thereupon he co-ordinates to these typical course-of-action patterns a personal type, a model of an actor whom he imagines as being gifted with consciousness. Yet it is a consciousness restricted to containing nothing but all the elements relevant to the performance of the course-of-action patterns under observation and relevant, therewith, to the scientist's problem under scrutiny. He ascribes, thus, to this fictitious consciousness a set of typical in-order-to motives corresponding to the goals of the observed course-of-action patterns and typical because-motives upon which the in-order-to motives are founded. Both types of motives are assumed to be invariant in the mind of the imaginary actor-model.

---

[52] To this section cf. in addition to the literature mentioned in footnotes 30 and 43, Alfred Schutz: "The Problem of Rationality in the Social World," *Economica*, Vol. X, May 1943, pp. 130–149.

COMMON-SENSE AND SCIENTIFIC INTERPRETATION   41

Yet these models of actors are not human beings living within their biographical situation in the social world of everyday life. Strictly speaking, they do not have any biography or any history, and the situation into which they are placed is not a situation defined by them but defined by their creator, the social scientist. He has created these puppets or homunculi to manipulate them for his purpose. A merely specious consciousness is imputed to them by the scientist, which is constructed in such a way that its presupposed stock of knowledge at hand (including the ascribed set of invariant motives) would make actions originating from it subjectively understandable, provided that these actions were performed by real actors within the social world. But the puppet and his artificial consciousness is not subjected to the ontological conditions of human beings. The homunculus was not born, he does not grow up, and he will not die. He has no hopes and no fears; he does not know anxiety as the chief motive of all his deeds. He is not free in the sense that his acting could transgress the limits his creator, the social scientist, has predetermined. He cannot, therefore, have other conflicts of interests and motives than those the social scientist has imputed to him. He cannot err, if to err is not his typical destiny. He cannot choose, except among the alternatives the social scientist has put before him as standing to his choice. Whereas man, as Simmel has clearly seen,[53] enters any social relationship merely with a part of his self and is, at the same time, always within and outside of such a relationship, the homunculus, placed into a social relationship is involved therein in his totality. He is nothing else but the originator of his typical function because the artificial consciousness imputed to him contains merely those elements which are necessary to make such functions subjectively meaningful.

Let us very briefly examine some of the implications of this general characterization. The homunculus is invested with a system of relevances originating in the scientific problem of his constructor and not in the particular biographically determined situation of an actor within the world. It is the scientist who defines what is to his puppet a Here and a There, what is within his reach, what is to him a We and a You or a They. The scientist

[53] See footnote 33 above.

determines the stock of knowledge his model has supposedly at hand. This stock of knowledge is not socially derived and, unless especially designed to be so, without reference to social approval. The relevance system pertinent to the scientific problem under scrutiny alone determines its intrinsic structure, namely, the elements "about" which the homunculus is supposed to have knowledge, those of which he has a mere knowledge of acquaintance and those others which he just takes for granted. With this is determined what is supposed to be familiar and what anonymous to him and on what level the typification of the experiences of the world imputed to him takes place.

If such a model of an actor is conceived as interrelated and interacting with others – they, too, being homunculi – then the general thesis of reciprocal perspectives, their interlocking, and, therewith, the correspondence of motives is determined by the constructor. The course-of-action and personal types supposedly formed by the puppet of his partners, including the definition of their systems of relevances, roles, motives, have not the character of a mere chance which will or will not be fulfilled by the supervening events. The homunculus is free from empty anticipations of the Other's reactions to his own actions and also from self-typifications. He does not assume a role other than that attributed to him by the director of the puppet show, called the model of the social world. It is he, the social scientist, who sets the stage, who distributes the roles, who gives the cues, who defines when an "action" starts and when it ends and who determines, thus, the "span of projects" involved. All standards and institutions governing the behavioral pattern of the model are supplied from the outset by the constructs of the scientific observer.

In such a simplified model of the social world pure rational acts, rational choices from rational motives are possible because all the difficulties encumbering the real actor in the everyday life-world have been eliminated. Thus, the concept of rationality in the strict sense already defined does not refer to actions within the common-sense experience of everyday life in the social world; it is the expression for a *particular* type of constructs of *certain specific* models of the social world made by the social scientist for certain specific methodological purposes.

Before, discussing the particular functions of "rational" models of the social world, however, we have to indicate some principles governing the construction of scientific models of human action in general.

5) Postulates for scientific model constructs of the social world

We said before that it is the main problem of the social sciences to develop a method in order to deal in an objective way with the subjective meaning of human action and that the thought objects of the social sciences have to remain consistent with the thought objects of common sense, formed by men in everyday life in order to come to terms with social reality. The model constructs as described before fulfill these requirements if they are formed in accordance with the following postulates:

a) The postulate of logical consistency

The system of typical constructs designed by the scientist has to be established with the highest degree of clarity and distinctness of the conceptual framework implied and must be fully compatible with the principles of formal logic. Fulfillment of this postulate warrants the objective validity of the thought objects constructed by the social scientist, and their strictly logical character is one of the most important features by which scientific thought objects are distinguished from the thought objects constructed by common-sense thinking in daily life which they have to supersede.

b) The postulate of subjective interpretation

In order to explain human actions the scientist has to ask what model of an individual mind can be constructed and what typical contents must be attributed to it in order to explain the observed facts as the result of the activity of such a mind in an understandable relation. The compliance with this postulate warrants the possibility of referring all kinds of human action or their result to the subjective meaning such action or result of an action had for the actor.

c) *The postulate of adequacy*

Each term in a scientific model of human action must be constructed in such a way that a human act performed within the life-world by an individual actor in the way indicated by the typical construct would be understandable for the actor himself as well as for his fellow-men in terms of common-sense interpretation of everyday life. Compliance with this postulate warrants the consistency of the constructs of the social scientist with the constructs of common-sense experience of the social reality.

V. SCIENTIFIC MODEL CONSTRUCTS OF RATIONAL ACTION PATTERNS

All model constructs of the social world in order to be scientific have to fulfill the requirements of these three postulates. But is not any construct complying with the postulate of logical consistency, is not any scientific activity by definition a rational one?

This is certainly true but here we have to avoid a dangerous misunderstanding. We have to distinguish between rational constructs of models of human actions on the one hand, and constructs of models of rational human actions on the other. Science may construct rational models of irrational behavior, as a glance in any textbook of psychiatry shows. On the other hand, common-sense thinking frequently constructs irrational models of highly rational behavior, for example, in explaining economic, political, military and even scientific decisions by referring them to sentiments or ideologies presupposed to govern the behavior of the participants. The rationality of the construction of the model is one thing and in this sense all properly constructed models of the sciences – not merely of the social sciences – are rational; the construction of models of rational behavior is quite another thing. It would be a serious misunderstanding to believe that it is the purpose of model constructs in the social sciences or a criterion for their scientific character that irrational behavior patterns be interpreted as if they were rational.

In the following we are mainly interested in the usefulness of scientific – therefore rational – models of rational behavior patterns. It can easily be understood that the scientific construct of a perfect rational course-of-action type, of its corresponding personal type and also of rational interaction patterns is, as a matter of principle, possible. This is so because in constructing a model of a fictitious consciousness the scientist may select as relevant for his problem merely those elements which make rational actions or reactions of his homunculi possible. The postulate of rationality which such a construct would have to meet can be formulated as follows:

The rational course-of-action and personal types have to be constructed in such a way that an actor in the life-world would perform the typified action if he had a perfectly clear and distinct knowledge of all the elements, and only of the elements, assumed by the social scientist as being relevant to this action and the constant tendency to use the most appropriate means assumed to be at his disposal for achieving the ends defined by the construct itself.

The advantage of the use of such models of rational behavior in the social sciences can be characterized as follows:

1) The possibility of constructing patterns of social interaction under the assumption that all participants in such interaction act rationally within a set of conditions, means, ends, motives defined by the social scientist and supposed to be either common to all participants or distributed among them in a specific manner. By this arrangement standardized behavior such as so-called social roles, institutional behavior, etc., can be studied in isolation.

2) Whereas the behavior of individuals in the social life-world is not predictable unless in empty anticipations, the rational behavior of a constructed personal type is by definition supposed to be predictable, within the limits of the elements typified in the construct. The model of rational action can, therefore, be used as a device for ascertaining deviating behavior in the real social world and for referring it to "problem-transcending data," that is, to non-typified elements.

3) By appropriate variations of some of the elements several models or even sets of models of rational actions can be constructed for solving the same scientific problem and compared with one another.

The last point, however, seems to require some comment. Did we not state earlier that all constructs carry along a "subscript" referring to the problem under scrutiny and have to be revised if a shift in the problem occurs? Is there not a certain contradiction between this insight and the possibility of constructing several competing models for the solution of one and the same scientific problem?

The contradiction disappears if we consider that any problem is merely a locus of implications which can be made explicit or, to use a term of Husserl's,[54] that it carries along its inner horizon of unquestioned but questionable elements.*

In order to make the inner horizon of the problem explicit we may vary the conditions within which the fictitious actors are supposed to act, the elements of the world of which they are supposed to have knowledge, their assumed interlocked motives, the degree of familiarity or anonymity in which they are assumed to be interrelated, etc. For example, as an economist concerned with the theory of oligopoly,[55] I may construct models of a single firm or of an industry or of the economic system as a whole. If restricting myself to the theory of the individual firm (say, if analyzing the effects of a cartel agreement on the output of the commodity concerned), I may construct a model of a producer acting under conditions of unregulated competition, another of a producer with the same cost-conditions acting under the cartel restrictions imposed upon him and with the knowledge of similar restrictions imposed on the other suppliers of the "same" commodity. We can then compare the output of "the" firm in the two models.

All these models are models of rational actions but not of actions performed by living human beings in situations defined by them. They are assumed to be performable by the personal types constructed by the economist within the artificial environment in which he has placed his homunculi.

---

[54] As to the concept of horizon, see Helmut Kuhn, "The Phenomenological Concept of Horizon" in *Philosophical Essays in Memory of Edmund Husserl*, edited by Marvin Farber, Cambridge, 1940, pp. 106-124 and Ludwig Landgrebe in Husserl, *Erfahrung und Urteil*, secs. 8-10.

[55] I gratefully acknowledge the permission of my friend, Professor Fritz Machlup, to borrow the following examples from his book *The Economics of Seller's Competition Model Analysis of Seller's Conduct*, Baltimore, 1952, p. 4ff.

* See, for example, "Concept and Theory Formation in the Social Sciences," pp. 63-65. (M.N.)

VI. CONCLUDING REMARKS

The relationship between the social scientist and the puppet he has created reflects to a certain extent an age-old problem of theology and metaphysics, that of the relationship between God and his creatures. The puppet exists and acts merely by the grace of the scientist; it cannot act otherwise than according to the purpose which the scientist's wisdom has determined it to carry out. Nevertheless, it is supposed to act as if it were not determined but could determine itself. A total harmony has been pre-established between the determined consciousness bestowed upon the puppet and the pre-constituted environment within which it is supposed to act freely, to make rational choices and decisions. This harmony is possible only because both, the puppet and its reduced environment, are the creation of the scientist. And by keeping to the principles which guided him, the scientist succeeds, indeed, in discovering within the universe, thus created, the perfect harmony established by himself.

CONCEPT AND THEORY FORMATION IN THE SOCIAL SCIENCES [1]

The title of my paper refers intentionally to that of a Symposium held in December, 1952, at the annual meeting of the American Philosophical Association.[2] Ernest Nagel and Carl G. Hempel contributed highly stimulating comments on the problem involved, formulated in the careful and lucid way so characteristic of these scholars. Their topic is a controversy which for more than half a century has split not only logicians and methodologists but also social scientists into two schools of thought. One of these holds that the methods of the natural sciences which have brought about such magnificent results are the only scientific ones and that they alone, therefore, have to be applied in their entirety to the study of human affairs. Failure to do so, it has been maintained, prevented the social sciences from developing systems of explanatory theory comparable in precision to those offered by the natural sciences and makes debatable the empirical work of theories developed in restricted domains such as economics.

The other school of thought feels that there is a basic difference in the structure of the social world and the world of nature. This feeling led to the other extreme, namely the conclusion that the methods of the social sciences are *toto coelo* different from those of the natural sciences. In order to support this position a variety of arguments was proffered. It has been maintained that the social sciences are idiographic, characterized by individualizing conceptualization and seeking singular assertory propositions,

[1] Paper presented at the 33rd Semi-Annual Meeting of the Conference on Methods in Philosophy and the Sciences, New York, May 3, 1953.
[2] Published in the volume *Science, Language and Human Rights* (American Philosophical Association, Eastern Division, Vol. I), Philadelphia, 1952, pp. 43-86 (referred to as SLH).

whereas the natural sciences are nomothetic, characterized by generalizing conceptualization and seeking general apodictic propositions. The latter have to deal with constant relations of magnitude which can be measured and can perform experiments, whereas neither measurement nor experiment is practicable in the social sciences. In general, it is held that the natural sciences have to deal with material objects and processes, the social sciences, however, with psychological and intellectual ones and that, therefore, the method of the former consists in explaining, that of the latter in understanding.

Admittedly, most of these highly generalized statements are untenable under closer examination, and this for several reasons. Some proponents of the characterized arguments had a rather erroneous concept of the methods of the natural sciences. Others were inclined to identify the methodological situation in one particular social science with the method of the social sciences in general. Because history has to deal with unique and non-recurrent events, it was contended that all social sciences are restricted to singular assertory propositions. Because experiments are hardly possible in cultural anthropology, the fact was ignored that social psychologists can successfully use laboratory experiments at least to a certain extent. Finally, and this is the most important point, these arguments disregard the fact that a set of rules for scientific procedure is equally valid for all empirical sciences whether they deal with objects of nature or with human affairs. Here and there, the principles of controlled inference and verification by fellow scientists and the theoretical ideals of unity, simplicity, universality, and precision prevail.

This unsatisfactory state of affairs results chiefly from the fact that the development of the modern social sciences occurred during a period in which the science of logic was mostly concerned with the logic of the natural sciences. In a kind of monopolistic imperialism the methods of the latter were frequently declared to be the only scientific ones and the particular problems which social scientists encountered in their work were disregarded. Left without help and guidance in their revolt against this dogmatism, the students of human affairs had to develop their own conceptions of what they believed to be the methodology of the social sciences. They did it without sufficient philosophical knowledge and stopped their effort when they reached a level of generalization which seemed to justify their deeply felt conviction that the goal of their inquiry could not be reached by adopting the methods of the natural sciences without modification or implementation. No wonder that their arguments are frequently ill-founded, their formulations insufficient, and that many misunderstandings obfuscate the controversy. Not what social scientists *said* but what they *meant* is therefore our main concern in the following.

The writings of the late Felix Kaufmann [3] and the more recent contributions by Nagel [4] and Hempel [5] have criticized many fallacies in the arguments proposed by social scientists and prepared the ground for another approach to the problem. I shall here concentrate on Professor Nagel's criticism of the claim made by Max Weber and his school that the social sciences seek to "understand" social phenomena in terms of "meaningful" categories of human experience and that, therefore, the "causal functional" approach of the natural sciences is not applicable in social inquiry. This school, as Dr. Nagel sees it, maintains that all socially significant human behavior is an expression of motivated psychic states, that in consequence the social scientist cannot be satisfied with viewing social processes simply as concatenations of "externally related" events, and that the establishment of correlations or even of universal relations of concomitance cannot be his ultimate goal. On the contrary, he must construct "ideal types" or "models of motivations" in terms of which he seeks to "understand" overt social behavior by imputing springs of action to the actors involved in it. If I understand Professor Nagel's criticism correctly, he maintains:

1) That these springs of action are not accessible to sensory observation. It follows and has frequently been stated that the social scientist must imaginatively identify himself with the participants and view the situation which they face as the actors themselves view it. Surely, however, we need not undergo other men's psychic experiences in order to know that they have them or in order to predict their overt behavior.

---

[3] Especially his *Methodology of the Social Sciences*, New York, 1941.
[4] *SLH*, pp. 43–64.
[5] *SLH*, pp. 65–86.

2) That the imputation of emotions, attitudes, and purposes as an explanation of overt behavior is a twofold hypothesis: it assumes that the agents participating in some social phenomenon are in certain psychological states; and it assumes also definite relations of concomitance between such states, and between such states and overt behavior. Yet none of the psychological states which we imagine the subjects of our study to possess may in reality be theirs, and even if our imputations should be correct none of the overt actions which allegedly issue from those states may appear to us understandable or reasonable.

3) That we do not "understand" the nature and operations of human motives and their issuance in overt behavior more adequately than the "external" causal relations. If by meaningful explanation we assert merely that a particular action is an instance of a pattern of behavior which human beings exhibit under a variety of circumstances and that, since some of the relevant circumstances are realized in the given situation, a person can be expected to manifest a certain form of that pattern, then there is no sharp gulf separating such explanations from those involving merely "external" knowledge of causal connections. It is possible to gain knowledge of the actions of men on the evidence supplied by their overt behavior just as it is possible to discover and know the atomic constitution of water on the evidence supplied by the physical and chemical behavior of that substance. Hence the rejection of a purely "objective" or "behavioristic" social science by the proponents of "meaningful connections" as the goal of social sciences is unwarranted.

Since I shall have to disagree with Nagel's and Hempel's findings on several questions of a fundamental nature, I might be permitted to start with a brief summary of the no less important points on which I find myself happily in full agreement with them. I agree with Professor Nagel that all empirical knowledge involves discovery through processes of controlled inference, and that it must be statable in propositional form and capable of being verified by anyone who is prepared to make the effort to do so through observation[6] – although I do not believe, as Professor Nagel does, that this observation has to be sensory in the precise meaning of this term. Moreover, I agree with him that "theory"

[6] *SLH*, p. 56.

means in all empirical sciences the explicit formulation of determinate relations between a set of variables in terms of which a fairly extensive class of empirically ascertainable regularities can be explained.[7] Furthermore, I agree wholeheartedly with his statement that neither the fact that these regularities have in the social sciences a rather narrowly restricted universality, nor the fact that they permit prediction only to a rather limited extent, constitutes a basic difference between the social and the natural sciences, since many branches of the latter show the same features.[8] As I shall try to show later on, it seems to me that Professor Nagel misunderstands Max Weber's postulate of subjective interpretation. Nevertheless, he is right in stating that a method which would require that the individual scientific observer identify himself with the social agent observed in order to understand the motives of the latter, or a method which would refer the selection of the facts observed and their interpretation to the private value system of the particular observer, would merely lead to an uncontrollable private and subjective image in the mind of this particular student of human affairs, but never to a scientific theory.[9] But I do not know of any social scientist of stature who ever advocated such a concept of subjectivity as that criticized by Professor Nagel. Most certainly this was not the position of Max Weber.

I also think that our authors are prevented from grasping the point of vital concern to social scientists by their basic philosophy of sensationalistic empiricism or logical positivism, which identifies experience with sensory observation and which assumes that the only alternative to controllable and, therefore, objective sensory observation is that of subjective and, therefore, uncontrollable and unverifiable introspection. This is certainly not the place to renew the age old controversy relating to the hidden presuppositions and implied metaphysical assumptions of this basic philosophy. On the other hand, in order to account for my own position, I should have to treat at length certain principles of phenomenology. Instead of doing so, I propose to defend a few rather simple propositions:

[7] *SLH*, p. 46.
[8] *SLH*, pp. 60 ff.
[9] *SLH*, pp. 55–57.

1) The primary goal of the social sciences is to obtain organized knowledge of social reality. By the term "social reality" I wish to be understood the sum total of objects and occurrences within the social cultural world as experienced by the common-sense thinking of men living their daily lives among their fellow-men, connected with them in manifold relations of interaction. It is the world of cultural objects and social institutions into which we all are born, within which we have to find our bearings, and with which we have to come to terms. From the outset, we, the actors on the social scene, experience the world we live in as a world both of nature and of culture, not as a private but as an intersubjective one, that is, as a world common to all of us, either actually given or potentially accessible to everyone; and this involves intercommunication and language.

2) All forms of naturalism and logical empiricism simply take for granted this social reality, which is the proper object of the social sciences. Intersubjectivity, interaction, intercommunication, and language are simply presupposed as the unclarified foundation of these theories. They assume, as it were, that the social scientist has already solved his fundamental problem, before scientific inquiry starts. To be sure, Dewey emphasized, with a clarity worthy of this eminent philosopher, that all inquiry starts and ends within the social cultural matrix; to be sure, Professor Nagel is fully aware of the fact that science and its self-correcting process is a social enterprise.[10] But the postulate of describing and explaining human behavior in terms of controllable sensory observation stops short before the description and explanation of the process by which scientist B controls and verifies the observational findings of scientist A and the conclusions drawn by him. In order to do so, B has to know what A has observed, what the goal of his inquiry is, why he thought the observed fact worthy of being observed, *i.e.*, relevant to the scientific problem at hand, etc. This knowledge is commonly called understanding. The explanation of how such a mutual understanding of human beings might occur is apparently left to the social scientist. But whatever his explanation might be, one thing is sure, namely, that such an intersubjective understanding between scientist B and scientist A occurs neither by scientist B's

[10] *SLH*, p. 53.

observations of scientist A's overt behavior, nor by introspection performed by B, nor by identification of B with A. To translate this argument into the language dear to logical positivism, this means, as Felix Kaufmann [11] has shown, that so-called protocol propositions about the physical world are of an entirely different kind than protocol propositions about the psycho-physical world.

3) The identification of experience with sensory observation in general and of the experience of overt action in particular (and that is what Nagel proposes) excludes several dimensions of social reality from all possible inquiry.

a) Even an ideally refined behaviorism can, as has been pointed out for instance by George H. Mead,[12] merely explain the behavior of the observed, not of the observing behaviorist.

b) The same overt behavior (say a tribal pageant as it can be captured by the movie camera) may have an entirely different meaning to the performers. What interests the social scientist is merely whether it is a war dance, a barter trade, the reception of a friendly ambassador, or something else of this sort.

c) Moreover, the concept of human action in terms of commonsense thinking and of the social sciences includes what may be called "negative actions," *i.e.*, intentional refraining from acting,[13] which, of course, escapes sensory observation. Not to sell certain merchandise at a given price is doubtless as economic an action as to sell it.

d) Furthermore, as W. I. Thomas has shown,[14] social reality contains elements of beliefs and convictions which are real because they are so defined by the participants and which escape sensory observation. To the inhabitants of Salem in the seventeenth century, witchcraft was not a delusion but an element of their social reality and is as such open to investigation by the social scientist.

e) Finally, and this is the most important point, the postulate of sensory observation of overt human behavior takes as a model a particular and relatively small sector of the social world,

---

[11] *Op. cit.*, p. 126.
[12] *Mind, Self and Society*, Chicago, 1937.
[13] See Max Weber, *The Theory of Social and Economic Organization*, translated by A. M. Henderson and Talcott Parsons, New York, 1947, p. 88.
[14] See W. I. Thomas, *Social Behavior and Personality*, edited by E. H. Volkart, New York, 1951, p. 81.

namely, situations in which the acting individual is given to the observer in what is commonly called a face-to-face relationship. But there are many other dimensions of the social world in which situations of this kind do not prevail. If we put a letter in the mailbox we assume that anonymous fellow-men, called postmen, will perform a series of manipulations, unknown and unobservable to us, with the effect that the addressee, possibly also unknown to us, will receive the message and react in a way which also escapes our sensory observation; and the result of all this is that we receive the book we have ordered. Or if I read an editorial stating that France fears the re-armament of Germany, I know perfectly well what this statement means without knowing the editorialist and even without knowing a Frenchman or a German, let alone without observing their overt behavior.

In terms of common-sense thinking in everyday life men have knowledge of these various dimensions of the social world in which they live. To be sure, this knowledge is not only fragmentary since it is restricted principally to certain sectors of this world, it is also frequently inconsistent in itself and shows all degrees of clarity and distinctness from full insight or "knowledge-about," as James [15] called it, through "knowledge of acquaintance" or mere familiarity, to blind belief in things just taken for granted. In this respect there are considerable differences from individual to individual and from social group to social group. Yet, in spite of all these inadequacies, common-sense knowledge of everyday life is sufficient for coming to terms with fellow-men, cultural objects, social institutions – in brief, with social reality. This is so, because the world (the natural and the social one) is from the outset an intersubjective world and because, as shall be pointed out later on, our knowledge of it is in various ways socialized. Moreover, the social world is experienced from the outset as a meaningful one. The Other's body is not experienced as an organism but as a fellow-man, its overt behavior not as an occurrence in the space-time of the outer world, but as our fellow-man's action. We normally "know" what the Other does, for what reason he does it, why he does it at this particular time and in these particular circumstances. That means that we experience our fellow-man's action in terms of his

[15] *Principles of Psychology*, Vol. I, pp. 221f.

motives and goals. And in the same way, we experience cultural objects in terms of the human action of which they are the result. A tool, for example, is not experienced as a thing in the outer world (which of course it is also) but in terms of the purpose for which it was designed by more or less anonymous fellow-men and its possible use by others.

The fact that in common-sense thinking we take for granted our actual or potential knowledge of the meaning of human actions and their products, is, I suggest, precisely what social scientists want to express if they speak of understanding or *Verstehen* as a technique of dealing with human affairs. *Verstehen* is, thus, primarily not a method used by the social scientist, but the particular experiential form in which common-sense thinking takes cognizance of the social cultural world. It has nothing to do with introspection; it is a result of processes of learning or acculturation in the same way as the common-sense experience of the so-called natural world. *Verstehen* is, moreover, by no means a private affair of the observer which cannot be controlled by the experiences of other observers. It is controllable at least to the same extent to which the private sensory perceptions of an individual are controllable by any other individual under certain conditions. You have just to think of the discussion by a trial jury of whether the defendant has shown "pre-meditated malice" or "intent" in killing a person, whether he was capable of knowing the consequences of his deed, etc. Here we even have certain "rules of procedure" furnished by the "rules of evidence" in the juridical sense and a kind of verification of the findings resulting from processes of *Verstehen* by the Appellate Court, etc. Moreover, predictions based on *Verstehen* are continuously made in common-sense thinking with high success. There is more than a fair chance that a duly stamped and addressed letter put in a New York mailbox will reach the addressee in Chicago.

Nevertheless, both defenders and critics of the process of *Verstehen* maintain, and with good reason, that *Verstehen* is "subjective." Unfortunately, however, this term is used by each party in a different sense. The critics of understanding call it subjective, because they hold that understanding the motives of another man's action depends upon the private, uncontrollable, and unverifiable intuition of the observer or refers to his private value system. The social scientists, such as Max Weber, however, call *Verstehen* subjective because its goal is to find out what the actor "means" in his action, in contrast to the meaning which this action has for the actor's partner or a neutral observer. This is the origin of Max Weber's famous postulate of subjective interpretation, of which more will have to be said in what follows. The whole discussion suffers from the failure to distinguish clearly between *Verstehen* 1) as the experiential form of common-sense knowledge of human affairs, 2) as an epistemological problem, and 3) as a method peculiar to the social sciences.

So far we have concentrated on *Verstehen* as the way in which common-sense thinking finds its bearing within the social world and comes to terms with it. As to the epistemological question: "How is such understanding or *Verstehen* possible?" Alluding to a statement Kant made in another context, I suggest that it is a "scandal of philosophy" that so far a satisfactory solution to the problem of our knowledge of other minds and, in connection therewith, of the intersubjectivity of our experience of the natural as well as the socio-cultural world has not been found and that, until rather recent times, this problem has even escaped the attention of philosophers. But the solution of this most difficult problem of philosophical interpretation is one of the first things taken for granted in our common-sense thinking and practically solved without any difficulty in each of our everyday actions. And since human beings are born of mothers and not concocted in retorts, the experience of the existence of other human beings and of the meaning of their actions is certainly the first and most original empirical observation man makes.

On the other hand, philosophers as different as James, Bergson, Dewey, Husserl, and Whitehead agree that the common-sense knowledge of everyday life is the unquestioned but always questionable background within which inquiry starts and within which alone it can be carried out. It is this *Lebenswelt*, as Husserl calls it, within which, according to him, all scientific and even logical concepts originate; it is the social matrix within which, according to Dewey, unclarified situations emerge, which have to be transformed by the process of inquiry into warranted assertibility; and Whitehead has pointed out that it is the aim of science to produce a theory which agrees with experience by explaining the thought-objects constructed by common sense through the mental constructs or thought objects of science.* For all these thinkers agree that any knowledge of the world, in common-sense thinking as well as in science, involves mental constructs, syntheses, generalizations, formalizations, idealizations specific to the respective level of thought organization. The concept of Nature, for instance, with which the natural sciences have to deal is, as Husserl has shown, an idealizing abstraction from the *Lebenswelt*, an abstraction which, on principle and of course legitimately, excludes persons with their personal life and all objects of culture which originate as such in practical human activity. Exactly this layer of the *Lebenswelt*, however, from which the natural sciences have to abstract, is the social reality which the social sciences have to investigate.

This insight sheds a light on certain methodological problems peculiar to the social sciences. To begin with, it appears that the assumption that the strict adoption of the principles of concept and theory formation prevailing in the natural sciences will lead to reliable knowledge of social reality is inconsistent in itself. If a theory can be developed on such principles, say in the form of an ideally refined behaviorism – and it is certainly possible to imagine this – then it will not tell us anything about social reality as experienced by men in everyday life. As Professor Nagel himself admits,[16] it will be highly abstract, and its concepts will apparently be remote from the obvious and familiar traits found in any society. On the other hand, a theory which aims at explaining social reality has to develop particular devices foreign to the natural sciences in order to agree with the common-sense experience of the social world. This is indeed what all theoretical sciences of human affairs – economics, sociology, the sciences of law, linguistics, cultural anthropology, etc. – have done.

This state of affairs is founded on the fact that there is an essential difference in the structure of the thought objects or mental constructs formed by the social sciences and those formed by the natural sciences.[17] It is up to the natural scientist and to

---

[16] *SLH*, p. 63.
[17] Some of the points dealt with in the following are presented more elaborately in "Common-Sense and Scientific Interpretation of Human Action".

* See "Common-Sense and Scientific Interpretation of Human Action," p. 3f. (M.N.)

him alone to define, in accordance with the procedural rules of his science, his observational field, and to determine the facts, data, and events within it which are relevant for his problem or scientific purpose at hand. Neither are those facts and events pre-selected, nor is the observational field pre-interpreted. The world of nature, as explored by the natural scientist, does not "mean" anything to molecules, atoms, and electrons. But the observational field of the social scientist – social reality – has a specific meaning and relevance structure for the human beings living, acting, and thinking within it. By a series of common-sense constructs they have pre-selected and pre-interpreted this world which they experience as the reality of their daily lives. It is these thought objects of theirs which determine their behavior by motivating it. The thought objects constructed by the social scientist, in order to grasp this social reality, have to be founded upon the thought objects constructed by the common-sense thinking of men, living their daily life within their social world. Thus, the constructs of the social sciences are, so to speak, constructs of the second degree, that is, constructs of the constructs made by the actors on the social scene, whose behavior the social scientist has to observe and to explain in accordance with the procedural rules of his science.

Thus, the exploration of the general principles according to which man in daily life organizes his experiences, and especially those of the social world, is the first task of the methodology of the social sciences. This is not the place to outline the procedures of a phenomenological analysis of the so-called natural attitude by which this can be done. We shall briefly mention only a few problems involved.

The world, as has been shown by Husserl, is from the outset experienced in the pre-scientific thinking of everyday life in the mode of typicality. The unique objects and events given to us in a unique aspect are unique within a horizon of typical familiarity and pre-acquaintanceship. There are mountains, trees, animals, dogs – in particular Irish setters and among them my Irish setter, Rover. Now I may look at Rover either as this unique individual, my irreplaceable friend and comrade, or just as a typical example of "Irish setter," "dog," "mammal," "animal," "organism," or "object of the outer world." Starting from here, it can be shown that whether I do one or the other, and also which traits or qualities of a given object or event I consider as individually unique and which as typical, depends upon my actual interest and the system of relevances involved – briefly, upon my practical or theoretical "problem at hand." This "problem at hand," in turn, originates in the circumstances within which I find myself at any moment of my daily life and which I propose to call my biographically determined situation. Thus, typification depends upon my problem at hand for the definition and solution of which the type has been formed. It can be further shown that at least one aspect of the biographically and situationally determined systems of interests and relevances is subjectively experienced in the thinking of everyday life as systems of motives for action, of choices to be made, of projects to be carried out, of goals to be reached. It is this insight of the actor into the dependencies of the motives and goals of his actions upon his biographically determined situation which social scientists have in view when speaking of the subjective meaning which the actor "bestows upon" or "connects with" his action. This implies that, strictly speaking, the actor and he alone knows what he does, why he does it, and when and where his action starts and ends.

But the world of everyday life is from the outset also a social cultural world in which I am interrelated in manifold ways of interaction with fellow-men known to me in varying degrees of intimacy and anonymity. To a certain extent, sufficient for many practical purposes, I understand their behavior, if I understand their motives, goals, choices, and plans originating in *their* biographically determined circumstances. Yet only in particular situations, and then only fragmentarily, can I experience the Others' motives, goals, etc. – briefly, the subjective meanings they bestow upon their actions, in their uniqueness. I can, however, experience them in their typicality. In order to do so I construct typical patterns of the actors' motives and ends, even of their attitudes and personalities, of which their actual conduct is just an instance or example. These typified patterns of the Others' behavior become in turn motives of my own actions, and this leads to the phenomenon of self-typification well known to social scientists under various names.

Here, I submit, in the common-sense thinking of everyday life, is the origin of the so-called constructive or ideal types, a concept which as a tool of the social sciences has been analyzed by Professor Hempel in such a lucid way. But at least at the common-sense level the formation of these types involves neither intuition nor a theory, if we understand these terms in the sense of Hempel's statements.[18] As we shall see, there are also other kinds of ideal or constructive types, those formed by the social scientist, which are of a quite different structure and indeed involve theory. But Hempel has not distinguished between the two.

Next we have to consider that the common-sense knowledge of everyday life is from the outset socialized in many respects.

It is, first, structurally socialized, since it is based on the fundamental idealization that if I were to change places with my fellow-man I would experience the same sector of the world in substantially the same perspectives as he does, our particular biographical circumstances becoming for all practical purposes at hand irrelevant. I propose to call this idealization that of the reciprocity of perspectives.*

It is, second, genetically socialized, because the greater part of our knowledge, as to its content and the particular forms of typification under which it is organized, is socially derived, and this in socially approved terms.

It is, third, socialized in the sense of social distribution of knowledge, each individual knowing merely a sector of the world and common knowledge of the same sector varying individually as to its degree of distinctness, clarity, acquaintanceship, or mere belief.

These principles of socialization of common-sense knowledge, and especially that of the social distribution of knowledge, explain at least partially what the social scientist has in mind in speaking of the functional structural approach to studies of human affairs. The concept of functionalism – at least in the modern social sciences – is not derived from the biological concept of the functioning of an organism, as Nagel holds. It refers to the socially distributed constructs of patterns of typical

---

[18] *SLH*, pp. 76ff. and 81.
* See "Common-Sense and Scientific Interpretation of Human Action," p. 11f. (M.N.)

motives, goals, attitudes, personalities, which are supposed to be invariant and are then interpreted as the function or structure of the social system itself. The more these interlocked behavior patterns are standardized and institutionalized, that is, the more their typicality is socially approved by laws, folkways, mores, and habits, the greater is their usefulness in common-sense and scientific thinking as a scheme of interpretation of human behavior.

These are, very roughly, the outlines of a few major features of the constructs involved in common-sense experience of the intersubjective world in daily life, which is called *Verstehen*. As explained before, they are the first level constructs upon which the second level constructs of the social sciences have to be erected. But here a major problem emerges. On the one hand, it has been shown that the constructs on the first level, the commonsense constructs, refer to subjective elements, namely the *Verstehen* of the actor's action from his, the actor's, point of view. Consequently, if the social sciences aim indeed at explaining social reality, then the scientific constructs on the second level, too, must include a reference to the subjective meaning an action has for the actor. This is, I think, what Max Weber understood by his famous postulate of subjective interpretation, which has, indeed, been observed so far in the theory formation of all social sciences. The postulate of subjective interpretation has to be understood in the sense that all scientific explanations of the social world *can*, and for certain purposes *must*, refer to the subjective meaning of the actions of human beings from which social reality originates.

On the other hand, I agreed with Professor Nagel's statement that the social sciences, like all empirical sciences, have to be objective in the sense that their propositions are subjected to controlled verification and must not refer to private uncontrollable experience.

How is it possible to reconcile these seemingly contradictory principles? Indeed, the most serious question which the methodology of the social sciences has to answer is: How is it possible to form objective concepts and an objectively verifiable theory of subjective meaning-structures? The basic insight that the concepts formed by the social scientist are constructs of the constructs formed in common-sense thinking by the actors on the social scene offers an answer. The scientific constructs formed on the second level, in accordance with the procedural rules valid for all empirical sciences, are objective ideal typical constructs and, as such, of a different kind from those developed on the first level of common-sense thinking which they have to supersede. They are theoretical systems embodying testable general hypotheses in the sense of Professor Hempel's definition.[19] This device has been used by social scientists concerned with theory long before this concept was formulated by Max Weber and developed by his school.

Before describing a few features of these scientific constructs, let us briefly consider the particular attitude of the theoretical social scientist to the social world, in contradistinction to that of the actor on the social scene. The theoretical scientist – qua scientist, not qua human being (which he is, too) – is not involved in the observed situation, which is to him not of practical but merely of cognitive interest. The system of relevances governing common-sense interpretation in daily life originates in the biographical situation of the observer. By making up his mind to become a scientist, the social scientist has replaced his personal biographical situation by what I shall call, following Felix Kaufmann,[20] a scientific situation. The problems with which he has to deal might be quite unproblematic for the human being within the world and vice versa. Any scientific problem is determined by the actual state of the respective science, and its solution has to be achieved in accordance with the procedural rules governing this science, which among other things warrant the control and verification of the solution offered. The scientific problem, once established, alone determines what is relevant for the scientist as well as the conceptual frame of reference to be used by him. This and nothing else, it seems to me, is what Max Weber means when he postulates the objectivity of the social sciences, their detachment from value patterns which govern or might govern the behavior of the actors on the social scene.

How does the social scientist proceed? He observes certain facts and events within social reality which refer to human action

[19] *SLH*, pp. 77ff.
[20] *Op. cit.*, pp. 52 and 251.

and he constructs typical behavior or course-of-action patterns from what he has observed. Thereupon he co-ordinates to these typical course-of-action patterns models of an ideal actor or actors, whom he imagines as being gifted with consciousness. Yet it is a consciousness restricted so as to contain nothing but the elements relevant to the performing of the course-of-action patterns observed. He thus ascribes to this fictitious consciousness a set of typical notions, purposes, goals, which are assumed to be invariant in the specious consciousness of the imaginary actor-model. This homunculus or puppet is supposed to be interrelated in interaction patterns to other homunculi or puppets constructed in a similar way. Among these homunculi with which the social scientist populates his model of the social world of everyday life, sets of motives, goals, roles – in general, systems of relevances – are distributed in such a way as the scientific problems under scrutiny require. Yet – and this is the main point – these constructs are by no means arbitrary. They are subject to the postulate of logical consistency and to the postulate of adequacy. The latter means that each term in such a scientific model of human action must be constructed in such a way that a human act performed within the real world by an individual actor as indicated by the typical construct would be understandable to the actor himself as well as to his fellow-men in terms of common-sense interpretation of everyday life. Compliance with the postulate of logical consistency warrants the objective validity of the thought objects constructed by the social scientist; compliance with the postulate of adequacy warrants their compatibility with the constructs of everyday life.*

As the next step, the circumstances within which such a model operates may be varied, that is, the situation which the homunculi have to meet may be imagined as changed, but not the set of motives and relevances assumed to be the sole content of their consciousness. I may, for example, construct a model of a producer acting under conditions of unregulated competition, and another of a producer acting under cartel restrictions, and then compare the output of the same commodity of the same firm in

* See "Common-Sense and Scientific Interpretation of Human Action," p. 43f. (M.N.)

the two models.[21] In this way, it is possible to predict how such a puppet or system of puppets might behave under certain conditions and to discover certain "determinate relations between a set of variables, in terms of which ... empirically ascertainable regularities... can be explained." This, however, is Professor Nagel's definition of a theory.[22] It can easily be seen that each step involved in the construction and use of the scientific model can be verified by empirical observation, provided that we do not restrict this term to sensory perceptions of objects and events in the outer world but include the experiential form, by which common-sense thinking in everyday life understands human actions and their outcome in terms of their underlying motives and goals.

Two brief concluding remarks may be permitted. First, a key concept of the basic philosophic position of naturalism is the so-called principle of continuity, although it is under discussion whether this principle means continuity of existence, or of analysis, or of an intellectual criterion of pertinent checks upon the methods employed.[23] It seems to me that this principle of continuity in each of these various interpretations is fulfilled by the characterized device of the social sciences, which even establishes continuity between the practice of everyday life and the conceptualization of the social sciences.

Second, a word on the problem of the methodological unity of the empirical sciences. It seems to me that the social scientist can agree with the statement that the principal differences between the social and the natural sciences do not have to be looked for in a different logic governing each branch of knowledge. But this does not involve the admission that the social sciences have to abandon the particular devices they use for exploring social reality for the sake of an ideal unity of methods which is founded on the entirely unwarranted assumption that only methods used by the natural sciences, and especially by physics, are scientific ones. So far as I know, no serious attempt has ever been made by the proponents of the "unity of science" movement to answer

[21] See Fritz Machlup, *The Economics of Seller's Competition: Model Analysis of Seller's Conduct*, Baltimore, 1952, pp. 9 ff.
[22] *SLH*, p. 46; see also pp. 51–52 above.
[23] See Thelma Z. Lavine, "Note to Naturalists on the Human Spirit," *Journal of Philosophy*, Vol. L, 1953, pp. 145–154, and Ernest Nagel's answer, *ibid.*, pp. 154–157.

or even to ask the question whether the methodological problem of the natural sciences in their present state is not merely a special case of the more general, still unexplored, problem how scientific knowledge is possible at all and what its logical and methodological presuppositions are. It is my personal conviction that phenomenological philosophy has prepared the ground for such an investigation. Its outcome might quite possibly show that the particular methodological devices developed by the social sciences in order to grasp social reality are better suited than those of the natural sciences to lead to the discovery of the general principles which govern all human knowledge.

CHOOSING AMONG PROJECTS OF ACTION

I. THE CONCEPT OF ACTION

Our purpose here is the analysis of the process by which an actor in daily life determines his future conduct after having considered several possible ways of action. The term "action" shall designate human conduct as an ongoing process which is devised by the actor in advance, that is, which is based upon a preconceived project. The term "act" shall designate the outcome of this ongoing process, that is, the accomplished action. Action, thus, may be covert – for example, the attempt to solve a scientific problem mentally – or overt, gearing into the outer world. But not all projected conduct is also purposive conduct. In order to transform the forethought into an aim and the project into a purpose, the intention to carry out the project, to bring about the projected state of affairs, must supervene. This distinction is of importance with respect to covert actions. My phantasying may be a projected one, and therefore, an action within the meaning of our definition. But it remains mere fancying unless what W. James called the voluntative "fiat" supervenes and transforms my project into a purpose. If a covert action is more than "mere fancying," namely purposive, it shall be called for the sake of convenience a "performance." In case of an overt action, which gears into the outer world and changes it, such a distinction is not necessary. An overt action is always both projected and purposive. It is projected by definition because otherwise it would be mere conduct and since it has become overt, that is, manifested in the outer world, the voluntative fiat which transfers the project into a purpose, the inner command "Let us start!" must have preceded.

Action may take place – purposively or not – by commission or omission. The case of purposively refraining from action deserves, however, special attention. I may bring about a future state of affairs by non-interference. Such a projected abstaining from acting may be considered in itself as an action and even as a performance within the meaning of our definition. If I project an action, then drop this project, say because I forget about it, no performance occurs. But if I oscillate between carrying out and not carrying out a project and decide for the latter, then my purposive refraining from acting is a performance. I may even interpret my deliberation whether or not to carry out a projected action as a choice between two projects, two anticipated states of affairs, one to be brought about by the action projected, the other by refraining from it. The deliberation of the surgeon whether or not to operate upon a patient or of the businessman whether or not to sell under given circumstances are examples of situations of this kind.

II. THE TIME STRUCTURE OF THE PROJECT *

According to Dewey's pregnant formulation, deliberation is "a dramatic rehearsal in imagination of various competing possible lines of action... It is an experiment in making various combinations of selected elements of habits and impulses to see what the resultant action would be like if it were entered upon." [1] This definition hits the point in many respects. All projecting consists in an anticipation of future conduct by way of phantasying. We have only to find out whether it is the future ongoing process of the action as it rolls on phase by phase or the outcome of this future action, the act imagined as having been accomplished, which is anticipated in the phantasying of projecting. It can easily be seen, that it is the latter, the act that will have been accomplished, which is the starting point of all of our projecting. I have to visualize the state of affairs to be brought about by my future action before I can draft the single steps of my future acting from which this state of affairs will result. Metaphorically speaking, I have to have some idea of the structure to be erected before I can draft the blueprints. In order to project my future

[1] John Dewey, *Human Nature and Conduct*, III, Modern Library edit., p. 190.
* Cf. "On Multiple Realities," p. 214f. (M.N.)

action as it will roll on I have to place myself in my phantasy at a future time when this action *will* already *have been* accomplished, when the resulting act *will* already *have been* materialized. Only then may I reconstruct the single steps which will have brought forth this future act. What is thus anticipated in the project is, in our terminology, not the future action, but the future act, and it is anticipated in the Future Perfect Tense, *modo futuri exacti*. This time perspective peculiar to the project has rather important consequences. First, I base my projecting of my forthcoming act in the Future Perfect Tense upon my knowledge of previously performed acts which are typically similar to the prescribed one, upon my knowledge of typically relevant features of the situation in which this projected action will occur, including my personal biographically determined situation. But this knowledge is my knowledge now at hand, now, at the time of projecting, and must necessarily be different from that which I shall have when the now merely projected act will have been materialized. Until then I shall have grown older and if nothing else has changed, at least the experiences I shall have had while carrying out my project will have enlarged my knowledge. In other words, projecting like any other anticipation carries along its empty horizons which will be filled in merely by the materialization of the anticipated event. This constitutes the intrinsic uncertainty of all forms of projecting.

Second, the particular time perspective of the project explains the relationship between the project and the various forms of motives.

III. IN-ORDER-TO AND BECAUSE MOTIVE

It is frequently stated that actions within the meaning of our definition are motivated behavior. Yet the term "motive" is equivocal and covers two different sets of concepts which have to be distinguished. We may say that the motive of the murderer was to obtain the money of the victim. Here "motive" means the state of affairs, the end, which the action has been undertaken to bring about. We shall call this kind of motive the "in-order-to motive." From the point of view of the actor this class of motives refers to his future. In the terminology suggested, we may say that the projected act, that is the pre-phantasied state of affairs to be brought about by the future action constitutes the in-order-to motive of the latter. What is, however, motivated by such an in-order-to motive? It is obviously not the projecting itself. I may project in my phantasy to commit a murder without any supervening intention to carry out such a project. Motivated by the way of in-order-to, therefore, is the "voluntative fiat," the decision: "Let's go!" which transforms the inner fancying into a performance or an action gearing into the outer world.

Over against the class of in-order-to motives we have to distinguish another one which we suggest calling the "because" motive. The murderer has been motivated to commit his acts because he grew up in an environment of such and such a kind, because, as psycho-analysis shows, he had in his infancy such and such experiences, etc. Thus, from the point of view of the actor, the because-motive refers to his past experiences. These experiences have determined him to act as he did. What is motivated in an action in the way of "because" is the project of the action itself. In order to satisfy his needs for money, the actor had the possibility of providing it in several other ways than by killing a man, say by earning it in a remunerative occupation. His idea of attaining this goal by killing a man was determined ("caused") by his personal situation or, more precisely, by his life history, as sedimented in his personal circumstances.

The distinction between in-order-to motives and because motives is frequently disregarded in ordinary language which permits the expression of most of the "in-order-to" motives by "because" sentences, although not the other way around. It is common usage to say that the murderer killed his victim *because* he wanted to obtain his money. Logical analysis has to penetrate the cloak of language and to investigate how this curious translation of "in-order-to" relations into "because" sentences becomes possible.

The answer seems to be a twofold one and opens still other aspects of the implications involved in the concept of motives. Motive may have a subjective and an objective meaning. Subjectively it refers to the experience of the actor who lives in his ongoing process of activity. To him, motive means what he has actually in view as bestowing meaning upon his ongoing action, and this is always the in-order-to motive, the intention of bringing about a projected state of affairs, of attaining a preconceived goal. As long as the actor lives in his ongoing action, he does not have in view its because motives. Only when the action has been accomplished, when in the suggested terminology it has become an act, he may turn back to his past action as an observer of himself and investigate by what circumstances he has been determined to do what he did. The same holds good if the actor grasps in retrospection the past initial phases of his still ongoing action. This retrospection may even be merely anticipated *modo futuri exacti*. Having, in my projecting phantasy, anticipated what I shall have done when carrying out my project, I may ask myself why I was determined to take this and no other decision. In all these cases the genuine because motive refers to past or future perfect experiences. It reveals itself by its very temporal structure only to the retrospective glance. This "mirror-effect" of temporal projection explains why, on the one hand, a linguistic "because form" may and is frequently used for expressing genuine "in-order-to relations" and why, on the other hand, it is impossible to express genuine because relations by an "in-order-to" sentence. In using the linguistic form "in-order-to", I am looking at the ongoing process of action which is still in the making and appears therefore in the time perspective of the future. In using the linguistic "because" form for expressing a genuine in-order-to relationship, I am looking at the preceding project and the therein *modo futuri exacti* anticipated act. The genuine because motive, however, involves, as we have seen, the time perspective of the past and refers to the genesis of the projecting itself.

So far we have analyzed the subjective aspect of the two categories of motives, that is, the aspect from the point of view of the actor. It has been shown that the in-order-to motive refers to the attitude of the actor living in the process of his ongoing action. It is, therefore, an essentially subjective category and is revealed to the observer only if he asks what meaning the actor bestows upon his action. The genuine because motive, however, as we have found, is an objective category, accessible to the observer who has to reconstruct from the accomplished act, namely from the state of affairs brought about in the outer world by the actor's action, the attitude of the actor to his action. Only insofar as the actor turns to his past and, thus, becomes an observer of his own acts, can he succeed in grasping the genuine because motives of his own acts.

The mixing-up of the subjective and objective point of view as well as of the different temporal structures inherent in the concept of motives has created many difficulties in understanding the process by which we determine our future conduct. The problem of genuine because motives has age-old metaphysical connotations. It refers to the controversy between determinists and indeterminists, the problem of free will and *"librum arbitrium."* This controversy is of no concern to us here although we hope to learn from the treatment it has received from some philosophers such as Bergson and Leibniz important insights for our main problem, the process of choosing between projects and the determination of our future actions. Yet the time structure of all projecting is of highest importance to us: our analysis has shown that it always refers to the actor's stock of knowledge at hand at the time of projecting and, nevertheless, carries along its horizon of empty anticipations, the assumption that the projected act will go on in a typically similar way as had all the typically similar past acts known to him at the time of projecting. This knowledge is an exclusively subjective element, and for this very reason the actor, as long as he lives in his projecting and acting, feels himself exclusively motivated by the projected act in the way of in-order-to.

IV. FANCYING AND PROJECTING

It is also the reference of projecting to a stock of knowledge at hand which distinguishes projecting from mere fancying. If I fancy to be superman or to be endowed with magic powers and dream what I will then perform, this is not projecting. In pure phantasy I am not hampered by any limits imposed by reality. It is in my discretion to ascertain what is within my reach and to determine what is within my power. I may freely fancy that all or some or none of the conditions upon which the attaining of my fancied goal by fancied means in a fancied situation depends will have been fulfilled. In such a pure phantasying my mere wish defines my possible chances. It is a thinking in the optative mode.

Projecting of performances or overt actions, however, is a motivated phantasying, motivated by the anticipated supervening intention to carry out the project. The practicability of the project is a condition of all projecting which could be translated into a purpose. Projecting of this kind is, thus, phantasying within a given or better within an imposed frame, imposed by the reality within which the projected action will have to be carried out. It is not, as mere phantasying is, a thinking in the optative mode but a thinking in the potential one. This potentiality, this possibility of executing the project requires, for instance, that only ends and means believed by me to be within my actual or potential reach may be taken into account by my projecting in fancy; that I am not allowed to vary fictitiously in my phantasying those elements of the situation which are beyond my control; that all chances and risks have to be weighed in accordance with my present knowledge of possible occurrences of this kind in the real world; briefly, that according to my present knowledge the projected action, *at least as to its type*, would have been feasible, its means and ends, *at least as to their types*, would have been available if the action had occurred in the past. The italicized restriction is important. It is not necessary that the "same" projected action in its individual uniqueness, with its unique ends and unique means has to be pre-experienced and, therefore, known. If this were the case, nothing novel could ever be projected. But it is implied in the notion of such a project that the projected action, its end and its means, remain compatible and consistent with these typical elements of the situation which, according to our experience at hand at the time of projecting, have warranted so far the practicability, if not the success, of *typically* similar actions in the past.

V. THE FOUNDATION OF PRACTICABILITY

What are, however, these elements of the situation with which the projected action has to remain consistent and compatible in order to be anticipated as feasible, and what constitutes their typicality? Without entering into the detailed analysis of this highly complicated problem, we may, very roughly, distinguish two sets of experiences upon which the assumption of the practicability of the projected action is founded.

a) *The world as taken for granted*

The first set consists of the actor's experiences and his opinions, beliefs, assumptions, referring to the world, the physical and the social one, which he takes for granted beyond question at the moment of his projecting. This set of experiences has stood the test so far and is, therefore, without question accepted as given, although as given merely "until further notice." This does not mean that the experiences, beliefs, etc., taken for granted are themselves consistent and compatible with one another. But their intrinsic inconsistency and incompatibility is discovered and they themselves put into question only if a novel experience not subsumable under the so far unquestioned frame of reference turns up. Yet, even without being questioned, the realm of the world as taken for granted is the domain within which alone doubt and questioning becomes possible and, in this sense, it is at the foundation of any possible doubt.

The unquestioned experiences are from the outset experienced as typical ones, that is, as carrying along open horizons of anticipated similar experiences. For example, the unquestioned outer world is from the outset experienced not as an arrangement of individual unique objects dispersed in space and time, but as "mountains," "trees," "animals," "fellow-men." I may have never seen an animal of the kind I am seeing now but I know that this is an animal and in particular a dog. I may reasonably ask "What kind of dog is this?" The question presupposes that I have grasped the newly experienced object as a dog showing all the typical features and the typical behavior of a dog and not, say, of a cat. In other words, the dissimilarity of this particular dog from all other kinds of dogs which I know stands out and becomes questionable merely by reference to the similarity it has to my unquestioned experiences of typical dogs.

We can neither enter here into a more detailed investigation of the typicality of our pre-predicative experience which Husserl has outlined in such a masterful way nor into the social foundation of these types – which are either socially derived or socially approved or both and which are handed down by the typifying medium *par excellence*, namely, common language. It must suffice to point out that all knowledge taken for granted has a highly socialized structure, that is, it is assumed to be taken for granted not only by *me* but by *us*, by *"everyone"* (meaning "every one who belongs to us"). This socialized structure gives this kind of knowledge an objective and anonymous character: it is conceived as being independent of my personal biographical circumstances. The typicalness and the objective character of our unquestioned experiences and beliefs also inheres in those dealing with relations of causality and finality, of means and ends, and, therefore, with the practicability of human actions (ours and those of our fellow-men), within the domain of things taken for granted. For this very reason there is an objective chance taken for granted that future actions typically similar to those which have been proved as practicable in the past will also be practicable in the future.

We said before that our experiences, beliefs, and opinions taken for granted might be inconsistent and incompatible with one another. We now have to amplify this statement by saying that each element of the realm taken for granted beyond question has necessarily an equivocal character of indeterminateness. Let us recall the simple example mentioned in an earlier essay.* Suppose that one of the beliefs unquestionably taken for granted could be formulated by the proposition "S is p." Now S, taken without question, as it appears to be given to us, is not only p but also q, r, and many other things. As long as this interrelationship is not put into question the expression "S is p" is elliptical in the sense that the full statement should read: "S is, among many other things such as q and r, also p." In other words, within the

* "Common-Sense and Scientific Interpretation of Human Action," pp. 8–9. (M.N.)

unquestionably given world the propositions "S is p" and "S is q" are until counterproof both open possibilities, not contradicting each other, either having its equal right and its equal weight. If I, with respect to an element S of the world taken for granted, assert: "S is p," I do so because for my purpose at hand at this particular moment I am interested only in the p-being of S and am disregarding as not relevant to such purpose the fact that S is also q and r. The famous principle discovered by Spinoza "*Omnis definitio est negatio*" points, of course on another level, in the same direction.

b) The biographically determined situation

What, however, constitutes my purpose at hand at this particular moment? This question leads us to the second set of our experiences upon which the practicability of future actions is founded. It consists of the experiences which I, the actor, have of my biographically determined situation at the moment of any projecting. To this biographically determined situation belongs not only my position in space, time, and society but also my experience that some of the elements of the world taken for granted are imposed upon me, while others are either within my control or capable of being brought within my control and, thus principally modifiable. For instance these things are within my reach, those things outside of it, be it that they were formerly within my reach and might be brought into it again, or that they never have been within my reach but are in yours, my fellow-man's reach and might be brought within mine if I, being here, change places with you, being there. This factor is of great importance for our problem because all my projecting is based upon the assumption that any action occurring within the sector of the world under my actual or potential control will be practicable. But that is not all. At any given moment of my biographically determined situation I am merely concerned with some elements, or some aspects of both sectors of the world taken for granted, that within and that outside my control. My prevailing interest – or more precisely the prevailing system of my interests, since there is no such thing as an isolated interest – determines the nature of such a selection. This statement holds good independently of the precise meaning given to the term "interest" and independently also of the assumption made as to the origin of the system of interests.[2] At any rate, there is such a selection of things and aspects of things relevant to me at any given moment, whereas other things and other aspects are for the time being of no concern to me or even out of view. All this is biographically determined, that is, the actor's actual situation has its history; it is the sedimentation of all his previous subjective experiences. They are not experienced by the actor as being anonymous but as unique and subjectively given to him and to him alone.

VI. DOUBTING AND QUESTIONING

The subjectively determined selection of elements relevant to the purpose at hand out of the objectively given totality of the world taken for granted gives rise to a decisive new experience: the experience of doubt, of questioning, of choosing and deciding, in short, of deliberation. Doubt might come from various sources; only one case important for our problem at hand will be discussed here. We said that there is no such thing as an isolated interest, that interests are from the outset interrelated with one another into systems. Yet interrelation does not necessarily lead to complete integration. There is always the possibility of overlapping and even conflicting interests and consequently of doubt whether the elements selected from our surrounding world taken for granted beyond question are really relevant to our purpose at hand. Is it indeed the p-being of S which I have to take into consideration and not its being q? Both are open possibilities within the general frame of the world taken for granted without question until counterproof. But now my biographically determined situation compels me to select either the p-being or the

[2] Because what is commonly called interest is one of the basic features of human nature, the term will necessarily mean different things to different philosophers in accordance with their basic conception of human existence in the world. We venture to suggest that the various solutions offered for the explanation of the origin of the interests might be grouped into two types: one which is concerned with the because motives, the other with the in-order-to motives constituting the so called interests. Leibniz, with his theory of the "small perceptions" determining all of our activities, might be considered as a representative of the first, Bergson's view that all of our perceptions are determined by our activities as an example of the second.

q-being of S as relevant for my purpose at hand. What has been unquestioned so far has now to be put into question, a situation of doubt occurs, a true alternative has been created. This situation of doubt, created by the selection of the actor in his biographically determined situation from the world taken for granted is what alone makes deliberation and choice possible. The fact that all choosing between projects refers to the situation of doubt has been acknowledged explicitly or implicitly by the greater number of the philosophers dealing with this problem. We quote the following passage from Dewey who has formulated the question in his masterful plastic language: In deliberation, Dewey says, "each conflicting habit and impulse takes its turn in projecting itself upon the screen of imagination. It unrolls a picture of its future history, of the career it would have if it were given head. Although overt exhibition is checked by the pressure of contrary propulsive tendencies, this very inhibition gives habit a chance at manifestation in thought... In thought as well as in overt action, the objects experienced in following out a course of action attract, repel, satisfy, annoy, promote and retard. Thus deliberation proceeds. To say that at last it ceases is to say that choice, decision, takes place. What then is choice? Simply hitting in imagination upon an object which furnishes an adequate stimulus to the recovery of overt action... Choice is not the emergence of preference out of indifference. It is the emergence of a unified preference out of competing preferences." [3]

This analysis is in substance entirely acceptable also to those who are unable to share Dewey's fundamental view of interpreting human conduct in terms of habit and stimulus. Yet behind the problem discussed by Dewey another one emerges. What makes (in his terminology) habits and impulses conflict? What causes the pressure of contrary propulsive tendencies inhibiting one another? Which among our many preferences are competing and capable of being unified by the decision? In other words: I can choose only between projects which stand to choice. I am in a dilemma before an alternative. But what is the origin of such an alternative? It seems to us that Husserl has, although on another level, made a significant contribution to answering these questions.

[3] *Op. cit.*, pp. 190ff.

VII. PROBLEMATIC AND OPEN POSSIBILITIES ACCORDING TO HUSSERL

We owe to Husserl's investigation on the origin of the so-called modalizations of predicative judgments (such as certainty, possibility, probability) in the pre-predicative sphere the important distinction between what he calls problematic and open possibilities. This distinction is vital for the understanding of the problem of choice.

According to Husserl, any object of our experience is originarily pregiven to our passive reception; it affects us, imposing itself upon the ego. Thus, it stimulates the ego to turn to the object, to attend to it, and this turning to the object is the lowest form of activity emanating from the ego. Philosophers have frequently described this phenomenon as the receptivity of the ego, and psychologists have analyzed it under the heading of attention. Attention is first of all the tending of the ego toward the intentional object, but this tending is merely the starting point of a series of active *cogitationes* in the broadest sense: the initial phase of the starting activity carries along an intentional horizon of later phases of activity which will fulfill or not fulfill what has been anticipated in an empty way in a continuous synthetic process until the activity reaches its end or is interrupted, eventually in the form: "and so on." Taking as an example our actual belief in the existence of an outer object perceived, we find that the ego's interest in this object induces it to manifold other activities, for instance to compare the image it has of the appearance of the perceptional object with other images of the same object, or to make accessible its back side if it appears from the front side, and so on. Each single phase of all these tendencies and activities carries along its specific horizon of protentional expectations, of anticipations, that is, of what may occur in the later phases of the fulfilling activity. If these expectations are not fulfilled there are several alternatives: (1) It may happen that the process is hampered for one reason or another either because the object disappears from the perceptional field or is covered by another object or because the original interest is superseded by another, stronger one. In these cases the process stops with the constitution of one single image of the object; (2) It may also happen that our interest in the perceptual object continues but that our anticipations are not fulfilled but disappointed by the supervening phases of the process. Here again two cases have to be distinguished: (a) the disappointment of our expectations is a complete one, for instance, the back side of this object which we expected to be an evenly red-colored sphere turns out to be not red but green and not spherical but deformed. This "not... but otherwise," this superimposition of a new meaning of the object over the pre-constituted meaning of the same object, whereby the new meaning supersedes the old one, leads in our example to the complete annihilation of the anticipating intention. The first impression ("this is an evenly red-colored sphere") is "stricken out," negated; (b) yet it is possible that the first impression, instead of being completely annihilated, becomes merely doubtful in the course of the ongoing process. Is this something in the store window, a human being, say an employee occupied with window dressing, or a clothed dummy? There is a conflict between belief and belief, and for a certain time both perceptual apperceptions may coexist. While we doubt, neither of these two beliefs is cancelled; either of them continues in its own right; either is motivated, nay, even postulated, by the perceptual situation; but postulate stands against postulate, one contests the other and is contested by the other. Only our resolution of this doubt will annihilate one or the other. In case of a doubtful situation both beliefs of the alternative have the character of being "questionable," and that which is questionable is always contested in its being, namely, contested by something else. The ego oscillates between two tendencies to believe. Both beliefs are merely suggested as possibilities. The ego is in conflict with itself: it is inclined to believe now this, now that. This inclination means not merely the affective tendency of suggested possibilities, but these possibilities, says Husserl, are suggested to *me* as being, *I* follow now this, now that possibility in the process of taking a decision, bestow now on the one, now on the other validity in an act of "taking sides" although always hampered in carrying it through. This following of the ego is motivated by the weight of the possibilities themselves. Following actively one of the possibilities over at least a certain period, I make, so to speak, an instantaneous decision, deciding for this possibility. But, then, I cannot proceed further because of the exigency of the counterpossibility which, too, will obtain its fair trial and makes me inclined to believe it. The decision is reached in a process of clarification of the contesting tendencies by which either the weakness of the counterpossibilities becomes more and more visible or by which new motives arise which reinforce the prevailing weight of the first.

Possibilities and counterpossibilities, contesting with one another, and originating in the situation of doubt are called by Husserl *problematic or questionable possibilities*, questionable, because the intention to decide in favor of one of them is a questioning intention. Only in the case of possibilities of this kind, that is of possibilities "for which something speaks," can we speak of likelihood. It is more likely that this is a man means: more circumstances speak for the possibility that this is a man than for the possibility that this is a dummy. Likelihood is, thus, a weight which belongs to the suggested beliefs in the existence of the intentional objects. From this class of problematic possibilities, originating in doubt, has to be distinguished the class of *open possibilities* originating in the unhampered course of empty anticipations. If I anticipate the color of the unseen side of an object of which I know only the front side that shows some pattern or patches, any specific color I anticipate is merely contingent, but not, that the unseen side will show "some" color. All anticipation has the character of indeterminacy, and this general indeterminacy constitutes a frame of free variability; what falls within the frame is one element among other elements of possibly *nearer* determination, of which I merely know that they will fit in the frame but which are otherwise entirely undetermined. This exactly is the concept of open possibilities.

The difference between problematic and open possibilities is first one of their origin. The problematic possibilities presuppose tendencies of belief which are motivated by the situation and in contest with one another; for each of them speaks something, each has a certain weight. None of the open possibilities has any weight whatsoever, they are all equally possible. There is no alternative preconstituted, but within a frame of generality all possible specifications are equally open. Nothing speaks for one which would speak against the other. An undetermined general intention, which itself shows the modality of certainty – although of an empirical or presumptive certainty – "until further notice" – carries along an implicit modalization of the certainty peculiar to its implicit specifications. On the other hand, the field of problematic possibilities is unified: in the unity of contest and of being apprehended by disjunctive oscillation A, B, and C become known as being in opposition and, therefore, united. To be sure, it is quite possible that only one of these contesting possibilities stands out consciously whereas the others remain unnoticed in the background as empty and thematically unperformed representations. But this fact does not invalidate the pregivenness of a true alternative.

Thus far we have considered Husserl. His theory of choosing between alternatives is the more important for our problem, as we will remember that any project leads to a true problematic alternative. Each project to do something carries with it the problematic counterpossibility of not doing it.

As mentioned before, the aim of Husserl's theory of open and problematic possibilities was the investigation of the origin of the so-called modalizations of judgment in the pre-predicative sphere, and for this very reason he took as examples of cogitations the perceiving of objects in the outer world. He frequently stresses, however, the general character of this theory which refers to activities of all kinds.

We think that our analysis of the two sets of experiences warranting the practicability of projected actions converges with the outcome of Husserl's distinction. The world as taken for granted is the general frame of open possibilities, none of them having its specific weight, none of them as long as believed beyond question, contesting the others. All are believed to be of empirical or presumptive certainty until further notice, that is, until counterproof. It is the selection made from things taken for granted by the individual in his biographically determined situation that transforms a selected set of these open possibilities into problematic ones which stand from now on to choice: each of them has its weight, requires its fair trial, shows the conflicting tendencies of which Dewey speaks. How can this procedure of choosing be more precisely described?

VIII. CHOOSING AMONG OBJECTS WITHIN REACH

To simplify the problem let us first consider the case in which I do not have to choose between two or more future states of affairs to be brought forth by my own future actions but between two objects, A and B, both actually and equally within my reach. I oscillate between A and B as between two equally available possibilities. A as well as B has a certain appeal to me. I am now inclined to take A, which inclination is then overpowered by an inclination to take B, this is again replaced by the first one, which finally prevails: I decide to take A and to leave B.

In this case everything takes place as described so far. A true alternative, preconstituted by our previous experiences, stands to choice: The objects A and B are equally within our reach, that is, obtainable with the same effort. My total biographical situation, that is, my previous experiences as integrated into my actually prevailing system of interests, creates the principally problematic possibilities of conflicting preferences, as Dewey expresses it. This is the situation which most of the modern social sciences assume to be the normal one underlying human action. It is assumed that man finds himself at any time placed among more or less well defined problematic alternatives or that a set of preferences enables him to determine the course of his future conduct. Even more, it is a methodological postulate of modern social science that the conduct of man has to be explained *as if* occurring in the form of choosing among problematic possibilities. Without entering here into details we want to give two illustrations:

Man acting in the social world among and upon his fellow-men finds that the preconstituted social world imposes upon him at any moment several alternatives among which he has to choose. According to modern sociology, the actor has "to define the situation." By doing so he transforms his social environment of "open possibilities" into a unified field of "problematic possibilities" within which choice and decision – especially so-called "rational" choice and decision – becomes possible. The sociologist's assumption that the actor in the social world starts with the definition of the situation is, therefore, equivalent to the methodological postulate, that the sociologist has to describe the observed social actions *as if* they occurred within a unified field of true alternatives, that is, of problematic and not of open possibilities. Likewise the so-called "marginal principle," so important for modern economics, can be interpreted as the scientific postulate for dealing with the actions of the observed economic subjects *as if* they had to choose between pregiven problematic possibilities.

IX. CHOOSING AMONG PROJECTS

We have studied so far the process of choosing between two objects actually within my reach, both equally obtainable. At first glance it might appear that the choice between two projects, between two courses of future action occurs in exactly the same manner. As a matter of fact, most of the students of the problem of choice have failed to make any distinction. Perhaps the old distinction between τεχνή ποιητική and τεχνή κτητική, between the art of producing and the art of acquiring, taken over by Plato and Aristotle from the Sophists, refers to this problem. The chief differences between the two situations seem to be these: in the case of choosing between two or more objects, all of them actually within my reach and equally available, the problematic possibilities are, so to speak, ready made and well circumscribed. As such their constitution is beyond my control, I have to take one of them or to leave both of them as they are. Projecting, however, is of my own making and in this sense within my control. But before I have rehearsed in my imagination the future courses of my actions, the outcome of my projecting action has not been brought within my reach and, strictly speaking, there are at the time of my projecting no problematic alternatives between which to choose. Anything that will later on stand to choice in the way of a problematic alternative has to be produced by me, and in the course of producing it, I may modify it at my will within the limits of practicability. Moreover – and this point seems to be decisive – in the first case, the alternatives which stand to my choice coexist in simultaneity in outer time: here are the two objects A and B, I may turn away from one of them and return to it; here it is still and unchanged. In the second case, the

PROJECTS OF ACTION 85

several projects of my own future actions do not coexist in the simultaneity of outer time: The mind by its phantasying acts creates in succession in inner time the various projects, dropping one in favor of the other and returning to, or more precisely, recreating, the first. But by and in the transition from one to the succeeding states of consciousness I have grown older, I have enlarged my experience, I am, returning to the first, no longer the "same" as I was when originally drafting it, and, consequently, the project to which I return is no longer the same as that which I dropped; or, perhaps more exactly, it is the same, but modified. In the first case, what stands to choice are problematic possibilities coexistent in outer time; in the second case, the possibilities to choose between are produced successively and exclusively in inner time, within the *durée*.

X. BERGSON'S THEORY OF CHOICE

Bergson, who has emphasized more than any other philosopher the importance of the two time dimensions – inner *durée* and spatialized time – for the structure of our conscious life, investigated, in his first book, the *Essai sur les données immédiates de la conscience* (1899), the problem of choice under this aspect. He handles it in connection with his criticism of the deterministic and indeterministic doctrines. Both determinists and indeterminists, so his argument runs, base their conclusions upon an associationistic psychology. They substitute for the inner *durée* with its continuous succession and the interconnected stream of consciousness the spatialized time in which there is juxtaposition of seemingly isolated experiences. They show us an ego hesitating between two opposite sentiments going from one to the other and finally deciding for one of them. The ego and the sentiments by which it is moved are, thus, assimilated to well defined things which remain unchanged through the whole course of the operation. However, the ego by the very fact that it has experienced the first sentiment has changed before it experiences the second one. Hence it modifies, at any moment in the course of deliberation not only itself but also the sentiments which act (*agite*) upon it. Thus, a dynamic series of interpenetrating states of consciousness is created which enforce one another and lead to a free act by a natural evolution. If I am choosing between two possible actions X and Y and go in turn from one to the other, this means, says Bergson, that I am living through a series of states of mind which can be referred to two groups according to my prevailing inclinations to X or to its opposite. But even these opposite inclinations have merely one single real existence, X and Y being symbols merely for different tendencies of my personality at successive moments of my *durée*. There are not in the strict sense two opposite states but a series of successive and different states which the ego runs through, growing and expanding continuously as it passes between the imaginary tendencies which change during the process of deliberation as the ego changes itself. Thus the way of speaking of two tendencies or two directions is purely a metaphorical one: in reality there are neither two tendencies, nor two directions but just an ego which lives and develops by its very hesitations until the free action detaches itself from it like too ripe a fruit. Associationistic psychology, used equally by both determinists and indeterminists, assumes, however, that the ego in the state of deliberation oscillates between two – we would add, problematic – possibilities which they conceive as if these two possibilities were two coexisting points in space, as if the road run through by the consciousness of the ego so far bifurcated at a certain point and as if the ego, placed at the crossroad, had to take its decision which way to follow. He who makes such an assumption commits the fallacy of placing himself at a moment when the action has already been accomplished but of looking nevertheless at the process of the actor's activity as if the bifurcation of the road had existed before the deliberation took place and the decision was made. Onrolling time and time past, *durée* and spatialized time, are thus confused and the irreversibility and irretrievability of time disregarded. There was no bifurcation, no traced ways before the action was accomplished, there was even no direction and no question of a way; and only the accomplished action has traced the way. Deliberation cannot be conceived as an oscillation in space; it consists rather in a dynamic process in which the ego as well as its motives are in a continuous stage of becoming. The ego, infallible in its immediate findings, feels itself free and declares this; but in any attempt to explain its freedom it succumbs by necessity to a spatial symbolism with all its fallacies.

Thus far we have considered Bergson. Translated into the terminology of the present discussion, his criticism is directed against the assumption that problematic possibilities existed with respect to projects at a time when all possibilities were still open ones. The ego living in its acts knows merely open possibilities; genuine alternatives become visible only in interpretative retrospection, that is, when the acts have been already accomplished, and thus the becoming has been translated into existence. Remembering our terminological distinction between action and act, we may say that, according to Bergson, all actions occur within open possibilities and that problematic possibilities are restricted to past acts.

We have no issue with this theory (although it is obviously modelled after a special class of actions, namely actions gearing into the outer world), except that it tells only half the story. To be sure, Bergson, too, points out that the ego in self-interpretation of its past acts has the illusion of having chosen between problematic possibilities. But he fails to add that it is the accomplished act and not the action which is anticipated *modo futuri exacti* in the project. Projecting, as we have seen, is retrospection anticipated in phantasy. In this anticipated retrospection, and only in it, the projected action is phantasied as accomplished; the ways after the bifurcation – to keep to Bergson's metaphor – have been traced, although merely as pencil strokes on a map and not as trails in the landscape. The ego phantasying one project after the other, runs, growing and expanding, through a series of successive states and behaves, while doing so, exactly as described by Bergson, dealing merely within the open possibilities inherent to each projecting, as explained before. But what has been projected in such a projecting (or better, in such a series of successive phantasying activities), is the *modo futuri exacti* anticipated accomplished acts, the outcome, therefore, of the actions to be performed, not the actions themselves as they will go on. These various anticipated acts are now problematic alternatives within a unified field *modo potentiali*, they have their quasi-coexistence and stand now to choice. But their coexistence is merely a quasi-coexistence, that is, the projected acts are merely imagined as coexistent; they are not ready made and equally available within my reach. Still they are all within my control and they remain in their quasi-existence until my decision to carry one of them out has been reached. This decision consists in the supervening intention to turn one of these projects into my purpose. As we have seen, this transition requires a voluntative "fiat" which is motivated by the in-order-to motive of the chosen project.

Motives, says Leibniz,[4] induce man to act but do not necessitate him. He is free to choose to follow or not to follow his inclinations or even to suspend such a choice. He has the freedom of reasonable deliberation; reason will be his guide in weighing the pros and cons of each possibility. We may translate this statement into our language as follows: As soon as the possibilities of my future action have been constituted as problematic possibilities within a unified field, that is, as soon as two or more projects stand to choice, the weight of each of them can be ascertained by operations of judgment. The "art of deliberation," the procedure by which conflicting motives after having past the scrutiny of reason lead finally to an act of volition, has been carefully analyzed by Leibniz. As will be seen presently, he comes very close to Husserl's concept of an instantaneous decision and Bergson's concept of the free act which detaches itself from the ego like too ripe a fruit.

XI. LEIBNIZ'S THEORY OF VOLITION

Leibniz handles this problem in his "Theodizee" within a moral-theological setting. In presenting his theory here, we have detached his general analysis from this context and replaced the terms "good" and "evil" as used by Leibniz by "positive" and "negative weight" (of the problematic possibilities involved), leaving it for the time being intentionally open what should be understood by "positive" and "negative weight."

Like most of the problems handled in the Theodizee, Leibniz's analysis of volition originates in a polemic with Bayle. Bayle

---

[4] And according to him motives are always founded upon "perceptions" in the broad sense in which he uses this term, that is, including the "small perceptions."

compared the soul to a balance where the reasons and inclinations of action take the place of weights. According to him, we may explain what happens in acts of decision by the hypothesis that the balance is in equilibrium as long as the weights in both scales are equal but inclines to one or the other side if the content of one of the two scales is heavier than the other. An emerging argument gives additional weight, a new idea shines more brilliantly than an old one, the fear of a heavy displeasure may outweigh several expected pleasures. One has the greater difficulties in arriving at a decision the more the opposite arguments approach an equal weight. This simile seems to Leibniz inadequate for several reasons. First, not only two but mostly more eventualities stand to choice; secondly, volitive intentions are present in every phase of deliberation and decision; thirdly, there is no such thing as an equilibrium from which to start. It is for these reasons that Leibniz takes over from the Schoolmen the notions of "antecedent" and "subsequent" volitions which he uses, after having introduced his own concept of an "intermediate" volition, in a very original way for explaining the mechanism of choice.

According to this theory will has various phases. Generally speaking, it can be said that will consists in the inclination to bring about some action in proportion with its inherent positive weight. This kind of will may be called antecedent will (*volonté antécédente*) because it is unconnected and considers each positive weight separately as positive without proceeding to combinations. This will would produce its effect if there were not some stronger counterarguments which would bar it from becoming effective. The intermediate will (*volonté moyenne*) originates in such counterarguments. It proceeds to combinations such as attaching a negative weight to the positive one, and if the latter still outweighs the former, the will will continue to tend toward this combination. With respect to the final will, the decretory and decisive one, the intermediate will may be considered as an antecedent one although it follows the pure and primitive antecedent will. The final and decisive volition results from the conflict of all the antecedent wills and their combinations, those which respond to the positive as well as those which respond to the negative weights. It is by the concourse of all these particular wills that the total volition originates, as in mechanics the composed movement results from all tendencies which concur in one and the same mobile body and satisfies equally each of them by realizing all of them simultaneously. It is this consequent final volition which determines the direction of the act and of which it is said that everyone performs what he is willing to perform provided he can perform it. Reasoning has, thus, its function in determining our choice and in transforming the *volontés antécédentes* into the *volonté finale*. But this function is limited in various respects. To begin with, choice of the preferable always takes place within the limits of the state of our knowledge (and this knowledge consists in the totality of our pre-experiences). But this knowledge is not homogeneous, it is either distinct or confused. Only distinct knowledge is the realm of Reason, our senses and our passions furnish merely confused thoughts and we are in their bondage as long as we do not succeed in basing our actions on distinct knowledge. This situation is frequently complicated by the fact that our confused thoughts are felt clearly whereas our distinct thoughts are only potentially clear: they could be clear if we were willing to make the necessary efforts to explicate their implications, for instance by penetrating into the meaning of words or symbols, etc. Secondly – and here Leibniz shares Locke's point of view – man's mind is inclined to make misjudgments in comparing present pleasures and displeasures with future ones, disregarding that this future will become a present and then appear in full proximity. Leibniz compares this phenomenon with the spatial perspective: a small distance in time may deprive us completely of the sense of the future, as if the future object had disappeared entirely. What, then, is left of future things is frequently merely a name or a blind thought (*cogitationes caecae*). In such a case it may occur that we do not even raise the question whether future goods should be preferred but act according to our vague impressions. But even if we do, if we entertain the question, it may be that we anticipate future events in the wrong way or doubt that our decision will lead to the anticipated consequences. Thirdly, the perfect balancing of the reasons which determine our choice may be compared with the procedure of an accountant in establishing a balance sheet. No item must be omitted, each has to receive its appropriate evaluation, all of them have to be arranged correctly and finally summed up exactly. In each of these activities of reasoning errors can be committed. Fourthly, in order to come to a correct estimate of the consequences of our choice (to a "perfectly rational decision," as modern scientists would say) we would need the mastery of several techniques today not less undeveloped than at the time of Leibniz. We would need a technique for availing ourselves of what we know (*l'art de s'aviser au besoin ce qu'on sait*); a technique for estimating the likelihood of future events, in particular the consequences of our decisions; and finally a technique for ascertaining the positive and negative weights of the problematic possibilities to choose between or as Leibniz calls them, the values of goods and evils. Only then could we hope to master what Leibniz terms the art of consequences.

As in Husserl's and Bergson's theories, it is also here the ego which in the living process of its stream of consciousness creates the possibilities that stand to choice, and it is the same ego which makes the final decision in the course of this process. The "perceptions" which are to Leibniz nothing else than changes of the mind itself create by their solicitations the inclinations, that is, the various "*volontés antécédentes*," which as soon as the scrutinizing reason interferes are partially counterbalanced by the "*volontés moyennes.*" Tendency is, thus, succeeded by countertendency until the "in-order-to motive" of the prevailing project leads to the "*volonté conséquente, décrétoire et définitive*," to the voluntative fiat: "Let us start!" To Bergson choice is merely a series of events in the inner *durée* and never an oscillating between two sets of factors which coexist in spatialized time; deliberation with all its contesting tendencies can only be conceived as a dynamic process in which the ego, its sentiments, its motives and goals are in a state of continuous becoming until this development leads to the free act. To Husserl the situation of doubt in which the ego is in conflict with itself creates the unified field of problematic possibilities; in a series of successive instantaneous but not final decisions the ego takes the side of one of the competing possibilities and counterpossibilities and ascertains what might be in favor of each of them. This process continues until the situation of doubt ceases, either, as Husserl says, because a decision has been made with a bad logical conscience or because doubt has been transformed into empirical certainty, which, as merely empirical, he calls a "certainty good until further notice." Husserl studies in terms of modalization the constitution of problematic possibilities as the precondition of all possible choice; Bergson describes, in an analysis of the time perspectives involved, the process of choosing itself; Leibniz follows the interplay of volitive intentions which leads to the final "fiat" of decision. All three theories converge because all of them place themselves in the midst of the ongoing flux of consciousness of the actor who is about to make his choice and do not retrospectively reconstruct what has happened if once a decision has been reached, a reconstruction which appertains to the so-called objective point of view of the observer or of the ego that turns in self-interpretation back to its past experiences as an observer of itself.

But still, and for good reasons, the actor's experiences of the past are taken into account. To Bergson the actual state of mind of an individual is as it is merely because it has lived through all its past experiences in their peculiar intensity and their peculiar sequence. In a passage of the same work not reported by us he demonstrates the impossibility of the scientist Peter's deciding how Paul will act in a concrete situation. The assumption that Peter is able to make any such prediction would presuppose that he has lived through every experience of Paul's and exactly with the same intensity and with the same sequence as Paul did, that consequently, Peter's stream of consciousness has to be exactly the same as Paul's, in a word: that Peter has to be identical with Paul. Husserl's theory presupposes the whole sphere of prepredicative experiences in which alone the situation of doubt with its constitution of problematic possibilities originates and in which alone each possibility receives its "weight." And also the certitude into which doubt is transformed is merely an empirical one, a certitude consistent and compatible with our previous experiences. To Leibniz the "good" and the "evil," terms which we have translated by "positive and negative weight," refer to previous experiences of the actor as well as the scrutinizing activity of reason by which the different *"volontés antécédentes"* are transformed into *"volontés moyennes."*

XII. THE PROBLEM OF WEIGHT

We now have to examine the origin of the "weight" of possibilities and counterpossibilities, of Leibniz's "good" and "evil" as the inherent positive weight of *"volonté antécédente"* or negative of a *"volonté moyenne."* Let us keep to our example of choosing between two different projects. Can it be said that the "weight," the "good" or "evil," attributed to either of them is inherent to the specific project? It seems that such a statement is meaningless. The standards of weights, of good and evil, of positive and negative, briefly of evaluation, are not created by the projecting itself, but the project is evaluated according to a preexistent frame of reference. Any student of ethics is familiar with the age-old controversy on values and valuation here involved. For our problem, however, we need not embark upon discussing it. It is sufficient for us to point out that the problem of positive and negative weights transcends the actual situation of a concrete choice and decision and to give an indication of how this fact can be explained without having recourse to the metaphysical question of the existence and nature of absolute values.

In discussing earlier the notion of interest we observed that there is no such thing for the actor as an isolated interest. Interests have from the outset the character of being interrelated with other interests in a system. It is merely a corollary of this statement that also actions, motives, ends and means, and, therefore, projects and purposes are only elements among other elements forming a system. Any end is merely a means for another end; any project is projected within a system of higher order. For this very reason any choosing between projects refers to a previously chosen system of connected projects of a higher order. In our daily life our projected ends are means within a preconceived particular plan – for the hour or the year, for work or for leisure – and all these particular plans are subject to our plan for life as the most universal one which determines the subordinate ones even if the latter conflict with one another. Thus, any choice refers to pre-experienced decisions of a higher order, upon which the alternative at hand is founded – as any doubt refers to a pre-experienced empirical certainty which becomes questionable in the process of doubting. It is our pre-experience of this higher organization of projects which is at the foundation of the problematic possibilities standing to choice and which determines the weight of either possibility: its positive or negative character is positive or negative merely with reference to this system of higher order. For the purpose of this purely formal description, no assumption whatsoever is needed either as to the specific content of the higher system involved or as to the existence of so-called "absolute values," nor is any assumption needed as to the structure of our pre-knowledge, that is, as to its degree of clarity, explicitness, vagueness, etc. On the contrary, on any level of vagueness the phenomenon of choice can be repeated. As seen from the point of view of the actor in daily life, full clarity of all the elements involved in the process of choosing, that is, a *"perfectly"* rational action, is impossible. This is so because first, the system of plans upon which the constitution of alternatives is founded belongs to the because motives of his action and is disclosed merely to the retrospective observation, but hidden to the actor who lives in his acts oriented merely to his in-order-to motives which he has in view; secondly, because his knowledge, if our analysis is correct, is founded upon his biographically determined situation which selects the elements relevant to his purpose at hand from the world simply taken for granted, and this biographically determined situation as prevailing at the time of the projecting changes in the course of oscillating between the alternatives, if for no other reason than because of the experience of this oscillating itself.

XIII. SUMMARY AND CONCLUSION

Our analysis, which we have intentionally restricted to the daily life situation of choosing between projects, started from the world taken for granted beyond question as the general field of our open possibilities. Our biographically determined situation selects certain elements of this field as relevant for our purpose at hand. If this selection meets with no obstacle the project is simply transformed into a purpose and the action is carried out as a matter of course. If, by the very vagueness of our knowledge at hand at the time of projecting, a situation of doubt arises, then some of the formerly open possibilities become questionable, problematic. Some part of the world formerly taken for granted beyond question and therefore unquestioned has now been put into question. The decision re-transforms what has been made questionable into a certainty, but an empirical certainty that is again an unquestioned element of our knowledge, taken for granted until further notice.

Our analysis, in spite of its length, has had to remain very sketchy. The notions of "interest," "systems of interest," "relevance," and, first of all the concept of the world taken for granted and of the biographically determined situation are rather headings for groups of problems to be investigated. In concluding, we might be permitted to indicate just two questions important especially for the social sciences, to which the results of the preceding analysis might possibly be applied advantageously.

The first refers to the fellow-man's understanding of the actor's action, that is, to the observer of the ongoing or accomplished action within the social world. There is no warranty that the world as taken for granted subjectively by the actor is in the same way beyond question for the observer. The actor may suppose that what he takes for granted is beyond question also for "everyone belonging to us," but whether this assumption holds good for the particular fellow-man depends upon whether a genuine we-relation has been pre-established between both. Yet even if this is the case, the biographically determined situation and therewith the selection of the relevant elements among the open possibilities of the actor and the observer must necessarily be different. In addition, the observer does not participate in immediacy in the process of the actor's choice and decision even if some of its phases were communicated to him. He has to reconstruct from the accomplished overt behavior, from the act, the underlying in-order-to or because motives of the actor. Nevertheless, to a certain extent at least, man is capable of understanding his fellow man. How is this possible?

The second question refers to the nature of idealization and generalization made by the social scientist in describing the actions occurring within the social world. On the one hand the social scientist is not permitted to take the social world for granted, that is, as merely given. His "general plan" consists in putting this world into question, to inquire into its structure. On the other hand, *qua* scientist, not as man among fellow-men which he certainly also is, it is not his biographically determined situation, or at least not in the same sense as in the case of the actor in daily life, which ascertains what is relevant for his scientific performance. Can and does the social scientist refer to the same reality of the social world that appears to the actor? And if so, how is this possible?

Answering either question would require detailed investigations far beyond the limits of the present discussion.

PART II

*Phenomenology
and the Social Sciences*

SOME LEADING CONCEPTS OF PHENOMENOLOGY

I

An unsigned booknote in an issue of the *American Sociological Review*, discussing phenomenological literature, regrets that these writings are almost inaccessible even to many philosophers, to say nothing of social scientists. "We must apparently wait for popularized interpretations before much can be said about the relations of phenomenology and the social sciences." [1]

Unfortunately, this description of the situation is not exaggerated. So far, social scientists have not found an adequate approach to the phenomenological movement initiated by the basic writings of Edmund Husserl in the first three decades of our century. In certain quarters the phenomenologist is held to be a kind of crystal gazer, a metaphysician or ontologist in the deprecatory sense of the words, at any rate a fellow who spurns all the empirical facts and the more or less established scientific methods devised to collect and interpret them. Others, who are better informed, feel that phenomenology may have a certain significance for the social sciences, but they regard the phenomenologists as an esoteric group whose language is not understandable to an outsider and is not worth bothering with. A third group has formed a vague and mostly erroneous idea of what phenomenology means, on the basis of some of the slogans used by authors who merely pretend to be phenomenologists, without using Husserl's method (such as Theodor Litt), or used by phenomenologists (such as Max Scheler) in non-phenomenological writings dealing with subject matters of the social sciences.

Except for a few remarks in the final pages, the present paper

[1] *American Sociological Review*, Vol. 9, 1944, p. 344.

is not intended as a discussion of the relations of phenomenology and the social sciences, or even as a "popularized" interpretation of phenomenology for social scientists. An attempt to reduce the work of a great philosopher to a few basic propositions understandable to an audience not familiar with his thought is, as a rule, a hopeless undertaking. And in regard to Husserl's phenomenology there are also several special difficulties. The published part of his philosophy, characterized by a condensed presentation and highly technical language, is of a rather fragmentary character. He found it essential to start again and again with his inquiry into the basic foundation not only of philosophy itself but also of all scientific thinking. His aim was to show the implicit presuppositions upon which any science of the world of natural and social things, and even the current philosophy, are based. His ideal was to be a "beginner" in philosophy, in the truest sense of the word. Only by laborious analyses, by fearless consistency and by a radical change in our habits of thinking can we hope to reveal the sphere of a "first philosophy" which complies with the requirements of a "rigorous science" worthy of the name.

It is true that many sciences are commonly called rigorous sciences, the term referring usually to the possibility of presenting the scientific content in mathematical form. This is not the sense in which Husserl used the term. In order to prevent any misunderstanding it must be stressed that Husserl, a disciple of Weierstrass, was himself a trained mathematician who acquired his doctorate in mathematics on the basis of a thesis dealing with the philosophy of arithmetic. But his deep understanding of mathematical thinking, and his admiration for its achievements, did not blind him to its limitations. It was his conviction that none of the so-called rigorous sciences, which use mathematical language with such efficiency, can lead toward an understanding of our experiences of the world – a world the existence of which they uncritically presuppose, and which they pretend to measure by yardsticks and pointers on the scale of their instruments. All empirical sciences refer to the world as pre-given; but they and their instruments are themselves elements of this world. Only a philosophical doubt cast upon the implicit presuppositions of all our habitual thinking – scientific or not – can guarantee the "exactitude" not only of such a philosophical attempt itself but of all the sciences dealing directly or indirectly with our experiences of the world. Such an inquiry – so Husserl hopes – will also resolve the so-called fundamental crises of such sciences as logic, mathematics, physics, psychology, that have become apparent in our time and threaten their seemingly most secure results.

This outline of Husserl's general aim may explain the great difficulties encountered by a beginning student of phenomenology who attempts to attach to this philosophy one of the customary textbook labels, such as idealism, realism, empiricism. None of these school-classifications can be adequately applied to a philosophy that puts them all in question. Phenomenology, searching for a real beginning of all philosophical thinking, hopes when fully developed to end where all the traditional philosophies start. Its place is beyond – or better, before – all distinctions between realism and idealism.

In addition, these introductory remarks may help to remove a widespread misunderstanding of the nature of phenomenology – the belief that phenomonology is anti-scientific, not based upon analysis and description but originating in a kind of uncontrollable intuition or metaphysical revelation. Even many serious students of philosophy have been induced to classify phenomenology as metaphysics, because of its admitted refusal to accept uncritically the givenness of sensory perceptions, of biological data, of society and environment, as the unquestionable point of departure for philosophical investigation. Moreover, Husserl's use of certain unfortunate terms, such as *Wesensschau*, has prevented many from acknowledging phenomenology as a method of philosophical thinking.

For a method it is, and one as "scientific" as any. The following pages attempt to present a few examples, as far as possible in non-technical language, in order to show what the basic principles of this method are and how they work. This necessarily involves oversimplification and inexactitude. The only justification for such an endeavor is the hope of removing some of the current prejudices against phenomenology, and perhaps of inducing the reader to familiarize himself with Husserl's style of philosophical thinking.[2]

---

[2] Marvin Farber's paper, "Phenomenology," in *Twentieth Century Philosophy*, ed. by Dagobert D. Runes, New York, 1943, and the same author's excellent book, *The Foundation of Phenomenology: Edmund Husserl and the Quest for a Rigorous Science of Philosophy*, Cambridge, Mass., 1943, are to be regarded as the best introductions, and should be carefully studied before the reader turns to Husserl's own writings.

II

The search for a realm of indubitable truth as a starting point for philosophical thinking is not at all new in modern philosophy. On the contrary, it may be said that modern philosophy starts with the famous Cartesian attempt to attain absolute certainty by systematically casting doubt upon all our experiences which can be put in question. It is hardly necessary to enter into a discussion of the peculiar way taken by Descartes in his "Meditations" in his effort to establish "Cogito, ergo sum" as the indubitable certainty that lies at the basis of all our thinking. But it seems advisable to emphasize the importance of his basic thought, his insistence that any philosopher must at least once in his life make the radical effort to examine critically all the seemingly given data of his experiences and of the elements of his stream of thought; must, for this purpose, turn away from the uncritical attitude toward the world he lives in naively among his fellow-men, unconcerned whether this world of his daily life has the character of existence or of mere appearance. This fundamental discovery of Descartes opened an avenue of approach for all future philosophical thinking.

Descartes' meditations were the outstanding pattern for Husserl's phenomenology. But Husserl believed that Descartes' analysis was not radical enough. Holding in his hand the key to a great discovery, he hesitated to use it, hesitated to pursue the indispensable consequences. To be sure, he laid bare the indubitable "ego cogito" as the origin of all our knowledge, and thus defined the stream of thought as the field of all further philosophical investigation. But he was not aware of the implications hidden in both terms of this "ego cogito."

To start with the latter, Descartes handled the cogitations that appear within the stream of thought as isolated entities. Neither was he aware of the through and through interconnectedness of the stream of thought in inner time, nor did he make a sufficiently radical distinction between the act of thinking and the object of thought. The first problem, that of the interconnectedness of the stream of thought, will be dealt with later. The second one found its solution only through the discovery, by Franz Brentano, Husserl's teacher, of the *intentional* character of all our thinking. Any of our experiences as they appear within our stream of thought, Brentano held, are necessarily referred to the object experienced. There is no such thing as thought, fear, fantasy, remembrance as such; every thought is thought *of*, every fear is fear *of*, every remembrance is remembrance *of* the object that is thought, feared, remembered.

The technical term coined by Husserl to designate this relationship is "intentionality." The intentional character of all our cogitations necessarily involves a sharp distinction between the act [3] of thinking, fearing, remembering, and the objects to which these acts are referred. Husserl considerably deepened the inquiry into the intentional character of cogitations, and he frequently declared the field of intentionality to be the outstanding topic of phenomenological research. It will be necessary to return later to the implications carried by the concept of intentionality; here we are interested only in the fact that the Cartesian concept of the stream of cogitations may be considerably radicalized by pointing out their intentional character.

Another radicalization seems necessary with respect to Descartes' concept of the ego, whose indubitable existence was the outcome of his meditations. As we have seen, the Cartesian method involves an artificial change in the attitude that man observes in his daily life. In daily life we accept the existence of the world naively as it is, and only by means of philosophical doubt can the indubitability of the "ego cogitans" be reinstated. But after having made the important discovery of the field of transcendental subjectivity as the domain of certainty, Descartes dropped it immediately by identifying this ego with *mens sive animus sive intellectus*, thus substituting the human soul or mind *within* the world for the ego that can be discovered only by detaching from and reflecting upon the world. This is exactly the point where phenomenological criticism sets in, the point where Husserl started a Cartesian meditation all over again. In order to lay bare the pure field of consciousness Husserl developed the famous and frequently misunderstood technique of "phenomenological reduction," which will now be presented in broad outline. It is no more than a radicalized renewal of the Cartesian method.

---

[3] Husserl defined "acts" not as psychical activities, but as intentional experiences; see Farber, *The Foundation of Phenomenology* (cited above) pp. 343ff.

III

The phenomenologist does not deny the existence of the outer world, but for his analytical purpose he makes up his mind to suspend belief in its existence – that is, to refrain intentionally and systematically from all judgments related directly or indirectly to the existence of the outer world. Borrowing terms from mathematical technique, Husserl called this procedure "putting the world in brackets" or "performing the phenomenological reduction." There is nothing mysterious in these notions, which are merely names for the technical device of phenomenology for radicalizing the Cartesian method of philosophical doubt, in order to go beyond the natural attitude of man living within the world he accepts, be it reality or mere appearance.

It is an admittedly artificial change from man's attitude in his daily life toward the world and his belief in it to the attitude of the philosopher, who by his very problem is bound to reject any presupposition that does not stand the test of his critical doubt. The purpose of such a technique is only to reach a level of indubitable certainty which lies beyond the realm of mere belief – in other words, to disclose the pure field of consciousness. As will be shown below, this pure field of consciousness can be explored and described in its own right, can be analyzed and questioned about its genesis.[4] If this technique succeeds in attaining its goal – and the phenomenologist thinks it does – if it helps really to make possible an investigation within the purified sphere of conscious life, upon which all our beliefs are founded, then we may turn back later on from this aprioristically reduced sphere to the mundane one. Since to each empirical determination within the latter there necessarily corresponds a feature within the former, we may be confident that all our discoveries within the reduced sphere will stand the test also in the mundane sphere of our life within the world.

Although "phenomenological reduction" does not require any magic or mysterious faculty of mind, the technique of bracketing which it suggests is by no means a simple one if applied with the

---

[4] Husserl's term "genesis" refers to the process by which knowledge arises in its "origin-form" of self-givenness, and has nothing to do with the factual process of meanings arising out of a definite historical subjectivity; see *ibid.*, p. 167.

necessary radicalism. What we have to put in brackets is not only the existence of the outer world, along with all the things in it, inanimate and animate, including fellow-men, cultural objects, society and its institutions. Also our belief in the validity of our statements about this world and its content, as conceived within the mundane sphere, has to be suspended. Consequently, not only our practical knowledge of the world but also the propositions of all the sciences dealing with the existence of the world, all natural and social sciences, psychology, logic and even geometry – all have to be brought within the brackets. This means that none of their truths, tested or not by experiences and proofs within the mundane sphere, can be taken over in the reduced sphere without critical examination. And even more – I, the human being, am also, as a psycho-physiological unit, an element of this world that has to be bracketed, and so is my body and my mind or my soul or whatever name you prefer to give to the scheme of reference to which we relate our experiences of the world. In performing the phenomenological reduction I have to suspend belief also in my mundane existence as a human being within the world. Thus the process of reduction transcends the world in every respect, and the reduced sphere is in the very meaning of the word a transcendental one or, in the well understood meaning of the word, an aprioristic one.

But a student who is willing to try to perform this suppression of all natural habits of thinking may ask whether this phenomenological reduction does not lead toward an absolute nihilism. If I have annulled, so to speak, not only the world and my beliefs in it, not only all the results of sciences dealing with the world, but also myself as a psycho-physiological unit, what then remains? Is it not the only possible conclusion that nothing can be left outside the brackets when all the aforementioned elements have been bracketed?

The answer is emphatically no. What remains after the performance of the transcendental reduction is nothing less than the universe of our conscious life, the stream of thought in its integrity, with all its activities and with all its cogitations and experiences (both terms being used in the broadest – the Cartesian – sense, which includes not only perceptions, conceptions, judgments, but also acts of will, feelings, dreams, fantasies, etc.)

And now it is useful to remember what was said above with respect to the intentional character of all our cogitations. They are essentially and necessarily cogitations *of* something; they refer to intentional objects. This intentional character of our cogitations has not only been preserved within the reduced sphere; it has even been purified and made visible. My perception of this chair in the natural attitude corroborates my belief in its existence. Now I perform the transcendental reduction. I refrain from believing in the existence of this chair. Thereafter the chair perceived remains outside the bracketing, but the perception itself is without any doubt an element of my stream of thought. And it is not "perception as such," without any further reference; it remains "perception *of*" – specifically perception *of* this *chair*. I am no longer attaching to this perception, however, any judgment whether this chair is really an existing object in the outer world. It is not the corporeal thing "chair" to which my perception intentionally refers, but the intentional object of my preserved perception is "the chair *as I have perceived it*," the *phenomenon* "chair *as it appears to me*," which may or may not have an equivalent in the bracketed outer world. Thus the whole world is preserved within the reduced sphere in so far, but only in so far, as it is the intentional correlate of my conscious life – with the radical modification, however, that these intentional objects are no longer the things of the outer world as they exist and as they really are, but the phenomena as they appear to me. This difficult distinction requires further comment.

IV

I perceive the blossoming tree in the garden. This, my perceiving of the tree as it appears to me, is an indubitable element of the stream of my thought. And the same is valid for the phenomenon "blossoming-tree-as-it-appears-to-me," which is the intentional object of my perceiving. This phenomenon is independent of the fate of the real tree in the outer world. The tree in the garden may change its colors and shades by the interplay of sun and cloud, it may lose its blossoms, it may be destroyed by fire. The once perceived phenomenon "blossoming-tree-as-it-appears-to-me" remains untouched by all these events, and also remains untouched by the performance of the phenomenological reduction described above. A second perception may refer to the tree as it appears to me at that time, and may or may not be consistent with the first one. If it is, I may perform a synthesis, an identification of the two phenomena (or more correctly, of the second phenomenon actually perceived and the recollected phenomenon caught by the first perception). If the second perception is not consistent with the first, I may doubt either of them, or I may search for an explanation of their apparent inconsistency.

In any case, each act of perceiving and its intentional object are indubitable elements of my stream of thought; and equally certain is the doubt I may have about whether the "tree as it appears to me" has a correlate in the outer world. The foregoing example has illustrated the fact that my cogitations and their intentional objects are elements of my stream of thought which are not influenced by the changes that may happen to their correlates in the outer world. But this does not mean that the cogitations are not subject to modification by events happening within my stream of consciousness. In order to make this clear let us first distinguish between the act of perceiving and the perceived, between the *cogitare* and the *cogitatum* or, to use Husserl's technical term, between the Noesis and the Noema.[5]

There are modifications of the intentional object which are due to activities of the mind and are therefore noetical, and others which originate within the intentional object itself and are therefore noematical. It is impossible, of course, to enter here into a full discussion of these noetical-noematical modifications, the systematic exploration of which constitutes a vast field of phenomenological research. But merely in order to give some idea of the importance of the problems involved, I shall mention a few examples of the implications hidden within the appearing phenomenon itself.

[5] Students of William James' psychology will not err if they bring these notions into correlation with James' "thinking" and the "object thought of," provided they keep in mind the fact that James' psychological analysis refers exclusively to the mundane sphere, whereas Husserl operates within the phenomenologically reduced sphere; see A. Schutz, "William James' Concept of the Stream of Thought, Phenomenologically Interpreted," in *Philosophy and Phenomenological Research*, Vol. 1, 1941, pp. 442–52.

When, for the sake of abbreviation, I used language like "I am perceiving this chair" or "I am perceiving this blossoming cherry tree in the garden," I did not adequately describe what was perceived by those perceptions, but rather the outcome of a very complicated process of interpretation, in which the present perception was connected with previously experienced perceptions (cogitations) of the different aspects of this cherry tree when I walked around it, of this cherry tree as it appeared to me yesterday, of my experiences of cherry trees and of trees in general, of corporeal things and so on. The intentional object of my perceiving is a specific mixture of colors and shapes in a special perspective of distance, and it stands out over against other objects afterward called "my garden," "the heavens," "clouds." Interpretation of this total as "the blossoming cherry tree in my garden as it appears to me" is the outcome of a complicated reference to preexperienced cogitations. Nevertheless, all these preexperienced cogitations, referring to corporeal things, have produced a certain "universal style" of interpreting the noematic correlate of my perceiving activity. I may even say that the noema itself, the intentional object perceived, carries along many implications which may be explicated systematically.

Let us for the sake of simplification restrict our examples to the so-called perceptions of corporeal things. What I am perceiving is only one aspect of the thing. Not only when I move around do other aspects appear. In addition, the aspect of the thing caught by my perceiving act suggests other possible aspects: the front side of the house suggests its back, the facade the interior, the roof the unseen foundation and so on. All these moments together may be called the "inner horizon" of the perceived object, and it can be systematically explored by following the intentional indications within the noema itself. But there is an outer horizon too. The tree refers to my garden, the garden to the street, to the city, to the country in which I am living, and finally to the whole universe. Every perception of a "detail" refers to the "thing" to which it pertains, the thing to other things over against which it stands out and which I call its background. There is not an isolated object as such, but a field of perceptions and cogitations with a halo, with a horizon or, to use a term of William James, with fringes relating it to other things.

These groups of implications, which we have called the inner and the outer horizon, are concealed within the noema itself, and if I follow its intentional indications the noema itself seems to be modified; whereas the noetical side, the perceiving act, does not change.

From these noematical modifications have to be distinguished, for the purpose of analysis, the noetical modifications that are due to the perceiving activity itself. These are, for instance, the different attitudes peculiar to the perceiving act which in psychology textbooks are handled under the heading of "attention." There is also the important distinction between the originary experience of the experienced thing and such derived experiences as those based upon recollection or retention of previous experiences. (Without entering into this very complicated problem I may add that the distinction just made is very important for the solution of one of the greatest enigmas of all psychology, the problem of evidence: to the phenomenologist, evidence is not a hidden quality inherent in a specific kind of experience, but the possibility of referring derived experiences to an originary one.) This distinction is based upon the interconnectedness of the stream of thought in inner time: the present cogitation is surrounded by fringes of retentions and protentions connecting it with what just now happened and with what may be expected to happen immediately, and refers to cogitations of the more distant past by recollection and to the future by anticipations.

All this leads to an entirely new theory of memory and experience in inner time, and to the definite overthrow of the psychology of association. In radicalizing the insight into the through and through connectedness of our stream of experiences, phenomenology comes very close to the early writings of William James and to the doctrine of the Gestaltists.* But the basic concept of phenomenology leads also to an entirely new interpretation of logic. Before this can be made clear we have to turn for a moment to another topic.

---

* See Aron Gurwitsch, *Théorie du champ de la conscience*, Bruges, 1957. (M.N.)

V

So far this discussion has been deliberately restricted to the phenomenological interpretation of so-called real objects, of things in the outer world. It is now time to introduce Husserl's concept of "ideal objects." These are by no means of metaphysical origin, and have nothing to do with Plato's or Kant's ideas or with any kind of Berkeleyan or Hegelian idealism. An ideal object is, for instance, the concept of number and the whole system of numbers with which arithmetic and algebra deal; or the content of the Pythagorean theorem as a meaningful entity; or the meaning of a sentence or a book; or a notion like "the Hegelian philosophy" or "Calvin's concept of original sin"; or any of the so-called social and cultural objects which are meaningful and can at any time be made intentional objects of our cogitations.

It is the peculiarity of intentional objects that they are *founded* upon so-called "real" objects of the outer world, and that they can be communicated only by signs and symbols which are in turn perceptible things, such as the sound waves of the spoken word, or printed letters. Therefore phenomenology had to develop a very important theory of semantics. It is characteristic of a sign that it suggests another thing which belongs to quite another category. The well known sign for "root" suggests a specific mathematical notion that is entirely independent of the typographical shape of the root sign in different printing styles, and of whether this sign appears printed in a textbook, written with ink or pencil on paper or with chalk on the blackboard, whether I refer to it in speech by the sound sign "Wurzel" or "root" or "racine." And the same holds true for the specific sign system and for all sign systems or languages. They indicate the ideal objects but they are not themselves the ideal objects.

The thing of the outer world which will be interpreted as a sign, its meaning, its meaning within the system of the universe of discourse, its specific meaning within the context at hand – all these have to be sharply distinguished. A glance at the doctrines of certain logicians of our time who are pleased to reduce logic, science and even philosophy to a pre-given system of semantics shows the full importance of Husserl's distinction. This does not mean, however, that Husserl did not have a full understanding of the genuine problem of the *mathesis universalis*. Indeed, an outstanding contribution of phenomenology toward this problem is one of his "Logical Investigations" called "The Distinction of Independent and Dependent Meanings and the Idea of Pure Grammar."

VI

The theory of ideal objects opens an avenue of approach to another phenomenological insight, the importance of which is not limited, however, to our experiencing of ideal objects. As high school students we all learned to derive the Pythagorean theorem $a^2 + b^2 = c^2$ from certain other geometrical propositions by developing step by step certain conclusions from certain assured premises. This performance of many separate although interconnected mental operations disclosed to us the meaning of the theorem in question, and this meaning has since become our permanent possession. It is not necessary now for us to repeat this mental process of deriving the theorem, in order to understand its meaning. On the contrary, although some of us might have some difficulty if we had to prove why the sum of the squares of the sides of a right triangle must always be equal to the square of the hypotenuse, we do understand the meaning of this proposition, which we find ready at hand within the stock of our experience.

In more general terms, our mind builds up a thought by single operational steps, but in hindsight it is able to look in a single glance at this whole process and its outcome. We can even go a step further: our knowledge of an object, at a certain given moment, is nothing else than the sediment of previous mental processes by which it has been constituted. It has its own history, and this history of its constitution can be found by questioning it. This is done by turning back from the seemingly ready-made object of our thought to the different activities of our mind in which and by which it has been constituted step by step.

This is the kernel of Husserl's theory of constitution, and it gives an insight into one of his great contributions to the interpretation of logic.

VII

Our current school-logic is merely a refinement of the Aristotelian formal logic, which regards concepts as ready-made and works out operational rules for the technique of judgment, of conclusions, of deduction and subsumption and so on. This logic is based upon the assumption of a world in which there are things with qualities, relationships between things, species and genera, all of them representable by well circumscribed notions. The basic assumption of this kind of logic is the principle of predicability, according to the well known formula "S is P."

Phenomenological analysis shows, however, that there is a pre-predicative stratum of our experience, within which the intentional objects and their qualities are not at all well circumscribed; that we do not have original experiences of isolated things and qualities, but that there is rather a field of our experiences within which certain elements are selected by our mental activities as standing out against the background of their spatial and temporal surroundings; that within the through and through connectedness of our stream of consciousness all these selected elements keep their halos, their fringes, their horizons; that an anlysis of the mechanism of predicative judgment is warranted only by recourse to the mental processes in which and by which pre-predicative experience has been constituted. Formal logic must therefore be founded upon a logic of the underlying constitutional processes, which can be investigated only within the transcendental field made accessible by the phenomenological reduction.

This, in oversimplified outline, is Husserl's distinction between "Formal and Transcendental Logic." In his book of that name he shows that analyses of this kind lead to entirely new interpretations of certain basic concepts of our current logic, such as evidence, tautology, the principle of the excluded middle, and so on. He shows the presuppositions of formal logic which are derived from certain ontological assumptions; and he starts to investigate the role of intersubjectivity within the field of logic, which refers not to my private world but to the world common to all of us, and which alone explains the problem of intersubjective truth.

It is of course impossible to enter here into a discussion of these

SOME LEADING CONCEPTS

very intricate problems. The short catalogue given above can show only that questions of the greatest importance for all the sciences are at stake. I even venture to say that the many great performances in the field of logic for which our generation is indebted to Dewey's operationalism and James' pragmatism can find their justification only by recourse to the field of prepredicative experience. All the overt and covert ontological assumptions made by these schools have to be carefully analyzed in order to determine the sphere where these theories are legitimately applicable and yet avoid the mistake of considering them as general principles of our thought, which they are not.

VIII

Even a short account of the basic methods of Husserl's phenomenology would be incomplete without a mention of the important distinction between the empirical and the eidetical approach. According to Husserl, phenomenology aims to be an eidetical science, dealing not with existence but with essence (*Wesen*). Phenomenological methods can of course be applied with the greatest success within the empirical sphere as well. But only by recourse to the eidetical sphere can the aprioristic character of phenomenology as a *prima philosophia* and even as a phenomenological psychology be assured. I wish strongly to emphasize that the distinction between the empirical and the eidetical approaches has nothing to do with the distinction between the mundane and the reduced sphere, dealt with so far. Within the mundane sphere, too, eidetical science (*Wesenswissenschaft*) is possible.

The unfortunate terms *Wesen* and *Wesensschau* which Husserl chose for characterizing the eidetical approach have created many misunderstandings and have almost prevented readers of good will from studying Husserl's *Ideen*, which starts with an exposition of this method. The term *Wesen* has a metaphysical connotation in philosophical literature; the Greek term "eidetic" induces the reader to identify the "essence" with the Platonic idea; and the term *Wesensschau* suggests a kind of irrational intuition, like certain techniques of revelation accessible only to the mystic in ecstasy, which is used by the phenomenological esoteric in order to gaze at the eternal truths.

Actually, the eidetic approach, like the phenomenological reduction, is no more than another methodological device of investigation. The principle of this method is as follows. Let us assume that on the desk before me, illuminated by the lamp, stands a red wooden cube, of one-inch dimensions. In the natural attitude I perceive this thing as unquestionably real, having the qualities and characteristics I have mentioned. In the phenomenologically reduced sphere the phenomenon cube – the cube as it appears to me – keeps the same qualities as an intentional object of my perceiving act. But suppose I am interested in finding what are the qualities common to all cubes. I do not want to do so by the method of induction, which not only presupposes the existence of similar objects but also implies certain unwarranted logical assumptions. I have before me only this single concrete object perceived. I am free, however, to transform this perceived object in my fancy, by successively varying its features – its color, its size, the material of which it is made, its perspective, its illumination, its surroundings and background and so on. Thus I may imagine an infinite number of varied cubes. But these variations do not touch on a set of characteristics common to all imaginable cubes, such as rectangularity, limitation to six squares, corporeality. This set of characteristics, unchanged among all the imagined transformations of the concrete thing perceived – the kernel, so to speak, of all possibly imaginable cubes – I shall call the essential characteristics of the cube or, using a Greek term, the *eidos* of the cube. No cube can be thought of that would not have these essential features. All the other qualities and characteristics of the concrete object under scrutiny are non-essential. (Needless to say, I could use my red wooden cube as point of departure for other imagined variations in order to find the eidos of color, of corporeal thing, of object of perception, and so on.)

Thus eidetic investigations do not deal with concrete real things but with possibly imaginable things. It is in this sense that we must understand Husserl's frequently criticized dictum that phenomenology has to do not only with objects perceived but also with objects imagined, and that the latter are of even greater importance for the phenomenological approach.

Again we see that the eidetic approach is merely a methodological device for the solution of a special task. The phenomenologist, we may say, does not have to do with the objects themselves; he is interested in their *meaning*, as it is constituted by the activities of our mind.

The importance of this original method should not be underestimated. It leads to an entirely new theory of induction and association, and also it opens the way to a scientific ontology. Only by the eidetical method may we find, for instance, the real reason for so-called spheres of incompatibility; only by using it may we discover and describe the important relationship of foundation which subsists between certain ontological realms.

IX

The manifold applications of the few methodological principles chosen as examples cannot be discussed here. Nor will it be attempted to report Husserl's progress in exploring this new territory of scientific investigation, or the performance of the many scholars who consider themselves his students, although many of them have entirely misunderstood what he meant. The only aim of the present account has been to make it clear that phenomenology is a serious and difficult endeavor. Its job has only started, and the task ahead is enormous. But one thing, it is hoped, has been demonstrated: the results of phenomenological research cannot and must not clash with the tested results of the mundane sciences, or even with the proved doctrines of so-called philosophies of the sciences. As emphasized above, phenomenology has its field of research in its own right, and hopes to end where the others begin.

And now I am afraid I have to disappoint the reader. A trained phenomenologist would not regard the foregoing as an account of phenomenological *philosophy*. He would perhaps admit that one or two questions of what Husserl called phenomenological *psychology* have been touched on. Phenomenological philosophy deals with the activities of the transcendental ego, with the constitution of space and time, with the constitution of intersubjectivity, with the problems of life and death, with the problems of monads; indeed, it is an approach to the questions hitherto called metaphysical. Husserl's published writings deal only very fragmentarily with the foundations of phenomenological philosophy, although he spent the last twenty years of his life outlining these problems.[6] I believe, however, that under the present circumstances American scholars may be much more interested in the methods and results of phenomenological psychology which, correctly understood, converge with many features of James' psychology, with certain of G. H. Mead's basic concepts,* and finally, with Gestalt theory, which has gained many followers among American psychologists.

X

A few final remarks may briefly suggest where the importance of phenomenology lies for the social sciences. It must be clearly stated that the relation of phenomenology to the social sciences cannot be demonstrated by analyzing concrete problems of sociology or economics, such as social adjustment or theory of international trade, with phenomenological methods. It is my conviction, however, that future studies of the methods of the social sciences and their fundamental notions will of necessity lead to issues belonging to the domain of phenomenological research.[7]

To give just one example, all social sciences take the intersubjectivity of thought and action for granted. That fellow-men exist, that men act upon men, that communication by symbols and signs is possible, that social groups and institutions, legal and economic systems and the like are integral elements of our life-world, that this life-world has its own history and its special relationship to time and space – all these are notions that are explicitly or implicitly fundamental for the work of all social scientists. The latter have developed certain methodological devices – schemes of reference, typologies, statistical methods – in order to deal with the phenomena suggested by these terms. But the phenomena themselves are merely taken for granted. Man is

---

[6] See his article "Phenomenology," in *Encyclopaedia Britannica*, 14th ed.

[7] See "Phenomenology and the Social Sciences."

* See Maurice Natanson, *The Social Dynamics of George H. Mead*, Washington, D.C., 1956. (M.N.)

simply conceived as a social being, language and other systems of communication exist, the conscious life of the Other is accessible to me – in short, I can understand the Other and his acts and he can understand me and my doings. And the same holds good for the social and cultural objects created by men. They are taken for granted, and they have their specific meaning and way of existence.

But how does it happen that mutual understanding and communication are possible at all? How is it possible that man accomplishes meaningful acts, purposively or habitually, that he is guided by ends to be attained and motivated by certain experiences? Do not the concepts of meaning, of motives, of ends, of acts, refer to a certain structure of consciousness, a certain arrangement of all the experiences in inner time, a certain type of sedimentation? And does not interpretation of the Other's meaning and of the meaning of his acts and the results of these acts presuppose a self-interpretation of the observer or partner? How can I, in my attitude as a man among other men or as a social scientist, find an approach to all this if not by recourse to a stock of pre-interpreted experiences built up by sedimentation within my own conscious life? And how can methods for interpreting the social interrelationship be warranted if they are not based upon a careful description of the underlying assumptions and their implications?

These questions cannot be answered by the methods of the social sciences. They require a philosophical analysis. And phenomenology – not only what Husserl called phenomenological philosophy but even phenomenological psychology – has not only opened an avenue of approach for such an analysis but has in addition started the analysis itself.

PHENOMENOLOGY AND THE SOCIAL SCIENCES

The significance of Husserl's Phenomenology for the foundation of the social sciences will presumably become fully known only when the Husserl manuscripts which are relevant to this problem have been published. To be sure, the published works already contain the most important themes of thought pertaining to this subject. Husserl was constantly concerned with them from the time of writing the sixth *Logical Investigation*. But these important implicit themes remain scarcely noticed, not only because the extensive discoveries of phenomenology in the realm of pure logic and the general theory of knowledge have taken first place in the public discussions, but also because only in the later writings of the master has the problem of the social sciences been attacked systematically.

Even in these later writings Husserl proceeded with great hesitation. As is known, he had completed a second volume of the *Ideen* in 1913, as far as proof-reading. In this volume the problems of personality, intersubjectivity, and culture were to have been treated. Just before publication, misgivings concerning the result of his work befell this scholar, who was always a model of conscientiousness. He recognized that the attack on these problems presupposed carrying out still further analyses, especially the clarification of the constitutive activities of consciousness.

It was first in the *Formal and Transcendental Logic* (1929)

AUTHOR'S NOTE. – I wish to express my gratitude to Professor Richard H. Williams of the University of Buffalo for the great interest and the untiring efforts which he has devoted to the translation of my essay. The task of reproducing faithfully Husserl's language, which in the original German offers serious difficulties even to German readers, is, I believe, really creative work. To Professor Marvin Farber I am deeply indebted for his kind interest and his careful supervision of the text. To Professor Fritz Machlup I owe valuable suggestions concerning the English rendition.

that an avenue of approach was opened to this new thematic field, but again it proceeded from the point of view of purely logical problems. In this work can also be found [1] the starting-points toward considerations which were carried further in the postscript to the English translation of the *Ideen* and in the fifth *Cartesian Meditation* (both in 1931), and which would have found their complete presentation in an extensive series of essays planned under the title "The Crisis of European Sciences and Transcendental Phenomenology." [*] In the last conversations which the writer had the good fortune of having with Husserl, he repeatedly designated this series of essays as the summary and the crowning achievement of his life work. He was working continuously on them during the last three years of his life, but only the first essay appeared, in the journal *Philosophia* (Belgrade, 1936).[**] Then death took the pen from Husserl's hand and only the penetrating fragment which appeared in the *Revue internationale de Philosophie* [2] on "The Question about the Origin of Geometry" gives an indication of the extent of the work which had been begun in this period.

In the following paragraphs of this essay an attempt will be made to trace in concise form the initial phases of a phenomenological foundation of the social sciences which are contained in the writings referred to above. Following this, in the second part of the essay, the question concerning the independence of the social sciences will be raised and, going beyond Husserl, an inquiry will be made concerning the contribution which phenomenology can make to their concrete methodological problems. It goes without saying that all this must be limited to inadequate intimations.

---

[1] See especially *Formale und transzendentale Logik*, Secs. 94ff.
[2] Brussels, 1939, 1, 2.
[*] Published in 1954 as *Die Krisis der europäischen Wissenschaften und die transzendentale Phänomenologie*, (edited by Walter Biemel, Haag.) (M.N.)
[**] Under the title "Die Krisis der europäischen Wissenschaften und die transzendentale Phänomenologie" and hereafter referred to as "Krisis." (M.N.)

I

All sciences, be they related to objects of nature or to so-called cultural phenomena, are, for Husserl, a totality of human activities, namely, those of scientists working together. The fact of science itself belongs to that realm of objects which must be clarified by the methods of the cultural sciences, which in German are referred to as *Geisteswissenschaften*. Furthermore, the basis of meaning (*Sinnfundament*) in every science is the pre-scientific life-world (*Lebenswelt*) which is the one and unitary life-world of myself, of you, and of us all. The insight into this foundational nexus can become lost in the course of the development of a science through the centuries. It must, however, be capable in principle of being brought back into clarity, through making evident the transformation of meaning which this life-world itself has undergone during the constant process of idealization and formalization which comprises the essence of scientific achievement. If this clarification fails to occur, or if it occurs to an insufficient degree, and if the idealities created by science are directly and naïvely substituted for the life-world, then in a later stage in the development of science those problems of foundation and those paradoxes appear from which all positive sciences are suffering today; they ought to be remedied by an *ex post facto* critique of knowledge which comes too late.

Phenomenological philosophy claims to be a philosophy of man in his life-world and to be able to explain the meaning of this life-world in a rigorously scientific manner. Its theme is concerned with the demonstration and explanation of the activities of consciousness (*Bewusstseinsleistungen*) of the transcendental subjectivity within which this life-world is constituted. Since transcendental phenomenology accepts nothing as self-evident, but undertakes to bring everything to self-evidence, it escapes all naïve positivism and may expect to be the true science of mind (*Geist*) in true rationality, in the proper meaning of this term.

However, a whole series of difficult problems is already revealed by this point of departure. We shall select a few of the groups of problems treated by Husserl which are especially relevant to our topic.

1) First of all, how can a transcendental philosophy, such as constitutive phenomenology, risk the assertion that the life-world as viewed within the natural attitude remains its basis of meaning while at the same time the troublesome effort of phenomenological reduction is needed in order to bracket this natural world? This reduction thus creates the prerequisite of the investigation of the contributive intentionalities in which the world is constituted for transcendental subjectivity.

2) If the life-world as viewed within the natural attitude remains the basis of meaning of transcendental phenomenology, then not only I but also you and everyone belong to this life-world. My transcendental subjectivity, in the activities of which this world is constituted, must thus from the beginning be related to other subjectivities, in relation to the activities of which it authorizes and rectifies its own. And to this life-world, which is characterized as the single and unitary life-world of us all, belong indeed all the phenomena of social life from the simple Thou-relation to the most diverse types of social communities (including all the sciences as a sum total of the accomplishments of those who are engaged in science). In short, all that constitutes our own social world in its historical actuality, and all other social worlds concerning which history gives us knowledge, belongs to it. But must not the attempt to constitute the world from the activities of transcendental subjectivity necessarily lead to solipsism? Can it explain the problem of the *alter ego* and thereby of all social phenomena which are founded on the interaction of man with his fellows in the real life-world?

3) Can the assertion be justified that positive sciences have naïvely substituted idealities for the life-world, and thus have lost the connection with their basis of meaning, in view of the unquestionable success of the natural sciences and especially of mathematical physics in the control of this life-world? And is a special cultural science (*Geisteswissenschaft*) at all thinkable which would not necessarily refer to natural science, since the entire world of mind (*Geist*) seems to be based on things of the natural world and the psychical appears only in psychophysical connections? Must not, rather, a single style be demanded for all sciences which claim to be exact, and is not this style of the unified science precisely that of the mathematical sciences,

whose remarkable successes, even in their practical application, we must always gratefully admire?

4) If in fact the phenomenological method is able to prove its legitimate claim to the establishment of the cultural sciences, and if in this way it succeeds in bringing to light a style of thought peculiar to these sciences by an analysis of the constitutive activities of the transcendental subjectivity, would such a proof yield any contribution at all to the solution of the methodological problems of the concrete sciences of cultural phenomena (law, the economic and social world, art, history, etc.), since all these sciences are related to that mundane sphere which transcendental phenomenology has bracketed? Can any help at all be expected from phenomenology for the solution of all these questions? Is it not rather an affair of a psychology oriented to everyday life to solve this problem?

In the following paragraphs we shall attempt to draw together the answers to these questions which Husserl has given in diverse places in the writings cited above.

Ad 1. It should be pointed out at once that there is widespread misunderstanding to the effect that transcendental phenomenology denies the actual existence of the real life-world, or that it explains it as mere illusion by which natural or positive scientific thought lets itself be deceived. Rather, for transcendental phenomenology also there is no doubt that the world exists and that it manifests itself in the continuity of harmonious experience as a universe. But this indubitability must be made intelligible and the manner of being of the real world must be explained. Such a radical explanation, however, is only possible by proving the relativity of this real life-world, and of any imaginable life-world, to the transcendental subjectivity which alone has the ontic sense of absolute being.[3]

In order to uncover this sphere of the transcendental subjectivity at all, the philosopher, beginning his meditation within the natural attitude, must undertake that change in attitude which Husserl calls phenomenological epoché or transcendental phenomenological reduction. That is to say, he must deprive the world which formerly, within the natural attitude,

---

[3] Husserl, "Nachwort zu meinen *Ideen*," *Jahrbuch für Philosophie und phänomenologische Forschung*, Vol. XI, 1930, p. 562ff.

was simply posited as being, of just this posited being, and he must return to the living stream of his experiences of the world. In this stream, however, the experienced world is kept exactly with the contents which actually belong to it. With the execution of the epoché, the world in no way vanishes from the field of experience of the philosophically reflecting ego. On the contrary, what is grasped in the epoché is the pure life of consciousness in which and through which the whole objective world exists for me, by virtue of the fact that I experience it, perceive it, remember it, etc. In the epoché, however, I abstain from belief in the being of this world, and I direct my view exclusively to my consciousness of the world.

In this universe of the experiencing life of the transcendental subjectivity I find my entire cogitations of the life-world which surrounds me, a life-world to which also belong my life with others and its pertinent community-forming processes, which actively and passively shape this life-world into a social world. In principle all of these experiences found in my conscious life, if they are not themselves originarily giving and primally founding experiences of this life-world, can be examined concerning the history of their sedimentation. In this way, I can return fundamentally to the originary experience of the life-world in which the facts themselves can be grasped directly.

To interpret all this by showing the intentional accomplishments of the transcendental subjectivity makes up the enormous area of work of constitutive phenomenology. It is thus a true science of mind (Geist), and claims to be a method, in fact the only method, which seriously means to be a radical explanation of the world through mind.

Ad 2. But this life-world, which has constantly been referred to above, and which may only be constituted by the activities of my transcendental subjectivity, is certainly not my private world. To be sure, Others, fellow-men, also belong to it, indeed not only as other bodies or as objects of my experience of this world but as *alter egos*, that is to say, as subjectivities which are endowed with the same activities of consciousness as am I. The world which is experienced after the completion of the reduction to my pure life of consciousness is an intersubjective world, and that means that it is accessible to everyone. All cultural objects (books, tools, works of all sorts, etc.) point back, by their origin and meaning, to other subjects and to their active constitutive intentionalities, and thus it is true that they are experienced in the sense of "existing there for everybody." (Of course, this is only true "for everybody" who belongs to the corresponding community of culture – but that is a problem of a quite different character, which will be discussed later.)

Thus, for phenomenology the problem of the experience of Others need not be a dark corner which, to use a beautiful expression of Husserl,[4] is feared only by children in philosophy because the specter of solipsism or psychologism and relativism haunts it. The true philosopher, however, must light up this dark corner rather than run away from it.

In the fifth *Cartesian Meditation* Husserl offered the following solution of the problem, which we shall attempt to render in its main outline, as far as possible in his own words.[5]

After the execution of the epoché I can first eliminate from the thematic field within the transcendental universal sphere all the constitutive activities which are immediately or mediately related to the subjectivity of Others. In this way I reduce the universe of my conscious life to my own transcendental sphere (*transzendentale Eigensphäre*), to my concrete being as a monad. What is left by the abstractive elimination of the sense of other subjectivity is a uniformly connected stratum of the phenomenon "world" – Husserl calls it the primordial sphere – which is no longer a world objectively existing for everybody, but is my world belonging peculiarly to me alone. And thus, in the truest sense, it is my private world.

Within this reduced world-phenomenon, one object is distinguished from all others. I call it my body, and it is distinguished by the fact that I can control it in action and that I attribute sensorial fields to it in conformity with my experience. If I

---

[4] *Formale und transzendentale Logik*, p. 210.

[5] For this purpose we have not used the French translation but the original unpublished German manuscript *. A critique of the Husserlian establishment of the transcendental subjectivity, against which, in my opinion, certain important objections can be raised, must wait for another publication **.

* The German edition was published in 1950 as *Cartesianische Meditationen und Pariser Vorträge*, (edited by S. Strasser, Haag.) (M.N.)

** See Alfred Schutz, "Das Problem der transzendentalen Intersubjektivität bei Husserl," *Philosophische Rundschau*, Bd. 5, Heft 2, 1957, pp. 81–107. (M.N.)

reduce other human beings in a similar way, I get peculiar corporealities; if I reduce myself as a human being, I get "my body" and "my mind" or me as a psychophysical unity, and in it my personal I which functions in my body, or which acts on and endures the exterior world by means of it. Now, in this reduced exterior world the "Other" also appears as a corporeality, but as a corporeality which I apprehend as a body, and indeed as a body of *another* by a process of appresentative pairing.[6]

The other corporeality, once experienced, continues indeed to manifest itself as a body through its changing but always concordant gestures, which appresentatively indicate a psychical side. This psychical side, at first only indicated by appresentation, has to be fulfilled by original experience. In this way an Other is appresentatively constituted in my monad as an ego that is not "I myself" but a second ego which mirrors itself in my monad. This second ego, however, is not simply there and given in and of itself, but is an *alter ego;* it is an Other which, in accordance with his constitutive sense, refers back to me, the ego of this *alter ego*. This "Other" is nevertheless not simply a duplicate of myself. The alien corporeality that is apperceived as an "Other" appears in my monadic sphere above all in the mode of the "there" (*illic*), while my own body is in the mode of the absolute "here" (*hic*). That which becomes appresented in this way does not derive from my own sphere of peculiarity; it is a coexistent ego in the mode of the *illic* and therefore an *alter ego*.

The first communality which exists between me, the primordial psychophysical I, and the appresentatively experienced Other, and which forms the foundation of all other intersubjective communities of a higher order, is the community of Nature, which belongs not only to my primordial sphere but also to that of the Other. There is, however, the difference that the Other's

---

[6] By *appresentation* Husserl understands a process of analogy, but this process is in no sense a conclusion by analogy. By it an actual experience refers back to another experience which is not given in actuality and will not be actualized. In other words the appresented does not attain an actual presence. For instance, by looking at the obverse of an object the reverse is appresented. *Pairing* ("accouplement" in the French translation) is a principal form of passive synthesis, which means of association. Its characteristic is that two data, distinguishable each from the other, are presented in the unity of consciousness; they constitute as a pair a phenomenological unity of similarity established by pure passivity, although they appear distinct and regardless of whether or not they are noticed. Cf. *Méditations Cartésiennes*, Sec. 50 and 51, [and "Symbol, Reality and Society," p. 294f.] (M.N.)

world of Nature is seen as *illic* from my point of view, which is to say that the Other gets that aspect from it, which I should get if I myself were not *hic* but *illic*. In this way, every natural thing which is experienced or which can be experienced in my primordial sphere obtains a new appresentative stratum, namely, as the same natural thing in the possible manners of its givenness for the Other.

Starting from myself as the original constitutive monad, I thus get other monads, that is, Others as psychophysical subjects. These Others are not merely related by means of associative pairing to my psychophysical being in their capacity as being bodily opposite me; rather it is a question of an objective equalization, a mutual interrelatedness of my existence and that of all Others. For, as the body of the Other is appresented by me as an Other, so my body is experienced by the Other as his Other, and so forth. The same thing obtains for all subjects, that is, for this open community of monads which Husserl has designated as transcendental intersubjectivity.

It should be stressed that this transcendental intersubjectivity exists purely in me, the meditating ego. It is constituted purely from the sources of my intentionality, but in such a manner that it is the *same* transcendental intersubjectivity in every single human being (only in other subjective manners of appearance) in his intentional experiences. In this constitution of the transcendental intersubjectivity that of the single and uniformly objective world is also executed, and along with it the constitution of those peculiarly mental objectivities, especially those types of social communities, which have the character of personalities of a higher order.

Of special importance for our topic is the constitution of the specifically human, and that means cultural, worlds in their peculiar manner of objectivity.[7] According to Husserl, accessibility for everyone belongs in essence to the constitutive sense of Nature, of corporeality and of the psychophysical human being. *But the world of culture is of a limited kind of objectivity*, and with this it should be borne in mind that the life-world is given to me, and to everyone who retains the natural attitude primarily as his cultural world, namely, as a world of signification

---

[7] In this connection see especially *Méditations Cartésiennes*, Sec. 58.

which the human being in question historically takes a part in forming. The constitution of the world of culture, similar to the constitution of any "world," including the world of one's own stream of experience, has the lawful structure of a constitution, oriented with respect to a "null point" (*Nullglied*), i.e., to a personality. Here am I and my culture; it is accessible to me and to my cultural companions as a kind of experience of Others. Other cultural humanity and other culture can become accessible only by a complicated process of understanding, namely, on the basic level of the common Nature, which, in its specific spatio-temporal structure, constitutes the horizon of being for the accessibility to all the manifold cultural phenomena. As Nature is thus concretely and uniformly constituted, so human existence itself is referred to an existent life-world as a realm of practical activity, which, from the first, is endowed with human significations. All this is in principle accessible to the explication of a phenomenological constitutive analysis which, proceeding from the apodictic ego, must finally reveal the transcendental meaning of the world in its full concretion, which is the continuous life-world of us all.

Ad 3. It was stated above that the natural sciences generally, and especially the natural sciences which use mathematics, have lost their relation to their basis of meaning, namely the life-world. How can this reproach be justified, when it has just been shown that it is precisely this universal Nature which constitutes itself concretely and uniformly in intersubjectivity, and which must almost be considered as the form of access to the worlds of other culture, in their manner of oriented constitution? We may reply first of all that Nature as the object of the natural sciences does not mean precisely the same thing as Nature as a constitutive element of the life-world. That which the naïvely living human being takes for natural reality is not the objective world of our modern natural sciences; his conception of the world, as valid for him in its subjectivity, obtains with all its gods, demons, etc. *Nature in this sense, as an element of the life-world, is thus a concept which has its place exclusively in the mental* (geistig) *sphere.* It constitutes itself in our everyday meaningful experience as this experience develops in our historically determined being.

Let us take geometry as an example. When we, in our perceptual life-world, direct our view by abstraction to merely spatial and temporal figures we experience, it is true, "solids." However, they are not the ideal solids of geometry, but they are solids as we actually realize them, with the same content which is the true content of our experience.[8] To the world which is pre-given to our everyday experience belongs the spatio-temporal form, in which are included the corporeal figures ordered within it, and in which we ourselves live in conformity with our personal, bodily manner of being. But here we find nothing of geometrical idealities, of geometrical space or of mathematical time with all their forms.[9] Concretely empirical figures are given to us, in our life-world, merely as forms of a material, of a "sensory fullness"; thus they are given with that which is represented by the so-called specific sense-qualities (color, odor, etc.). But pure geometry deals with solids in the corporeal world only in pure abstraction; that is to say, only with abstract figures in the spatio-temporal framework, which are, as Husserl recognizes, purely ideal "meaning figures," meaning-creations of the human mind. This is not to say that geometrical existence is psychological or personal existence in the personal sphere of consciousness. On the contrary, geometrical existence is of the same kind as the existence of meaning-structures, and it is objective for everyone who is a geometer or understands geometry.

Geometrical figures, axioms, and propositions, just as most structures of the world of culture, have an *ideal objectivity;* they can always be *reactivated* as identically the same. That is to say, the meaning-producing activity which has led to their sedimentation can be re-executed. But reactivation in this sense is also explication of the meaning which lies implicated in the abbreviations of this sedimentation, by referring it back to the primal evidence. The possibility always remains open for examining the primal evidence of a tradition, for example, of geometrical or of any other deductive science, which works on through the centuries. If this does not occur, then the original activities which are found within the fundamental concepts of this deductive science and their foundation in pre-scientific materials remain undisclosed. The tradition in which these

[8] Husserl, "Krisis," pp. 98ff.
[9] *Ibid.*, pp. 125ff.

sciences are handed down to us is then emptied of meaning, and the basis of meaning to which these sciences refer, namely the life-world, is forgotten.[10] But according to Husserl, this is the situation in modern times not only with respect to geometry and mathematics, including all natural sciences using mathematics, but also with respect to traditional logic.[11]

The fundamental idea of modern physics is that nature is a *mathematical* universe. Its ideal is exactitude, which means an ability to recognize and determine the things of nature in absolute identity, as the substratum of an absolutely identical, methodically unequivocable and discernible character. In order to achieve this ideal, physics makes use of measurement and of the mathematical methods of calculation and formulae. In this way it seeks to create an entirely new kind of prediction for the corporeal world, and to be able to calculate the occurrences in this world in terms of a compelling necessity. But on the one hand, the sensory fullness of solids in the life-world and the changes of this fullness are not capable of being mathematized, and on the other hand, pre-scientific intuitable nature does not lack this predictability. In the world perceptible by our senses, changes in the spatio-temporal positions of solids, changes in their form and fullness, are not accidental and indifferent, but they are dependent on each other in sensuously *typical* ways. The basic style of our visible immediate world is empirical. This universal, and indeed causal, style makes possible hypotheses, inductions, and predictions, but in pre-scientific life they all have the character of the approximate and typical.[12] Only when the ideal objectivities become substituted for the empirical things of the corporeal world, only when one abstracts or co-idealizes the intuitable fullness, which is not capable of mathematization, does the *fundamental hypothesis* of the entire realm of mathematical natural science result, namely, that a universal inductivity might prevail in the intuitable world, an inductivity which suggests itself in everyday experience but which remains concealed in its infinity. Consequently, this

[10] Husserl, "Die Frage nach dem Ursprung der Geometrie," pp. 203-226, and especially pp. 209-217.
[11] In relation to this last point, about logic, cf. *Formale und transzendentale Logik*, Sec. 73-81, Sec. 94ff.
[12] Cf. "Krisis," pp. 101-105.

universal causality of the mathematical sciences is also an idealization. Now it is doubtless true, says Husserl, that in the remarkable structure of the natural sciences this hypothesis holds good in infinity, and precisely in its prediction of events in the life-world. But in spite of all verification it still remains a hypothesis and thus an unclarified supposition of mathematical natural science.

The natural scientist, in unquestioned tradition, accepts the inherited idealizations and unclarified suppositions as technics (τεχνή) without becoming conscious of the shift which the originally living meaning of the aim to get knowledge of the world itself has experienced.[13] In the process of mathematization of the natural sciences, says Husserl, we measure the life-world for a well-fitting garment of ideas. In just this way we get possibilities for a prediction which goes far beyond the accomplishments of everyday anticipation, concerning the occurrences in the intuitable life-world. But everything which represents the life-world to the natural scientists as "objectively actual and true nature" is clothed by this garment of symbols and disguised. The cloak of ideas has the effect that we take a method to be true being, in order infinitely to improve upon the *raw* predictions which are the only ones possible within the actual experiences of the life-world. But the proper meaning of methods, formulae, and theories remains unintelligible as long as one does not reflect about the historical meaning belonging to their primordial establishment.

With the enormous success of the mathematical natural sciences has come the fact that modern philosophy and critique of knowledge generally perceive the prototype of scientific thought in their methods. The consequence is a dualistic cleavage into a real and self-contained corporeal world, and a mental world, which latter, however, remains dependent upon the natural world and is not brought to any independent status in its own right. The further consequence is that even this mental world ought to be explained *more geometrico* according to the unclarified rationalism of the mathematical natural sciences, or, as Husserl terms it, by means of physicalistic rationalism. Above all, psychology ought to be treated objectivistically, where

[13] "Krisis," pp. 113–116 and pp. 132ff.

objectivistic should mean that in the realm of the world which is self-evidently given through experience one will search for the "objective truths" without inquiring about the subjective activities of the mind, out of which alone the ontic sense of the pre-given life-world is constituted. For the life-world is a subjective formation resulting from the activities of the experiencing pre-scientific life. Inasmuch as the intuitable life-world, which is purely subjective, has been forgotten in the thematic interest of natural science, and also of objectivistic psychology, the working subject, namely the human being himself who is pursuing his science, has in no way become thematic. It is only in purely cultural scientific knowledge that the scientist does not become confounded by the objection of the self-disguise of his activity. It is consequently erroneous if the social sciences contend with the natural sciences for an equal warrant. As soon as they grant to the natural sciences their objectivity as their own independent attribute, the social sciences themselves fall into objectivism, for only mind (*Geist*) has being in itself and is independent. To regard nature as something in itself alien to mind and then to found the cultural sciences on the natural sciences, and thus supposedly to make them exact, is an absurdity. The cultural scientists, blinded by naturalism, have completely neglected even to raise the problem of a universal and true cultural science.

Ad 4. But is it an affair of the cultural sciences at all, in the sense of that term as used today, to make inquiries concerning the problem of a universal science of the mind in Husserl's sense? Is this task not specifically a philosophical, or more properly a phenomenological problem that becomes visible only in the transcendental sphere, and thus only after that mundane world, which alone is the topic and ought to be the topic of all efforts of the concrete sciences of culture, has been bracketed? The ideal of history, to recount the past "as it then actually was" (von Ranke) is also, with certain modifications, the ideal of all other sciences of culture, i.e., to determine what society, the state, language, art, economy, law, etc., actually are in our mundane life-world and its historicity, and to determine how the meaning of each can be made intelligible in the sphere of our mundane experience. And should not an appeal be made to psychology in this sphere for a solution of the problem of a universal cultural science?

For Husserl there is also no doubt that all the hitherto existing cultural and social sciences are related in principle to phenomena of mundane intersubjectivity. Hence, the transcendental constitutive phenomena, which only become visible in the phenomenologically reduced sphere, scarcely come within the view of the cultural sciences. However, a psychology from which a solution of the problems of the cultural sciences might be expected must become aware of the fact that it is not a science which deals with empirical facts. It has to be a science of essences, investigating the correlates of those transcendental constitutional phenomena which are related to the natural attitude. Consequently, it has to examine the invariant, peculiar, and essential structures of the mind; but that is to say it examines their *a priori* structure.[14] The concrete description of the spheres of consciousness as it has to be undertaken by a true descriptive psychology within the natural attitude remains, however, the description of a closed sphere of the intentionalities. That is to say, it requires not only a concrete description of the experiences of consciousness, as in the Lockean tradition, but also necessarily the description of the conscious (intentional) "objects in their objective sense"[15] found in active inner experiences. But such a true *psychology of intentionality* is, according to Husserl's words, nothing other than a *constitutive phenomenology of the natural attitude*.[16]

In this eidetic mundane science (thus in the psychological apperception of the natural attitude), which stands at the beginning of all methodological and theoretical scientific problems of all the cultural and social sciences, all analyses carried through in phenomenological reduction essentially retain their validation. It is precisely here that the tremendous significance of the results achieved by Husserl for all the cultural sciences lies.

---

[14] "Nachwort zu meinen *Ideen*," p. 553; cf. p. 14 of Boyce Gibson's translation of *Ideas*.
[15] *Ibid.*, p. 565.
[16] *Ibid.*, p. 567.

II

In the above résumé of some of the most important lines of thought of the later philosophy of Husserl, the concept of the life-world is revealed in its entire and central significance as the basis of meaning of all sciences, including natural sciences and including also philosophy in so far as it wishes to appear as an exact science. Thus, every reflection finds its evidence only in the process of recurring to its originally founding experience within this life-world, and it remains the endless task of thought to make intelligible the intentional constitution of the contributive subjectivity in reference to this its basis of meaning. We, however, who live naïvely in this life-world, encounter it as already constituted. We are, so to speak, born into it. We live in and endure it, and the living intentionality of our stream of consciousness supports our thinking, by which we orient ourselves practically in this life-world, and our action, by which we intervene in it.

Our everyday world is, from the outset, an intersubjective world of culture. It is intersubjective because we live in it as men among other men, bound to them through common influence and work, understanding others and being an object of understanding for others. It is a world of culture because, from the outset, the life-world is a universe of significations to us, i.e., a framework of meaning (*Sinnzusammenhang*) which we have to interpret, and of interrelations of meaning which we institute only through our action in this life-world. It is a world of culture also because we are always conscious of its *historicity*, which we encounter in tradition and habituality, and which is capable of being examined because the "already-given" refers back to one's own activity or to the activity of Others, of which it is the sediment. I, the human being born into this world and naïvely living in it, am the center of this world in the historical situation of my actual "Now and Here"; I am the "null point toward which its constitution is oriented." [17] That is to say, this world has significance and meaning first of all by me and for me.

In what follows we intend to try to clarify this topic by drawing from Husserl's course of ideas some fundamental

[17] Cf. above, pp. 126–127.

consequences not found in his own writings, for the knowledge of the structure of the social sciences.

This world, built around my own I, presents itself for interpretation to me, a being living naïvely within it. From this standpoint everything has reference to my actual historical situation, or as we can also say, to my pragmatic interests which belong to the situation in which I find myself here and now. The place in which I am living has not significance for me as a geographical concept, but as my home. The objects of my daily use have significance as my implements, and the men to whom I stand in relationships are my kin, my friends, or strangers. Language is not a substratum of philosophical or grammatical considerations for me, but a means for expressing my intentions or understanding the intentions of Others. Only in reference to me does that relation to Others obtain its specific meaning which I designate with the word "We." In reference to Us whose center I am, Others stand out as "You," and in reference to You, who refer back to me, third parties stand out as "They." My social world with the *alter egos* in it is arranged, around me as the center, into associates (*Umwelt*), contemporaries (*Mitwelt*), predecessors (*Vorwelt*), and successors (*Folgewelt*),[18] whereby I and my different attitudes to Others institute these manifold relationships. All this is done in various degrees of *intimacy* and *anonymity*.

Furthermore, the life-world is arranged into fields (*Zentren*) of different relevance according to my current state of interest, each one of which has its own peculiar center of density and fullness, and its open but interpretable horizons. In this connection, the categories of *familiarity* and *strangeness* and the very important category of *accessibility* enter into consideration. This last category refers to the grouping of my environments according to (1) that which actually lies within the extent of my reach,

[18] The translation of these terms follows the usage in an article by Alfred Stonier and Karl Bode concerning Dr. Schutz's work, "A New Approach to the Methodology of the Social Sciences," *Economica*, Vol. IV, 1937, pp. 406–424. These terms are developed at length in Dr. Schutz's *Der sinnhafte Aufbau der sozialen Welt*, Vienna, 1932, 2nd ed. 1960. The *Umwelt* is the immediate world within which direct and relatively intimate experience of Others is possible. The *Mitwelt* is a world of mediate, but contemporary, experience within which indirect and relatively anonymous experience of Others can be obtained. The *Vorwelt* refers to experiences of the historical past. The *Folgewelt* refers to the future, of which no experience is possible, but toward which an orientation may exist. – TRANSLATOR'S NOTE.

seeing and hearing, or has once lain there and might at will be brought back into actual accessibility; (2) that which is or was accessible to others and might thus potentially be accessible to me if I were not here (*hic*) but there (*illic*);[19] (3) the open horizons of that which in free variation can be thought of as attainable.

To this it should be added that I assume everything which has meaning for me also has meaning for the Other or Others with whom I share this, my life-world, as an associate, contemporary, predecessor, or successor. This life-world presents itself also to them for interpretation. I know about their perspectives of relevance and their horizons of familiarity or strangeness; indeed I also know that with segments of my meaningful life I belong to the life-world of Others as Others belong to my life-world. All this is a manifold orientation for me, the naïve human being. I posit meaningful acts in the expectation that Others will interpret them meaningfully, and my schema of positing is oriented with respect to the Others' schema of interpretation. On the other hand, I can examine everything which, as a product of Others, presents itself to me for meaningful interpretation as to the meaning which the Other who has produced it may have connected with it. Thus, on these reciprocal acts of positing meaning and of interpretation of meaning, my social world of mundane intersubjectivity is built; it is also the social world of Others, and all other social and cultural phenomena are founded upon it.

All this is self-evident to me in my naïve life just as it is self-evident to me that the world actually exists and that it is actually *thus*, as I experience it (apart from deceptions which subsequently in the course of experience prove to be mere appearances). No motive exists for the naïve person to raise the transcendental question concerning the actuality of the world or concerning the reality of the *alter ego*, or to make the jump into the reduced sphere. Rather, he posits this world in a *general thesis* as meaningfully valid for him, with all that he finds in it, with all natural things, with all living beings (especially with human beings), and with meaningful products of all sorts (tools, symbols, language systems, works of art, etc.). Hence, the naïvely living person (we are speaking of healthy, grown-up,

[19] Cf. above, pp. 125–126.

and wide-awake human beings) automatically has in hand, so to speak, the meaningful complexes which are valid for him. From things inherited and learned, from the manifold sedimentations of tradition, habituality, and his own previous constitutions of meaning, which can be retained and reactivated, his *store of experience* of his life-world is built up as a closed meaningful complex. This complex is normally unproblematical for him, and it remains controllable by him in such a way that his momentary interest selects from this store of experience those things which are relevant to the demand of the situation. The experience of the life-world has its special style of verification. This style results from the process of the harmonization of all single experiences. It is co-constituted, last but not least, by the perspectives of relevance and by the horizons of interest which are to be explicated.

All that has been said so far, however, is no more than chapter-headings for an extensive exploration. For the present, it will suffice to keep firmly in mind that a special motivation is needed in order to induce the naïve person even to pose the question concerning the meaningful structure of his life-world, even *within the general thesis*. This motivation can be very heterogeneous; for example, a newly appearing phenomenon of meaning resists being organized within the store of experience, or a special condition of interest demands a transition from a naïve attitude to a reflection of a higher order. So-called rational action can be given as an example of the latter. Rational action is given when all the ends of action and all the means which will lead to it are clearly and distinctly presented, as, for example, in the case of economic action. If such a motivation for leaving the natural attitude is given, then by a process of reflection the question concerning the structure of meaning can always be raised. One can always reactivate the process which has built up the sediments of meaning, and one can explain the intentionalities of the perspectives of relevance and the horizons of interest. Then all these phenomena of meaning, which obtain quite simply for the naïve person, might be in principle exactly described and analyzed even *within the general thesis*. To accomplish this on the level of mundane intersubjectivity is the task of the mundane cultural sciences, and to clarify their specific methods is precisely a part of that constitutive phenomenology of the natural attitude of which we have been speaking. Whether one will call this science Intentional Psychology or, better, General Sociology, since it must always be referred back to mundane intersubjectivity, is a quite secondary question.

All science presumes a special attitude of the person carrying on science; it is the attitude of the disinterested observer. In this manner it is distinguished above all from the attitude of the person who lives naïvely in his life-world and who has an eminently practical interest in it. With the transition to this attitude, however, all categories of experience of the life-world undergo a fundamental modification. As a disinterested observer, not as a private person, which certainly he also is, the scientist does not participate in the life-world as an actor, and he is no longer carried along by the living stream of intentionalities. The person living naïvely in the life-world can become, as we have said, motivated so as to raise the question concerning the structure of its meaning. But, although he reflects in this manner, he in no way loses his practical interest in it, and he still remains the center, the "null point," of this his world, which is oriented with regard to him. *But to make up his mind to observe scientifically this life-world means to determine no longer to place himself and his own condition of interest as the center of this world, but to substitute another null point for the orientation of the phenomena of the life-world.* What this null point is and how it comes to be constituted as a type (economic man, subject of law, etc.) depends upon the particular problem-situation which the scientist has chosen. The life-world, as an object of scientific investigation, will be for the investigator *qua* scientist predominantly the life-world of Others, the observed. This does not alter the fact that the scientist, who is *also* a human being among human beings in this single and uniform life-world and whose scientific work is in itself a working-together with Others in it, constantly refers and is obliged to refer in his scientific work to his own experience of the life-world. But it must always be clearly borne in mind that the disinterested observer has to a certain extent departed from the living stream of intentionalities. *Together with the substitution of another null point for the framework of orientation, every meaning-reference which was self-evident to the naïve person, in reference to his own I, has now undergone a fundamental specific modification*.[20] It remains for each social and cultural science to develop the type of such modification proper to it, that is, *to work out its particular methods*. In other words, each of these sciences must give the equation of transformation according to which the phenomena of the life-world become transformed by a process of idealization.

For idealization and formalization have just the same role for the social sciences as the one which Husserl has stated for the natural sciences, except that it is not a question of *mathematizing the forms* but of developing a *typology of "fullnesses"* (*Füllen*). Also, in the social sciences the eminent danger exists that their idealizations, in this case typologies, will not be considered as methods but as true being. Indeed this danger is even greater in the sciences which deal with the human being and his life-world, because they are always obliged to work with a highly complex material involving types of a higher order. This material does not refer back immediately to the subjective activity of individuals, which is always the chief problem if it is in the sphere of mundane apperception.

In relation to these problems it is the great contribution of Max Weber [21] in his "verstehende Soziologie" to have given the principles of a method which attempts to explain all social phenomena in the broadest sense (thus all objects of the cultural sciences) in relation to the "intended meaning" which the actor connects with his action. At the same time, he has given the main characteristics of the style of method of these sciences in his theory of the ideal type and its laws of formation. But, it seems to me, these methods can only become fully intelligible by means of the far-reaching investigations of a constitutive phenomenology of the natural attitude.

Such a science will find more than a guide in Husserl's in-

---

[20] For example, the social scientist does not study the concrete action (*Handeln*) of human beings, like you and me and everyone in our daily lives, with our hopes and fears, mistakes and hates, happiness and misery. He analyzes only certain definite sequences of activity (*Handlungsabläufe*) as types, with their means-end relations and their chains of motivation; and he constructs (obviously, according to quite definite structural laws) the pertinent ideal personality types with which he peoples the segment of the social world he has selected as an object of his scientific research.

[21] An excellent presentation of his theory is to be found in English in Talcott Parsons, *The Structure of Social Action*, New York, 1937.

vestigations in the area of transcendental phenomenology, for, as we have already said, in essence all analyses carried out in phenomenological reduction must retain their validation in the correlates of the phenomena investigated within the natural sphere. Therefore, it is to be the task of this science to apply the whole treasure of knowledge opened up by Husserl to its own area. We mention only Husserl's analysis of time, his theory of signs and symbols, of ideal objects, of occasional judgments, and finally his teleological interpretation of history. To develop the program of such a science, even in its main characteristics, beyond the mere suggestion given above, would go far beyond our present limits.[22]

---

[22] I have presented several of the main principles in *Der sinnhafte Aufbau der sozialen Welt*, Vienna 1932, 2nd edition 1960.

HUSSERL'S IMPORTANCE FOR THE SOCIAL SCIENCES*

Husserl was not conversant with the concrete problems of the social sciences. However the problems of intersubjectivity, of empathy, and of the status of society and community as subjectivities of a higher order occupied him since the first draft of *Ideen II*. When I asked him once why he had refrained from publishing the second volume, he answered that at that time he had not found a solution to the problem of the constitution of intersubjectivity. He believed he had done so in the Fifth *Cartesian Meditation*. The topic of the *Lebenswelt* became thematic in the posthumous parts of the *Krisis* study.

There is no need to present Husserl's pertinent theories to readers familiar with his writings; a critical discussion of their shortcomings has been given elsewhere.[1] Yet it might be useful to give a brief account of the treatment of these problems by a few thinkers who based or believed they were basing their discussion on Husserl's philosophy.

Unfortunately, the first group of Husserl's close personal students believed that concrete problems of the social sciences could be solved by direct application of the method of eidetic reduction to unclarified notions of common-sense thinking or to equally unclarified concepts of the empirical social sciences. It is entirely compatible with my profound respect for Edith Stein as a person and thinker to state that her [2] and Gerda Walther's [3] naive use of the eidetic method in analyzing the

---

[1] As to *Ideen II*: *Philosophy and Phenomenological Research*, Vol. XIII, March 1953, pp. 394–413; as to the Fifth *Cartesian Meditation*: *Philosophische Rundschau*, Bd. V, 1957, pp. 81–107.

[2] Edith Stein, "Beiträge zur philosophischen Begründung der Psychologie und der Geisteswissenschaften," *Jahrbuch für Philosophie und phänomenologische Forschung*, Bd. V, pp. 1–285; "Untersuchung über den Staat," *ibid.*, Bd. VII, pp. 1–125.

[3] Gerda Walther, "Zur Ontologie der sozialen Gemeinschaften," *ibid.*, Bd. VI, pp. 1–159.

* Some preliminary remarks concerned with the author's personal reminiscences of Edmund Husserl which appear in the original published version of this article have been omitted here. (M.N.)

problems of social relations, of community, and of the state led them to the formulation of certain apodictic and purportedly aprioristic statements which have contributed toward discrediting phenomenology among social scientists.

Even Max Scheler used the same unfortunate approach in the concluding chapters of his *Formalismus* [4] when he attempted to analyze the nature of society and community in its various forms. Later on, when this remarkable thinker became more and more involved in the concrete problems of the social sciences and came to be an eminent sociologist in his own right, he abandoned, it seems to me, many of the theories developed in this book. There his phenomenological analysis of the eidetic structure of the hierarchy of values had led him to a conception of the Person as the center of spiritual acts. But he hypostasized this idea of the individual person by assuming a *Gesamtperson*, a collective person, whose concrete spiritual acts are directed toward supravital values such as the legal order, the state, the church. The nature of the collectively determined acts supposedly performed by the *Gesamtperson* remains entirely unclarified and, for this very reason, so does the nature of the four forms of sociality distinguished by him: 1) the herd or mass, 2) the community based on life shared (*Lebensgemeinschaft*), 3) Society in the narrower sense, and 4) the communion of love based on the idea of salvation in God.

Yet as early as in the second edition of his book, *The Nature of Sympathy*,[5] Scheler applied phenomenological methods to the question of our grounds for assuming the reality of other selves and the possibility and limits of our understanding them, stating that this problem is virtually *the* problem for any theory of knowledge in the social sciences. During his later phase he recognized that sociology has to be founded upon a fully elaborated philosophical anthropology. He then applied the methods of ideation to the nature of man within the world, the natural as well as the socio-cultural one. The biological nature of man is at the foundation of his system of needs and their rank of

---

[4] Max Scheler, *Der Formalismus in der Ethik und die materiale Wertethik*, 4. Auflage (*Ges. Werke*, Bd. 2), Bern 1954, pp. 506–572.
[5] Max Scheler, *Wesen und Formen der Sympathie*, 2. Auflage, Bonn 1922, pp. 244–307; English Translation: *The Nature of Sympathy*, New Haven 1954, pp. 213–264.

order, his spiritual nature determines the forms of his knowledge, and both are at the foundation of his social and cultural reality. Scheler promised to show in his book on metaphysics,[6] which he was unable to finish, that Husserl's phenomenological reduction is a particular epistemological technique specific to the philosophical attitude although it appears to have been presented by its author in terms of a logical methodology.[7] Scheler postulates as a prerequisite of any phenomenological reduction a theory of the nature of reality and our experiencing of it. He criticizes Husserl for having identified "being real" with "having a position in time." According to Scheler, the general thesis of reality in the natural attitude and its anthropomorphic character, as well as the *structure* of the "relative natural conception of the world," accepted as given and unquestioned, can be analyzed by phenomenological methods. The *content* of this relative natural attitude, however, changes from group to group and within the same group in the course of historical evolution. To describe its features is the task of the empirical social sciences.

If I correctly understand Professor Merleau-Ponty's pertinent statements,[8] then his view of the applicability of phenomenological methods to the problems of the social sciences comes very close to Scheler's latest position. Merleau-Ponty quotes Husserl's letter to Lucien Levy-Bruhl of 1935 in which he stated that, as an anthropological fact, historical relativism incontestably has its legitimate place as a station on the road leading to the intentional analysis of the structure of the social world. And Merleau-Ponty sums up his own position by stating that, from the phenomenological point of view, the social is not merely an object but, first of all, my situation lived through in a vivid present by means of which also the whole historical past becomes accessible to me; the social appears to me always as a variation of a single life in which I partake and in terms of which my fellow-man is to me always another I, an *alter ego*.

This is precisely the point where Ortega y Gasset [9] deviates

---

[6] Max Scheler, *Die Wissensformen und die Gesellschaft*, Leipzig 1926, p. 352, 460.
[7] *loc. cit.*, pp. 160ff.
[8] Maurice Merleau-Ponty, "Le philosophe et la sociologie," *Cahiers Internationaux de Sociologie*, Vol. X, 1951, pp. 50–69.
[9] Ortega y Gasset, *El Hombre y la Gente*, Madrid 1957; English Translation (to which quotations refer): *Man and People*, New York 1957, Chs. IV–VII.

from Husserl's view. According to Ortega, the I finds its reality in its immanence, that is, in the radical solitude of its personal life which is patent to it. The Other's human life, however, is to me latent and hypothetical, a second-degree reality; his I is a *quasi*-I, transcending my own and merely com-present but never present to me. To be sure, I normally take these second-degree realities for granted as if they were radical ones. Then I am unaware of my genuine life in its solitude and truth, but I live in a socially conditioned reality in terms of which the Other is he with whom I can and must enter into relations. The Other's capacity for corresponding to my actions, the resulting reciprocity of our acts, is the first social fact and fundamental for the constitution of a common environment. Ortega refers to Husserl's statement that the meaning of the notion "man" implies from the outset reciprocal existence with Others, a community of men, men in society. To Ortega, as to Husserl, the presence of the Other's body is an indication of the Other's compresent inwardness. But although the Other's body belongs to my world, the Other's world remains strange to me. Ortega criticizes [10] at length Husserl's theory (developed in the Fifth *Cartesian Meditation*) construing the constitution of the *alter ego* in my own intentionality on the ground that Husserl tries to grasp the Other as an *alter ego* by an analogical projection or transposition from my body to the Other's body. Husserl fails to take into account that I observe merely the exteriority of the Other's body, whereas I experience my own body from within. This difference can never be reduced to that of the perspective of Here and There. Moreover, how could transference by empathy, as suggested by Husserl, be possible if I am a male and the Other a female? To Ortega the *ego* is something that I alone am, and to speak of an *alter ego* means merely that there is something in the abstract Other which corresponds to that which the *ego* is in me. Yet in spite of the common environment established by the Other's capacity of co-responding with me, the Other's radical reality remains as inaccessible to me as mine is to him, and the common world in which we live is neither mine nor his; this objective world – Ortega calls it the humanized world – is just the correlate of the society into which we are born. In this

[10] *loc. cit.*, esp. pp. 121-128.

world the Other is first an abstract He; then he might be individualized and turn into a You. The I, however, in its concreteness appears last. It is the Other who makes me discover my boundaries, dividing me from him and my world from his. My concrete I, thus emergent, is experienced by me as an Other and particularly as a You, as an *"alter tu"*. Society and community, state and collectivities, are experienced by me in the anonymity of "someone," of "people," doing just what "is done." In sharing their world, I cease to be an individual person with individual convictions. I turn into a social automaton, enter a state of inauthenticity (to borrow a term from Heidegger not used by Ortega), simply repeating "what is thought, said, or done." In brief: I am socialized, submitting to the socializing force of usage which exercises constraint upon me. There is, however, no such thing as a collective soul or a collective consciousness in Durkheim's sense; social relations are always interindividual.

Ortega's theory starts admittedly from Husserl's notion of a comprehensive environment as the foundation of the constitution of sociality. Like Husserl, he fails to note that it is merely the experience of the Other's existence which makes comprehension of a supposedly common environment possible, so that the whole reasoning becomes circular. Having rejected – not without some justification – Husserl's view on the constitution of the *alter ego* in the transcendental sphere and, therewith, on the constitution of a common intersubjective world, he rejects – for still better reasons – Husserl's conception of the collectivity as a subjectivity of a higher order. In the inauthenticity of the humanized world the Other is not experienced as an *alter ego*, but as the socialized I in terms of an *alter tu*. To be sure, Ortega carries on his analysis within the natural attitude and does not take into account the fact that Husserl's concern in the Cartesian Meditations was the constitution of transcendental intersubjectivity within the phenomenologically reduced sphere. In both spheres, however, the problem remains open: How is a common world in terms of common intentionalities possible?

Although this problem remains a central one for any phenomenological research, the fact that it has so far not found a satisfactory solution does not impair the outstanding importance of Husserl's life work for the foundation of the social sciences.

For these sciences do not have to deal with the philosophical aspects of intersubjectivity, but with the structure of the *Lebenswelt* as experienced by men in their natural attitude, by men, that is, who are born into this socio-cultural world, have to find their bearings within it, and have to come to terms with it. This world is pre-given to them and taken by them unquestionably for granted – "unquestionably" in the sense that it is unquestioned until further notice but may be called into question at any time. In the natural attitude I take it for granted that fellow-men exist, that they act upon me as I upon them, that – at least to a certain extent – communication and mutual understanding among us can be established, and that this is done with the help of some system of signs and symbols within the frame of some social organization and some social institutions – none of them of my own making.

Max Weber has shown that all phenomena of the socio-cultural world originate in social interaction and can be referred to it. According to him, it is the central task of sociology to understand the meaning which the actor bestows upon his action (the "subjective meaning" in his terminology).* But what is action, what is meaning, and how is understanding of such meaning by a fellow-man possible, be he a partner of the social interaction, or merely an observer in everyday life, or a social scientist? I submit that any attempt to answer these questions leads immediately to problems with which Husserl was concerned and which he has to a certain extent solved. I propose to give a short and, of course, entirely inadequate outline of some of the main problems of the social sciences, selected at random, to which certain results of Husserl's researches can be and partially have been fruitfully applied.

1) Let us for the present purpose define meaningful action as conduct motivated in terms of a preconceived project. That which is projected is the anticipated state of affairs to be brought about by the action. Projecting is, then, rehearsing the future course of action in phantasy. What is the nature of such a phantasm? It is, in the language of *Ideen I*, a neutrality-modification of a positing presentation (*Neutralitätsmodifikation der*

---

* See "Common-Sense and Scientific Interpretation of Human Action," pp. 24–25, and "Concept and Theory Formation in the Social Sciences," pp. 56–57, 62ff. (M.N.)

setzenden Vergegenwärtigung).[11] Moreover, the relation of the preconceived project to its motives on the one hand and to the ensuing action on the other hand becomes understandable only by an analysis of the consciousness of inner time such as that proposed by Husserl.

2) Any action refers by its being projected to pre-experiences organized in what may be called the stock of knowledge actually at hand, which is, thus, the sedimentation of previous experiencing acts together with their generalizations, formalizations, and idealizations. It is at hand, actually or potentially recollected or retained, and as such the ground of all of our protentions and anticipations. These, in turn, are subject to the basic idealizations of "and so forth and so on" ("*und so weiter*") and "I can do it again" ("*Ich kann immer wieder*") described by Husserl.[12]

Moreover, this stock of knowledge actually at hand contains zones of manifold degrees of clarity and distinctness. It carries along infinite open horizons of the unknown but potentially knowable. It shows relevance structures of various types, all of them founded upon the attentional modifications [13] originating in our practical, theoretical, or axiological interest. These manifold dimensions of the stock of knowledge at hand are the outcome of synthetic operations of our consciousness by which polythetically constituted acts are grasped monothetically,[14] in brief, the outcome of all the manifold performances on the higher level which Husserl has described in *Ideen I*, especially in the last part of this book.[15] Any successful analysis of the problem of the stock of knowledge at hand has to be based on these conceptions and their implications; such an analysis is of basic importance for many concrete problems of the social sciences, since culture can be defined in terms of shared knowledge which is socially derived and socially approved.

3) All acting involves choosing, and this not merely in cases where several courses of action stand to choice. Even with respect to a single project there is the choice whether it should be carried

---

[11] *Ideen I*, Secs, 111, 114; *Zeitbewusstsein*, Sec. 17 and *Beilage* II.
[12] *Formale und transzendentale Logik*, Sec. 74; *Erfahrung und Urteil*, Secs. 51b, 58, 61.
[13] *Ideen I*, Secs. 92, 113, 116.
[14] *Ideen I*, Sec. 119; *Erfahrung und Urteil*, Secs. 24, 50.
[15] *Ideen I*, Secs. 147ff.

out or dropped. Husserl's theories of open and problematic possibilities,[16] of the various meanings of the term "I can" [17] and of the problems of "formal praxis" [18] open the way towards an analysis of choice within the natural attitude, basic for all the social sciences.

4) If I experience my fellow-man in a so-called face-to-face relationship, then I share with him a common environment of which his body is an element to me as mine is to him. Husserl's analyses, carried out in the transcendentally reduced sphere,[19] of the environment as seen from "Here" (*hic*) and from "There" (*illic*), are of special importance if applied to the *Lebenswelt* as experienced in the natural attitude. The "*hic*" is the zero point of the system of co-ordinates in terms of which the individual groups the *Lebenswelt* into zones within actual and potential reach, each of which carries along open horizons of undetermined determinability. The Other's system of co-ordinates has a zero point which is, as seen from my "Here," a "There," but which is a "Here" to him. The "reciprocity of perspectives" * – to use a term so dear to sociologists – is founded on the open possibility of an interchange of the standpoints, that is – metaphorically speaking – on the establishment of a formula of transformation by which the terms of one system of co-ordinates can be translated into terms of the other. All this does not refer merely to perspectives originating in the location in space, but also to those determined by the particular socio-cultural situation in its particular historicity.

5) Husserl's analyses of the consciousness of inner time with its interplay of protentions and retentions make it understandable that the I can partake in the Other's stream of consciousness in a vivid present, whereas the I can grasp – and then only in the reflective attitude – merely past phases of its own stream of consciousness.

6) As Husserl has clearly seen, the Other's conscious life is not originally accessible to me, but merely in terms of appresentation.[20] Objects or events in the outer world perceived by me –

---
[16] *Erfahrung und Urteil*, Sec. 21c. See: "Choosing among Projects of Action."
[17] *Ideen II*, Sec. 60.
[18] *Ideen I*, Secs. 116, 147.
[19] *Cartesianische Meditationen*, Sec. 54.
[20] e.g. *Ideen I*, Sec. 1; *Cartesianische Meditationen*, Secs. 49ff.
* See "Common-Sense and Scientific Interpretation of Human Action," pp. 11–12. (M.N.)

the Other's body as an expressional field, the Other's bodily movements or their outcome, such as cultural objects – are interpreted by me as signs and symbols of events in the Other's consciousness. Husserl has investigated the nature and constitution of these objects of a higher order, as he calls them (*fundierte Gegenstände*). In his *Logical Investigations*[21] he had already dealt, although in a rather fragmentary manner, with the theory of signs and symbols in terms of meaning and expression, of meaning-endowing and meaning-fulfilling acts, of indications, significant signs, etc. It seems to me,[22] however, that Husserl's theory of appresentation as developed in his later works can be fruitfully applied to the relationship between the sign and the significatum, the symbol and the symbolized, and also to the analysis of the constitution of the great symbolic systems such as language, myth, religion, art, etc., all of which are essential elements of the *Lebenswelt* and accordingly of highest interest to the social sciences. Such a theory would also have to deal with the problem of multiple levels of reality and their interconnection, and with the foundation of all of them upon the paramount reality of the *Lebenswelt*. Moreover, it has to be shown how these systems are, on the one hand, constitutive for a particular culture and society and, on the other hand, how they are socially derived.

7) The social world has particular dimensions of proximity and distance in space and time and of intimacy and anonymity. Each of these dimensions has its specific horizonal structure, and to each of them belongs a specific experiential style. These experiences are pre-predicative, and their style is that of typologies formed differently for experiences relating to contemporaries, predecessors, and successors. Husserl's analyses of the pre-predicative experience and of the nature of types (although not applied by him to the social world) are of particular importance here.[23] Taking them as a point of departure, it can be explained why we interpret the actions of our fellow-men in terms of course-of-action types and of personal types, and why we have to undergo a self-typification in order to come to terms with them

---

[21] *Logische Untersuchungen*, Bd. II, Erste und Zweite Untersuchung.
[22] See "Symbol, Reality and Society."
[23] *Erfahrung und Urteil*, Secs. 8, 22, 24, 25, 26, 80, and especially Sec. 83(a) and (b).

by establishing a universe of communicative comprehension. The social sciences study this problem under the heading of "social roles" and in terms of the so-called subjective and objective interpretation of the meaning of action (Max Weber). On the other hand, all typifications of common-sense thinking are themselves integral elements of the concrete historical sociocultural *Lebenswelt* within which they prevail as taken for granted and as socially approved. Their structure determines among other things the social distribution of knowledge and its relativity and relevance to the concrete social environment of a concrete group in a concrete historical situation. Here are the legitimate problems of relativism, historicism, and of the so-called sociology of knowledge.

In summing up, we may say that the empirical social sciences will find their true foundation not in transcendental phenomenology, but in the constitutive phenomenology of the natural attitude. Husserl's signal contribution to the social sciences consists neither in his unsuccessful attempt to solve the problem of the constitution of the transcendental intersubjectivity within the reduced egological sphere, nor in his unclarified notion of empathy as the foundation of understanding, nor, finally, in his interpretation of communities and societies as subjectivities of a higher order the nature of which can be described eidetically; but rather in the wealth of his analyses pertinent to problems of the *Lebenswelt* and designed to be developed into a philosophical anthropology. The fact that many of these analyses were carried out in the phenomenologically reduced sphere, and even more, that the problems dealt with became visible only after this reduction was performed, does not impair the validity of their results within the realm of the natural attitude. For Husserl himself has established once and for all the principle that analyses made in the reduced sphere are valid also for the realm of the natural attitude.*

---

* See "Phenomenology and the Social Sciences," p. 132 and p. 139. (M.N.)

SCHELER'S THEORY OF INTERSUBJECTIVITY AND THE GENERAL THESIS OF THE ALTER EGO

I. SCHELER'S CONCEPT OF MAN

In order to make Scheler's theory of intersubjectivity and its role within his philosophical thought fully understandable we must glance at his concept of a philosophical anthropology. It is outlined in an essay called "The Place of Man in the Cosmos," [1] one of the last papers published in his lifetime, to serve as a prelude to two never finished volumes on anthropology and metaphysics. Here Scheler develops a scheme of five interrelated levels of psychical existence in the world. 1) The lowest one is characterized by an *emotional impulse* [2] without consciousness, without even sensations and perceptions. This kind of psychical existence is not directed towards a goal although it indisputably shows certain tendencies. The vegetative life of the plant takes place exclusively on this level, but the human being also participates in it, e.g., by the rhythm between sleep and waking. In this sense, sleep is the vegetative state of man. 2) The second form of psychical existence is that of *instinctive life*.[3] Instinctive behavior is meaningful as it is oriented to an end; it is performed rhythmically; it does not serve the individual but the species; it is innate and hereditary; it is independent of the number of attempts which have to be made in order to succeed, and therefore it is, so to speak, ready-made from the beginning. This level is characteristic of the lower animals. It can be defined as a unity of pre-knowledge and action, as there is no more knowledge at hand than is necessary for the performance of the next step. By its directedness towards *specific* elements of the environment it is distinguished from the level of emotional impulse; by its chief

---

[1] *Die Stellung des Menschen im Kosmos*, Darmstadt, 1928.
[2] *L.c.*, pp. 16ff.
[3] *L.c.*, pp. 24ff.

function of "creative dissociation" (that is, by singling specific sensations and perceptions out of diffuse complexes of experiences) it is separated from the next level, namely, 3) the level of *associative memory*.[4] This is the level of "conditioned reflexes." To it corresponds a behavior tested in an increasing number of attempts performed according to the principle of success and failure, the faculty of forming habits and traditions, and other forms of associative regularities as imitation and learning – all this, however, by half-unconscious tradition and not by spontaneous recollection. 4) The fourth level is that of *practical intelligence*.[5] An animal behaves intelligently if it acts spontaneously and appropriately in new situations, and this independently of the number of previous attempts to solve a certain task impulsively. Such behavior presupposes insight into the interconnectedness of the environment and its elements and, therefore, a productive (not merely a reproductive) thinking which is capable of anticipating a state of affairs never before experienced and of grasping relations like "similar," "analogous," "means for obtaining something," "cause of something," etc. The well-known researches of Prof. W. Koehler [6] have proved that higher mammals are capable of genuine intelligent acts in the indicated sense.

But if mammals are intelligent, does anything other than a gradual difference exist between man and animal? Scheler rejects both prevailing schools of thought, the one which restricts intelligent acts exclusively to human beings as well as the so-called "*homo-faber*-theory" which reduces the differences between man and animal to one of degree. Of course, in so far as human nature pertains to the sphere of vitality, in so far as its psychical life shows impulses, instincts, associative memory, intelligence and choice, it participates in all the realms of organic life thus far enumerated. And in so far, but only in so far, as human nature shows the same structure as the nature of other living beings it is accessible to experimental psychology.[7]

[4] *L.c.*, pp. 31ff.
[5] *L.c.*, pp. 39ff.
[6] W. Koehler, *Intelligenzpruefungen an Menschenaffen, Abhandlungen der preussischen Akademie der Wissenschaften*, and *The Mentality of Apes*, 1925.
[7] Cf. the excellent criticism of the limits of experimental methods in psychology by Prof. Gordon W. Allport in his presidential address at the Forty-seventh Annual Meeting of the American Psychological Association, 1939: "The Psychologist's

5) But man is also something else.⁸ The principle which constitutes the specific exceptional position of man within the cosmos is not derived from the evolution of life; it stands rather over against the life and its manifestations. The old Greek philosophers acknowledged the existence of this principle and called it "logos" or Reason. But Scheler prefers the term "Geist" (Mind) which includes not only "reason," and this means the faculty of thinking in ideas, but also the power of intuitive perception of essences (*Wesensgehalten*) and certain classes of volitive and emotional acts such as those of kindness, love, repentance, awe, etc. The center of activity, correlated to the level of "Mind," is called by Scheler "Person" and has to be distinguished from the other centers of vitality which he calls "psychical centers."

The realm of the Mind is the realm of freedom: freedom from dependence on the organic life, freedom from the bondage of impulses, freedom also from an environment in which the animal is immersed. Whereas the animal experiences its environment as a system of centers of resistances and reactions whose structure it carries along as the snail does its shell wherever it moves, the Mind and therefore the Person has the faculty of transforming those environmental centers of resistance into "objects" and the closed "environment" itself into the open "world." Unlike the animal, man may also objectify his own physical and psychical experiences. The animal hears and sees but without knowing *that* it does so and it experiences even *its* impulses but just as attractions and repulsions emanating from things in its environment. Thus, the animal has consciousness, but not self-consciousness; it is not master of itself. Man, however, is the only being which is able to be a Self and to place itself not only above the world but even above itself. He can do so, because he is not only a soul (*anima*) but a Person – "persona cogitans" in the sense of Kant's doctrine of the transcendental apperception, the "cogitare" being the condition of all possible inner and outer experience and therefore of all objects of experience.⁹ But this means also

---

Frame of Reference," *Psychological Bulletin*, Vol. XXXVII, pp. 1–26, especially p. 14ff. Also Prof. R. S. Woodworth, "Successes and Failures of Experimental Psychology," *Science*, Vol. XCIII, pp. 265 ff., especially p. 269 f.

⁸ Scheler, *Stellung des Menschen im Kosmos*, pp. 44ff.

⁹ In his book, *Der Formalismus in der Ethik und die materiale Wertethik*, p. 388 ff.,

that Mind and its correlate, Person, is principally not objectifiable. Mind is pure actuality and Person is nothing else than a self-constituted integration of acts. Moreover, even other people are not objectifiable in so far as their Persons are in question. Being merely the locus of acts the totality of which co-determines each single act, a Person is accessible only for another Person by co-achieving these acts, by thinking with, feeling with, willing with the Other.[10]

II. SCHELER'S CONCEPT OF PERSON

In a previous book [11] Scheler had worked out the concept of the Person, which is basic for all his philosophizing. He distinguishes there sharply between the I and the Person. The experienced I (*Erlebnis-ich*) is under any aspect an *object* of our thought. It is given to our inner experience as a datum from which psychology and even descriptive psychology must abstract in order to operate with experiences or thoughts as such without referring to the thinker. On the other hand, an act can never be objectified. It is never "given" to our outer or inner experience and can only be experienced by performing it. And much less can the correlate of the different forms and categories of acts, the Person, be considered as an object. The Person manifests himself exclusively by performing the acts in which he lives and by which he experiences himself. Or as far as other Persons are concerned, they can be experienced by co-performance, pre-performance or re-performance of the other Persons' acts, but without objectifying the Person.[12] To avoid misunderstanding,

Scheler has criticized Kant's concept of the identity of the objects. If the object were nothing else than what can be indentified by an I, the I too would be an object – and that, Scheler thinks, is indeed the case. For Kant, however, the I must not be an object – as it is the condition of all objects. But Kant's underlying tenet that the existence of the world depends on the possibility of its being experienced by an I is according to Scheler merely the consequence of Kant's "transcendental qualms" that things in themselves, once left alone, might behave quite differently if we do not bind them from the beginning by the laws of our experience.

[10] *Stellung des Menschen im Kosmos*, p. 58ff.
[11] *Der Formalismus in der Ethik und die materiale Wertethik*, [*Neuer Versuch der Grundlegung des ethischen Personalismus*. First published in Vol. I and II of *Jahrbuch für Philosophie und phänomenologische Forschung*, 1913 and 1916; second edition, 1921], hereafter designated *Ethik;* Cf. especially Chapter VI.
[12] *Ethik*, p. 401f. Nicolas Berdyaev makes a similar distinction between "Ego and Personality" in his *Solitude and Society*, p. 159ff. From a quite different angle Neo-

says Scheler, a distinction must be made between acts belonging to the Person and mere "functions" belonging to the I such as seeing, hearing, tasting, bodily feelings, all kinds of attention, etc. The functions presuppose a body, they are correlated to the environment, they have their origin within the I, they are psychical. Acts, however, are not psychical in this sense; they do not necessarily presuppose a body, but they are psychophysically indifferent;[13] their correlate is not the environment, but the world. To be sure, this world is an individual world correlated to an individual Person. But the Person is never a part of this world, and the term "correlated" does not mean anything else than that the individual Person experiences himself within his individual world.[14]

The term "I," however, always implies, according to Scheler, a reference to its double antithesis: the outer world on the one hand and the "Thou" on the other. The term "Person" is free from such connotations. God may be a Person but not an I; He neither has a "thou" nor an outer world. A Person acts, takes a walk, for example. This cannot be done by an I. Language tolerates the use of the phrase "I am acting, I am walking." But this "I" is not the name for the "Self" as an experience of my psychical life, rather an "occasional" expression, whose meaning changes with the man who actually uses it; it merely marks the linguistic form of adressing the "first person," as the grammarians call it. If I say, "I am perceiving myself," then the "I" does not mean the psychical I, but merely designates the speaker; and the "myself" does not mean "my Self," but leaves open the question whether "I" perceive the "me" by outer or inner perception. On the other hand, if I say, "I perceive my Self," the I means the speaker and the "my Self" means the psychical Self as an object of inner perception. A Person, therefore, might

Thomists distinguish "individuality" as apart from "personality" as a whole (cf. e.g., Jacques Maritain: *Du Régime temporel et de la liberté*). It is not possible to enter here into a discussion of G. H. Mead's very interesting interpretation of the problem in *Mind, Self and Society* and *The Philosophy of the Act;* his approach to it is a quite different one. The student of Mead will, however, find that certain special views of Mead and Scheler converge.

[13] Here, as generally in his theory of the Person, Scheler's thought converges with certain aspects of William Stern's personalistic psychology. Stern, too, characterizes the being of the personalities as "meta-psycho-physical." (*Person und Sache*).

[14] *Ethik*, pp. 403, 408–410.

just as well take a walk as perceive his Self, e.g., if this Person makes psychological observations. But the psychical Self, which the Person perceives in such a case, can just as little "perceive" as it can walk or act. A Person, on the other hand, may perceive his Self, his body, his outer world, but it is not possible to render a Person the object of (his own or an other Person's) perceiving acts.[15] The Person does not exist, except in the performance of his acts. Any attempt to objectify the Person or his acts – be this objectifying a perceiving, thinking, recollecting, expecting – transforms his existence into a transcendental idea.[16] Of course, acts can be "given" either in their naive performance or in reflection. But this means simply that a reflective knowledge accompanies the act without rendering it an object. Grasping an act as an object by another reflective act is therefore impossible.[17]

The account of Scheler's theory of the I would be incomplete without a short reference to the specific experiences a man has of his body. Although the concept "human body" already refers to a human being to which this body belongs, either as his own body or as the body of another man, this does not mean that it is the reference of the human body to a Self which makes the experience of the body possible. And on the other hand, says Scheler, it would be wrong to assume that a man has necessarily to refer first to his experiences of his own Self and then to the experience of his own body, if he wants to comprehend another Self or another body.[18]

We shall not criticize this basic theory of Scheler, although the inconsistency of several of the above theses is obvious. We have presented his ideas just for the purpose of making clear his more rounded doctrine of the understanding of the *alter ego*. Later we shall again meet some of Scheler's principle tenets and have the opportunity of dealing with them.

---

[15] *Ethik*, pp. 404ff.
[16] *Ethik*, p. 405.
[17] *Ethik*, pp. 388, 401, 405.
[18] *Ethik*, pp. 415–440, especially p. 427.

III. SCHELER'S THEORY OF INTERSUBJECTIVITY

a) The problems involved

As a result of his studies in the theory of sympathy,[19] Scheler passes in review the contributions of contemporary psychologists and philosophers to the solution of the problem of intersubjectivity and wonders why the results are so unsatisfactory. He comes to the conclusion that the failure of all efforts to deal with this topic has been caused by the lack of clear distinctions between the different problems involved and by neglect of the sequence in which these problems have to be raised. His first task, therefore, is to establish a catalogue of questions to be solved. There are six questions he enumerates:[20]

1) Is the relation between man and fellow-men just a factual one or does the concept of man already presuppose society, and this quite independently of the factual existence of a concrete ego within a concrete social world (ontological problem)?

2) a) By what reason am I, e.g., the writer of these lines, well-founded in my belief that other people and their conscious life do really exist? b) Furthermore, how is the reality of another's consciousness accessible to me (logico-epistemological problem)?

3) Which individual experiences have already to be presupposed and which activities of consciousness must be considered as already performed, before knowledge about an alter ego might emerge at all (problems of constitution)? For instance, does knowledge about other people's consciousness presuppose self-consciousness? Does it presuppose knowledge of Nature in the meaning of a real outer world? Does knowledge of other people's psychical and mental life presuppose an apperception of the Other's body and its interpretation as a field of expression? Questions of this order, [21] however, cannot be answered by

---

[19] First published in 1913 under the title, *Phänomenologie der Sympathiegefühle*, second rewritten edition, 1923, under the title, *Wesen und Formen der Sympathie*. We refer to this second edition (hereafter cited as *Sympathie*).

[20] *Sympathie*, pp. 248–269.

[21] Scheler has answered some of these questions in his later writings in a way which differs partially from his opinions as presented in this paper. Cf., e.g., "Probleme einer Soziologie des Wissens" in his book, *Die Wissensformen und die Gesellschaft*, Leipzig, 1926, pp. 48–54.

solutions which are valid only for the attitudes and experiences of a well-educated adult living in the Occidental civilization of our time. They have to be valid independently of those accidental factors. They are not problems of an empirical but of a *transcendental psychology*.

4) The *empirical psychological* problems of understanding other people are of a quite different kind. Any sort of empirical psychology already presupposes not only that fellow-men do really exist, but also that the organization of their consciousness enables them to retain their perceptions, outer and inner experiences, sensations, feelings, etc., in memory; furthermore, that they can communicate those experiences by statements, and that these statements are understandable.[22] And in so far as "empirical psychology" may be taken as equivalent to "experimental psychology" it presupposes furthermore the objectifiability of the psychical as such and includes the ill-founded supposition that the same psychical events may recur in a multitude of subjects and may be reproduced by experiments. But the Person and his acts cannot be objectified and only that part of human existence which pertains to levels below the realm of mind and freedom are accessible to experiments. For the Person and his manifestations are not open to perception in the same sense as are the objects of nature. It is within the free will of the Person to disclose or conceal his acts or to keep silent, and this is quite another thing than merely not speaking. Nature cannot conceal itself and therefore neither can man, in so far as his animate existence belongs to Nature. It is necessarily open to discovery, and the pure acts of animate existence manifest themselves – at least in principle – in the somatico-physiological events correlated with them.

5) Metaphysical problems involved in the theory of the alter ego. There is a certain unity of style between basic metaphysical assumptions and the logico-epistemological approach to the problem of intersubjectivity. The so-called "theory of inference," for example, is only compatible with a very definite metaphysical standpoint, namely, the Cartesian assumption of two separate

[22] An excellent presentation of the problems of empirical psychology related to "understanding personality" may be found in Prof. Gordon W. Allport's book, *Personality, a Psychological Interpretation*, New York, 1937, Part V, pp. 499–549.

substances, the physical and the psychical, influencing one another; it would be incompatible, however, with the metaphysical assumption of an epiphenomenological parallelism.

6) Value problems connected with the existence of alter-egos. There is no doubt that certain moral acts such as those of love, responsibility, duty, gratitude refer by their nature to the existence of alter egos. Scheler calls them "essentially social acts" ("Wesenssoziale Akte") because they cannot be construed as pre-social acts on which sociality only later supervenes. For Scheler, these acts in particular constitute the proof for his theory that in each individual sociality is always present and that not only is the human individual a part of society but that society is also an integral part of the individual. Let us examine this theory more closely.

According to Scheler,[23] the belief in the existence of alter egos is not based on acts of theoretical cognition. A person-like being, capable of all kinds of emotional acts such as love, hate, will, etc., but incapable of theoretical acts – i.e., objectifying cognitions – would not at all lack any evidence of the existence of Others. The "essentially social feelings" alone are sufficient to establish the scheme of reference of society as an ever-present element of his consciousness. There is no Robinson Crusoe conceivable in the theory of mind who had not from the beginning some kind of knowledge of the existence of a community of human beings to which he belongs. There never has been a radical solipsist who said: "There are no communities of human beings and I do not belong to any of them. I am alone in the world." All a solipsistic Crusoe might pretend is: "I know that there are communities of human beings in the world and I know that I pertain to one or several of them. But I do not know the individuals constituting them, nor do I know the empirical groups which constitute such a community at all." We have, says Scheler, to distinguish between the empty knowledge *about* the existence of some alter ego and some community as such and the knowledge *of* [24] one or more concrete fellow-men and social groups. As far as the latter are concerned the supposition of some philosophers (like Driesch) is

---

[23] *Sympathie*, pp. 269–273; *Ethik*.
[24] We are borrowing here, in order to present Scheler's thought adequately, the terms, "knowledge about" and "knowledge of," from W. James' *Principles of Psychology*, Vol. I, p. 221.

erroneous that all knowledge of a concrete other person is based on the perception of his bodily movements. This is only one of the sources of my knowledge of Others and not at all the most important one. Other experiences, the knowledge of a system of interpretable signs, for instance, are sufficient for the belief in the existence of other persons.

b) Inference and empathy

But how is it possible that our experiences, which are supposed to be referred to concrete Others, lead to the conviction of their existence? There prevail in the contemporary literature two theories, the theory of inference or analogy, and the theory of empathy, which pretend to offer a solution not only for the empirical problem (cf. above ad 4) but also for the transcendental problem (cf. above ad 3) here involved.[25] The theory of inference pretends that we discover other people's thought by a process of reasoning by analogy, inferring from the Other's "expressive" bodily gestures his state of mind which is supposed to be analogous to our state of mind (disclosed by inner experience) if we perform the "same" gesture. The other theory consists in the hypothesis that the ego acquires a belief in the psychical existence of Others by a process of empathy in the manifestations of the Other's body. The followers of the first school of thought praise the conclusiveness of their hypothesis, which leads in their opinion to wellfounded evidence of the alter ego's existence, whereas the theory of empathy results only in a blind belief in it. The defenders of the theory of empathy rejoin that we have also merely a blind belief in the existence of our past experiences which are just "images" in our memory and that we even cannot go beyond a blind belief in the existence of the outer world.

Scheler's criticism of both theories goes in two directions. First, he proves for either theory that it is inconsistent in itself; secondly he shows that both of them are based on a common fallacy. Scheler's arguments against the theory of inference may be condensed as follows: 1) Animals, very young children and

[25] *Sympathie*, pp. 274-280; cf., the fine presentation and the important criticism of both theories in G. W. Allport's *Personality*, *l.c.*, pp. 523-533.

primitives, who obviously lack the faculty of inferring by analogy, also have the conviction of the existence of their fellow-beings and catch expressions of the Other's physical life. Koehler, Stern, Koffka, Levy-Bruhl have moreover proved that expression is the genuine experience of those beings and that all learning creates for them a disenchantment with and not a progressive animation of the world. 2) Except for self-observation in mirrors, etc., we have knowledge of our bodily gestures by sensations or motions and positions of our body, whereas other people's gestures are given to us first of all as optical phenomena having no analogy whatsoever to our kinesthetic sensations. Hence, all inference by analogy to Others' gestures already presupposes the psychical existence of the Others and our knowledge even of their experiences. 3) We suppose also the animate existence of animals like birds and fish whose expressive gestures are entirely different from ours. 4) The theory of inference conceals the logical fallacy called "quaternio terminorum." The only logically correct inference would be that where expressive bodily gestures exist which are analogous to my own, my Self must exist once more over there, and this would lead to a reduplication of my stream of thought. It is not understandable how – avoiding an obvious *quaternio terminorum* – an other Self, different from my own, should be posited by such a conclusion.

The theory of empathy, on the other hand, is not an explanation of the origin of our knowledge of Others, but just a hypothesis which explains the reason of our belief in the Other's existence. It would be a pure accident if the Other's body to which we ascribe our empathetic feelings were really animated. For, interpretation of the Other's gesture as expression can only be the consequence of and not the proof for his existence. Furthermore, this theory, too, suffers from the same *quaternio terminorum* as the theory of inference and would lead at best to the assumption that my own Self exists twice or several times but not that another Self does exist.

But all this criticism does not hit the basic fallacy of both hypotheses, namely, the suppositions 1) that the first thing given to each of us is his own Self and 2) that the first thing we can grasp of another human being is the appearance of his body, together with its movement and gestures. Both theories assume as self-evident that these statements are true and that only on this conviction do we base our belief in the existence of *alter egos*. But in doing so both theories underestimate the difficulties of self-perception and overestimate the difficulties in perceiving other people's thought.

The first statement involves, according to Scheler,[26] the idea that anybody can only think his own thoughts, feel his own feelings, etc., and that this fact constitutes the individual substratum "Self" for him. But the only thing self-evident is the tautology that *if* such a substratum were once supposed, all thoughts and feelings thought and felt by this "Self" would pertain to this substratum. On the other hand, it is certain that we think our own thought, as well as other people's thought, feel also other people's feelings, accept or reject other people's will. There are even situations where we cannot distinguish whether a thought is ours or not. Then an experience is given to us without any mark indicative of the individual stream of consciousness to which it belongs. This fact Scheler considers as very important. To be sure, any experience pertains to a Self, and this Self is necessarily an individual Self which is present in any of its experiences and not just constituted through the interconnectedness of those experiences. But to which individual Self an experience may belong, whether it be our own or another's experience, is not necessarily and genuinely determined by the emerging experience itself. On the contrary, a stream of experiences flows along, indifferent in respect to the distinction between Mine and Thine, which contains intermingled and undifferentiated my own and Others' experiences. Within this stream eddies gradually constitute themselves which attract more and more of the stream's elements and are attributed by and by to different individuals. Scheler [27] goes even a step further. Basing his conclusions on the results of modern child-psychology, which reveal that the discovery of the child's own individuality is a relatively late one, he maintains that man lives from the beginning rather "in" other people's experiences than in his individual sphere.[28]

[26] *Sympathie*, pp. 281–287.
[27] *Sympathie*, p. 285.
[28] In his *Ethik*, p. 543ff., he distinguishes even within any "finite Person" two elements, namely, an "individual Person" (*Einzelperson*) and a "total Person" (*Ge-*

c) Scheler's perceptional theory of the alter ego

But how can inner experience remain undetermined? Is inner experience not *ipso facto* self-experience? And is it possible to catch the alter ego and its stream of thought by inner experience? Scheler thinks [29] that the traditional identification of inner experience (inner perception) and self-experience is ill-founded. On the one hand, I may perceive myself – as I may perceive anybody else – by outer perception, too. A glance in the mirror will prove this. On the other hand, I may seize by inner perception other people's experiences as I perceive my present and past experiences. Of course, the inner perception of other people's experiences requires a certain set of conditions, among them that my own body undergoes certain influences emanating from the Other's body. For instance, my ear has to be affected by the sound waves of words spoken by the Other if I am to understand what he says. But these conditions do not determine the act of my perceiving as such: they are just the consequence of the fact that to any act of possible inner perception belongs an act of a possible outer perception, which in turn refers to an outer object affecting the senses. Only the *specific* content of my perception of other people's thought is therefore conditioned by the processes which happen between my and the Other's body. This, however, has nothing to do with the principle that I may perceive other people's experience by inner perception. Exactly as our inner perception embraces not only our present state of mind but also the whole past of our stream of thought, it embraces also *as a possibility* the whole realm of minds as an undifferentiated stream of experiences. And not otherwise than we perceive our present self as emergent from the background of all our past life do we also become aware of our self as standing out against the background of a (more or less indistinctly felt) all-embracing consciousness which contains my experiences as well as the experiences of all the other minds. Both time-honored metaphysical theories on the relations between mind and body – the theory of the reciprocal influence of two substances as well as the

---

samtperson), the former being constituted by his individual acts, the latter by his social acts. Both are aspects of one concrete total of Person and World. This theory recalls W. James' interpretation of the Social Self (*Principles of Psychology*, Vol. I, p. 293ff.) and its development by G. H. Mead.

[29] *Sympathie*, pp. 284–293.

so-called psycho-physical parallelism – exclude even the possibility of perceiving the Other's experiences. Both confine man in a kind of psychical jail where he has to wait and see what the metaphysical nexus of causality might magically project on its walls. But both theories misinterpret the role of the body as the great selector and analyst for the contents of all our outer and inner perceptions.

This concept of the role of the body in the processes of experiencing other people's thought leads Scheler [30] to the conclusion that the only category of the Other's experiences which cannot be caught by direct perception is the Other's experiences of his body, its organs, and of the sensuous feelings attached to them; and it is exactly these bodily feelings which constitute the separation between man and fellow-man. Conversely, as far as man lives only in his bodily feelings he does not find any approach to the life of the alter ego. Only if he elevates himself as a Person above his pure vegetative life does he gain experience of the Other.

But what else shall we perceive of the Other than its body and its gestures? Scheler [31] thinks that we certainly perceive in the Other's smile his joy, in his tears his suffering, in his blushing his shame, in his joined hands his praying, in the sounds of his words his thought – all this without empathy and without any inference by analogy. We start reasoning only if we feel induced to distrust our perceptions of the Other's experiences – as, e.g., if we feel we have misunderstood him or if we discover that we have to deal with an insane individual. But even those "inferences" are based on perceptions of the Other which are rather complicated. In looking at him I not only perceive his eyes, but also that he looks at me, and even that he does so as if he would prevent my knowing that he looks at me. If we really ask what the object of our perception of the Other is, we have to answer that we perceive neither the Other's body nor his Soul or Self or Ego, but a totality, undivided into objects of outer and inner experiences. The phenomena arising out of this unity are psycho-physically indifferent. They might be analyzed as color qualities, form-units, units of movements, or changes in the position of his bodily organs. But by no worse reasoning might they be inter-

[30] *Sympathie*, p. 295ff.
[31] *Sympathie*, p. 301ff.

preted as "expressions" of the Other's thought which cannot be broken down into parts of expressive character, but show the structure of a unit (for instance, a physiognomical unit).

This, in outline, is Scheler's own theory of understanding the Other. He calls it [32] "Wahrnehmungstheorie des fremden Ich" (perceptional theory of the alter ego). Its interrelation with Scheler's anthropology and its concept of the Person is obvious: as far as man remains entangled in his bodily feelings he cannot find an approach to the Other's life. Nobody can seize the Other's bodily feelings. Only as a Person does he find access to the other Persons' streams of thought. But the Person is not the I. The Person and his acts can never be objectified. It is the I which always is objectifiable. And as no intentional reflections upon the Person and his acts are possible, other Person's acts can be seized only by co-performing, pre-performing and re-performing them.

But this reference to Scheler's other theories already reveals a certain inconsistency which is not fully explicable by the fact that Scheler partially worked out these theories later in his philosophical development without revising his perceptional theory of the alter ego in his published writings. The following observations try to explain the reasons for this fact.

IV. CRITICAL OBSERVATIONS

a) *Intersubjectivity as a transcendental problem*

One of Scheler's deepest insights is the distinction between the different levels on which the problem of the alter ego has to be dealt with. Unfortunately, it seems that in constructing his own theory, he forgets to adhere to the distinction discovered by himself. To the theories of inference and empathy he objects first of all that they pretend not only to be valid for the empirical psychological level but also to explain our belief in the existence of alter egos and hence to offer a solution of the transcendental constitutional problems here involved. According to his well-founded criticism, these theories fail in attaining at least the

[32] *Sympathie*, p. 253.

latter goal. That is why Scheler designs his own perceptional theory. But what is its contribution to the solution of the transcendental problem? The hypothesis that there exists a stream of experiences, indifferent in respect to the distinction between mine and thine, which contains our own experiences as well as the experiences of all other minds. Consequently, the sphere of the "We" is pregiven to the sphere of the I; the sphere of the Self emerges relatively late from the background of an all-embracing consciousness. However, he supports this theory not by analyses within the transcendental sphere, but by references to empirical facts taken from the psychology of children and primitives.

As a metaphysical hypothesis Scheler's theory is neither better nor worse than other metaphysical hypotheses on this topic. Incidentally, the idea of a suprapersonal consciousness has many ancestors in metaphysics. Most heterogeneous thinkers have formed such a basic assumption. Hegel, Bergson, the founders of "psychical research," certain German sociologists who try to combine Marx and Kant [33] are among them. But it is hard to see why Scheler's assumption should be of greater help for the solution of the problem of the alter ego than, for instance, Leibniz's monadology. For the problem of transcendental phenomenology as a science founded on accurate analysis of the transcendental field [34] Scheler's hypothesis does not offer the desired solution.

To be sure, it must be frankly admitted that the problem of the alter ego is the real crux of any transcendental philosophy. Husserl,[35] for example, clearly sees the eminent danger of solipsism as the consequence of the transcendental reduction. He tries courageously to "light up this dark corner, feared only by children in philosophy because the specter of solipsism haunts it"* and offers a solution of the alter ego problem in the fifth of his *Méditations Cartésiennes* [36] – unfortunately, without succeeding in eliminating the existent difficulties. Having performed the transcendental reduction and analyzed the constitutional problems of the consciousness built up by the activities of the

---

[33] For instance, Max Adler, *Kant und Marx*.
[34] Edmund Husserl, *Philosophie als strenge Wissenschaft*.
[35] Husserl, *Formale und transcendentale Logik*, p. 210.
[36] *Méditations Cartésiennes*, V, especially Secs. 44–45.
* See "Phenomenology and the Social Sciences," p. 124. (M.N.)

transcendental subjectivity, he singles out within the transcendental field what he calls "my own peculiar sphere" by eliminating all the constitutive activities which are immediately or mediately related to the subjectivity of Others. This is done by abstracting from all the "meanings" referring to Others and consequently by withdrawing from surrounding Nature its character of intersubjectivity. Nature is then no longer common to us all. What remains is strictly my private world in the most radical sense. Within this my own peculiar sphere, however, certain objects emerge which by "passive synthesis" called "Pairing" (*accouplement*) or "coupling" are interpreted as analogous to my own body and are therefore apperceived as other people's bodies.[37] Furthermore, I interpret in the same manner the Other's bodily movements as gestures and their concordant behavior as an expression of his psychical life. In this way, the Other is constituted within my monad as an Ego that is not "I myself" but a second, an *alter ego*.

There are several difficulties here. First, it is hard to understand how the abstraction from all meanings referring to Others could be performed in the required radical manner in order to isolate my own peculiar sphere, since it is exactly the non-reference to the Other which constitutes the line of demarcation of the sphere of what is peculiar to my own concrete transcendental ego. Hence, *some* meaning related to Others must necessarily subsist in the very criterion of non-reference to Others. Secondly, the processes of passive synthesis called by Husserl "Pairing" and sometimes even empathy seem to carry along some of the fallacies criticized so strikingly by Scheler. Thirdly, a special difficulty arises from the general conception of the transcendental reduction. This reduction has left nothing but the unified stream of my consciousness. This stream is, so to speak, closed; open only for my inner experience and my reflective glance – a monad without a window. On the other hand, this stream of consciousness refers

[37] This "pairing" is, according to Husserl, in no sense an *inference* by analogy. It is rather a form of passive synthesis, by which, as in the process of association, an actual experience refers back to another experience which does not attain actual presence, but is merely "appresented." Thus, both data, the presented and the appresented one which it indicates, are constituted as a pair in a unity of similarity. It is probable that the unpublished manuscripts of Husserl contain more extended descriptions of the process so characterized. [Cf. "Symbol, Reality, and Society," p. 294ff.] (M.N.)

intentionally to my life-world which, as "appearance," has been kept intact with its full content within the transcendental reduction, although I have suspended belief in its real existence. In the natural attitude I know that this life-world is not my private world but from the beginning an intersubjective one common to us all. Thus, I have also knowledge of Others and their inner life, and this knowledge cannot be given up for lost by performing the phenomenological reduction. The fact that Husserl feels induced to apply within the reduced sphere the device of abstracting from the meaning of "Others" proves this statement rather than refutes it. Of course, all the knowledge acquired within the life-world has to be restated after the reduction in terms of the transcendental sphere before the question how such knowledge might be constituted by the activities of my transcendental subjectivity can be raised. The re-statement of the concept of Others in terms of the transcendental sphere reveals that the Others also are monads without windows. Each monad is capable of performing the transcendental reduction and of keeping intact as I do, all the intentional life of its stream of consciousness which is directed to the same common life-world (although put in brackets). Hence, the Others, too, would have their transcendental subjectivity. There would exist, consequently, a cosmos of monads, and that indeed is the outcome of Husserl's fifth *Méditation Cartésienne*. But it must be earnestly asked whether the transcendental Ego in Husserl's concept is not essentially what Latin grammarians call a "singular tantum," that is, a term incapable of being put into the plural. Even more, it is in no way established whether the existence of Others is a problem of the transcendental sphere at all, i.e., whether the problem of intersubjectivity does exist between transcendental egos (Husserl) or Persons (Scheler); or whether intersubjectivity and therefore sociality does not rather belong exclusively to the mundane sphere of our life-world.

b) Intersubjectivity as a mundane problem

In view of such overwhelming difficulties, in the following considerations we will set aside the transcendental problems and turn to the mundane sphere of our life-world. Our first question is whether within this sphere Scheler's proposition, that the sphere of the "We" is given to each of us prior to the sphere of the I, proves true. If we retain the natural attitude as men among other men, the existence of Others is no more questionable to us than the existence of an outer world. We are simply born into a world of Others, and as long as we stick to the natural attitude we have no doubt that intelligent fellow-men do exist. Only if radical solipsists or behaviorists demand proof of this fact does it turn out that the existence of intelligent fellow-men is a "soft datum" and incapable of verification (Russell).[38] But in their natural attitude even those thinkers do not doubt this "soft datum." Otherwise they could not meet Others in congresses where it is reciprocally proved that the intelligence of the Other is a questionable fact. As long as human beings are not concocted like homunculi in retorts but are born and brought up by mothers, the sphere of the "We" will be naively presupposed. So far we may agree with Scheler that the sphere of the "We" is pregiven to the sphere of the I.

But there is a serious objection: obviously only in reference to "me," the individual who acts and thinks, do Others obtain the specific meaning which I designate with the pronoun "we"; and only in reference to "us," whose center I am, do Others stand out as "you"; and in reference to you, who refer back to me, third parties stand out as "they." [39] To be sure, in acting and thinking in daily life, I am not aware that all these objects of my acts and thoughts which I call Others and "we" and "you" and "they" are relative to my Self and that only my existence within this world as a Self makes this relationship and relativity possible. I just live along amidst other human beings which I group under the relations of we and you as I live amidst objects of the outer world which I group under the relations of left and right. In this naive attitude I am not aware of myself. I am, as Husserl says, living in my acts and thoughts, and in doing so, I am exclusively directed towards the objects of my acts and thoughts. Then my

---

[38] B. Russell, *Our Knowledge of the External World*, London, 1922, Lecture III, pp. 72ff.; also R. Carnap, *Scheinprobleme der Philosophie*, Berlin, 1928.

[39] This might be considered as a supplement to Koffka's well-known location of the Ego: according to Koffka the Ego is that which lies between right and left, between before and behind, between past and future. But this location could be given in social terms, too.

stream of thought seems to be an anonymous flux. "It thinks," not "I think," is the formula proposed by James,[40] and Dewey [41] even rejects the term "stream of thought" and wants to speak just of an "ongoing course of experienced things."

All this is valid, if I live naively in my acts directed towards their objects. But I may always, as Dewey says in such a pregnant way, "stop and think." [42] Still remaining in the natural attitude, and this means without performing the transcendental reduction, I may always turn in an act of reflection from the objects of my acts and thoughts to my acting and thinking. In doing so, I render my previous acts and thoughts objects of another, the reflective thought by which I grasp them. Then my "Self," which has been hidden as yet by the objects of my acts and thoughts, emerges. It does not merely enter the field of my consciousness in order to appear on its horizon or at its center; rather, it alone constitutes this field of consciousness. Consequently, all the performed acts, thoughts, feelings reveal themselves as originating in *my* previous acting, *my* thinking, *my* feeling. The whole stream of consciousness is through and through the stream of my personal life, and my Self is present in any of my experiences.[43]

[40] *Principles of Psychology*, Vol. I, p. 224.
[41] E.g., in his paper: "The Vanishing Subject in the Psychology of James," *Journal of Philosophy*, Vol. XXXVII, p. 22.
[42] *How We Think*, Boston, 1910; and *Human Nature and Conduct*, New York, 1922.
[43] A. Gurwitsch in discussing a theory of Jean-Paul Sartre has dealt with this problem in a paper entitled "A Non-Egological Conception of Consciousness," *Philosophy and Phenomenological Research*, Vol. I, 1941, pp. 325–338. The chief argument of Sartre-Gurwitsch against the egological theory maintained in the present paper runs as follows: as long as we do not adopt the attitude of reflection the ego does not appear. By reflection is meant the grasping of an act A by an act B in order to make the former the object of the latter. The act B, however, in its turn is not grasped by a third act and made its object. The grasping act itself is experienced with a non-reflective attitude exactly as in the case of an act bearing on some object other than a mental fact belonging to the same stream of consciousness. To be sure, by an act of reflection the grasped act may acquire a personal structure and a relation to the ego which it did not have before it was grasped. But the grasping act deals with the ego as an object only. It is the ego of the grasped and not of the grasping act. On the other hand, the grasped act has been experienced before it was grasped, and although reflection entails a modification of the acts grasped by it, this means only that all of the act's structure and components are disentangled and rendered explicit but that none of them is given rise to by reflection. Reflection is disclosing, not producing. How, then, may reflection give rise to a new object, namely, the ego, which did not appear before the act A was grasped? The answer offered is that the ego appears through rather than in the grasped act. It is the synthetic unity of certain psychic objects as dispositions, actions, and certain qualities such as virtues, faults, talents, etc. These psychic objects have their support in the ego, which may never be appre-

Scheler, in drafting his perceptional theory of the alter ego, does not distinguish between the naïve attitude of living in the acts and thoughts whose objects the others are and the attitude of reflection upon those acts and thoughts. Probably his supposition that intentional reflection upon acts is impossible prevents him from embarking on such analyses.[44] But if we introduce the distinction between the two characterized attitudes the following objections can be made against Scheler's theory:

1) The statement that we live rather in Others than in our own individual life becomes true only for the naïve attitude in which we direct our acts and thoughts towards other people as their object.

2) There is no such thing as an experience "given" to me that would not indicate which individual stream of consciousness it belongs to. As soon as I turn to the stream of experiences, and this means as soon as I adopt the reflective attitude, this stream is through and through the stream of *my* experiences.

3) The fact that some of my experiences refer to other people's thought cannot destroy their character as belonging to my and

hended directly but merely in a reflection as appearing behind the dispositions at the horizon. The ego exists neither *in* the acts of consciousness nor *behind* these acts. It stands *to* consciousness and *before* consciousness: it is the noematic correlate of reflective acts. Hence it follows that no evidence of the ego is apodictic. It is open to doubt.

It is not possible to enter here into a thorough discussion of Sartre-Gurwitsch's argument, which seems to me not at all conclusive. If they admit that the grasping act B deals with the ego at all (although with the ego of the grasped act as an object only and not with the ego of the grasping act), then this ego is grasped by act B as performing act A (or more precisely, as having performed act A, since reflection can only refer to the past). If a third act C grasps the act B and through it the act A, the ego with which act C deals is grasped as having performed act B as well as act A, and it is grasped as the same and identical ego notwithstanding all the modifications it undergoes in and by the flux of the stream of experiences in inner time. Furthermore, it is not clear why the ego in the reflection may never be apprehended directly but merely appear behind the dispositions at the horizon. Even the term "horizon" already refers to an egological consciousness to which alone "frame," "horizon," "disposition," "act," and other terms used by Sartre and Gurwitsch, become meaningful. The same becomes valid for the examples quoted by Gurwitsch in order to illustrate his thesis. If he says that there is no egological moment involved if I see my friend in adversity and help him and that what is given to me is just "my-friend-in-need-of-aid," it must be stated that any single element of the hyphenated term "my," "friend," "need," "aid," already refers to the ego for which alone each of them may exist.

[44] Scheler makes that supposition rather incidentally and without more conclusive proof in discussing the theory of the Person, *Ethik*, p. 388 and p. 49. His statement involves, of course, the abandonment of a basic principle of phenomenology, namely, that any kind of experience can be grasped by a reflective act. Cf. Husserl's *Ideen*, e.g., Secs. 45, 78.

only my individual sphere. In thinking the thoughts of another, I think them as "other people's thoughts thought by me." In suffering with other people I am from the beginning directed to "other people's suffering as reproduced by me." That I might be in doubt whether the origin of one of my thoughts lies within my stream of thought or someone else's makes that thought no less mine now; the Other's thought, together with my doubt, is now a content of my experience.

4) The results of modern studies in the psychology of children and primitives, purporting to show that children and primitive man only slowly become aware that they are individuals, cannot and will not be contested.[45] But these results just prove that the technique of reflection is acquired very late by the child and the primitive man and that they live *in* their acts, directed towards their object; they may then become also objects of their own acts.

Scheler's attitude towards the problem of self-consciousness is a very inconsistent one. On the one hand, he admits that any experience pertains to a Self and that this Self is an individual Self which is present in any of its experiences.[46] Furthermore, he admits the possibility that man can grasp his own Self by inner perception. It is, of course, the prerogative of the Person to grasp this Self which is always an object and never the subject of such a perceiving activity.[47] But as man is also a Person he has the faculty of being a Self, whereas the animal has consciousness without self-consciousness. It hears and sees without knowledge *that* it does so.[48] On the other hand, Scheler denies that any intentional reflections toward acts are possible, since the Person and his acts can never be objectified.[49]

The reasons for this strange conception are: a) the inconsistency in the notion of the Person. The origin of Scheler's idea of the Person must be looked for in his philosophy of religion and ethics. Only subsequently was the idea of the non-objectifiable Person of the deity and the free subject of ethical acts put into the

---

[45] Cf. the summary of reasons for the infant's lack of self-consciousness, G. W. Allport, *Personality*, p. 16ff.
[46] Cf. above, pp. 162–163, and *Sympathie*, p. 284f.
[47] Cf. above p. 154f and *Ethik*, p. 404.
[48] Cf. above pp. 153–154 and *Stellung des Menschen*, p. 51.
[49] Cf. above p. 154f and *Ethik*, pp. 388, 401.

service of a half-phenomenological theory of cognition and merged with the concept of the transcendental subjectivity. b) A second reason lies in the artificial distinction between mere "functions" belonging to the Self and "acts" belonging to the Person; c) and thirdly, the necessity of maintaining the concept of a supra-individual consciousness in order to build up several of his theories in the field of sociology and philosophy of history.[50]

But there is another reason which might have led the philosopher to deny the possibility of grasping acts by reflection. Although he nowhere refers to the following problem, it might have been at the root of his concept.

V. THE GENERAL THESIS OF THE ALTER EGO AND ITS TIME STRUCTURE

We have just characterized the two different attitudes: one of living in our acts, being directed towards the objects of our acts; and the other, the reflective attitude, by which we turn to our acts, grasping them by other acts. We have to glance now at the time-structure of both attitudes. In adopting the first we live in our present and are directed towards the immediate future which we anticipate by our expectations. These expectations – Husserl calls them, as the counterpart of retentions, "protentions" [51] – belong, of course, to our present acting. They are elements of our present, although referring to the immediate future. They pull the future, so to speak, continuously into our present. This present, of course, is not a mere mathematical point on the line of time. On the contrary, to borrow a term from James,[52] it is a specious present, and the great G. H. Mead has devoted one of his most excellent books [53] to the study of its structure. Living in our acts means living in our specious present or, as we may call it, in our vivid present. But as we stated above, in living thus we are not aware of our ego and of the stream of our thought. We cannot

---

[50] Especially in his "Probleme einer Soziologie des Wissens" in *Die Wissensformen und die Gesellschaft*. Cf. Howard Becker and Helmut O. Dahlke, "Max Scheler's Sociology of Knowledge," *Philosophy and Phenomenological Research*, Vol. II, 1942.
[51] E.g., *Ideen*, p. 77f.
[52] *Principles of Psychology*, Vol. I, p. 609.
[53] *The Philosophy of the Present*, Chicago, 1932.

approach the realm of our Self without an act of reflective turning. But what we grasp by the *reflective* act is never the present of our stream of thought and also not its specious present; it is always its past. Just now the grasped experience pertained to my present, but in grasping it I know it is not present any more. And, even if it continues, I am aware only by an afterthought that my reflective turning towards its starting phases has been simultaneous with its continuation. The whole present, therefore, and also the vivid present of our Self, is inaccessible for the reflective attitude. We can only turn to the stream of our thought as if it had stopped with the last grasped experience. In other words, self-consciousness can only be experienced *modo praeterito*, in the past tense.

Now let us go back again to the naïve attitude of daily life in which we live in our acts directed towards their objects. Among those objects which we experience in the vivid present are other people's behavior and thoughts. In listening to a lecturer, for instance, we seem to participate immediately in the development of his stream of thought. But – and this point is obviously a decisive one – our attitude in doing so is quite different from that we adopt in turning to our own stream of thought by reflection. We catch the Other's thought in its vivid presence and not *modo praeterito;* that is, we catch it as a "Now" and not as a "Just Now." The Other's speech and our listening are experienced as a vivid simultaneity.[54] Now he starts a new sentence, he attaches word to word; we do not know how the sentence will end, and before its end we are uncertain what it means. The next sentence joins the first, paragraph follows paragraph; now he has expressed a thought and passes to another, and the whole is a lecture among other lectures and so on. It depends on circumstances how far we want to follow the development of his thought. But as long as we do so, we participate in the immediate present of the Other's thought.

The fact that I can grasp the Other's stream of thought, and

[54] We use the term "simultaneity" in the same precise sense as Bergson in his book, *Durée et Simultanéité, A propos de la théorie d'Einstein*, Paris, 1923, p. 66: "I call simultaneous two fluxes which are for my consciousness either one or two indifferently according as my consciousness perceives them together as one single flow if it pleases to give them one undivided act of attention, or, on the other hand, distinguishes them in their full length if it prefers to divide its attention, but without cutting them in two."

this means the subjectivity of the alter ego in its vivid present,[55] whereas I can grasp my own self only by way of reflection on its past, leads us to a definition of the alter ego: the alter ego is that subjective stream of thought which can be experienced in its vivid present. In order to bring it into view we need not fictitiously stop the Other's stream of thought nor need we transform its "Nows" into "Just Nows." It is simultaneous with our own stream of consciousness, we share together the same vivid present – in a word: we grow old together. The alter ego, therefore, is that stream of consciousness whose activities I can seize in their present by my own simultaneous activities.

This experience of the Other's stream of consciousness in vivid simultaneity I propose to call the *general thesis of the alter ego's existence*. It implies that this stream of thought which is not mine shows the same fundamental structure as my own consciousness. This means that the Other is like me, capable of acting and thinking; that his stream of thought shows the same through and through connectedness as mine; that analogous to my own life of consciousness his shows the same time-structure, together with the specific experiences of retentions, reflections, protentions, anticipations, connected therewith and its phenomena of memory and attention, of kernel and horizon of the thought, and all the modifications thereof. It means, furthermore, that the Other can live, as I do, either in his acts and thoughts, directed towards their objects or turn to his own acting and thinking; that he can experience his own Self only *modo praeterito*, but that he may look at my stream of consciousness in a vivid present; that, consequently, he has the genuine experience of growing old with me as I know that I do with him.

As a potentiality each of us may go back into his past conscious life as far as recollection goes, whereas our knowledge of the Other remains limited to that span of his life and its manifestations observed by us. In this sense each of us knows more of himself than of the Other. But in a specific sense the contrary is true. In so far as each of us can experience the Other's thoughts and acts in the vivid present whereas either can grasp his own

---

[55] It is not necessary to refer to an example of social interrelationship bound to the medium of speech. Whoever has played a game of tennis, performed chamber music, or made love has caught the Other in his immediate vivid present.

only as a past by way of reflection, I know more of the Other and he knows more of me than either of us knows of his own stream of consciousness. This present, common to both of us, is the pure sphere of the "We." And if we accept this definition, we can agree with Scheler's tenet that the sphere of the "We" is pregiven to the sphere of the Self – although Scheler never had in mind the theory we have just outlined. We participate without an act of reflection in the vivid simultaneity of the "We," whereas the I appears only after the reflective turning. And our theory also converges (on another level, to be sure) with Scheler's statement that acts are not objectifiable and that the Other's acts can be experienced only by co-performing them. For we cannot grasp our own acting in its actual present; we can seize only those of our acts which are past; but we experience the Other's acts in their vivid performance.

All that we have described as the "general thesis of the alter ego" is a description of our experiences in the mundane sphere. It is a piece of "phenomenological psychology," as Husserl calls it in antithesis to "transcendental phenomenology." [56] But the results of an analysis of the mundane sphere, if true, cannot be impugned by any basic assumption (metaphysical or ontological) which might be made in order to explain our belief in the existence of Others. Whether or not the origin of the "We" refers to the transcendental sphere at all, our immediate and genuine experience of the alter ego within the mundane sphere cannot be gainsaid. In any event, however, the general thesis of the alter ego, as outlined above, is a sufficient frame of reference for the foundation of empirical psychology and the social sciences. For all our knowledge of the social world, even of its most anonymous and remote phenomena and of the most diverse types of social communities, is based upon the possibility of experiencing an alter ego in vivid presence.[57]

---

[56] Husserl, article on "Phenomenology," *Encyclopaedia Britannica*, 14th ed.
[57] This has been outlined in my book: *Der sinnhafte Aufbau der sozialen Welt*, Vienna, 1932, 2nd edition 1960.

VI. THE PERCEPTION OF THE ALTER EGO

But is this experience of the alter ego a perception and, if so, an inner perception, as Scheler claims? This seems to be rather a terminological question as Husserl has already pointed out.[58] If we do not understand the term perception in the restricted meaning of "adequate perception," that is, an originary, evidence-giving experience, but just as the more or less well-founded belief of apperceiving a thing as present, then we may call our experience of the Other's thought a perception. If I listen to somebody I perceive him as such; moreover, I perceive him talking, proving, doubting, wanting, etc. And within the same limits I can also say that I perceive his wrath, his suffering, etc. But is such a perception an *inner* one? If we accept Husserl's definition that inner perception takes place, if the objects of the perception pertain to the same stream of experiences as the perceptions themselves, then, of course, all our perceptions of the Other's thoughts are outer or transcendent perceptions. They are beliefs in the existence of their objects, which are neither better nor worse founded than our belief in the existence of all the other objects in the outer world. But if we accept Scheler's definition that inner experience refers to all the objects of psychical or mental life, then our experiences of other people's thought might be by no worse a reason subsumed under the term of inner perceptions. It seems that we have in a similar way as Scheler to distinguish between our experience of the *existence* of Others, that is, the general thesis of the alter ego, and our knowledge of or about the Others' specific *thoughts*. The first, according to our theory, is really an inner experience in the radical meaning of Husserl, as our Self participates likewise in the vivid simultaneity of the "We" which belongs, therefore, to our stream of consciousness. To this extent at least the "We" is always and from the beginning connected with the Self. But our experience of other peoples' *thoughts* is a transcendent one, and our belief in the existence of those thoughts, therefore, a principally dubitable belief.

This, of course, does not mean, that our knowledge of the Other's existence, or even of his thoughts, refers immediately to

[58] *Logische Untersuchungen*, Vol. II, p. 34f.

the Other's psycho-physical existence and especially to the perceiving of his body. Scheler is certainly right if he underlines again and again that the mere existence of a frame of reference referring to the Other, of a system of interpretable signs or symbols, for instance, is sufficient for the belief in the existence of other persons. We have to add that also any production and any tool, any work of art and any manufactured thing refers to its producer. It is the frozen result of human activities and by reproducing the acts which led to its existence, we always may win access to other people's stream of thought without referring necessarily to other people's bodies. We understand a symphony without thinking of the composer's writing hand. Nevertheless, the function of the body is most important for the knowledge of the Other's thought.

VII. THE PROBLEM OF PERSPECTIVES RELATED TO INTERSUBJECTIVITY

Scheler has described many features of this function. The Other's body is to him first of all a field of expression. But there is nothing in the world which would not have, under certain conditions, a certain expressive value or, more correctly, to which we could not attribute such a value. Any great painter's still-life or landscape is an example. For, to be a "field of expression" is not a quality which would inhere in the things. The world is given to us as an object of possible interpretation. We might interpret it by attributing to it our own extroverted feelings. Expression is, then, our own feelings projected into an object of the outer world.[59]

The chief function of the body, however, for the problem of understanding the alter ego is, according to Scheler, its role as the great selector and analyst of the contents of our inner and outer experiences. We know from other writings of Scheler that this thought converges with some well known theories of Bergson and James and that it contains in a nutshell the pragmatic theory of cognition afterwards developed by him.[60] It was not possible to

[59] This, of course, is just *one* meaning of the most ambiguous term "expression." Cf. G. W. Allport, *Personality*, p. 464ff.
[60] "Erkenntnis und Arbeit" in *Die Wissensformen und die Gesellschaft*.

embark within the frame of the present discussion upon a presentation and criticism of this interesting theory. But another function of the body seems to be of the greatest importance for the interpretation of the common life-world and the problem of the alter ego. It was described by Husserl in his *Méditations Cartésiennes* [61] and as it leads to a new grouping of the problems connected with the alter ego it may find its place here as a kind of conclusion. My own body is for me the center of orientation in the spatio-temporal order of the world. It alone is given to me as the center of the "Here," whereas the Other's body is given to me as being "There." This "There" is modifiable by my own kinesthetic movements. The reason for the fact that my own body can be interpreted like any other movable solid in space lies in my faculty of transforming any "There" into a "Here" if I change my position, e.g., by walking around. This implies that I may perceive from "There" the same things as from "Here" but from an angle which attaches to my being There. The Other, therefore, cannot be identical with my self, as his body stays for him in the center of his absolute "Here," whereas his "Here" remains for me always a "There." I attribute to him the same perspectives which I should have if I were not "Here," but "There," and vice versa. The objects of the outer world perceived by both of us are the same, but they appear to me in the perspective "seen from Here" and to him in the perspective "seen from There"; this means as they would appear to me if I transformed my present "There" by my kinesthetic movements into a new "Here."

This, it seems, Leibniz also had in view when he says that any monad mirrors the whole universe but under another perspective. And in fact, the principle of perspectives developed by Husserl for the problem of space has to be applied to the whole structural field of our interconnected experiences. What was pointed out for the perspectives of the "Here" and "There" has to be worked out (although not immediately referring to the body) in a further development of the general thesis of the alter ego by analyses of the time-bound perspectives of "Now" and "Then," the social perspectives of "We" and "They" and the personal perspectives of familiarity and strangeness. Scheler's theory of the alter ego is

[61] L.c., Sec. 53f.

just a first step into this enormous field open to phenomenological psychology. And only a careful investigation of all the implications of the general thesis of the alter ego will bring us nearer to the solution of the enigma of how man can understand his fellow-man. All empirical psychology and all social sciences, however, take such a solution for granted.

SARTRE'S THEORY OF THE ALTER EGO [1]

Even those students of Sartre's philosophical work [2] who with the present writer consider his basic position untenable have to acknowledge his endeavors to find a new approach to the problem of intersubjectivity. The questions of the Other's existence and its multifarious manifestations are carefully investigated in subtle analyses under the most various aspects.[3] To discuss some of them is the purpose of the following study. It is undertaken in the belief that Sartre's pertinent inquiry represents the most valuable part of his thought and that it can be discussed in relative independence of the fundamental issue of existentialism.

I. SARTRE'S CRITICISM OF THE REALISTIC AND THE IDEALISTIC APPROACH TO THE PROBLEM OF INTERSUBJECTIVITY [4]

Sartre rejects both the realistic and the idealistic attempt to prove by a process of cognition the human existence of the Other as a certainty. The realist posits the outer world as real and within it the Other's body as given. However, he will never

---

[1] Jean-Paul Sartre, *L'Être et le Néant*, Paris, 1943.
[2] See for a condensed presentation of Sartre's system, Herbert Marcuse, "Existentialism: Remarks on Jean-Paul Sartre's *L'Être et le Néant*," *Philosophy and Phenomenological Research*, Vol. VIII, 1948, pp. 309-326. The best critical discussion of Sartre's philosophical position can be found in Jean Wahl's "Essai sur le Néant d'un problème," *Deucalion, Cahiers de Philosophie*, No. 1, Paris, 1946, pp. 40-72, and the following papers by Alphonse De Waelhens: "Heidegger et Sartre," *Deucalion*, No. 1, pp. 15-40; "Zijn en Niet-zijn, Over de philosophie van Jean-Paul Sartre," *Tijdschrift voor Philosophie*, 71 Jaargang, 1945, pp. 35-116; "J.-P. Sartre, *L'Être et le Néant*," *Erasmus*, Vol. I, Amsterdam, pp. 522-539.
[3] Chiefly in the third part of *L'Être et le Néant*, pp. 275-507.
[4] *Ibid.*, pp. 275-288.

succeed in proving that this given body is more than *a* body, that it is the body of a fellow-man, unless he has silently presupposed the existence of the Other's mind as a certainty and thus taken refuge in the idealistic thesis. Whether he takes the position of the radical behaviorist, affirming the existence of the Other as certain (although admitting that our knowledge of it is merely probable) or whether he believes that our knowledge of the Other's mind is revealed by a process of reasoning by analogy or by empathy or sympathy does not make much difference. It is still possible that the Other is nothing but his body, and in any case the human existence of the Other remains merely conjectural.

To the idealist the Other is just my presentation, a phenomenon referring to other phenomena. Yet the group of phenomena relating to the Other's existence is from the outset distinguished by their appearing in organized forms such as gestures, actions, expressions, conduct. These organized forms necessarily refer to an organizing unity placed beyond my experience and principally inaccessible to me. It is the basic thesis of idealism that the subject's organizing all its impressions into a system is a condition of all possible experience. How is this thesis compatible with the assumption that the Other as a synthetic unity of *his* experiences organizes my experiences of him? Do we perhaps have to assume a causal relationship between Paul's rage and the redness of Paul's face as experienced by me? This is not possible. The notion of causality – at least in Kant's system – refers necessarily to a relationship between phenomena belonging to one and the same individual consciousness. In fact, Kant's causality is nothing else than the unification of the moments of my inner time under the form of irreversibility. How can it be assumed that causality unifies the time of my consciousness with that of another? What temporal relationship should be established between the Other's decision to express himself (an event belonging to his consciousness) and the expression itself (which is a phenomenon belonging to my experience)? Neither by simultaneity nor by succession can an instant of my inner time be conceived as being connected with an instant of the inner time of the Other's consciousness unless on the assumption of a mysterious pre-established harmony. And even on such an assumption the two fluxes would still remain unconnected, since for either consciousness the unifying synthesis of moments into a flux originates in an act of the subject.

But the idealist may argue that the notion of "the Other" has no constitutive function at all, that it is merely a regulative concept, a hypothesis *a priori* in order to justify the apparent unity of our experiences relating to it. This position is not tenable either. First, the very perception of the Other as a mere object would still refer to a coherent system of presentations which is not mine since it does not originate within my field of consciousness. Moreover, there is a set of phenomena which occur only by reason of the Other's existence, that is, by reason of a system of significations and experiences radically different from mine. In truth, it is not the Other who constitutes my experience of him as a concrete and knowable object; it is rather a certain type of my experiences which induces me to constitute the Other as another subject. Through my experiences of the Other I am continually looking at the Other's sentiments and volitions, his thoughts and his character. The Other is not only he whom I see, but also he who sees me. I look at him and at his set of experiences, within which I have my place as an object among other objects. By trying to determine the concrete nature of the system of the Other's experiences and my place therein, I necessarily have to transcend the field of my own experiences and to destroy the unity of my consciousness. Consequently, the notion of "the Other" can never be interpreted as a merely regulative idea.

The Other, an object of my thought, is by this very thought posited as a subject: this is the dilemma of idealism. Its solution can be attempted either by abandoning entirely the notion of the Other, proving that it is unnecessary for the constitution of my experience, or by positing a real and extra-empirical communication between my and the Other's consciousness. The first attempt leads to solipsism; the second to Sartre's own existentialistic interpretation.

A third attempt, the assumption of a plurality of systems of experiences not interrelated and quite exterior to one another, shares a hidden presupposition with the realistic position. This presupposition is rooted in the fact that, empirically, the Other appears to me at the occasion of my perceiving his body and that this body is spatially separated from my own body. The realist, trying to seize the Other through the medium of his body, believes himself to be separated from the Other in the same way as objects of the outer world are separated from one another. The idealist, although reducing my and the Other's body to mere systems of presentations, assumes, nevertheless, a spatial distance between the two streams of consciousness, one being exterior to the other. Thus, only a third observer, external to myself and the Other could ascertain the truth of my and the Other's coexistence. Clearly, this assumption would lead to an infinite regress, which only a theological notion of God and the Creation of the world such as is offered by Leibniz may try to overcome.

II. SARTRE'S CRITICISM OF HUSSERL, HEGEL, AND HEIDEGGER

Husserl, Hegel, and Heidegger have tried to solve the problem without resorting either to solipsism or to the assumption of a personal God. None of them has succeeded.[5]

a) Husserl *

Husserl's main argument – as Sartre sees it – consists in the thesis that the reference to the Other is a necessary condition for the existence of the world. The universe, as it reveals itself to consciousness, is from the outset inter-monadic. If, says Sartre, I consider in solitude or in the company of others this table or this tree, the Other is always present in the form of a layer of constitutive significations, which belong to the object considered as such. And since my psycho-physical ego is also part of this world, the same world which has to be bracketed in performing the phenomenological reduction, the general meaning of "the Other" appears to be a necessary prerequisite of the constitution of my empirical ego. Thus, if I doubted the existence of my friend Peter (or of the empirical egos of Others in general) I

---

[5] *L'Être et le Néant*, pp. 288–291; Sartre refers to Husserl's *Formale und transzendentale Logik* and the *Méditations Cartésiennes*; a presentation of Husserl's theory of the alter ego will be found in Section V of the present paper.

* *L'Être et le Néant*, pp. 288 ff. (M.N.)

should have to doubt also the existence of my own empirical ego, which has no privileged position over the empirical egos of my fellow-men. It is not my empirical ego, but my transcendental subjectivity (which is entirely different from the former), that has such a privileged position. Conversely, the general meaning of "the Other" does not refer to the empirical fellow-man given to my experience, but to the transcendental subjectivity to which he refers. But, then, the very problem to be investigated is not that of the parallelism prevailing between empirical egos (which never has been seriously doubted by anybody), but that of the interrelationship existing between transcendental subjects which are beyond my experience. If the phenomenologist answers that the transcendental subjectivity refers from the outset to other subjects as a condition for the *constitution* of the noematic totality, it is easy to answer that it refers to them merely as *meanings* and not as Beings really existing beyond the world. Such a reference would have a merely hypothetical character and the function of a unificatory concept; such a concept would, by necessity, be valid only for and within the world, whereas the "Other" (as transcendental subjectivity) remains outside the world. Husserl, so Sartre believes, can never arrive at an understanding of the possible meaning of the extramundane being of the Other. He has established knowledge as the yardstick for Being by defining Being as the indication of an infinite series of operations to be effectuated. This position is exactly the opposite of Sartre's. But even if one admits that knowledge is the measure of Being, then the being of the Other has to be defined by the knowledge he has of himself and not by that which I have of him. The Other, as he knows himself, escapes my knowledge completely unless I make the impossible presupposition that the Other is identical with me. Husserl, so Sartre states, has understood this difficulty by defining the Other, as he reveals himself to our concrete experience, as an *absence*. Yet – at least within the frame of Husserl's philosophy – we cannot have a fulfilled intuition of an absence. Thus, the Other is merely the object of empty intentionalities, the empty noema which corresponds to my intentionalities directed toward him as he appears concretely within my experience; and this experience is unified and constituted with the help of a transcendental concept.

Husserl, as Sartre sums up his criticism, has not succeeded in overcoming the basic dilemma of the idealistic position. He answers the solipsist that the existence of the Other is certain to the same extent as the existence of the world (including my psycho-physical existence within it). But the solipsist does not say anything else: it is as certain, but not more certain. And, the solipsist would add, the existence of both of them will depend upon my experience.

b) Hegel [6]

Thus, Husserl's attempt to overcome the solipsistic argument proves to be a failure, and Sartre thinks that even as a construction it is inferior to Hegel's theory developed in his *Phenomenology of Mind*. To Hegel (as opposed to Husserl) the notion of the Other is not merely indispensable for the constitution of the world and my empirical ego, but also for the very existence of my consciousness as self-consciousness. As self-consciousness the ego seizes itself as itself. But the resulting equation ' I am I" has to be made explicit; the I has to posit itself as an object in order to attain the next stage of development, that of the consciousness of the general Self, which recognizes itself in self-consciousness and in that of the Ego. The concept of the Other is, thus, the mediator; the Other appears at the same time as my Self since self-consciousness is identical with itself by *excluding* the Other. Such exclusion takes a double form: by the very fact of being myself, I exclude the Other; by the very fact of being himself, the Other, whom I exclude, excludes me. Hegel, unlike Husserl, avoids establishing a one-way relationship between the *ego cogito* and the Other, who has to be constituted by such cogitations. He assumes from the outset a reciprocal relationship, which he defines as the "seizure of the Self of one in the Self of the Other." The existence of the Other is the condition for the seizure of the Self by itself, and the latter, in turn, the condition for any *cogito*.

This is indeed an ingenious attempt to overcome the solipsistic argument: my self-consciousness depends upon the reality of the Other, and the Other's self-consciousness upon my own reality. Nevertheless it remains unsatisfactory to Sartre. It sticks to the

[6] *L'Être et le Néant*, pp. 291–300.

basic idealistic position by trying to solve the underlying ontological problems in terms of cognition. But the consciousness characterized by the proposition "I am I" is by definition an entirely empty notion and must not be identified with the concrete consciousness I have of the world, myself, and the Other.

Hegel is a victim of his *epistemological optimism*, which consists in the assumption that an accord can be established between my and the Other's consciousness, between the recognition of myself by the Other and the recognition of the Other by myself. Yet, what I am for the Other, what he is for me, what I am for myself, and what he is for himself are not commensurable. I experience my self and he experiences his as a subject, but both of us experience the Other's self as an object. How could I recognize myself in the Other if the Other is first of all an object to me? How can I seize the Other, as he really is for himself, namely as a subject? Sartre calls this situation the ontological separation of the one and the Other.

Moreover, Hegel is the victim of his *ontological optimism*, which consists in the assumption that the relationship between consciousnesses can be studied as such, without taking one particular concrete consciousness as the starting point and system of reference. In truth, Hegel does not investigate the relationship of his own concrete consciousness with that of the Other; he is not concerned with the rapport between Ego and Alter-Ego; he merely studies the mutual rapports prevailing between the consciousness of Others, all of them being to him – Hegel – just objects. From such a position the "scandal of the plurality of consciousnesses" can at best be described, but not surmounted; there is no hope of refuting with its help the solipsistic argument.

c) *Heidegger* [7]

Heidegger tries to overcome the difficulty by establishing between the I and the Other a relationship of being. According to him, human reality is "being-in-the-world" and as such from the outset "being-with" (*Mitsein*), namely "being-with-Others."

---

[7] *Ibid.*, pp. 301–307; cf. Martin Heidegger, *Sein und Zeit*, Halle, 1929, especially pp. 114–130, 231–300; also Waelhens, "Heidegger et S$_a$rtre," *loc. cit.*

This "being-with" is an essential structure of my own being, and the Other, therefore, is not a particular existence, which I encounter within the world, but the "ek-centric" term which contributes to my own existence. My being is not a "being-for" but a "being-with" the Other. In the commonplace situation of everyday life, in the state of inauthenticity (*Uneigentlichkeit*), I realize my being with Others not as a relationship of mutual knowledge but as a dullish existence in the form of anonymity and the Other as "anyone" (*Man*). In the inauthentic state I am not a self, for neither I nor the Other is determined; as interchangeable terms, I and he partake in the social everyday life as "anyone." Only by following the "call of conscience," by determining myself to my own death as the possibility of my innermost existence, do I attain my individual selfhood, my authentic state. In becoming authentic myself, I transform also the hitherto anonymous Other into a state of authenticity.

Yet, Sartre asks, does Heidegger's concept of being with the Others solve the problem indeed? Is it not this very coexistence and its type which has to be investigated? Can the concept of an undistinguished anonymity explain the establishment of a rapport between two *concrete* beings, my concrete "being-with" Peter or Anny? If, as Heidegger thinks, the ontological relationship between me and the Other has an aprioristic character, is this *a priori* not merely valid within the limits of my experience and does my concrete being with the Other not transcend my experience?

The "being-with," conceived as a structure of my being, isolates me in the same manner as the solipsistic argument. Designed to overcome the idealistic fallacy, it still preserves the concrete human reality as a constitutive element of the self.

III. SARTRE'S OWN THEORY OF THE OTHER'S EXISTENCE

After having criticized Husserl's, Hegel's, and Heidegger's theories, Sartre formulates the following criteria for a valid theory of the Other's existence.[8] 1. Such a theory need not *prove*

---

[8] *L'Être et le Néant*, pp. 307–310.

the Other's existence, the affirmation of which is rooted in a "pre-ontological" understanding. 2. The Cartesian *cogito* is the only possible point of departure in order to find (not reasons for my belief in the Other's existence, but) the Other himself as being-not-me. 3. The Other does not have to be grasped as an object of our cogitations, but in his existence "for us" as affecting our actual concrete being. 4. The Other has to be conceived as being "not me," but this negation is not an external spatial one; it is an internal negation, defined by Sartre as a synthetic and active connection between two terms, either of which constitutes itself by negating the other. Sartre hopes that his own theory of the Other's existence will comply with these requirements.

In the reality of everyday life I am surrounded by objects, some of which, so I affirm, are fellow-men. In order to clarify the meaning of such an affirmation, Sartre [9] analyzes the entrance of another man into my perceptional field. Before the Other appeared the objects within my perceptional field seemed to be grouped around myself as the center in certain objective measurable distances; they had properties relating to my subjectivity, although believed by me to be objective ones. With the appearance of a fellow-man, this apparent unity of my universe breaks asunder. The objects are no longer defined exclusively by measurable distances from my own position, but also from his; their properties, to be objective, have to persist from his as well as from my point of view; briefly, I perceive the objects as not only perceived by me, but as perceived also by him, the Other. To be sure, the Other at this level is still an object among other objects; but he is distinguished from all the other objects by the fact that he is the object which perceives what I perceive and which, at least as a possibility, perceives me as being an object. And here the turning-point has been attained: How can I possibly be the object for an object, I, who can never be an object for myself? Can my objectivity originate in the objectivity of the world, since I am precisely he by whose existence there is an objective world at all? In my very possibility of being an object for the Other, the Other reveals himself as a subject. My seeing an object as "being probably a man" refers to my probably being seen by him, and

[9] *Ibid.*, pp. 310ff.

this rapport is taken by Sartre as an irreducible fact. The Other is he who looks at me.

If another looks at me, a basic change occurs in my way of being. I become "self-conscious" in both meanings of this word, namely, aware of myself as being an object for another, placed in a situation not defined by me, and ashamed or proud of this fact. I am no longer myself but by reference to the Other. He, by merely looking at me, becomes the limit of my freedom. Formerly, the world was open to my possibilities; now it is he, the Other, who defines me and my situation within the world from his point of view, thus transforming my relations to objects into factors of *his* possibilities. The world and my existence within it is no longer "world for me"; it has become "world for the Other." My own possibilities are turned into probabilities beyond my control. I am no longer the master of the situation, or at least the situation has gained a dimension which escapes me. I have become a utensil with which and upon which the Other may act. I realize this experience not by way of cognition, but by a sentiment of uneasiness or discomfort, which, according to Sartre, is one of the outstanding features of the human condition.

Being looked at by the Other [10] confers upon me a new dimension of space: by becoming an object for the Other I discover myself to be at a distance from the Other, a distance, however, which is not of my, but of his making. And, on the other hand, the Other's looking at me reveals to me a new experience of time, namely, simultaneity, defined by Sartre (strangely enough) as the time relationship between two beings not connected by any other relationship.[11] The same object is co-present with me to Paul, as it is co-present with Paul to me; and my present becomes presence to the Other, and vice versa.

Any concrete experience of being looked at reveals to me in the way of a genuine *cogito* that I am existing for all living fellow-men. The "Other" may take the structure of an individual, a type, a collectivity, an anonymous audience or public, or (we may add) what G. H. Mead calls the "Generalized Other." [12] The emergent Me-object may take various social roles: in my relationship with

---
[10] It is very hard to find an adequate English term for Sartre's concept *"le regard d'autrui."*
[11] *L'Être et le Néant*, p. 325.
[12] *Mind, Self, and Society*, pp. 152–163.

Asiatic people I discover myself as a European, with young people as an old man, with workmen as a bourgeois, etc. Thus my being for myself is from the outset also being-for-the-Other.

But all this is merely half the story. Having once constituted the Other as a subjectivity, I can objectify him again. If, for instance, my reaction to the glance of the Other is shame, fear, or pride, these reactions contain references to myself as a subject which may induce me to constitute the Other as an object. I discover him, then, as being within the world, as placed in a certain situation defined by me as endowed with certain properties and characteristics, briefly as an object among other objects, as a utensil among all my other utensils. Moreover, by defining the objectified Other by his relations to other objects, I have defined him in his totality; he is known to me not merely as his body, but in his full being within such and such a situation. My unknown neighbor in the subway is defined by my knowing him as being in New York, travelling in such and such a direction, reading this newspaper. All this is known to me not by the intermediary of signs (which would refer to the Other's subjectivity); the objectified Other *is* all these relations; he is determined by the total organization of *my* world, of which he is an autonomous, but intra-mundane center. This distinguishes the Other as an object from the Other as a subject. Only the former can be known to me as a co-extensive totality within the world. The latter can never be an object of any kind of knowledge, and the objects of the world do not refer to him; he transcends the world and escapes seizure.

By objectifying the Other, I, the previously objectified Me, regain my subjectivity and self. I become again a self, my self; nevertheless, the Other is merely an object to me to the extent to which I am an object to him. The type of the Other's objectification depends, therefore, upon my and his situation and upon the factual circumstance whether he can see me and I him. It refers, therefore, to the relationship between my and the Other's body.

Sartre's extended investigations of this problem constitute perhaps the most interesting part of his system and would deserve a separate study. Space permits merely a few indications.

IV. SARTRE'S THEORY OF THE BODY [13]

Sartre distinguishes three "ontological dimensions" of my own body: 1) my body in its factual being, in its being-in-itself; I exist as my body; 2) my body in its being-for-the-Other, as used and known by the Other; 3) my experience of myself as being known to the Other by reason of my body. In order to analyze these dimensions, it would be useless to turn to physiology. Physiological knowledge never refers to my experience of my own body, but necessarily always to experiences of the bodies of other people.

1) My own body in its factual being [14] is experienced by me first of all as the carrier of my "five senses," hence as the center of orientation and reference of my perceptional field. I do not "see" this center, however, I *am* this center. Next I experience my body as the instrument of my actions, capable of handling other instruments. But, again, I do not "handle" my hand which uses the hammer; I *am* my hand. As center of the perceptional field my body determines my point of view; as center of my actions it determines the starting point of my future possibilities and choices. As both, my body is experienced not merely as my physiological structure, but as everything determining my point of view and point of departure: my race, my nationality, my birth, my past. Thus, my body refers to consciousness; it *is* consciousness, although not reflective, but merely affective consciousness, namely the pure non-positing seizure of a contingency, the pure apprehension of the self as factual existence. It is this apprehension of my body which Sartre, for reasons important from another point of view than ours for his existential doctrine (and, by the way, very arbitrarily), identifies with the feeling of nausea.

2) Curiously enough, Sartre does not, as he has promised, analyze the meaning of my body for the Other, but instead the meaning the Other's body has for me,[15] stating expressly [16] that

---

[13] *L'Être et le Néant*, pp. 356-428; Sartre's statements as presented in this section should be compared with Husserl's theories condensed in the following section V.

[14] *L'Être et le Néant*, pp. 368-404.

[15] *Ibid.*, pp. 404-418.

[16] "*Il revient au même d'étudier la façon dont mon corps apparaît à autrui ou celle dont le corps d'autrui m'apparaît*" (p. 405).

both problems are identical. We have seen that, according to Sartre, I seize the Other originally as a subject for which I am an object and objectify him in a second move, thus regaining my own subjectivity. Consequently, the Other exists for me *first*, and I seize him only *thereafter* in his body. Unlike my own, his body has the character of a secondary structure. As such it is to me an instrument among all the other instruments to be used by me, a utensil like all the other objects of my outer world. My own body is privileged among all other instruments by my *being* this instrument. The Other's body is privileged among all other objects because it functions as their possible center of reference and because all these other objects may be used by him as his instruments. Moreover, the Other's body reveals itself to me as the sum total of his sense organs, that is, the factual contingency of the Other's existence, its pure being-in-itself. In an empty way I have knowledge of the fact that the (objectified) Other has knowledge of the world (including myself) but I have no knowledge – not even an empty one – of his acts of knowing, neither of what he knows nor of how he knows it. The contingency consists in the fact that the Other's body is "here," although it could be elsewhere. Yet its "being-here" translates itself into its "being-as-such-and-such," that is, pertaining to this race, class, environment, etc. The Other's body is thus given to me from the outset as a body within a situation, and for this very reason I cannot separate the Other's body from the Other's actions. (Only the corpse is no longer within a situation, that is, within the synthetic unity of life). Peter's body is not first a hand which might afterwards reach for a glass. Peter's-reaching-for-a-glass occurs as a significant unit within spatial and temporal limits defined by the situation. Spatially, Peter's gesture remains significant to me even if the glass is hidden from my view; temporally, I seize this gesture, as it is revealed to me in the present act, in terms of the future state of affairs which this act tends to bring about. Thus, Peter's body is the totality of its significant relations to the world and not distinguished from Peter's being-for-me.

Sartre believes that this theory avoids the reference of the Other's body to a "mysterious psyche." The significations just described *are* this psyche itself. They do not refer to something "beyond the body." They refer merely to the world and to other significations. Expressive gestures in particular, do not indicate a hidden affect lived through by any psyche. The frowning brows, the clenched fists, etc., do not *indicate* the Other's wrath; they *are* his wrath.[17] The "psychical object," therefore, is entirely given in the perception of the bodily gestures and their reference to other gestures. This seems to be the behavioristic position, but the behaviorists have not understood their own arguments. They believed that there is only one type of perception and have overlooked the fact that to each type of reality there corresponds a particular type of perception. The type peculiar to the expressive ways of conduct of the Other is to perceive them as understandable; their meaning is an element of their being as color is an element of the being of paper. The Other's body in its ongoing action is given to me in immediacy as transcending its present by each particular signification towards an end belonging to its future.

3) The third dimension [18] of my experience of my own body originates in the shock of meeting the Other, who looks at me. My body no longer exclusively determines my point of view: the Other takes a view of it and even one which I myself am unable to take. My sense organs, incapable of seizing themselves, are now experienced as being seized by the Other. My body, hitherto the instrument which I *am* and which cannot be used by any other instrument, is now experienced as being for the Other an instrument among all *his* other instruments. Simultaneously, my body escapes me, becomes alienated from me; my body-for-me becomes body-for-the-Other. It appears that the Other accomplishes with respect to me a function which I can never perform: he sees me as I am. Finally, I come to accept looking at myself with the Other's eyes. I stop experiencing *being* my body and start to have cognizance of it.

Language teaches me the structure which my body has for the Other, and the conceptual framework based upon language is

---

[17] Sartre does not refer here to Max Scheler's similar perceptional theory of the alter ego, developed in his *Phänomenologie der Sympathiegefühle*, first edition 1913, second re-written edition under the title *Wesen und Formen der Sympathie*, 1923; see "Scheler's Theory of Intersubjectivity and the General Thesis of the Alter Ego".

[18] *L'Être et le Néant*, pp. 418–428.

entirely derived from my social intercourse with the Other. Thus a system of verbal correspondences emerges which designate first of all my body as it appears to the Other, but which I use to determine how my body appears to me. It is on this level that the assimilation of the Other's body with my own body by way of analogy takes place: my body for the Other is what the Other's body is for me.[19] This, however, presupposes that I have met the Other first in his objectifying subjectivity and then as object, and also that I have experienced my own body as an object. Analogy or similarity can never originally constitute the object-body of the Other and the objectivity of my own body. On the contrary, these two objectivities have to be presupposed before the principle of analogy or similarity can come into play. I must first by an act of reflective thought constitute my body as an object of my cognizance. The conceptual notion of my body, thus constituted, will however always and necessarily be in terms of the conceptual cognition that the Other has of my body. In other words, the notion I have of my own body will never be reconcilable with the factual being of my body in its being-in-itself. The constituted concept of my body refers in an empty way to its perpetual alienation. Yet I do not live this alienation; I just constitute it, thus transcending the given factual existence towards a quasi-object which is no longer given to me but merely of a significative character.

V. ON HUSSERL'S THEORY OF THE OTHER

A critical investigation of Sartre's contribution to the alter ego problem outlined very roughly in the preceding pages would have to start with his sometimes ingenious analysis of the solipsistic argument in modern philosophy. We restrict ourselves to his criticism of Husserl's theory, which seems to be important enough to provoke a serious discussion among phenomenologists.

Sartre is right in stating that in terms of Husserl's philosophy the problem of the Other could be explained only as a relationship

---

[19] This and the following sentences seem to be very important. Nevertheless Sartre has anticipated this outcome of his analysis of the third ontological dimension when starting his analysis of the second one. See footnote 16 above.

between transcendental subjects. Such an explanation cannot be found in Husserl's published writings. Doubtless, Husserl speaks frequently of an intermonadic universe and thus obviously assumes a plurality of transcendental egos. However, it is one of the most difficult problems of phenomenology – perhaps an insoluble one – to reconcile the notion of *the* transcendental ego as the source of the constitution of the world with the idea of a plurality of coexistent transcendental subjects.[20] Our main source, Husserl's fifth *Cartesian Meditation*,[21] does not show how the Other is constituted as a transcendental subjectivity, but merely how he is constituted as a mundane psycho-physical unity. A very condensed account of Husserl's fifth *Meditation* might be found useful in this connection. It will show that Sartre's analyses of my body are more indebted to Husserl's teachings and less original than one may suppose.

Husserl's main argument runs as follows: Having performed the phenomenological reduction, I may, in a second step, eliminate from the reduced sphere all "strange" elements, that is, all the "meanings" referring to the Other. In doing so, I gain my "own reduced world," my "own peculiar sphere" (*Eigenheitlichkeit*) which is the sphere of "Nature as experienced by me" (in contradistinction to the intersubjective Nature, common to all of us). Within this, my strictly private world, I find my own body distinct from all the other objects as the carrier of my field of perceptions, as the functioning organ of my kinesthetic movements, as the sum total of my organs which I command in the mode of "I can" and "I act." Briefly, I find myself as a psychophysical unity, acting in and by my body within the world, and being affected by the world through my body. This I – the human, personal I as it is apperceived within this sphere of *Eigenheitlichkeit* – is the sum total of the actualities and potentialities of my stream of experiences. Yet this does not mean that all experiences belonging to my peculiar sphere are just modifications of my self-consciousness. The intentionalities of my experiences within this private world transcend this sphere of "*Eigenheitlich-*

---

[20] See "*Scheler's Theory of Intersubjectivity and the general Thesis of the Alter Ego*," p. 164f.
[21] *Méditations Cartésiennes*, Paris, 1935, especially Secs. 44–55. See also the excellent outline of its content in Marvin Farber, *The Foundation of Phenomenology*, pp. 528–536.

keit"; they refer to the "objective Nature," nature not merely for me, but for me and the Others, and therewith to the coexistence of Others. The Other emerges within the sphere of *Eigenheitlichkeit* first of all as an object of the outer world which I interpret by an act of apperception by analogy, called by Husserl "appresentation," as being similar to my own body and, therefore, as being "another human body." However, this assimilating apperception is by no means an inference by analogy. Appresentation originates in passive synthesis, called "pairing" or "coupling," [22] which is characterized by the fact that what is appresented can never come to real presence. The appresenting term of the pair, my own body and mind within my strictly private sphere, is permanently given to me in real presence. The appresented term in this sphere – the object apperceived as another body, even more: as the body of another psycho-physical unity, briefly, as the Other is, however, given to me in the form of a non-intuitive anticipation. Yet this empty anticipation can be fulfilled by other appresentations, all of them referred to my experience of my own psycho-physical I. I may, then, interpret the Other's bodily movements as gestures and their concordance as an expression of the Other's psychical life. Thus, the Other is never experienced in the modus of self-giving but by permanent reference to my objectified I within my primordial sphere. The Other is, phenomenologically, an "intentional modification" of "my" I, which, in turn, receives this character as *"my"* I by the contrast in the process of "pairing" or "coupling" just described. Whereas my body is necessarily given to me as the center of the "Here," the Other's body is given to me as being always "There," thus as coexistent with me. But my appresentation indicates that his body is always in the center of *his* absolute "Here," whereas his "Here" remains for me always a "There." This coexistant I is, therefore, not my I (reduplicated) but another I – the I of the Other. From the appresentation of the other I, starting from the Other's body, I arrive by additional appresentations, by empathy (*Einfuehlung*) to the grasping of the Other's mental and psychical life of a higher order.*

---

[22] Cf. Husserl's *Erfahrung und Urteil*, esp. Secs. 33-46.

* Cf. "Scheler's Theory of Intersubjectivity and the General Thesis of the Alter Ego," p. 177f. and "Phenomenology and the Social Sciences," p. 125t. (M.N.)

Thus far we have considered Husserl, from whom Sartre, as can easily be seen, has borrowed widely in working out his own theory. Nevertheless, Sartre's statement that Husserl has not succeded in explaining the problem of intersubjectivity in terms of a relationship between transcendental subjectivities seems to be correct. The appresenting term of the coupling is not my transcendental ego but my own self-given life as a psychophysical I within my primordial sphere, that is, as a modification of my mundane I within the world. And what is appresented by this "pairing" is first the object in the outer world interpreted as the body of another human being, which, as such, indicates the mental life of the Other – the Other, however, still as a mundane psychophysical unity within the world, as a fellow-man, therefore, and not as a transcendental Alter Ego. Husserl, so it seems, has shown in a masterful way how within the mundane sphere man and fellow-man are compossible and coexistent, how within this sphere the Other becomes manifest, how within it concordant behavior, communication, etc., occur. Yet he has not shown the possibility of a coexisting transcendental Alter Ego constituted within and by the activities of the transcendental ego. This, however, would be necessary in order to overcome the solipsistic argument in the transcendental sphere.

VI. CRITICAL OBSERVATIONS CONCERNING SARTRE'S OWN THEORY

Having thus agreed with Sartre's criticism of Husserl, we now have to investigate whether his own theory has overcome the fundamental difficulties involved in the problem of the constitution of the Other. Sartre states clearly that his theory does not aim at proving the Other's existence, as our belief in it is rooted in a pre-ontological understanding. Nevertheless it is the Cartesian *cogito* which is the only starting point for grasping the Other as being not-me, a not-me, however, which is not an object but a subject. By looking at me, the Other makes me an object, limits my freedom, transforms me into a utensil of his possibilities. To be sure, in a second move, I may objectify again the Other-subject, regaining, thus, my own subjectivity.

Professor De Waelhens in his excellent reviews of Sartre's book [23] states correctly that this theory is just a refinement of Hegel's dialectic of the relationship between Master and Servant, it being understood that both may change their roles at any instant. And he points out correctly that according to Sartre a relationship between the I-subject and the Other-subject is impossible. Either I am the object and the Other is the subject or vice versa.[24] This principle is not only consistently applied to the aforementioned general theory of the Other's existence and of the three ontological dimensions of my own body. It is also the backbone of Sartre's subtle analyses of concrete human relationships [25] such as love, seduction, indifference, sexual desire, hatred, etc., in which he attempts to show that each of these attitudes can be reduced either to my masochistic submission to the alienation of my freedom by the Other or to my sadistic transformation of the Other's subjectivity into my instrument. Even Sartre's theory of the "We" distinguishes a We-subject and a We-object.[26] We cannot embark upon a detailed presentation of these theories nor show how deeply the alternative subject-object is rooted in Sartre's basic concepts of the antitheses between Being and Nothingness, Being-in-itself and Being-for-itself, freedom and alienation.

Sartre has correctly criticized Hegel for not having taken one particular concrete consciousness as the starting point and system of reference.[27] But Sartre himself becomes a victim of such "optimism" As a starting point of his analysis he takes it tacitly for granted that my experiencing the Other and the Other's experiencing me are simply interchangeable. For instance, instead of analyzing the meaning of my body for the Other, as he promised to do, he offers merely an analysis of the meaning the Other's body has for me.[28] He says, moreover, that by objectifying the Other, the Other is an object to me merely to the extent to which I am an object to him.[29] It will not be denied

---

[23] See footnote 2.
[24] "*Ces deux tentatives [pro-jet d'objectivation d'autrui ou d'assimilation d'autrui] que je suis sont opposées. Chacune d'elles est la mort de l'autre, c'est-à-dire que l'échec de l'une motive l'adoption de l'autre.*" *L'Être et le Néant*, p. 430.
[25] *Ibid.*, pp. 428–484.
[26] *Ibid.*, pp. 484–507.
[27] Cf. above p. 186.
[28] *L'Être et le Néant*, p. 405, cf. footnote 16.
[29] *Ibid.*, p. 356.

that the demonstration of such an interchangeability might be the *outcome* of any analysis of intersubjective relationship. Yet it cannot be taken for granted as its *"starting point"* without committing *a petitio principii*.[30] The whole problem of constituting the Other consists in answering the question: How is such an interchangeability possible? Sartre's criticism of the solipsistic argument can be applied to his own theory. For even if we were prepared to admit with him that our belief in the Other's *existence* needs no proof since it is rooted in a pre-ontological understanding, we should have to show how we can arrive at an understanding of the *concrete* Other's *concrete behavior* without falling back upon the solipsistic argument. Scheler [31] has clearly seen that here two different problems have to be distinguished. So has Sartre. But he has disregarded the chief problem of all the social sciences and of our existence in the "human reality" of the social world, namely, the concrete understanding of the Other whose existence is taken for granted. He did so because his basic position leads him into several inextricable difficulties.

Sartre's first difficulty originates in the equivocation hidden in the seemingly clean-cut antithetic terms "subject" and "object" as used by him. On the one hand, "subject" means to him being-for-itself, and "object" being-in-itself. As such, the subject is a center of activity, the object a utensil; the subject projects its possibilities, the object is always projected. On the other hand, "subject" means to Sartre the Cartesian *cogito* as it appears to itself, and "object" the *cogitatum* as it appears to me, the subject. Now Sartre holds that my experience of being looked at determines me in my being an object, in my being-for-the-Other, even if I was mistaken in my belief that a concrete Other was looking at me.[32] Yet, he states, I am not constituted by this fact as an object for the Other, the subject.[33] I am looking at my self with the eyes of the Other. Nevertheless, so Sartre continues,[34] the Other-subject, the Other as he is for himself, can never be

---
[30] Cf. footnote 19.
[31] See, "*Scheler's Theory of Intersubjectivity and the General Thesis of the Alter Ego*," pp. 156–159.
[32] *L'Être et le Néant*, p. 335.
[33] *Ibid.*, p. 334.
[34] *Ibid.*, p. 354.

known or conceived by me as such. The objects of this world do not refer to him, the Other-subject, but to the objectified Other, who is just one object among other objects. In other words, in being looked at I turn into an object for the Other-subject, whose subjectivity escapes me entirely. And objectifying the Other, I again seize the Other merely as an object. How is all this, if true, compatible with the assumption that my experiencing the Other and his experiencing me are interchangeable? And how is it compatible with the thesis that by being looked at I abandon my freedom, I become a utensil for the Other, that Other who under all circumstances escapes me in his being for himself? But whatever answer may be given to these questions, Sartre's theory, as will be shown presently, is at variance with a correct description of human reality.

Another difficulty consists in Sartre's ambiguous concept of action. To me the subject, the being-for-itself, the world is an organized system of my practical possibilities, centered around myself, that is, my body. By my action I seize one of these possibilities, committing myself to the chosen project. With the appearance of the Other this organized structure breaks asunder and a substructure of practical possibilities not of my making and and choice, but of his, the Other's, emerges. The Other's possibilities of freedom constitute the limits of my own. But how can I ascertain the realm of the Other's practical possibilities? And are we speaking of the Other-subject or the Other-object? The Other as a subject, as he appears to himself, escapes me entirely and so does consequently the system of his possibilities. I know of his subjectivity merely by my being looked at, that is, being looked at by any Other, whatever his concrete system of possibilities and projects may be. The Other as an object, however, is, so we learn from Sartre, by necessity conceived as interrelated with other objects. His gestures refer to other gestures, their significations (to me) to other relations with the outer world which are also significant (to me). Thus, the objectified Other has no freedom of action within open possibilities, or better: his possibilities are dead possibilities, referring to other objective aspects (I have) of the Other.[35] My action has, therefore, quite another meaning to me than the action of the Other. We have no

[35] *Ibid.*, p. 358.

issue with this latter statement considered as such. But *why from Sartre's position should we, then, assume that the Other acts at all, that he like me, has open possibilities?* Why assume that he has freedom, which to Sartre [36] is the first condition of action? And how can we come to an understanding of what the Other's action means to him, the actor? How can we relate our own conduct to that of the Other and orient the former in its course with reference to the latter? How explain, in a word, social action and social relationship? [37]

Moreover, Sartre's concept of situation and freedom of action does not describe human reality. In the mundane sphere of everyday life I conceive myself as well as the Other as a center of activity, each of us living among things to be handled, instruments to be used, situations to be accepted or changed. Yet my possibilities, my instruments, my situation have their specific structure as they appear to me, his as they appear to him. Each of us "defines his situation" as the sociologists call it. In order to use an object as an instrument, I have to bring it within my reach; in order to engage in a project, I have to acknowledge it as being relevant. What is relevant to the Other, what is within his reach, certainly does not coincide with what is relevant to me and within my reach, if for no other reason than that I am "Here" and he is "There." [38] Yet recognizing that the Other lives in a setting not defined by me does not transform him into my utensil. He remains within his situation (as defined by him) a center of activity; I can understand him as being not me, his activities as being not mine, his instruments as being beyond my reach, his projects as being outside my accepted possibilities. All the social sciences deal with the problem of how to interpret the Other's actions as they appear to me by understanding the meaning which the actor, the Other, bestows upon them. The theories of empathy, sympathy, reasoning by analogy are admittedly unsatisfactory attempts to solve this problem by the general postulate: I have to understand what the Other means by his action in the same way in which I would understand my own

---

[36] *Ibid.*, pp. 508ff.; see also Marcuse *loc. cit.*, 319–325.

[37] The student of the work of Max Weber will recognize in the preceding sentences a paraphrase of his famous definitions. [See "Concept and Theory Formation in the Social Sciences." (M.N.)]

[38] Cf. "On Multiple Realities," especially p.222f.

analogous action in terms of *my* system of relevance then prevailing if I were "There" (that is at the Other's place in the broadest sense of this term) instead of "Here." (But even this "There" will never be my actual "Here.") Yet this is quite another problem than the ontological transformation of myself into an object by recognizing the Other's subjectivity or than that of objectifying the Other in order to regain my own subjectivity.

All these problems are not explained, not even touched upon, by Sartre's assumption of the magic power vested in the Other's looking at me. Sartre analyzes at length the situation of a jealous lover, caught by another man while peeping through a keyhole.[39] Under the Other's eye he loses the freedom of his ignoble possibilities; he turns into what the Other sees he is. But, we have to add, he does so merely if he is not "caught unawares" but becomes aware that he is caught. Sartre's theory of the *"regard"* presupposes what I once called a mutual "tuning-in" relationship between me and the Other* This becomes perfectly clear if we consider what our lover experienced *before* he was caught. Through the keyhole he observed not just a moving shape similar to a human body, but from the outset another man behaving in this and that way, moving freely within a situation, exclusively defined by him, the actor, who lived in his action unaware that he was doing so under the eyes of anyone. The man looked at through the keyhole proves to be another subject acting within the freedom of his possibilities.

Yet we do not have to stick to the one-way relationship between observer and observed in order to show that the Other can be experienced as a concrete subjectivity in the freedom of his concrete action. If Peter speaks to Paul, then Peter neither seizes himself as being an object for Paul, nor Paul as his objectified instrument. Peter addresses Paul because he anticipates that Paul will inderstand him, and this implies that Paul will be able and willing to co-perform by his listening and interpreting activity the single steps in which Peter builds up, while speaking, the meaning of his message.[40] The ongoing speech as such is an

---

[39] *L'Être et le Néant*, pp. 317ff., Marcuse *loc. cit.*, p. 317.
[40] "On Multiple Realities," pp. 218–222.
* Alfred Schutz, "Making Music Together: A Study in Social Relationship," *Social Research*, Vol. 18, 1951, pp. 76–97. (M.N.)

occurrence in the outer world and in outer time. But this process is strictly simultaneous with Paul's inner time in which he performs polythetically the interpretation of Peter's speech. This answers Sartre's question [41] how an instant of Peter's inner time can be conceived as being connected by simultaneity with Paul's inner time. Peter's activity of speaking presupposes Paul's activity of listening and vice versa. Both seize one another as a co-performing subjectivity.

Sartre's theory, in spite of his many admirably subtle analyses, has nothing to contribute to the elucidation of this mechanism. His attempt to overcome epistemological solipsism leads to an unrealistic construction which involves, so to speak, a practical solipsism. Either the Other looks at me and alienates my liberty, or I assimilate and seize the liberty of the Other. Thus, mutual interaction in freedom has no place within Sartre's philosophy.

---

[41] *L'Être et le Néant*, p. 281; see also above p. 181.

PART III

Symbol, Reality, and Society

ON MULTIPLE REALITIES

In a famous chapter of his *Principles of Psychology* William James analyzes our sense of reality.[1] Reality, so he states, means simply relation to our emotional and active life. The origin of all reality is subjective, whatever excites and stimulates our interest is real. To call a thing real means that this thing stands in a certain relation to ourselves. "The word 'real' is, in short, a fringe." [2] Our primitive impulse is to affirm immediately the reality of all that is conceived, as long as it remains uncontradicted. But there are several, probably an infinite number of various orders of realities, each with its own special and separate style of existence. James calls them "sub-universes" and mentions as examples the world of sense or physical things (as the paramount reality), the world of science, the world of ideal relations, the world of "idols of the tribe", the various supernatural worlds of mythology and religion, the various worlds of individual opinion, the worlds of sheer madness and vagary.[3] The popular mind conceives of all these sub-worlds more or less disconnectedly, and when dealing with one of them forgets for the time being its relations to the rest. But every object we think of is at last referred to one of these subworlds. "Each world whilst it is attended to is real after its own fashion; only the reality lapses with the attention." [4]

With these remarks James' genius has touched on one of the most important philosophical questions. Intentionally restricting his inquiry to the psychological aspect of the problem, he has refrained from embarking upon an investigation of the many

[1] *Loc. cit.*, Vol. II, Chapter XXI, pp. 283–322.
[2] *Ibid.*, p. 320.
[3] *Ibid.*, pp. 291ff.
[4] *Ibid.*, p. 293.

implications involved. The following considerations, fragmentary as they are, attempt to outline a first approach to some of them with the special aim of clarifying the relationship between the reality of the world of daily life and that of theoretical, scientific contemplation.

I. THE REALITY OF THE WORLD OF DAILY LIFE

1) The natural attitude of daily life and its pragmatic motive

We begin with an analysis of the world of daily life which the wide-awake, grown-up man who acts in it and upon it amidst his fellow-men experiences within the natural attitude as a reality.

"World of daily life" shall mean the intersubjective world which existed long before our birth, experienced and interpreted by Others, our predecessors, as an organized world. Now it is given to our experience and interpretation. All interpretation of this world is based upon a stock of previous experiences of it, our own experiences and those handed down to us by our parents and teachers, which in the form of "knowledge at hand" function as a scheme of reference.

To this stock of experiences at hand belongs our knowledge that the world we live in is a world of well circumscribed objects with definite qualities, objects among which we move, which resist us and upon which we may act. To the natural attitude the world is not and never has been a mere aggregate of colored spots, incoherent noises, centers of warmth and cold. Philosophical or psychological analysis of the constitution of our experiences may afterwards, retrospectively, describe how elements of this world affect our senses, how we passively perceive them in an indistinct and confused way, how by active apperception our mind singles out certain features from the perceptional field, conceiving them as well delineated things which stand out over against a more or less unarticulated background or horizon. The natural attitude does not know these problems. To it the world is from the outset not the private world of the single individual but an intersubjective world, common to all of us, in which we have not a theoretical but an eminently practical interest. The world of everyday life is the scene and also the object of our actions and interactions. We have to dominate it and we have to change it in order to realize the purposes which we pursue within it among our fellow-men. We work and operate not only within but upon the world. Our bodily movements – kinaesthetic, locomotive, operative – gear, so to speak, into the world, modifying or changing its objects and their mutual relationships. On the other hand, these objects offer resistance to our acts which we have either to overcome or to which we have to yield. Thus, it may be correctly said that a pragmatic motive governs our natural attitude toward the world of daily life. World, in this sense, is something that we have to modify by our actions or that modifies our actions.

2) The manifestations of man's spontaneous life in the outer world and some of its forms

But what has to be understood under the term "action" just used? How does man with the natural attitude experience his own "actions" within and upon the world? Obviously, "actions" are manifestations of man's spontaneous life. But neither does he experience all such manifestations as actions nor does he experience all of his actions as bringing about changes in the outer world. Unfortunately the different forms of all these experiences are not clearly distinguished in present philosophical thought and, therefore, no generally accepted terminology exists.

In vain would we look for help to modern behaviorism and its distinction between overt and covert behavior, to which categories a third, that of subovert behavior, has sometimes been added in order to characterize the manifestation of spontaneity in acts of speech. It is not our aim here to criticise the basic fallacy of the behavioristic point of view or to discuss the inadequacy and inconsistency of the trichotomy just mentioned. For our purpose it suffices to show that the behavioristic interpretation of spontaneity can contribute nothing to the question we are concerned with, namely, how the different forms of spontaneity are experienced by the mind in which they originate. At its best, behaviorism is a scheme of reference useful to the observer of other people's behavior. He, and only he, might be interested in considering the activities of men or animals under a relational scheme of reference such as stimulus-response, or organism-environment, and only from his point of view are these categories accessible at all. Our problem, however, is not what occurs to man as a psychophysiological unit, but the attitude he adopts toward these occurrences – briefly, the subjective meaning man bestows upon certain experiences of his own spontaneous life. What appears to the observer to be objectively the same behavior may have for the behaving subject very different meanings or no meaning at all.

Meaning, as has been shown elsewhere,[5] is not a quality inherent in certain experiences emerging within our stream of consciousness but the result of an interpretation of a past experience looked at from the present Now with a reflective attitude. As long as I live *in* my acts, directed toward the objects of these acts, the acts do not have any meaning. They become meaningful if I grasp them as well-circumscribed experiences of the past and, therefore, in retrospection. Only experiences which can be recollected beyond their actuality and which can be questioned about their constitution are, therefore, subjectively meaningful.

But if this characterization of meaning has been accepted, are there any experiences at all of my spontaneous life which are subjectively not meaningful? We think the answer is in the affirmitive. There are the mere physiological reflexes, such as the knee jerk, the contraction of the pupil, blinking, blushing; moreover certain passive reactions provoked by what Leibniz calls the surf of indiscernible and confused small perceptions; furthermore, my gait, my facial expression, my mood, those manifestations of my spontaneous life which result in certain characteristics of my handwriting open to graphological interpretation, etc. All these forms of involuntary spontaneity are experienced while they occur, but without leaving any trace in memory; as experiences they are, to borrow again a term from Leibniz, most suitable for this peculiar problem, perceived but not apperceived. Unstable and undetachable from surrounding

---

[5] A. Schutz, *Der sinnhafte Aufbau der sozialen Welt*, 2nd ed., Vienna, 1960, pp. 29–43, 72–93.

experiences as they are, they can neither be delineated nor recollected. They belong to the category of *essentially actual experiences*, that is, they exist merely in the actuality of being experienced and cannot be grasped by a reflective attitude.[6]

Subjectively meaningful experiences emanating from our spontaneous life shall be called *conduct*. (We avoid the term "behavior" because it includes in present use also subjectively non-meaningful manifestations of spontaneity such as reflexes.) The term "conduct" – as used here – refers to all kinds of subjectively meaningful experiences of spontaneity, be they those of inner life or those gearing into the outer world. If it is permitted to use objective terms in a description of subjective experiences – and after the preceding clarification the danger of misunderstanding no longer exists – we may say that conduct can be overt or covert. The former shall be called *mere doing*, the latter *mere thinking*. However, the term "conduct" as used here does not imply any reference to intent. All kinds of so-called automatic activities of inner or outer life – habitual, traditional, affectual ones – fall under this class, called by Leibniz the "class of empirical behavior."

Conduct which is devised in advance, that is, which is based upon a preconceived project, shall be called *action*, regardless of whether it is overt or covert. As to the latter, it has to be distinguished whether or not there supervenes on the project an intention to realize it – to carry it through, to bring about the projected state of affairs. Such an intention transforms the mere forethought into an aim and the project into a purpose. If an intention to realization is lacking, the projected covert action remains a phantasm, such as a day-dream; if it subsists, we may speak of a purposive action or a *performance*. An example of a covert action which is a performance is the process of projected thinking such as the attempt to solve a scientific problem mentally.

As to the so-called overt actions, that is, actions which gear

---

[6] As to the "reflective attitude" cf. Marvin Farber, *The Foundation of Phenomenology*, Cambridge, 1943, pp. 523ff.; also pp. 378ff.; cf. furthermore Dorion Cairns: "An Approach to Phenomenology," in *Philosophical Essays in Memory of Edmund Husserl*, ed. by M. Farber, Cambridge, 1940; p. 8 f. The concept of "essentially actual experiences," however, cannot be found in Husserl's writings. Husserl's view was that, as a matter of principle, every act can be grasped in reflection.

into the outer world by bodily movements, the distinction between actions without and those with an intention to realization is not necessary. Any overt action is a performance within the meaning of our definition. In order to distinguish the (covert) performances of mere thinking from those (overt) requiring bodily movements we shall call the latter *working*.

Working, then, is action in the outer world, based upon a project and characterized by the intention to bring about the projected state of affairs by bodily movements. Among all the described forms of spontaneity that of working is the most important one for the constitution of the reality of the world of daily life. As will be shown very soon, the wide-awake self integrates in its working and by its working its present, past, and future into a specific dimension of time; it realizes itself as a totality in its working acts; it communicates with Others through working acts; it organizes the different spatial perspectives of the world of daily life through working acts. But before we can turn to these problems we have to explain what the term "wide-awake self," just used, means.

3) *The tensions of consciousness and the attention to life*

One of the central points of Bergson's philosophy is his theory that our conscious life shows an indefinite number of different planes, ranging from the plane of action on one extreme to the plane of dream at the other. Each of these planes is characterized by a specific tension of consciousness, the plane of action showing the highest, that of dream the lowest degree of tension. According to Bergson, these different degrees of tension of our consciousness are functions of our varying interest in life, action representing our highest interest in meeting reality and its requirements, dream being complete lack of interest. *Attention à la vie*, attention to life, is, therefore, the basic regulative principle of our conscious life. It defines the realm of our world which is relevant to us; it articulates our continuously flowing stream of thought; it determines the span and function of our memory; it makes us – in our language – either live within our present experiences, directed toward their objects, or turn back in a reflective attitude to our past experiences and ask for their meaning.[7]

By the term *"wide-awakeness"* we want to denote a plane of consciousness of highest tension originating in an attitude of full attention to life and its requirements. Only the performing and especially the working self is fully interested in life and, hence, wide-awake. It lives within its acts and its attention is exclusively directed to carrying its project into effect, to executing its plan. This attention is an active, not a passive one. Passive attention is the opposite to full awakeness. In passive attention I experience, for instance, the surf of indiscernible small perceptions which are, as stated before, essentially actual experiences and not meaningful manifestations of spontaneity. Meaningful spontaneity may be defined with Leibniz as the effort to arrive at other and always other perceptions. In its lowest form it leads to the delimitation of certain perceptions transforming them into apperception; in its highest form it leads to the performance of working which gears into the outer world and modifies it.

The concept of wide-awakeness reveals the starting point for a legitimate [8] pragmatic interpretation of our cognitive life. The state of full awakeness of the working self traces out that segment of the world which is pragmatically relevant, and these relevances determine the form and content of our stream of thought: the form, because they regulate the tension of our memory and therewith the scope of our past experiences recollected and of our future experiences anticipated; the content, because all these experiences undergo specific attentional

---

[7] The presentation given above does not strictly follow Bergson's terminology but it is hoped that it renders adequately his important thought. Here is a selection of some passages of Bergson's writings significant for our problem: *Essai sur les données immédiates de la conscience*, Paris, 1889, pp. 20ff; pp. 94–106; *Matière et Mémoire*, Paris, 1897, pp. 189–195; 224–233; Le rêve (1901) [in *L'Energie spirituelle*, Paris, 1919, pp. 108–111]; L'effort intellectuel (1902) [*ibid.*, pp. 164–171]; "Introduction à la métaphysique" (1903) [in *La Pensée et le Mouvant*, Paris, 1934, pp. 233–238]; "Le souvenir du présent et la fausse reconnaissance" (1908) [*L'Energie spirituelle*, pp. 129–137]; "La conscience et la vie" (1911) [*ibid.*, pp. 15–18]; "La perception du changement" (1911) [in *La Pensée et le Mouvant*, pp. 171–175; pp. 190–193]; "Fantômes de vivants" et "recherche psychique" (1913) [*L'Energie spirituelle*, pp. 80–84]; "De la position des problèmes" (1922) [*La Pensée et le Mouvant*, pp. 91ff].

[8] With very few exceptions, vulgar pragmatism does not consider the problems of the constitution of conscious life involved in the notion of an *ego agens* or *homo faber* from which as a giveness most of the writers start. For the most part, pragmatism is, therefore, just a common-sense description of the attitude of man within the world of working in daily life, but not a philosophy investigating the presuppositions of such a situation.

modifications by the preconceived project and its carrying into effect. This leads us immediately into an analysis of the time dimension in which the working self experiences its own acts.

4) The time perspectives of the "ego agens" and their unification

We start by making a distinction that refers to actions in general, covert and overt between action as an ongoing process, as acting in progress (*actio*) on the one hand, and action as performed act, as the thing done (*actum*) on the other hand. Living in my acting-in-progress, I am directed toward the state of affairs to be brought about by this acting. But, then, I do not have in view my experiences of this ongoing process of acting. In order to bring them into view I have to turn back with a reflective attitude to my acting. As Dewey once formulated it, I have to stop and think. If I adopt this reflective attitude, it is, however, not my ongoing acting that I can grasp. What alone I can grasp is rather my performed act (my past acting) or, if my acting still continues while I turn back, the performed initial phases (my present acting). While I lived in my acting in progress it was an element of my vivid present. Now this present has turned into past, and the vivid experience of my acting in progress has given place to my recollection of having acted or to the retention of having been acting. Seen from the actual present in which I adopt the reflective attitude, my past or present perfect acting is conceivable only in terms of acts performed by me.

Thus I may either live in the ongoing process of my acting, directed toward its object, and experience my acting in the Present Tense (*modo presenti*), or I may, so to speak, step out of the ongoing flux and look by a reflective glance at the acts performed in previous processes of acting in the Past Tense or Present Perfect Tense (*modo praeterito*). This does not mean that – according to what was stated in a previous section – merely the performed acts are meaningful but not the ongoing actions. We have to keep in mind that, by definition, action is always based upon a preconceived project, and it is this reference to the preceding project that makes both the acting and the act meaningful.

But what is the time structure of a projected action? When projecting my action, I am, as Dewey puts it,[9] rehearsing my future action in imagination. This means, I anticipate the outcome of my future action. I look in my imagination at this anticipated action as the thing which *will have been* done, the act which *will have been* performed by me. In projecting, I look at my act in the Future Perfect Tense, I think of it *modo futuri exacti*. But these anticipations are empty and may or may not be fulfilled by the action once performed. The past or present perfect act, however, shows no such empty anticipations. What was empty in the project has or has not been fulfilled. Nothing remains unsettled, nothing undecided. To be sure, I may remember the open anticipations involved in projecting the act and even the protentions accompanying my living in the ongoing process of my acting. But now, in retrospection, I remember them in terms of my *past* anticipations, which have or have not come true. Only the performed act, therefore, and never the acting in progress can turn out as a success or failure.

What has been stated so far holds good for all kinds of actions. But now we have to turn to the peculiar structure of working as bodily performance in the outer world. Bergson's and also Husserl's investigations have emphasized the importance of our bodily movements for the constitution of the outer world and its time perspective. We experience our bodily movements simultaneously on two different planes: inasmuch as they are movements in the outer world we look at them as events happening in space and spatial time, measurable in terms of the path run through; inasmuch as they are experienced together from within as happening changes, as manifestations of our spontaneity pertaining to our stream of consciousness, they partake of our inner time or *durée*. What occurs in the outer world belongs to the same time dimension in which events in inanimate nature occur. It can be registered by appropriate devices and measured by our chronometers. It is the spatialized, homogeneous time which is the universal form of objective or cosmic time. On the other hand, it is the inner time or *durée* within which our actual experiences are connected with the past by recollections and retentions and

---

[9] *Human Nature and Conduct*, New York, 1922, Part III, Section III: "The Nature of Deliberation."

with the future by protentions and anticipations. In and by our bodily movements we perform the transition from our *durée* to the spatial or cosmic time, and our working actions partake of both. In simultaneity we experience the working action as a series of events in outer and in inner time, unifying both dimensions into a single flux which shall be called the *vivid present*. The vivid present originates, therefore, in an intersection of *durée* and cosmic time.

Living in the vivid present in its ongoing working acts, directed toward the objects and objectives to be brought about, the working self experiences itself as the originator of the ongoing actions and, thus, as an undivided total self. It experiences its bodily movements from within; it lives in the correlated essentially actual experiences which are inaccessible to recollection and reflection; its world is a world of open anticipations. The working self, and only the working self, experiences all this *modo presenti* and, experiencing itself as the author of this ongoing working, it realizes itself as a unity.

But if the self in a reflective attitude turns back to the working acts performed and looks at them *modo praeterito* this unity goes to pieces. The self which performed the past acts is no longer the undivided total self, but rather a partial self, the performer of this particular act that refers to a system of correlated acts to which it belongs. This partial self is merely the taker of a rôle or – to use with all necessary reserve a rather equivocal term which James and Mead have introduced into the literature – a Me.

We cannot enter here into a thorough discussion of the difficult implications here involved. This would require a presentation and criticism of G. H. Mead's rather incomplete and inconsistent attempt to approach these problems. We restrict ourselves to pointing to the distinction Mead makes between the totality of the acting self, which he calls the "I," and the partial selves of performed acts, the takers of rôles, which he calls the "Me's." So far, the thesis presented in this paper converges with Mead's analysis. And there is, furthermore, agreement with Mead's statement that the "I" gets into experience only after it has carried out the act and thus appears experientially as a part of the Me, that is, the Me appears in our experience in memory.[10]

For our purpose the mere consideration that the inner experiences of our bodily movements, the essentially actual experiences, and the open anticipations escape the grasping by the reflective attitude shows with sufficient clearness that the past self can never be more than a partial aspect of the total one which realizes itself in the experience of its ongoing working.

One point relating to the distinction between (overt) working and (covert) performing has to be added. In the case of a mere performance, such as the attempt to solve a mathematical problem mentally, I can, if my anticipations are not fulfilled by the outcome and I am dissatisfied with the result, cancel the whole process of mental operations and restart from the beginning. Nothing will have changed in the outer world, no vestige of the annulled process will remain. Mere mental actions are, in this sense, revocable. Working, however, is irrevocable. My work has changed the outer world. At best, I may restore the initial situation by countermoves but I cannot make undone what I have done. That is why – from the moral and legal point of view – I am responsible for my deeds but not for my thoughts. That is also why I have the freedom of choice between several possibilities merely with respect to the mentally projected work, before this work has been carried through in the outer world or, at least, while it is being carried through in vivid present, and, thus, still open to modifications. In terms of the past there is no possibility for choice. Having realized my work or at least portions of it, I chose once for all what has been done and have now to bear the consequences. I cannot choose what I want to have done.

---

[10] Cf. G. H. Mead, *Mind, Self, and Society*, Chicago, 1934, pp. 173–175, 196–198, 203; "The Genesis of the Self," reprinted in *The Philosophy of the Present*, Chicago, 1932, pp. 176–195, esp. pp. 184ff.; "What Social Objects Must Psychology Presuppose?," *Journal of Philosophy* Vol. VIII, 1910, pp. 174–180; "The Social Self," *Journal of Philosophy*, Vol. X, 1913, pp. 374–380. See also Alfred Stafford Clayton's excellent book on G. H. Mead: *Emergent Mind and Education*, New York, 1943, pp. 136–141, esp. p. 137. It is doubtless Mead's merit to have seen the relations between act, self, memory, time, and reality. The position of the present paper is of course not reconcilable with Mead's theory of the social origin of the self and with his (modified) behaviorism which induces him to interpret all the beforementioned phenomena in terms of stimulus-response. There is much more truth in the famous chapter (X) of James' *Principles of Psychology*, in which not only the distinction between Me and I can be found, but also its reference to bodily movements, memory, and the sense of time.

So far our analysis has dealt with the time structure of action – and, as a corollary, with the time structure of the self – within the insulated stream of consciousness of the single individual, as if the wide-awake man within the natural attitude could be thought of as separated from his fellow-men. Such a fictitious abstraction was, of course, merely made for the sake of clearer presentation of the problems involved. We have now to turn to the social structure of the world of working.

5) *The social structure of the world of daily life*

We stated before that the world of daily life into which we are born is from the outset an intersubjective world. This implies on the one hand that this world is not my private one but common to all of us; on the other hand that within this world there exist fellow-men with whom I am connected by manifold social relationships. I work not only upon inanimate things but also upon my fellow-men, induced by them to act and inducing them to react. Without entering here into a detailed discussion of the structure and constitution of social relationship, we may mention just as an example of one of its many forms that my performed acts may motivate the Other to react, and vice versa. My questioning the Other, for instance, is undertaken with the intention of provoking his answer, and his answering is motivated by my question. This is one of the many types of "social actions." It is that type in which the "in-order-to motives" of my action become "because motives" of the partner's reaction.*

Social actions involve communication, and any communication is necessarily founded upon acts of working. In order to communicate with Others I have to perform overt acts in the outer world which are supposed to be interpreted by the Others as signs of what I mean to convey. Gestures, speech, writing, etc., are based upon bodily movements. So far, the behavioristic interpretation of communication is justified. It goes wrong by identifying the vehicle of communication, namely the working act, with the communicated meaning itself.

Let us examine the mechanism of communication from the point of view of the interpreter. I may find as given to my

* See "Choosing Among Projects of Action," p. 69 f. (M.N.)

interpretation either the ready-made outcome of the Other's communicating acts or I may attend in simultaneity the ongoing process of his communicating actions as they proceed. The former is, for instance, the case, if I have to interpret a signpost erected by the Other or an implement produced by him. The latter relation prevails, if I am listening to my partner's talk. (There are many variations of these basic types, such as the reading of the Other's letter in a kind of quasi-simultaneity with the ongoing communicating process.) He builds up the thought he wants to convey to me step by step, adding word to word, sentence to sentence, paragraph to paragraph. While he does so, my interpreting actions follow his communicating ones in the same rhythm. We both, I and the Other, experience the ongoing process of communication in a vivid present. Articulating his thought, while speaking, in phases, the communicator does not merely experience what he actually utters; a complicated mechanism of retentions and anticipations connects within his stream of consciousness one element of his speech with what preceded and what will follow to the unity of the thought he wants to convey. All these experiences belong to his inner time. And there are, on the other hand, the occurrences of his speaking, brought about by him in the spatialized time of the outer world. Briefly, the communicator experiences the ongoing process of communicating as a working in his vivid present.

And I, the listener, experience for my part my interpreting actions also as happening in my vivid present, although this interpreting is not a working, but merely a performing within the meaning of our definitions. On the one hand, I experience the occurrences of the Other's speaking in outer time; on the other hand, I experience my interpreting as a series of retentions and anticipations happening in my inner time interconnected by my aim to understand the Other's thought as a unit.

Now let us consider that the occurrence in the outer world – the communicator's speech – is, while it goes on, an element common to his and my vivid present, both of which are, therefore, simultaneous. My participating in simultaneity in the ongoing process of the Other's communicating establishes therefore a new dimension of time. He and I, *we* share, while the process lasts, a common vivid present, *our* vivid present, which enables him and me to say: "*We* experienced this occurrence together." By the We-relation, thus established, we both – he, addressing himself to me, and I, listening to him, – are living in our mutual vivid present, directed toward the thought to be realized in and by the communicating process. *We grow older together.*

So far our analysis of communication in the vivid present of the We-relation has been restricted to the time perspective involved. We have now to consider the specific functions of the Other's bodily movements as an expressional field open to interpretation as signs of the Other's thought. It is clear that the extension of this field, even if communication occurs in vivid present, may vary considerably. It will reach its maximum if there exists between the partners community not only of time but also of space, that is, in the case of what sociologists call a face-to-face relation.

To make this clearer let us keep to our example of the speaker and the listener and analyze the interpretable elements included in such a situation. There are first the words uttered in the meaning they have according to dictionary and grammar in the language used plus the additional fringes they receive from the context of the speech and the supervening connotations originating in the particular circumstances of the speaker. There is, furthermore, the inflection of the speaker's voice, his facial expression, the gestures which accompany his talking. Under normal circumstances merely the conveyance of the thought by appropriately selected words has been projected by the speaker and constitutes, therefore, "working" according to our definition. The other elements within the interpretable field are from the speaker's point of view not planned and, therefore, at best mere conduct (mere doing) or even mere reflexes and, then, essentially actual experiences without subjective meaning. Nevertheless, they, too, are integral elements of the listener's interpretation of the Other's state of mind. The community of space permits the partner to apprehend the Other's bodily expressions not merely as events in the outer world, but as factors of the communicating process itself, although they do not originate in working acts of the communicator.

Not only does each partner in the face-to-face relationship share the other in a vivid present; each of them with all manifestations of his spontaneous life is also an element of the other's surroundings; both participate in a set of common experiences of the outer world into which either's working acts may gear. And, finally, in the face-to-face relationship (and only in it) can the partner look at the self of his fellow-man as an unbroken totality in a vivid present. This is of special importance because, as shown before, I can look at my own self only *modo praeterito* and then grasp merely a partial aspect of this my past self, myself as a performer of a rôle, as a Me.

All the other manifold social relationships are derived from the originary experiencing of the totality of the Other's self in the community of time and space. Any theoretical analysis of the notion of environment" – one of the least clarified terms used in present social sciences – would have to start from the face-to-face relation as a basic structure of the world of daily life.

We cannot enter here into the details of the framework of these derived relationships. For our problem it is important that in none of them does the self of the Other become accessible to the partner as a unity. The Other appears merely as a partial self, as originator of these and those acts, which I do not share in a vivid present. The shared vivid present of the We-relation presupposes co-presence of the partners. To each type of derived social relationship belongs a particular type of time perspective which is derived from the vivid present. There is a particular quasi-present in which I interpret the mere outcome of the Other's communicating – the written letter, the printed book – without having participated in the ongoing process of communicating acts. There are other time dimensions in which I am connected with contemporaries I never met, or with predecessors or with successors; historical time, in which I experience the actual present as the outcome of past events; and many more. All of these time perspectives can be referred to a vivid present: my own actual or former one, or the actual or former vivid present of my fellow-man with whom, in turn, I am connected in an originary or derived vivid present. All this occurs in the different modes of potentiality or quasi-actuality, each type having its own forms of temporal diminution and augmentation and its appurtenant style of skipping in a direct move or "knight's move." There are furthermore the different forms of overlapping and interpenetrating of these different perspectives, their being put into and out of operation by a shift from one to the other and a transformation of one into the other, and the different types of synthesizing and combining or isolating and disentangling them. Manifold as these different time perspectives and their mutual relations are, they all originate in an intersection of *durée* and cosmic time.

In and by our social life within the natural attitude they are apprehended as integrated into a single supposedly homogeneous dimension of time which embraces not only all the individual time perspectives of each of us during his wide-awake life but which is common to all of us. We shall call it the civic or *standard time*. It, too, is an intersection of cosmic time and inner time, though, as to the latter, merely of a peculiar aspect of inner time – that aspect in which the wide-awake man experiences his working acts as events within his stream of consciousness. Because standard time partakes of cosmic time, it is measurable by our clocks and calendars. Because it coincides with our inner sense of time in which we experience our working acts, if – and only if – we are wide-awake, it governs the system of our plans under which we subsume our projects, such as plans for life, for work and leisure. Because it is common to all of us, standard time makes an intersubjective coordination of the different individual plan systems possible. Thus, to the natural attitude, the civic or standard time is in the same sense the universal temporal structure of the intersubjective world of everyday life within the natural attitude, in which the earth is its universal spatial structure that embraces the spatial environments of each of us.

6) *The strata of reality in the everyday world of working*

The wide-awake man within the natural attitude is primarily interested in that sector of the world of his everyday life which is within his scope and which is centered in space and time around himself. The place which my body occupies within the world, my actual Here, is the starting point from which I take my bearing in space. It is, so to speak, the center O of my system of coordinates. Relatively to my body I group the elements of my surroundings under the categories of right and left, before and behind, above and below, near and far, and so on. And in a similar way my actual Now is the origin of all the time perspectives under which I organize the events within the world such as the categories of fore and aft, past and future, simultaneity and succession, etc.

Within this basic scheme of orientation, however, the world of working is structurized in various strata of reality. It is the great merit of Mead [11] to have analyzed the structurization of the reality at least of the physical thing in its relationship to human action, especially to the actual manipulation of objects with the hands. It is what he calls the "manipulatory area" which constitutes the core of reality. This area includes those objects which are both seen and handled, in contradistinction to the distant objects which cannot be experienced by contact but still lie in the visual field. Only experiences of physical things within the manipulatory area permit the basic test of all reality, namely resistance, only they define what Mead calls the "standard sizes" of things which appear outside the manipulatory area in the distortions of optical perspectives.

This theory of the predominance of the manipulatory area certainly converges with the thesis suggested by this paper, namely, that the world of our working, of bodily movements, of manipulating objects and handling things and men constitutes the specific reality of everyday life. For our purpose, however, the otherwise most important distinction between objects experienced by contact and distant objects is not of primary importance. It could easily be shown that this dichotomy originates in Mead's basic behavioristic position and his uncritical use of the stimulus-response scheme. We, on the other hand, are concerned with the natural attitude of the wide-awake, grown-up man in daily life. He always disposes of a stock of previous experiences, among them the notion of distance as such and of the possibility of overcoming distance by acts of working, namely locomotions. In the natural attitude the visual perception of the distant object implies, therefore, the anticipation that the distant object can be brought into contact by locomotion, in which case the distorted perspective of the objects will disappear and their "standard sizes" reestablished. This anticipation like

---

[11] *The Philosophy of the Present*, Chicago, 1932, pp. 124ff.; *The Philosophy of the Act*, Chicago, 1938, pp. 103-106, 121ff., 151ff., 190-192, 196-197, 282-284.

any other may or may not stand the test of the supervening actual experience. Its refutation by experience would mean that the distant object under consideration does not pertain to the world of my working. A child may request to touch the stars. To the grown-up within the natural attitude they are shining points outside the sphere of his working, and this holds true even if he uses their position as a means for finding his bearings.

For our purposes, therefore, we suggest calling the stratum of the world of working which the individual experiences as the kernel of his reality the *world within his reach*. This world of his includes not only Mead's manipulatory area but also things within the scope of his view and the range of his hearing, moreover not only the realm of the world open to his actual but also the adjacent ones of his potential working. Of course, these realms have no rigid frontiers, they have their halos and open horizons and these are subject to modifications of interests and attentional attitudes. It is clear that this whole system of "world within my reach" undergoes changes by any of my locomotions; by displacing my body I shift the center O of my system of coordinates, and this alone changes all the numbers (coordinates) pertaining to this system.

We may say that the world within my actual reach belongs essentially to the present tense. The world within my potential reach, however, shows a more complicated time structure. At least two zones of potentiality have to be distinguished. To the first, which refers to the past, belongs what was formerly within my actual reach and what, so I assume, can be brought back into my actual reach again (*world within restorable reach*). The assumption involved is based upon the idealizations, governing all conduct in the natural sphere, namely, that I may continue to act as I have acted so far and that I may again and again recommence the same action under the same conditions. Dealing with the universal role of these idealizations for the foundation of logic and especially pure analytic, Husserl calls them the idealizations of the "and so on" and of the "I can do it again," the latter being the subjective correlate of the former.[12] To give an example: By an act of locomotion there came out of my reach what was formerly "world within my reach." The shifting of the

---

[12] *Formale und transzendentale Logik*, Sec. 74, p. 167.

center O of my system of coordinates has turned my former world in the *hic* into a world now in the *illic*.¹³ But under the idealization of the "I can do it again" I assume that I can retransform the actual *illic* into a new *hic*. My past world within my reach has under this idealization the character of a world which can be brought back again within my reach. Thus, for instance, my past manipulatory area continues to function in my present as a potential manipulatory area in the mode of *illic* and has now the character of a specific chance of restoration.*

As this first zone of potentiality is related with the past, so is the second one based upon anticipations of the future. Within my potential reach is also the world which neither is nor ever has been within my actual reach but which is nevertheless attainable under the idealization of "and so on" (*world within attainable reach*). The most important instance of this second zone of potentiality is the world within the actual reach of my contemporaneous fellow-man. For example, his manipulatory area does not – or at least does not entirely ¹⁴ – coincide with my manipulatory area because it is only to him a manipulatory area in the mode of the *hic*, but to me in the mode of the *illic*. Nevertheless, it is my attainable manipulatory area which would be my actual manipulatory area if I were in his place and indeed will turn into an actual one by appropriate locomotions.¹⁵

What has been stated with respect to the manipulatory area of the contemporaneous fellow-man holds good quite generally for the world within your, within their, within someone's reach. This implies not only world within the Other's actual reach, but also worlds within his restorable or attainable reach, and the whole system thus extended over all the different strata of the social world shows altogether all the shades originating in the perspectives of sociality such as intimacy and anonymity, strangeness

---

¹³ The terminology follows that used by Husserl in his *Méditations Cartésiennes* Secs. 53ff.

¹⁴ In the face-to-face relation – and this is an additional peculiarity of this paramount social relationship – the world within my reach and that within my partner's reach overlap and there is at least a sector of a world within my and his common reach.

¹⁵ G. H. Mead in his essay "The Objective Reality of Perspectives," reprinted in the *Philosophy of the Present*, comes to a similar conclusion: "Present reality is a possibility. It is what would be if we were there instead of here" (p. 173).

* Cf. "Phenomenology and the Social Sciences," p. 125f. and "Sartre's Theory of the Alter Ego," p. 201f. (M.N.)

and familiarity, social proximity and social distance, etc., which govern my relations with consociates, contemporaries, predecessors, and successors. All this cannot be treated here. For our purposes it is enough to show that the whole social world is a world within my attainable reach, having its specific chances of attainment.

Yet the specific chances of restoration, peculiar to the first, and of attainment, peculiar to the second zone of potentiality, are by no means equal. As to the former, we have to consider that what is now to me a mere chance of restorable reach was previously experienced by me as being within my actual reach. My past working acts performed and even the actions which in the past I had merely projected pertained to my world then within actual reach. On the other hand, they are related with my present state of mind which is as it is because the now past reality was once a present one. The anticipated possible reactualization of the once actual world within my reach is, therefore, founded upon reproductions and retentions of my own past experiences of fulfillments. The chance of restoring the once actual reach is, then, a maximal one.

The second zone of potentiality refers anticipatorily to future states of my mind. It is not connected with my past experiences, except by the fact that its anticipations (as all anticipations) originate in and have to be compatible with the stock of my past experiences actually at hand. These experiences enable me to weigh the likelihood of carrying out my plans and to estimate my powers. It is clear that this second zone is not at all homogeneous but subdivided into sectors of different chances of attainment. These chances diminish in proportion with the increasing spatial, temporal, and social distance of the respective sector from the actual center of my world of working. The greater the distance the more uncertain are my anticipations of the attainable actuality, until they become entirely empty and unrealizable.

7) The world of working as paramount reality; the fundamental anxiety; the epoché of the natural attitude

The world of working as a whole stands out as paramount over against the many other sub-universes of reality. It is the world of physical things, including my body; it is the realm of my locomotions and bodily operations; it offers resistances which require effort to overcome; it places tasks before me, permits me to carry through my plans, and enables me to succeed or to fail in my attempt to attain my purposes. By my working acts I gear into the outer world, I change it; and these changes, although provoked by my working, can be experienced and tested both by myself and others, as occurrences within this world independently of my working acts in which they originated. I share this world and its objects with Others; with Others, I have ends and means in common; I work with them in manifold social acts and relationships, checking the Others and checked by them. And the world of working is the reality within which communication and the interplay of mutual motivation becomes effective. It can, therefore, be experienced under both schemes of reference, the causality of motives as well as the teleology of purposes.

As we stated before, this world is to our natural attitude in the first place not an object of our thought but a field of domination. We have an eminently practical interest in it, caused by the necessity of complying with the basic requirements of our life. But we are not *equally* interested in all the strata of the world of working. The selective function of our interest organizes the world in both respects – as to space and time – in strata of major or minor relevance. From the world within my actual or potential reach those objects are selected as primarily important which actually are or will become in the future possible ends or means for the realization of my projects, or which are or will become dangerous or enjoyable or otherwise relevant to me. I am constantly anticipating the future repercussions I may expect from these objects and the future changes my projected working will bring about with respect to them.

Let us make clearer what is meant by "relevance" in this context. I am, for instance, with the natural attitude, passionately interested in the results of my action and especially in the question whether my anticipations will stand the practical test. As we have seen before, all anticipations and plans refer to previous experiences now at hand, which enable me to weigh my chances. But that is only half the story. *What* I am anticipating is one thing, the other, *why* I anticipate certain occurrences at all. What may happen under certain conditions and circumstances is one thing, the other, why I am interested in these happenings and why I should passionately await the outcome of my prophesies. It is only the first part of these dichotomies which is answered by reference to the stock of experiences at hand as the sediment of previous experiences. It is the second part of these dichotomies which refers to the system of relevances by which man within his natural atttiude in daily life is guided.

We cannot unfold here all the implications of the problem of relevance, upon one aspect of which we have just touched. But in a word, we want to state that the whole system of relevances which governs us within the natural attitude is founded upon the basic experience of each of us: I know that I shall die and I fear to die. This basic experience we suggest calling the *fundamental anxiety*. It is the primordial anticipation from which all the others originate. From the fundamental anxiety spring the many interrelated systems of hopes and fears, of wants and satisfactions, of chances and risks which incite man within the natural attitude to attempt the mastery of the world, to overcome obstacles, to draft projects, and to realize them.

But the fundamental anxiety itself is merely a correlate of our existence as human beings within the paramount reality of daily life and, therefore, the hopes and fears and their correlated satisfactions and disappointments are grounded upon and only possible within the world of working. They are essential elements of its reality but they do not refer to our belief in it. On the contrary, it is characteristic of the natural attitude that it takes the world and its objects for granted until counterproof imposes itself. As long as the once established scheme of reference, the system of our and other people's warranted experiences works, as long as the actions and operations performed under its guidance yield the desired results, we trust these experiences. We are not interested in finding out whether this world really does exist or whether it is merely a coherent system of consistent appearances. We have no reason to cast any doubt upon our warranted experiences which, so we believe, give us things as they really are. It needs a special motivation, such as the irruption of a "strange" experience not subsumable under the stock of knowledge at hand or inconsistent with it, to make us revise our former beliefs.

Phenomenology has taught us the concept of phenomenological *epoché*, the suspension of our belief in the reality of the world as a device to overcome the natural attitude by radicalizing the Cartesian method of philosophical doubt.[16] The suggestion may be ventured that man within the natural attitude also uses a specific *epoché*, of course quite another one than the phenomenologist. He does not suspend belief in the outer world and its objects, but on the contrary, he suspends doubt in its existence. What he puts in brackets is the doubt that the world and its objects might be otherwise than it appears to him. We propose to call this *epoché* the *epoché of the natural attitude*.[16a]

II. THE MANY REALITIES AND THEIR CONSTITUTION

In the beginning of this paper we referred to William James' theory of the many sub-universes each of which may be conceived as reality after its own fashion, whilst attended to. James himself has pointed out that each of these sub-universes has its special and separate style of existence; that with respect to each of these sub-universes "all propositions, whether attributive or existential, are believed through the very fact of being conceived, unless they clash with other propositions believed at the same time, by affirming that their terms are the same with the terms of these other propositions";[17] that the whole distinction of real and unreal is grounded on two mental facts – "first, that we are liable to think differently of the same; and second that, when we have done so, we can choose which way of thinking to adhere to and which to disregard." James speaks therefore of a "sense of reality" which can be investigated in terms of a psychology of belief and disbelief.

In order to free this important insight from its psychologistic

---

[16] Cf. Farber, *loc. cit.*, p. 526f.

[16a] Although the point of view of the present paper differs in many respects from his, I should like to call attention to Herbert Spiegelberg's very interesting paper "The Reality-Phenomenon and Reality" in *Philosophical Essays in Memory of Edmund Husserl* (*op.cit.*) pp. 84–105, which attempts an analysis of dubitability and dubiousness with respect to reality. According to Spiegelberg, reality-criteria are the phenomena of readiness, persistence, perceptual periphery, boundaries in concrete objects, independence, resistance, and agreement.

[17] James, *Principles*, Vol. II, p. 290.

setting we prefer to speak instead of many sub-universes of reality of *finite provinces of meaning* upon each of which we may bestow the accent of reality. We speak of provinces of *meaning* and not of sub-universes because it is the meaning of our experiences and not the ontological structure of the objects which constitutes reality.[18] Hence we call a certain set of our experiences a finite province of meaning if all of them show a specific cognitive style and are – *with respect to this style* – not only consistent in themselves but also compatible with one another. The italicized restriction is important because inconsistencies and incompatibilities of *some* experiences, all of them partaking of the same cognitive style, do not necessarily entail the withdrawal of the accent of reality from the respective province of meaning as a whole but merely the invalidation of the particular experience or experiences *within* that province. What, however, has to be understood under the terms "specific cognitive style" and "accent of reality"?

As an example let us consider again the world of everyday life as it was defined and analyzed in the preceding section. This world is certainly a "sub-universe" or "finite province of meaning" among many others, although one marked out as ultimate or paramount reality for the reasons mentioned in the last section. If we recapitulate the basic characteristics which constitute its specific cognitive style we find

1) a specific tension of consciousness, namely wide-awakeness, originating in full attention to life;

2) a specific *epoché*, namely suspension of doubt;

3) a prevalent form of spontaneity, namely working (a meaningful spontaneity based upon a project and characterized by the intention of bringing about the projected state of affairs by bodily movements gearing into the outer world);

4) a specific form of experiencing one's self (the working self as the total self);

5) a specific form of sociality (the common intersubjective world of communication and social action);

6) a specific time-perspective (the standard time originating in

---

[18] Cf. Husserl, *Ideas, General Introduction to Pure Phenomenology*, translated by Boyce Gibson, London-New York, 1931, Sec. 55, p. 168: "In a certain sense and with proper care in the use of words we may say that *all real unities are 'unities of meaning'*." (Italics Husserl's)

an intersection between *durée* and cosmic time as the universal temporal structure of the intersubjective world).

These are at least some of the features of the cognitive style belonging to this particular province of meaning. As long as our experiences of this world – the valid as well as the invalidated ones – partake of this style we may consider this province of meaning as real, we may bestow upon it the accent of reality. And with respect to the paramount reality of everyday life we, within the natural attitude, are induced to do so because our practical experiences prove the unity and congruity of the world of working as valid and the hypothesis of its reality as irrefutable. Even more, this reality seems to us to be the natural one, and we are not ready to abandon our attitude toward it without having experienced a specific *shock* which compels us to break through the limits of this "finite" province of meaning and to shift the accent of reality to another one.

To be sure, those experiences of shock befall me frequently amidst my daily life; they themselves pertain to its reality. They show me that the world of working in standard time is not the sole finite province of meaning but only one of many others accessible to my intentional life.

There are as many innumerable kinds of different shock experiences as there are different finite provinces of meaning upon which I may bestow the accent of reality. Some instances are: the shock of falling asleep as the leap into the world of dreams; the inner transformation we endure if the curtain in the theater rises as the transition into the world of the stageplay; the radical change in our attitude if, before a painting, we permit our visual field to be limited by what is within the frame as the passage into the pictorial world; our quandary, relaxing into laughter, if, in listening to a joke, we are for a short time ready to accept the fictitious world of the jest as a reality in relation to which the world of our daily life takes on the character of foolishness; the child's turning toward his toy as the transition into the play-world; and so on. But also the religious experiences in all their varieties – for instance, Kierkegaard's experience of the "instant" as the leap into the religious sphere – are examples of such a shock, as well as the decision of the scientist to replace all passionate participation in the affairs of "this world" by a disinterested contemplative attitude.

Now we are able to condense what we have found into the following theses:

1) All these worlds – the world of dreams, of imageries and phantasms, especially the world of art, the world of religious experience, the world of scientific contemplation, the play world of the child, and the world of the insane – are finite provinces of meaning. This means that (a) all of them have a peculiar cognitive style (although not that of the world of working within the natural attitude); (b) all experiences within each of these worlds are, with respect to this cognitive style, consistent in themselves and compatible with one another (although not compatible with the meaning of everyday life); (c) each of these finite provinces of meaning may receive a specific accent of reality (although not the reality accent of the world of working).

2) Consistency and compatibility of experiences with respect to their peculiar cognitive style subsists merely *within* the borders of the particular province of meaning to which those experiences belong. By no means will that which is compatible within the province of meaning P be also compatible within the province of meaning Q. On the contrary, seen from P, supposed to be real, Q and all the experiences belonging to it would appear as merely fictitious, inconsistent and incompatible and vice versa.

3) For this very reason we are entitled to talk of *finite* provinces of meaning. This finiteness implies that there is no possibility of referring one of these provinces to the other by introducing a formula of transformation. The passing from one to the other can only be performed by a "leap," as Kierkegaard calls it, which manifests itself in the subjective experience of a shock.*

4) What has just been called a "leap" or a "shock" is nothing else than a radical modification in the tension of our consciousness, founded in a different *attention à la vie*.

5) To the cognitive style peculiar to each of these different provinces of meaning belongs, thus, a specific tension of consciousness and, consequently, also a specific *epoché*, a prevalent form of spontaneity, a specific form of self experience, a specific form of sociality, and a specific time perspective.

---

* For a discussion of the transition from the paramount reality to other finite provinces of meaning experienced through a shock, cf. "Symbol, Reality and Society," p. 343f. (M.N.)

6) The world of working in daily life is the archetype of our experience of reality. All the other provinces of meaning may be considered as its modifications.[19]

It would be an interesting task to try a systematic grouping of these finite provinces of meaning according to their constitutive principle, the diminishing tension of our consciousness founded in a turning away of our attention from everyday life. Such an analysis would prove that the more the mind turns away from life, the larger the slabs of the everyday world of working which are put in doubt; the *epoché* of the natural attitude which suspends doubt in its existence is replaced by other *epochés* which suspend belief in more and more layers of the reality of daily life, putting them in brackets. In other words, a typology of the different finite provinces of meaning could start from an analysis of those factors of the world of daily life from which the accent of reality has been withdrawn because they do not stand any longer within the focus of our attentional interest in life. What then remains outside the brackets could be defined as the constituent elements of the cognitive style of experiences belonging to the province of meaning thus delimited. It may, then, in its turn, obtain another accent of reality, or, in the language of the archetype of all reality, namely the world of our daily life – of quasi-reality.

The last remark reveals a specific difficulty for all attempts at describing those quasi-realities. It consists in the fact that language – any language – pertains as communication κατ' ἐξοχήν to the intersubjective world of working and, therefore, obstinately resists serving as a vehicle for meanings which transcend its own presuppositions. This fact leads to the manifold forms of indirect communication, some of which we will meet

---

[19] A word of caution seems to be needed here. The concept of finite provinces of meaning does not involve any static connotation as though we had to select one of these provinces as our home to live in, to start from or to return to. That is by no means the case. Within a single day, even within a single hour our consciousness may run through most different tensions and adopt most different attentional attitudes to life. There is, furthermore, the problem of "enclaves," that is, of regions belonging to one province of meaning enclosed by another, a problem which, important as it is, cannot be handled within the frame of the present paper, which admittedly restricts itself to the outlining of a few principles of analysis. To give an example of this disregarded group of problems: any projecting within the world of working is itself, as we have seen, a phantasying, and involves in addition a kind of theoretical contemplation, although not necessarily that of the scientific attitude.

later on. Scientific terminology, for instance, is a special device to overcome the outlined difficulty within its limited field.

We cannot embark here upon the drafting of a thorough typology of the many realities according to the principles just outlined. We are especially interested in the relations between the provinces of the world of daily life and the worlds of the sciences, especially of the social sciences and their reality. We cannot, however, work out this problem with all its implications in a single step. We shall, therefore, proceed by stages and start with confronting the world of working with two typical examples of other finite provinces of meaning, namely, the world of imageries and the world of dreams. Based upon the results of our analyses of the cognitive style of these two provinces, we shall investigate the structure of the world of scientific contemplation.

III. THE VARIOUS WORLDS OF PHANTASMS

Under this heading we shall discuss some general characteristics of the cognitive style peculiar to a group of otherwise most heterogeneous finite provinces of meaning, none of them reducible to the other. This group is commonly known as that of fancies or imageries and embraces among many others the realms of day-dreams, of play, of fiction, of fairy-tales, of myths, of jokes. So far philosophy has not worked upon the problem of the specific constitution of each of these innumerable provinces of our imaginative life. Each of them originates in a specific modification which the paramount reality of our daily life undergoes, because our mind, turning away in decreasing tensions of consciousness from the world of working and its tasks, withdraws from certain of its layers the accent of reality in order to replace it by a context of supposedly quasi-real phantasms. For the problem at hand a fugitive survey of what all these worlds have in common has to be sufficient.

Living in one of the many worlds of phantasy we have no longer to master the outer world and to overcome the resistance of its objects. We are free from the pragmatic motive which governs our natural attitude toward the world of daily life, free also from the bondage of "interobjective" space and intersubjective standard time. No longer are we confined within the limits of our actual, restorable, or attainable reach. What occurs in the outer world no longer imposes upon us issues between which we have to choose nor does it put a limit on our possible accomplishments.

However, there are no "possible accomplishments" in the world of phantasms if we take this term as a synonym of "performable." The imagining self neither works nor performs within the meaning of the aforegiven definitions. Imagining may be projected inasmuch as it may be conceived in advance and may be included in a hierarchy of plans. But this meaning of the term "project" is not exactly the same in which we used it when we defined action as projected conduct. Strictly speaking, the opposite holds true, namely, that the projected action is always the imagined performed act, imagined in the future-perfect tense. Here we are not particularly interested in investigating whether all or merely some or no form of our imaginative life may be qualified as "action" or whether fancying belongs exclusively to the category of mere thinking. Yet it is of highest importance to understand that imagining as such always lacks the intention of realizing the phantasm; it lacks in other words the purposive "fiat." Using the language of Husserl's *Ideas* [20] we may say that all imagining is "neutral," it lacks the specific positionality of the thetic consciousness.

However, we have to distinguish sharply between imagining as a manifestation of our spontaneous life and the imageries imagined. Acting may be imagined as a true acting and even working within the meaning of our previous definitions; it may be imagined as referring to a preconceived project; as having its specific in-order-to and because motives;* as originating in choice and decision; as having its place within a hierarchy of plans. Furthermore, it may be imagined as endowed with an intention of realizing the project, to carry it through, and may be fancied as gearing into the outer world. All this, however, belongs to the imageries produced in and by the imagining act. The "performances" and "working acts" are merely imagined *as*

---

[20] *L.c.*, 306-312, especially Sec. 111, in particular the distinction between neutrality modification (in the strict sense) and phantasy.

* See "Choosing among Projects of Action," p. 69f. (M.N.)

performances and working acts, and they and the correlated categories bear, to borrow Husserl's term, "quotation-marks." Imagining itself is, however, necessarily inefficient and stays under all circumstances outside the hierarchies of plans and purposes valid within the world of working. The imagining self does not transform the outer world.

But how? Does not Don Quixote gear into the outer world if he attacks the windmills, imagining them to be giants? Is not what he does, determined by motives valid within the world of working, namely, his in-order-to motive to kill the giants and his because-motive to live up to his mission as a knight which involves the duty to fight bad giants wherever they are met? Is all this not included in the hierarchy of Don Quixote's life-plans?

The answer is that Don Quixote, acting as described, does not trespass the boundaries of the world of working. To him who is a fantast confronted with realities (as Eulenspiegel is a realist confronted with phantasms) there are no imagined giants in the reality of his world of working but real giants. Afterwards he will recognize that his interpretation of the object before him was invalidated by the succeeding events. This is the same experience we all have within the natural attitude if we discover that the distant something which we believed to be a tree turns out to be a man.[21] But then, Don Quixote reacts differently than we do in similar situations. He does not submit to the "explosion of his experience," he does not acknowledge his delusion and does not admit that the attacked objects have always been windmills and never giants. To be sure, he is compelled to concede the *actual* reality of the windmills to the resistance of which he succumbed, but he interprets this fact as if it did not belong to the real world. He explains it by the theory that, in order to vex him, his arch-enemy, the magician, must have transmogrified at the last moment the formerly no less real giants into windmills. And only now, by reaching this conclusion, has Don Quixote definitely withdrawn the accent of reality from the world of working and has bestowed such an accent upon the world of his imageries. Seen from the latter, the windmills are not realities but mere

---

[21] This situation has been carefully analyzed by Husserl, *Ideas*, Section 103 and in *Erfahrung und Urteil*, Prague, 1939, pp. 99ff. and 370ff.

appearances, mere phantasms. The existence of magicians and giants and the transformation of the latter into windmills, incompatible as it may be with the natural attitude prevalent in the world of working common to Don Quixote and Sancho Panza and the barber, is very well compatible with Don Quixote's other imageries in his finite province of private phantasms and, there, it is as "real" as anything.* – *Mutatis mutandis*, similar analyses could be made with respect to other quasi-realities such as the magic world of primitive men or the make-believe world of children's play, etc.

If we transform this result into more general terms, we find it corroborated by William James' statement that "any object which remains uncontradicted is *ipso facto* believed and posited as absolute reality." "If I merely dream of a horse with wings, my horse interferes with nothing else and has not to be contradicted. That horse, its wings, and its place, are all equally real. That horse exists no otherwise than as winged, and is moreover really there, for that place exists no otherwise than as the place of that horse, and claims as yet no connection with the other places of the world. But if with this horse I make an inroad into the *world otherwise known*, and say, for example, 'That is my old mare Maggie, having grown a pair of wings where she stands in her stall,' the whole case is altered; for now the horse and place are identified with a horse and place otherwise known, and *what is known of the latter objects is incompatible with what is perceived in the former.* 'Maggie in her stall with wings! Never!' The wings are unreal, then, visionary. I have dreamed a lie about Maggie in her stall." [22]

Husserl,[23] who has studied the problem involved more profoundly than any other philosopher, comes to the same conclusion. He distinguishes predications of existence (*Existenzialprädikationen*) and predications of reality (*Wirklichkeitsprädikationen*). The opposites to the former are the predications of non-existence, of the latter the predications of non-reality, of

---

[22] *Principles of Psychology*, Vol. II, p. 289.
[23] *Erfahrung und Urteil*, Sec. 74a, pp. 359ff.; cf. Farber, *l.c.*, pp. 525ff. It should be noted that the term "experience" is used here by Husserl in the restricted sense of *Erfahrung*.

* See Alfred Schutz, "Don Quixote and the Problem of Reality," published in Spanish in *Dianoia*, Vol. I, 1954, pp. 312–330. (M.N.)

fiction. Investigating the "origin" of predications of reality Husserl concludes:

"With the natural attitude there is at the outset (before reflection) no predicate 'real' and no category 'reality.' Only if we phantasy and pass from the attitude of living in the phantasy (that is the attitude of quasiexperiencing in all its forms) to the given realities, and if we, thus, transgress the single casual phantasying and its phantasm, taking both as examples for possible phantasying as such and fiction as such, then we obtain on the one hand the concepts fiction (respectively, phantasying) and on the other hand the concepts 'possible experience as such' and 'reality' ... We cannot say that he who phantasies and lives in the world of phantasms (the 'dreamer'), posits fictions *qua* fictions, but he has modified realities, 'realities as if' ... Only he who lives in experiences and reaches from there into the world of phantasms can, provided that the phantasm contrasts with the experienced, have the concepts fiction and reality." *

From our analysis of Don Quixote's conduct and the preceding quotation from Husserl we may derive another important insight. The compatibilities of experiences which belong to the world of working in everyday life do not subsist within the realm of imagery; however the logical structure of consistency, or, in Husserl's terms, the predications of existence and nonexistence, remain valid. I can imagine giants, magicians, winged horses, centaurs, even a *perpetuum mobile;* but not a regular decahedron, unless I stop – as I would have to do in full awakeness – at the blind juxtaposition of empty terms. Put otherwise: within the realm of imagery merely factual, but not logical incompatibilities can be overcome.

The corollary of this last statement is that chances of attainability and restorability of factual situations do not exist in the same sense within the world of phantasms as they exist within the world of working. What is a chance in the latter is in the former what Roman jurists call a *conditio potestativa*, that is, a circumstance controlled by the party involved, who decides whether or not to bring it about. The imagining individual masters his chances: he can fill the empty anticipations of

* *Erfahrung und Urteil*, Section 74a. (M.N.)

his imageries with any content he pleases; as to the anticipating of imagined future events he has freedom of discretion.

This remark leads us to the time perspectives of the world of imageries, which is of highest importance for its constitution. In his admirable investigations relating to the dimension of time of phantasms, Husserl [24] has pointed out that phantasms lack any fixed position in the order of objective time. Therefore, phantasms are not individualized, and the category of sameness is not applicable to them. The "same" phantasm may recur within the uninterrupted continuity of one single phantasying activity the unity of which is warranted by the continuity of inner time within which this activity occurs. But phantasms pertaining to different strands of phantasying activities or, in our terminology, pertaining to different finite provinces of meaning, cannot be compared as to their sameness or likeness. It is meaningless to ask whether the witch of one fairy tale is the same as the witch of another.

For our purpose it is not necessary to follow Husserl into the depth of the problems of constitutional analyses here involved. Yet it is important to point out that the imagining self can, in his phantasies, eliminate all the features of standard time except its irreversibility. It may imagine all occurrences as viewed, so to speak, through a time-retarder or through a time-accelerator. Their irreversibility, however, eludes any variation by phantasies because it originates within the *durée* which itself is constitutive for all activities of our mind and, therefore, also for our phantasying and the phantasms produced therein. Imagining, and even dreaming, I continue to grow old. The fact that I can remodel my past by a present imagining is no counter-evidence against this statement.

In my imagery I may fancy myself in any rôle I wish to assume. But doing so I have no doubt that the imagined self is merely a part of my total personality, one possible rôle I may take, a Me, existing only by my grace. In my phantasms I may even vary my bodily appearance, but this freedom of discretion has its barrier at the primordial experience of the boundaries of my body. They subsist whether I imagine myself as a dwarf or as a giant.

[24] *Erfahrung und Urteil*, Sects. 39–42, pp. 195–214.

Imagining can be lonely or social and then take place in We-relation as well as in all of its derivations and modifications. An instance of the first is day-dreaming, of the second the mutually oriented intersubjective make-believe play of children or some phenomena studied by mass psychology. On the other hand, the others and also any kind of social relationship, social actions, and reactions, may become objects of the imagining. The freedom of discretion of the imagining self is here a very large one. It is even possible that the phantasm may include an imagined cooperation of an imagined fellow-man to such an extent that the latter's imagined reactions may corroborate or annihilate my own phantasms.

IV. THE WORLD OF DREAMS

If full awakeness is the name for the highest tension of consciousness which corresponds to full attention to life, sleep may be defined as complete relaxation, as turning away from life.[25] The sleeping self has no pragmatic interest whatsoever in transforming its largely confused perceptions into a state of partial clarity and distinctness, in other words to transform them into apperceptions.[26] Nevertheless it continues to perceive as it continues to recollect and to think. There are the somatical perceptions of its own body, its position, its weight, its boundaries; perceptions of light, sound, warmth, etc., without any activity, however, of regarding, listening, attending to them, which alone would make the percepts apperceived; there continue, furthermore, the small perceptions, which, in the state of awakeness, by the very pragmatic orientation toward the tasks of life, remain indiscernible and ineffable – or as modern use likes to call them, unconscious. These small perceptions, escaping the censorship of the attention to life, gain high importance in the world of dreams. Although they do not become clear and distinct, but remain in a state of confusion, they are no longer concealed and disturbed by

[25] Cf. Bergson's lecture "Mécanisme du Rêve," 1901, reprinted in *L'Energie spirituelle*, pp. 91–116, esp. p. 111.
[26] That sleep is a state of consciousness which is free from apperceptions distinguishes the world of dreams from the world of phantasms. The imagining self continues to apperceive but the scheme of interpretation it applies to what it apperceives differs radically from that which the wide-awake self applies to the same apperceptions in the world of working.

the interference of *active*, pragmatically conditioned attention. It is the *passive* attention, that is, the total of the effects exercised by the small perceptions upon the intimate center of the personality which alone determines the interest of the dreamer and the topics which become themes of his dreams. It is the incomparable performance of Freud and his school to have clarified this reference of dreamlife to the unconscious, although his concept of the unconscious itself (and also his theory that the mental apparatus is – "topographically" – composed of an Id, Ego, and Super-ego) is a misunderstanding of the basic character of the intentionality of the stream of thought.[27]

The dreaming self neither works nor acts. This statement would be a mere truism had we not made a similar one with respect to the phantasying self. We have, therefore, to show briefly the principal modifications which the "bracketing of the world of working" undergoes in the provinces of phantasms on the one hand and in the province of dreams on the other. I suggest that the worlds of imageries are characterized by what we called the freedom of discretion, whereas the world of dreams lacks such freedom. The imagining self can "arbitrarily" fill its empty protentions and anticipations with any content and, strictly speaking, it is these fillings upon which the imagining self bestows the accent of reality. It may, as it pleases, interpret its "chances" as lying within its mastery. The dreamer, however, has no freedom of discretion, no arbitrariness in mastering the chances, no possibility of filling in empty anticipations. The nightmare, for instance, shows clearly the inescapableness of the happening in the world of dream and the powerlessness of the dreamer to influence it.

All this, however, does not mean that the life of dreams is confined exclusively to passive consciousness. On the contrary, most of the activities of mind which Husserl calls the activities of intentionality (and which, of course, are not to be confused with intentional actions) subsist, but without being directed toward objects of the outer world of working and without being

---

[27] But Freud himself – in contradistinction to many of his followers – has admitted that his "mental topography" is in every respect open to revision and like the whole theoretical superstructure of psychoanalysis still incomplete and subject to constant alteration. (Cf. Freud's article "Psychoanalysis" in *Encyclopaedia Britannica*, 14th ed., Vol. 18, p. 673.)

steered by active attention. Yet among these activities there are none of apperceiving and of volition. The life of dreams is without purpose and project.

But how can such a proposition be sustained, since Freud and his followers have taught us the predominant rôle of volitions and instincts within the world of dreams? I do not think that there is any contradiction. Actual volitions, actual projects, actual purposes, etc., do not exist in the life of dreams. What can be found of volitions, projects, purposes in dreams does not originate in the dreaming self. They are recollections, retentions, and reproductions of volitive experiences which originated within the world of awakeness. Now they reappear, although modified and reinterpreted according to the scheme of reference prevailing in the particular type of dream. We may consider the whole psychoanalytic technique of dream interpretation as an attempt to refer the contents of the dream to the originary experiences in the world of awakeness in which and by which they were constituted.

Generally speaking, the world of working or at least fragments of it are preserved within the world of dreams as recollections and retentions. In this sense we may say that the *attention à la vie* of the dreamer is directed to the past of his self. It is an attention in the tense of the past. The contents of dream life consist primarily in past or past perfect experiences which are re-interpreted by transforming previously confused experiences into distinctness, by explicating their implied horizons, by looking at their anticipations in terms of the past and at their reproduction in terms of the future. The sedimented experiences of the world of awakeness are, thus, so to speak, broken down and otherwise reconstructed – the self having no longer any pragmatic interest in keeping together its stock of experience as a consistently and coherently unified scheme of reference. But the postulates of consistency and coherence and of unity of experience themselves originate in pragmatic motives in so far as they presuppose clear and distinct apperceptions. They, and even certain logical axioms, such as the axiom of identity, do not, for this very reason, hold good in the sphere of dreams. The dreamer is frequently astonished to see now as compatible what he remembers as having been incompatible in the world of his awake life, and vice versa. All this Freud and psychoanalysis have thoroughly studied, and our present intention is restricted to translating some of their results, important for the topic at hand, into our language and to giving them their place within our theory.

I may dream myself as working or acting and this dream may be accompanied frequently by the knowledge that, "in reality," I am not working or acting. Then my dreamed working has its quasi-projects, quasi-plans, and their hierarchies, all of them originating in sedimented pre-experiences I had in the world of daily life. It happens frequently that the dreamed Me performs his work without any intention of carrying it through, without any voluntative fiat, and that this Me attains results with either disproportionately great or small effort.

The time perspective of the world of dreams has a very complicated stucture. Aft and fore, present, past and future seem to be intermingled, there are future events conceived in terms of the past, past and past-perfect events assumed as open and modifiable and, therefore, as having a strange character of futurity, successions are transformed into simultaneities and vice versa, etc. Seemingly – but only seemingly – the occurrences during the dream are separated and independent of the stream of the inner *durée*. They are, however, merely detached from the arrangement of standard time. They have no position in the order of objective time. They roll on within the subjectivity of inner *durée* although fragments of standard time, which was experienced by the past self and has fallen to pieces, are snatched into the world of dreams. The irreversibility of the *durée* subsists also in dream-life. Only the awakened mind which remembers its dream has sometimes the illusion of a possible reversibility.

This last remark reveals a serious difficulty for all analysis of the phenomena of the dream and also of imagery. As soon as I think of them I am no longer dreaming or imagining. I am wide-awake and use, speaking and thinking, the implements of the world of working, namely concepts which are subject to the principles of consistency and compatibility. Are we sure that the awakened person really can tell his dreams, he who no longer dreams? It will probably make an important difference whether he recollects his dream in vivid retention or whether he has to reproduce it. Whatever the case may be, we encounter the eminent dialectical difficulty that there exists for the dreamer no possibility of direct communication which would not transcend the sphere to which it refers. We can, therefore, approach the provinces of dreams and imageries merely by way of "indirect communication," to borrow this term from Kierkegaard, who has analyzed the phenomena it suggests in an unsurpassable way. The poet and the artist are much closer to an adequate interpretation of the worlds of dreams and phantasms than the scientist and the philosopher, because their categories of communication themselves refer to the realm of imagery. They can, if not overcome, at least make transparent the underlying dialectical conflict.

Within the modest limits of our purpose, we have no reason to shrink from the difficulty outlined. Our problem is to give an account of the specific cognitive style peculiar to the provinces of phantasms and dreams and to explain them as derivations from the cognitive style of experiencing the world of everyday life. We therefore feel entitled to apply categories derived from this world to the phenomena of imagery and dream. Nevertheless, the dialectical difficulty involved has to be understood in its full importance, since we will meet it again in the analysis of the world of scientific contemplation. Then we shall have to study the specific device which science has developed to overcome it, namely, the scientific method.

Concluding the fugitive remarks on the realm of dreams, we want to state that dreaming – as distinguished from imagining – is essentially lonely. We cannot dream together, and the alter ego remains always merely an object of my dreams, incapable of sharing them. Even the alter ego of which I dream does not appear in a common vivid present but in an empty fictitious quasi-We relation. The Other dreamed of is always typified, and this holds true even if I dream him to be in very close relationship to my intimate self. He is an alter ego only by my grace. Thus, the monad, with all its mirroring of the universe, is indeed without windows while it dreams.

V. THE WORLD OF SCIENTIFIC THEORY

In restricting the following analysis to the world as object of *scientific* contemplation we intentionally disregard for the present purpose the many forms of contemplative attitudes which we frequently adopt amidst our working activities and which in contradistinction to the practical attitudes of working could also be called theoretical attitudes. If we "sit down" in a major crisis of our life and consider again and again our problems, if we draft, reject, redraft projects and plans before making up our mind, if as fathers we meditate upon pedagogical questions or as politicians upon public opinion – in all these situations we indulge in theoretical contemplation in the wider sense of this term. But all this contemplative thinking is performed for practical purposes and ends, and for this very reason it constitutes an "enclave" [28] of theoretical contemplation within the world of working rather than a finite province of meaning.

Another type of contemplation which we intentionally disregard in the present section is pure meditation, such as religious meditation, which is not based upon a project to be brought about by application of operational rules. We have to deal exclusively with scientific theory.

Scientific theorizing – and in the following the terms theory, theorizing, etc., shall be exclusively used in this restricted sense – does not serve any practical purpose. Its aim is not to master the world but to observe and possibly to understand it.

Here I wish to anticipate a possible objection. Is not the ultimate aim of science the mastery of the world? Are not natural sciences designed to dominate the forces of the universe, social sciences to exercise control, medical science to fight diseases? And is not the only reason why man bothers with science his desire to develop the necessary tools in order to improve his everyday life and to help humanity in its pursuit of happiness? All this is certainly as true as it is banal, but it has nothing to do with our problem. Of course, the desire to improve the world is one of man's strongest motives for dealing with science, and the application of scientific theory leads of course to the invention of technical devices for the mastery of the world. But neither

[28] Cf. *Supra* footnote 19, page 233.

these motives nor the use of its results for "wordly" purposes is an element of the process of scientific theorizing itself. Scientific theorizing is one thing, dealing with science within the world of working is another. Our topic is the first one, but one of our chief problems will be to find out how it is possible that the life-world of all of us can be made an object of theoretical contemplation and that the outcome of this contemplation can be used within the world of working.

All theoretical cogitations are "actions" and even "performances" within the meaning of the definitions already given. They are actions because they are emanations of our spontaneous life carried out according to a project, and they are performances because the intention of carrying through the project to bring about the projected result supervenes. Thus, scientific theorizing has its own in-order-to and because motives, it is planned, and planned within a hierarchy of plans established by the decision to pursue and carry on scientific activities. (This "action-character" of theorizing alone would suffice to distinguish it from dreaming.) It is, furthermore, purposive thinking (and this purposiveness alone would suffice to distinguish it from mere fancying!), the purpose being the intention of realizing the solution of the problem at hand. Yet, theoretical cogitations are not acts of working, that is, they do not gear into the outer world. To be sure, they are based upon working acts (such as measuring, handling instruments, making experiments); they can be communicated only by working acts (such as writing a paper, delivering a lecture); and so on. All these activities performed within and pertaining to the world of working are either conditions or consequences of the theorizing but do not belong to the theoretical attitude itself, from which they can be easily separated. Likewise, we have to distinguish between the scientist *qua* human being who acts and lives his everyday life among his fellow-men and the theoretical thinker who is, we repeat, not interested in the mastery of the world but in obtaining knowledge by observing it.

This attitude of the "disinterested observer" is based upon a peculiar *attention à la vie* as the prerequisite of all theorizing. It consists in the abandoning of the system of relevances which prevails within the practical sphere of the natural attitude. The whole universe of life, that which Husserl calls the *Lebenswelt*, is pregiven to both the man in the world of working and to the theorizing thinker.[29] But to the former other sections and other elements of this world are relevant than to the latter. In a previous section [30] we have shown that for man within the natural attitude the system of relevances which governs him originates in what we called the basic experience of fundamental anxiety. The theoretical thinker once having performed the "leap" into the disinterested attitude is free from the fundamental anxiety and free from all the hopes and fears arising from it.[31] He, too, has anticipations which, on the one hand, refer back to his stock of sedimented experiences and, on the other hand, to its special system of relevances which will be discussed later. However, unlike man in daily life, he is not passionately interested in the question whether his anticipations, if fulfilled, will prove helpful for the solution of his practical problems, but merely whether or not they will stand the test of verification by supervening experiences. This involves – in the well-understood meaning of the aforegiven definition – a certain detachment of interest in life and a turning away from what we called the state of wide-awakeness.[32]

Since theoretical thought does not gear into the outer world, it is revocable within the meaning of this term as we have defined it.[33] That means it is subject to permanent revision, it can be undone, "struck out," "cancelled," modified, and so on, without creating any change in the outer world. In the process of theoretical thinking I may come back again and again to my premises, revoke my conclusions, annihilate my judgments,

---

[29] Cf. Husserl, "Die Krisis der europäischen Wissenschaften und die transzendentale Phänomenologie," *Philosophia*, Vol. I, Belgrad, 1936, pp. 124–129.

[30] Cf. *Supra* page 228.

[31] This does not mean that the fundamental anxiety is not the chief motive inducing human beings to start philosophizing. On the contrary, philosophy is one of the attempts – perhaps the principal one – to overcome the fundamental anxiety. An immortal Being – say an angel in the system of Thomas Aquinas – would not need to turn philosopher. But having performed the leap into the realm of theoretical contemplation, the human being exercises a peculiar *epoché* from the fundamental anxiety, putting it and all its implications in brackets.

[32] I hope that this statement will not be misunderstood as bearing any pejorative connotation. The term "wide-awakeness" as used here does not involve any valuation whatsoever. By no means is it the writer's opinion that life as such has a higher dignity than theoretical thought, a point of view advocated by certain so-called "philosophies of life," especially modish in Germany.

[33] *Supra* page 217.

enlarge or restrict the scope of the problem under scrutiny, etc.

The latter point has its corollary in the peculiarity of theoretical thought of being in a certain sense independent of that segment of the world which is within the reach of the thinker. This statement, of course, does not refer to the availability of certain *data* to which theoretical thinking may pertain, such as ultramicroscopic objects or the structure of the interior of the earth. As data they are – and in the latter case will probably forever remain – outside of our reach. But this does not prevent the building up of scientific theories concerning both sets of data. Biology and geology have developed methods to deal with them; they are for both sciences realities, although realities outside of our reach, realities *ex hypothesi*.[34] But this is not the point we have in view with our statement. As we have seen,[35] the concept of "world within our reach" depends upon our body which is conceived as center O of the system of coordinates under which we group the world. In turning to the sphere of theoretical thinking, however, the human being "puts in brackets" his physical existence and therewith also his body and the system of orientation of which his body is the center and origin. Consequently, unlike man in daily life, he does not look for solutions fitting his pragmatic personal and private problems which arise from his psycho-physical existence within this peculiar segment of the world which he calls his environment. The theoretical thinker is interested in problems and solutions valid in their own right for everyone, at any place, and at any time, wherever and whenever certain conditions, from the assumption of which he starts, prevail. The "leap" into the province of theoretical thought involves the resolution of the individual to suspend his subjective point of view. And this fact alone shows that not the undivided self but only a partial self, a taker of a rôle, a "Me," namely, the theoretician, "acts" within the province of scientific thought. This partial self lacks all "essentially actual" experiences

[34] In order to master or to influence these hypothetical realities we must, however, bring them within our reach. To give an example: The mere assumption that infantile paralysis is caused by an invisible virus of minute size which passes through the pores of earthenware filters may or may not be justified. But as long as this virus is outside of our reach – and, more precisely, outside our manipulatory sphere – we cannot prepare efficient measures to fight it – except an "antivirus," no less invisible and no less outside of our reach.

[35] *Supra* page 222f.

and all experiences connected with his own body, its movements, and its limits.

We may now sum up some of the features of the *epoché* peculiar to the scientific attitude. In this *epoché* there is "bracketed" (suspended): (1) the subjectivity of the thinker as a man among fellow-men, including his bodily existence as a psycho-physical human being within the world;[36] (2) the system of orientation by which the world of everyday life is grouped in zones within actual, restorable, attainable reach, etc.; (3) the fundamental anxiety and the system of pragmatic relevances originating therein. But within this modified sphere the life-world of all of us continues to subsist as reality, that is as the reality of theoretical contemplation, although not as one practical interest. With the shift of the system of relevances from the practical to the theoretical field all terms referring to action and performance within the world of working, such as "plan," "motive," "projects" change their meaning and receive "quotation marks."

We have now to characterize briefly the system of relevances prevailing within the province of scientific contemplation. This system originates in a voluntary act of the scientist by which he selects the object of his further inquiry, in other words, by the *stating of the problem at hand*. Therewith the more or less emptily anticipated solution of this problem becomes the supreme goal of the scientific activity. On the other hand, by the mere stating of the problem the sections or elements of the world which actually are or potentially may become related to it as relevant, as bearing upon the matter in hand, are at once defined. Henceforth, this circumscription of the relevant field will guide the process of inquiry. It determines, first of all, the so called "level" of the research. As a matter of fact, the term "level" is just another expression for the demarcation line between all that does and does not pertain to the problem under consideration, the former being the topics to be investigated, explicated, clarified, the latter, the other elements of the scientist's knowledge which,

---

[36] Needless to say, this form of *epoché* must not be confused with the *epoché* leading to the phenomenological reduction by which not only the subjectivity of the thinker but the whole world is bracketed. Theoretical thinking has to be characterized as belonging to the "natural attitude," this term *here* (but not in the text) being used in contradistinction to "phenomenological reduction." As to the ambiguity of the term "natural" cf. Farber, *l.c.*, p. 552.

because they are irrelevant to his problem, he decides to accept in their givenness, without questioning, as mere "data." In other words, the demarcation line is the locus of the points actually interesting the scientist and at which he has decided to stop further research and analysis. Secondly, the stating of the problem at once reveals its open horizons, the outer horizon of connected problems which will have to be stated afterwards, as well as the inner horizon of all the implications hidden within the problem itself which have to be made visible and explicated in order to solve it.

All this, however, does not mean that the decision of the scientist in stating the problem is an arbitrary one or that he has the same "freedom of discretion" in choosing and solving his problems which the phantasying self has in filling out its anticipations. This is by no means the case. Of course, the theoretical thinker may choose at his discretion, only determined by an inclination rooted in his intimate personality, the scientific field in which he wants to take interest and possibly also the level (in general) upon which he wants to carry on his investigations. But as soon as he has made up his mind in this respect, the scientist enters a preconstituted world of scientific contemplation handed down to him by the historical tradition of his science. Henceforth, he will participate in a universe of discourse embracing the results obtained by others, problems stated by others, solutions suggested by others, methods worked out by others. This theoretical universe of the special science is itself a finite province of meaning, having its peculiar cognitive style with peculiar implications of problems and horizons to be explicated. The regulative principle of constitution of such a province of meaning, called a special branch of science, can be formulated as follows: Any problem emerging within the scientific field has to partake of the universal style of this field and has to be compatible with the preconstituted problems and their solution by either accepting or refuting them.[37] Thus, the latitude for the discretion of the scientist in stating the problem is in fact a very small one.[38]

[37] As to the latter problem, cf. Felix Kaufmann *Methodology of the Social Sciences*, New York, 1944, Chapter IV.
[38] We disregard here – as surpassing the purpose of the present study – the many interdependencies among all possible systems of questions and answers (the Aristo-

No such latitude, however, has been left as soon as the problem has been stated. It is a shortcoming of our presentation of theoretical thinking that it represents an ongoing process in static terms. For a process it is, going on according to the strict rules of scientific procedure. To describe the epistemology and methodology involved is not within our present purpose.* To mention just a few of these rules: There is the postulate of consistency and compatibility of all propositions not only within the field of that special branch of science but also with all the other scientific propositions and even with the experiences of the natural attitude of everyday life insofar as they are safeguarded, although modified, within the finite province of theoretical contemplation; moreover, the postulate that all scientific thought has to be derived, directly or indirectly, from tested observation, that is, from originary immediate experiences of facts within the world; the postulate of highest possible clarity and distinctness of all terms and notions used, especially requiring the transformation of confused prescientific thought into distinctness by explicating its hidden implications; and many more. The logic of science and the methodology of the special branches of science have established the rules which guarantee the operational procedure of the scientific performance and the testing of its results. The total of these rules sets forth the conditions under which scientific propositions and, in particular, the system of those propositions which form the respective special branch of science can be considered as warranted – or, in our language, the conditions under which an accent of reality can be bestowed upon the finite province of meaning in question.

This leads us to an important distinction. As we have had to distinguish between the world of imagining and the world of imageries imagined,[39] now we have to distinguish between the theorizing cogitations and the intentional *cogitata* of such theorizing. By their intentionality the latter refer to the one objective world, the universe within which we all live as psychophysical human beings, within which we work and think, the

telian problem of a universal aporetic) and also the special problem of key-concepts, that is, of concepts the introduction of which divides the formerly homogeneous field of research into parts relevant or not for the topic under consideration.

[39] *Supra* page 235.

* See "Common-Sense and Scientific Interpretation of Human Action," p. 43f. (M.N.)

intersubjective life-world which is pregiven to all of us as the paramount reality from which all the other forms of reality are derived. "With the theoretical attitude the objects become theoretical objects, objects of an actual positing of *being*, in which the ego apprehends them as existent. This makes possible a comprehensive and systematic view of *all* objects, as possible substrates of the theoretical attitude." [39a]

But unlike the world of phantasms which always lack any fixed position in the order of objective time,[40] the intentional objects of theoretical contemplation, insofar as they are not "ideal objects of higher order," have their well defined place within the order of objective (cosmic) time; and insofar as they are "ideal objects of higher order" [41] they are founded upon objects having such a place in objective time.[42] This statement, however, covers merely the time structure of the *objects* of theoretical thought and does not refer to the perspective of time peculiar to the *process* of contemplative theorizing itself. The theoretical thinker, too, lives within his inner *durée;* he also grows old, since his stock of experiences changes permanently by the emergence and sedimentation of new experiences. The theorizing self, therefore, has its specific form of the past, namely the history of its pre-experiences and their sedimentations, and its specific form of the future, namely, the open horizons of the problem at hand (the "project" of the ongoing theorizing) which refer to other problems to be stated afterwards and to the methods by which they may be solved. But the time perspective which the theorizing self lacks is the vivid present constituted within the natural attitude by the bodily movements as an intersection of inner *durée* and objective (cosmic) time. Consequently, it cannot share a vivid present with Others in a pure We-relation and it even stays outside the different time perspectives of sociality originating in the vivid present of the We-relation. It does not, for this very reason, partake of the time structure of standard time, which, as we have seen, is nothing else than the intersubjective form of all the individual time

---

[39a] Farber, *l.c.*, p. 525.
[40] Cf. *Supra* page 239.
[41] Cf. Farber, *l.c.*, pp. 457, 460, and Husserl, VI. *Logische Untersuchungen*, Secs. 47–48.
[42] Cf. Farber, *l.c.*, p. 491.

perspectives, including the vivid present of the We-relation as well as all of its derivations. Insofar as scientific activity goes on within standard time (in working hours, according to time tables, etc.), it consists in acts of working within the world of everyday life which deal with science but not in acts of pure theorizing.

Although the theorizing self does not know the time dimension of the vivid present, it has, nevertheless, a particular specious present,[43] within which it lives and acts. This specious present is defined at any moment by the span of the projects conceived. Its "fore" embraces the problems previously stated as projected tasks the solution of which is just in progress; its "aft" consists in the anticipated outcome of the ongoing theorizing activities designed to bring about the solution of the problem at hand.

We have seen before that the theoretical thinker puts his physical existence and, thus, his body in brackets. He has no physical environment because there is no section of the world marked out as being within his immediate reach. We stated furthermore that the "actor" within the province of theoretical thought is never the "I" of the scientist as the unbroken totality of his personality but only a partial self, a Me. Now we have seen that the dimension of the vivid present and its derivation are inaccessible to the theorizing self. Consequently, it can never grasp – not even as a potentiality – the Other's self as an unbroken unit. All these statements can be summarized in a single one: The theorizing self is solitary; it has no social environment; it stands outside social relationships.

And now there arises with respect to the relationship between sociality and theoretical thought a dialectical problem similar to that which we encountered in our analysis of the world of dreams.[44]

Here, however, it has a twofold aspect: (1) How can the solitary theorizing self find access to the world of working and make it an object of its theoretical contemplation? (2) How can theoretical thought be communicated and theorizing itself be performed in intersubjectivity?

Ad (1). As long as theorizing deals with objects which exist

[43] The particular problems involved in the concept "specious present" cannot be analyzed here. For the present purpose a reference to William James' use of this term (*Principles of Psychology*, Vol. I, pp. 608ff. and pp. 641ff.) has to suffice.
[44] See *Supra* page 243f.

merely in objective time, as is the case in the sciences of nature and especially in those available for mathematical treatment, the dialectical problem in question does not become fully visible.[45] But the whole intersubjective world of working in standard time (including the working self of the thinker as a human being, his fellow-men, and their working acts) and even the problem how the existence of fellow-men and their thought can be experienced in the natural attitude is a topic of theoretical contemplation. It is the principal subject matter of the so-called social sciences. But how is it possible for the solitary thinker, with his theoretical attitude of disinterestedness and his aloofness from all social relationships to find an approach to the world of everyday life in which men work among their fellow-men within the natural attitude, the very natural attitude which the theoretician is compelled to abandon? How is this possible, since all working acts occur within standard time, within the vivid present of the We-relation or forms derived from it, that is, within the very dimension of time of which, as we have seen, theoretical contemplation does not partake? Moreover, only in the We-relation, in which there is a community of space and time (a common social environment in the pregnant sense), can man within the natural attitude experience the Other's self in its unbroken totality, whereas outside the vivid present of the We-relation, the Other appears merely as a Me, as a taker of a rôle, but not as a unity. How, then, can man in his full humanity and the social relationships in which he stands with Others be grasped by theoretical thought? Yet, that all this is possible is the unclarified presupposition of all theoretical social sciences. Furthermore, the theoretical social scientist has to refer to his stock of pre-experiences of the existence of Others, of their acting and working, and the meaning they bestow upon their acts and works. He has acquired these pre-experiences while living as a human being with Others in the everyday world of the natural attitude, the same attitude which he had to bracket in order to leap into the province of theoretical contemplation. We have to face the difficulty involved here in full earnestness. Only

---

[45] It appears, however, as soon as the scientific observer includes himself in the observational field, such as in the famous Heisenberg principle of uncertainty. If this is the case, so-called crises in the foundation of the science in question break out. They are just one form of the general dialectical situation outlined in the text.

then will we understand that the theoretical thinker while remaining in the theoretical attitude cannot experience originarily and grasp in immediacy the world of everyday life within which I and you, Peter and Paul, anyone and everyone have confused and ineffable perceptions, act, work, plan, worry, hope, are born, grow up and will die – in a word, live their life as unbroken selves in their full humanity. This world eludes the immediate grasp of the theoretical social scientist. He has to build up an artificial device, comparable to the aforementioned "indirect communication," in order to bring the intersubjective life-world in view – or better, not this world itself, but merely a likeness of it, a likeness in which the human world recurs, but deprived of its liveliness, and in which man recurs, but deprived of his unbroken humanity. This artificial device – called the method of the social sciences – overcomes the outlined dialectical difficulty by substituting for the intersubjective life-world a model of this life-world. This model, however, is not peopled with human beings in their full humanity, but with puppets, with *types;* they are constructed as though they could perform working actions and reactions. Of course, these working actions and reactions are merely fictitious, since they do not originate in a living consciousness as manifestations of its spontaneity; they are only assigned to the puppets by the grace of the scientist. But if, according to certain definite operational rules (the description of which is the business of a methodology of the social sciences),[46] these types are constructed in such a way that their fictitious working acts and performances remain not only consistent in themselves but compatible with all the pre-experiences of the world of daily life which the observer acquired within the natural attitude before he leaped into the theoretical province – then, and only then, does this model of the social world become a theoretical object, an object of an actual positing of being. It receives an accent of reality although not that of the natural attitude.

Ad (2). There is, however, another aspect of the dialectical problem involved which is not restricted to the question how

---

[46] Cf. Alfred Schutz, "The Problem of Rationality in the Social World," *Economica,* Vol. X, May 1943, pp. 131–149, esp. pp. 143ff.; and *Der sinnhafte Aufbau der sozialen Welt,* Vienna, 1932, 2nd edition, Vienna, 1960, esp. pp. 247–286.

sociality can be made the subject matter of theorizing but which refers in general to the sociality of theorizing itself. Theorizing – this term still used in the restricted meaning of scientific theorizing, and, therefore, excluding pure meditation – is, first, possible only within a universe of discourse that is pregiven to the scientist as the outcome of other people's theorizing acts. It is, secondly, founded upon the assumption that other people, too, can make the same subject matter, with which I deal in theoretical contemplation, the topic of their theoretical thought and that my own results will be verified or falsified by theirs as theirs by mine.[47] Yet this mutual corroborating and refuting, approving and criticizing presupposes communication, and communication is possible only outside the pure theoretical sphere, in the world of working. In order to communicate my theoretical thought to my fellow-men, I have, therefore, to drop the pure theoretical attitude, I have to return to the world of daily life and its natural attitude – that same world which as we have seen remains inaccessible to direct approach by theorizing. This seems to be a highly paradoxical situation, similar to that which we encountered in our analysis of dream life where we found that only he who no longer dreams can communicate his experiences as a dreamer.

This is just one form of the age-old problem which recurs in any type of pure meditation; it is the problem of indirect communication itself. To follow it from the beginning of philosophical thought up to our time would require the writing of a complete history of ideas. We, therefore, take just as an instance the particular form the problem has found in the latest phase of phenomenological theory. We find it in the first two of the three paradoxes besetting the phenomenologist, which Dr. Fink has developed in a now famous essay endorsed completely by Husserl as representing his own views.[48] Borrowing widely from Prof. Farber's excellent presentation,[49] we may sum up Fink-Husserl's argument as follows: After having performed the

---

[47] Cf. Husserl, *Formale und transzendentale Logik*. pp. 172–173, pp. 200–201, pp. 205–215, esp. 209 and 212.
[48] Eugen Fink, "Die phänomenologische Philosophie Edmund Husserls in der gegenwärtigen Kritik" with a preface by Edmund Husserl, *Kant-Studien*, Berlin, 1933, pp. 319–383.
[49] *L.c.*, Chapter XVII B, esp. pp. 558ff.

phenomenological reduction, the phenomenologist finds himself confronted with the difficulty of communicating his knowledge to the "dogmatist" who remains within the natural attitude. Does not this presuppose a common ground between them? This is the first form of the paradox. The problem involved is solved by showing that the phenomenologist does not leave the transcendental attitude and return to the natural one but that he places himself *"in"* the natural attitude as a transcendental situation that is seen through by him. The second paradox – called the "paradox of the phenomenological proposition," which interests us especially – is based upon the first. It relates to the mundane world-concepts and language which are alone at the disposal of the communicating phenomenologist. That is the reason why all phenomenological reports are inadequate because of the attempt to give a mundane expression to a non-worldly meaning, and this difficulty cannot be met by the invention of an artificial language. Farber has criticized this argument pointedly by showing that there is no "inner conflict" between mundane word-meaning and the indicated transcendent meaning itself.[50]

As we have shown, this problem is not a specific phenomenological one but far more general. It is more complicated in the sphere of transcendental phenomenology. Here we have the concept of a plurality of transcendental egos, a community of monads, which can communicate directly and immediately only by way of mundane bodily gestures in the broadest sense, including language. It is, however, a serious question whether intersubjectivity is a problem of the transcendental sphere at all; or whether sociality does not rather belong to the mundane sphere of our life-world.[51]

But the "paradox of communication" – the phenomenological as well as the mundane one with which the preceding analyses have dealt exclusively – exists only as long as we take what we called the finite provinces of meaning as ontological static entities, objectively existing outside the stream of individual

[50] *L.c.*, pp. 559–560. The third paradox called "the logical paradox of transcendental determinations," the most important of the three (although not for the problems of the present discussion) refers to the question whether logic is equal to the task of solving problems arising in the determination of basic transcendentla relations.
[51] Cf. "Scheler's Theory of Intersubjectivity and the General Thesis of the Alter Ego," esp. pp. 164–167.

consciousness within which they originate. Then, of course, the terms and notions, valid within one province, would not only, as is the case, require a through and through modification within the others, but would become therein entirely meaningless, comparable to coins peculiar to a country which cease to be legal tender when we cross the border. (But even then, to keep to this metaphor, we can exchange those coins for domestic currency of the new country.) The finite provinces of meaning are not separated states of mental life in the sense that passing from one to another would require a transmigration of the soul and a complete extinction of memory and consciousness by death, as the doctrine of metempsychosis assumes. They are merely names for different tensions of one and the same consciousness, and it is the same life, the mundane life, unbroken from birth to death, which is attended to in different modifications. As we have said before, my mind may pass during one single day or even hour through the whole gamut of tensions of consciousness, now living in working acts, now passing through a daydream, now plunging into the pictorial world of a painting, now indulging in theoretical contemplation. All these different experiences are experiences within my inner time; they belong to my stream of consciousness; they can be remembered and reproduced. And that is why they can be communicated in ordinary language in working acts to my fellow-man. We have frequently mentioned that working acts may be the "contents" of phantasms, of dreams, of theoretical contemplation. Why should not experiences originating in the finite provinces of phantasies, of dreams, of scientific theorizing become the contents of communicative working acts? If children play together in their make-believe world, if we discuss a work of art with a fellow beholder, if we indulge with Others in the same ritual, we are still in the world of working connected by communicative acts of working with the Other. And, nevertheless, both partners have leaped together from the finite province of meaning, called "world of everyday life," into the province of play, of art, or of religious symbols, etc. What formerly seemed to be a reality while attended to may now be measured by another yardstick and prove to be non-real or quasi-real; but this is so only under the specific form of a present non-reality, whose reality may be restored.

The paradox of communication arises, thus, only if we assume that sociality and communication can be realized within another finite province of meaning than the world of everyday life which is the paramount reality. But if we do not make such an unwarranted assumption then science becomes again included in the world of life. And, conversely, the miracle of συμφιλοσοφεῖν brings back the full humanity of the thinker into the theoretical field.

LANGUAGE, LANGUAGE DISTURBANCES, AND THE TEXTURE OF CONSCIOUSNESS

It is always a remarkable event in the evolution of scientific thought if certain essential ideas developed in one field are corroborated by the results of research in quite another discipline, especially if the investigations are carried out independently of one another, for different purposes, on different levels, and by entirely different methods. In such a case, the findings in either department of knowledge will interpret the achievements of the other. And if the analyses of certain outstanding modern philosophers relating to the texture of the human mind, especially to the origin of abstraction and typification, converge with the outcome of neurological and psychopathological studies in the field of language disturbance caused by lesions of the brain, the situation is one of enormous interest to the social scientist. He may rightly expect that such mutual confirmation will shed new light upon some of his most vital problems, namely, the relationship between human beings and their environment, on the one hand, and the function of language, on the other.

Every contemporary student of problems of language from the philosophical, psychological, or even linguistic angle has in one way or another become familiar with Professor Kurt Goldstein's life work relating to the study of defective language observed in connection with lesions of the brain cortex. He will also know the influence of Goldstein's findings on the philosophy of Ernst Cassirer and certain French existentialists. The following pages are inspired by Professor Goldstein's recent book,[1] in which he offers a comprehensive summary of his manifold outstanding contributions to this field. Our purpose is threefold: to present

[1] Kurt Goldstein, *Language and Language Disturbances, Aphasic Symptom Complexes and their Significance for Medicine and Theory of Language*, New York, 1948.

a part of the theoretical content of Professor Goldstein's book [2] and especially to analyze his concepts of the concrete and the categorial attitudes; to show the convergence of his findings with certain basic ideas of several modern philosophers; and, finally, to attempt some conclusions relating to the origin of types and the function of language.

I. GOLDSTEIN'S THEORY OF LANGUAGE

Professor Goldstein's book is designed primarily as a manual for clinical purposes, to aid in the examination of patients, in ascertaining the reasons for the disturbances, and in finding the appropriate therapeutic measures, consisting especially in systematic retraining. But it is not surprising that the author of *The Organism* (New York 1939) attacks the particular clinical problem at hand within a broad and well-founded psychological and philosophical framework. He has clearly seen that the procedure of the usual textbooks, which give ready-made clinical pictures of speech disturbances, cannot solve the problem. Starting from his organismic point of view, according to which pathological behavior is behavior of functions of parts of the organism isolated from the whole, he puts individual symptoms – that is, individual modifications of an individual behavior pattern – at the center of his interest. His basic question – basic, we believe, not only for this concrete research but for all sciences of human behavior – is this: Are symptoms, that is, modifications of behavior, the direct expression of a definite disturbance of function, or are there other factors involved which at least contribute to the production of symptoms? Goldstein proves that the same symptom may be produced in totally different ways: some deviations of behavior may be directly related to the underlying defect, while others are the expression of protective mechanisms which the organism utilizes against the disastrous effect of the defect. Moreover, a performance correct de facto may be attained in a quite incorrect (that is, abnormal) way and we may not be able

---

[2] The clinical sections, especially the careful case reports which fill about half the book, can unfortunately not be dealt with in this paper, though they contain a wealth of information for everyone concerned with language and speech.

to see this in the result. Impairment does not mean simply a disturbance of mental capacity in general but involves a disturbance in a qualitative way, a personality change. It consists mainly in an impairment of what Goldstein calls the "abstract attitude."

This term and its opposite, the concrete attitude, are of fundamental importance for the author's theory. In the concrete attitude we are given over passively and bound to the immediate experience of unique objects or situations. Our thinking and acting are determined by the immediate claims made by the particular aspect of the object or situation to which we have to react as it is imposed upon us. But the abstract attitude – also called the categorial or conceptual attitude – involves choosing a point of view from which we ascertain the situation, taking initiative, making a choice, keeping in mind simultaneously various aspects of a situation, grasping the essential, thinking the merely possible, thinking symbolically, and, in general, detaching the Ego from the outer world (p. 6). Goldstein believes that these two attitudes can always be distinguished in normal behavior. During all activity the concrete attitude is dominant, but abstraction is required for beginning an activity and, if the course of action is interfered with or disturbed, to correct disturbances and to continue properly the activity in question. There are various degrees of abstract behavior, the highest being the conscious and volitional act of directing any performance and of accounting for these activities to oneself or to Others; a less abstract degree of conceptual behavior is involved if unaccompanied by awareness of one's own doing. Also, the concrete behavior shows gradation: the most concrete way of dealing with situations and things consists in the grasping of merely one property of the situation, such as reacting only to one color or only to the form of an object or only to its practical use. Learned activities normally develop automatically, but pathological cases show clearly the dependence of such automatism upon the so-called abstract attitude (pp. 7ff.).

In view of the importance of the distinction between concrete and abstract attitudes, we shall have to examine their legitimacy later in our discussion. But these concepts are certainly sufficient and useful on the level of Professor Goldstein's investigation and lead him, as will be presently shown, to distinguish also between language belonging to the abstract attitude and concrete language.

Dealing primarily with problems of aphasia, Professor Goldstein is more concerned with what modern linguists, following Ferdinand de Saussure, call "speech" than with "language." He rejects the atomistic concept according to which language is regarded as based on images of words, motor and sensory, which are connected in various ways with one another, and with other images corresponding to objects, thoughts, and feelings. According to this theory, speaking and understanding are reproduction of these images, and language nothing but a conventional tool derived from expressive movements. Disturbances of speech were explained by lesion of circumscribed centers of the brain, which involves the assumption of separate "centers of conceptualization," "centers of concepts of words," and the like. This assumption found expression in "brain maps" and in the hypothesis that we are justified in inferring directly from a correlation between a localized defect and a defect in performance a relationship between the concerned area and a definite performance corresponding to the defect. But only defects, not performances, can be localized. All localizations of performances remain a theoretical interpretation. True, there is a differentiation between the periphery of the cortex and its central parts, the latter being, anatomically at least, relatively independent of the former. Yet this fact permits only the conclusion that separate parts contribute differently to the function of the brain, not that separate parts of the cortex are related to separate functions. Moreover, the "classic" theory of localization is based mainly on the material gained from post-mortems. It is very difficult in these circumstances to evaluate the degree of damage, especially to decide whether the preserved tissue was still functioning sufficiently to allow for a certain performance or not. The organism may react to the functional defect under certain conditions in such a way that the symptoms due to the localized defect are hidden.

Head, Jackson, Pierre Marie, and Goldstein himself have demonstrated the untenability of the theory of localization of so-called images (a result which, as will be shown, corroborates a basic assumption of Bergson's concept of mind). They gave the term "localization" a new meaning. Each performance (according to Goldstein's findings) is due to the function of the total organism in which the brain plays a particular rôle. In each performance the whole cortex is in activity, but the excitation is distributed in such a way that to each performance belongs an excitement of different structure in the cortex which corresponds to the "figure," while the process in the rest of the nervous system corresponds to the "ground" – both terms to be taken in the meaning of Gestalt psychology. Amnesic aphasia, for instance, explained by the older theory as a dissociation between object and word images, thus as a memory defect, turned out to be a consequence of a change of total personality, namely, an impairment of the so-called categorial or abstract attitude. Jackson had already stressed that speech does not consist in an unrelated succession of words, but in what he called "propositions" and that the value of the word can be judged only from its use in a special connection. Goldstein enlarges this idea. According to him, language is a means for the individual of coming to terms with the outer world and of realizing himself, especially of coming to terms with his fellows. Our way of speaking becomes understandable only if we take into consideration the special relation of the speaking person to the environment in the given situation.

With great care Professor Goldstein distinguishes between "inner speech" and external speech performances. Inner speech should not be confused with Wilhelm von Humboldt's concept of "inner speech form," that is, the special way by which people who speak the same language look at the world and express this perspective in a specific organization of linguistic forms. Inner speech is defined by Professor Goldstein as the totality of processes and experiences which occur when we are going to express our thoughts in external speech and when we perceive heard sounds as language. Inner speech is in close relation to what Goldstein calls the nonlanguage mental processes, such as the formation of meaningful images, fixed concepts, thoughts, series of such in the form of conclusions, and so on. For this reason, inner speech finds its expression in the organization of "inner speech form," in the selection of definite word categories by a special language, in its syntactical and grammatical structure; it varies in accordance with the situation in which it takes place, with the person of the listener, and our expectation of his grasping the present situation and the means of communication in the same way that we do. At the same time, inner speech is related to the instrumentalities of speech; but it must be kept in mind that both are not necessarily developed equally.

The insight is especially important for Goldstein's theory of the development of language in infancy. According to him, even the first sounds are closely linked to the intimate relationship between the child and the environment. They are from the outset *social* phenomena, although of a very primitive type. There is no separation between the child and the surrounding world; his activities (including speech) are embedded in a unitary totality of himself and the environment. "If the child is aware of his speech at all, this may be experience of motor and sensory phenomena belonging to a state of satisfaction in his trend to come to terms with the environment." This theory, closely related to certain views of Scheler (to which Professor Goldstein does not refer) is not in accord with Piaget's interpretation of the child's "egocentric speech" (p. 95). Piaget thinks that this first speech is not determined by a relation between child and environment, that the child thinks and speaks during this stage for himself. This kind of speech is more or less incomprehensible for the adult. Only later on – at about school age – when the social contacts of the child develop more and more, does egocentric speech decrease and the childs' language become socialized and thus understandable.

Professor Goldstein, endorsing Vigotsky's criticism of Piaget's theory and basing his conclusion on the general organismic pattern, according to which it would be very improbable that in a most important stage of life the child's language should have no special function in his development, finds another explanation for the change of language at school age, which he as well as Vigotsky recognizes. The language of the child corresponds to the primitive way in which he is able to understand the total situation, and his inner speech is closely bound to the external instrumentalities. Speech in this stage serves the purpose of mental orientation, of conscious understanding, of overcoming difficulties and obstacles. It takes place, however, under the illusion of being understood. If the child cannot experience that his speaking is understood, speaking diminishes and vice versa. Speech becomes more and more a phenomenon of inner life, and with increasing individualization (that is, distinction of the Ego and the world) detaches itself more and more from the external instrumentalities. Only later is the inner speech of the child transformed into the inner speech of the adult, which is determined by his totally different insight into the situation and changes with the latter. Observations of pathological cases show that the speech of patients has the character more of communication with Others than of speaking to oneself. It has lost its adequacy to the total situation and is determined more than normal speech by the instrumentalities. In normal inner speech concepts of letters, words, phrases, are more or less fixed wholes, patterns of which we are aware in the framework of an inner speech attitude and which we use as wholes in starting the speaking activity. The word, for instance, is normally experienced not as being composed of parts but as a simultaneous whole, as a phenomenon of a characteristic structure in which the sounds follow a definite sequence. In pathology, the character of simultaneity is lost, the word is dissolved into different parts, into letters and syllables; or again, one part experienced before as background may gain the character of figure and herewith abnormal importance. Thus, for instance, where patients show paraphasia (distortion of words or substitution of another word for the correct one) in spontaneous speech, repetition, finding words or names, they have to react in a definite way directed by a definite attitude and voluntary impulse. Yet, concomitantly with such reaction processes, others of a more voluntary character are going on in the background; they are represented by words in the "fringes." In his distress the patient looks for substitutions and then the processes in the fringes become more active: performances according to these fringes emerge passively and they are merely slightly altered by the defect that affects particularly the directed performance. This is the explanation of the astonishing fact that the "wrong" words are often uttered by patients with less paraphasia than the "right" ones.

In line with his general distinction between concrete and

abstract attitudes, Goldstein distinguishes between concrete and abstract language. The former consists of speech automatisms, of the instrumentalities of speech (such as sounds, words, series of words, sentences), of understanding of language in familiar situations, and finally, of emotional utterances. Abstract language belongs to the abstract attitude: it is volitional, propositional, rational language. Voluntary speech, conversational speech, speaking of isolated words or of series, repetition, naming of objects, reading – all depend in different degrees on the abstract attitude. Everyday language is a combination of both types of language. In a conversation, first automatisms may occur, then the appearance of words may be determined by the abstract attitude. The individual uses that form of language which permits him best to come to terms with the given situation in the effort to realize himself, particularly to express what he wants to express at the moment.

In cases of impairment of abstract language, the patient may be able to utter words but unable to use them as symbols. Naming an object in the true sense – that is, having the experience of a word which "means" this object – and considering the object named as representing a category is a performance of abstract language; pseudonaming or merely associating a sound complex with a concrete individual object is, however, a performance pertaining to concrete language. A patient to whom a knife is offered together with a pencil may call the knife a "pencil sharpener"; when the knife is offered with an apple he may call it an "apple parer," and so on; but the patient is unable to find the word "knife" as the symbol for the category of all these objects. Professor Goldstein concludes that to have sounds with an abstract meaning as symbols for ideas means the same with regard to language as the possibility of approaching the world in general with the abstract attitude. Of special interest is the fact that the so-called "small" words – prepositions, articles, pronouns, connectives – which occur easily in fluent speech, offer particular difficulties in voluntary word-finding. We are not dealing here with a primary motor defect but with an effect of missing attitude.

So far, we have discussed only the production of speech, but there are also disturbances on the receptive side of language.

Professor Goldstein's investigations of these kinds of disturbances led him to an excellent analysis of the complicated procedure involved in the understanding of the meaning of a word. Speech perception and speech understanding normally do not exist separately. But in pathological cases, the patient may perceive speech sounds as mere noises or differentiate them from other noises without recognizing them as speech; even if the patient recognizes sounds as language, he may not grasp the words; or he may grasp the words but not understand them, or not realize that a word presented at one moment is the same one presented a short time later; he may understand a word only under certain conditions, for example, if he sees the object to which the word belongs or if he is confronted with it among other words or if it belongs to the situation in which the patient is and in which he has understood certain other words.

We cannot consider in any greater detail the richness of Professor Goldstein's book and its importance for the most varied investigations. His analysis of disturbances of "intelligence" in aphasic patients yields remarkable results concerning the interrelationship between concepts and words, between the order of thought formation and the syntactical structure of language. In these investigations Goldstein always stresses the attitude of the speaker to the situation and to the listener, and especially the speaker's assumption that a number of things need not be expressed in language because the listener, on the basis of his knowledge of these elements belonging to the common situation, can be expected to complete correctly in his mind the unuttered ideas.

We must also forgo any discussion of Professor Goldstein's analysis of the processes of reading, writing, calculating, of musical performances, of the relationship between gesture and sound language, and of the especially interesting relationship between thought and speech in polyglot individuals. Instead of dwelling upon these topics, it is our intention to show how Professor Goldstein's findings are corroborated by the pertinent thought of certain philosophers such as Bergson, Cassirer, Merleau-Ponty, Gurwitsch, and Husserl. This study will serve also to examine Goldstein's basic concepts of the concrete and abstract attitudes.

II. PHILOSOPHICAL INTERPRETATIONS OF LANGUAGE DISTURBANCES

Henri Bergson. When Bergson first published his book *Matière et mémoire* (Paris 1897), he selected as the main topic of study the relationship between "matter," defined by him as the sum total of the images which surround me, and "perception of matter," defined as those same images referred to the possible action of a certain privileged image, namely, my body. Both idealism and realism find themselves in difficulties in explaining this relationship. How is it possible that the same images may be simultaneously referred to two different systems: the first being the system in which every image changes in itself, and that precisely in accordance with the real actions other images exercise upon it; the second being the system in which all the other images vary in reference to a single privileged one (my body) and do this differently in accordance with the manner in which they reflect the action of the privileged image. The realist starts from a given universe in which there is no center, and he can explain perceptions (and consciousness in general) merely as an epiphenomenon of events occurring within the brain, itself a part of matter. The idealist starts from the fact that there are perceptions grouped around the privileged image of my own body and that they change with modifications within the body. His difficulty is to explain the order of nature and he has to invent for this purpose some arbitrary hypothesis such as the pre-established harmony or the psychophysical parallelism. Both realism and idealism start from the erroneous assumption that it is the brain (and the central nervous system in general) that "manufactures" perceptions. Yet, according to Bergson, the functions of the brain consist merely in being a receptacle of stimuli, in building up motor performances, and in putting at the disposal of incoming stimuli the greatest possible number of motor tools. It is erroneous to imagine the organism as a kind of state within a state, as an instrument the purpose of which is first to fabricate perceptions and then to create motor activities. In truth, my nervous system is simply interposed as a kind of conductor between those objects which affect my body and those upon which I may exercise influence, and the main problem consists in explaining how our consciousness makes a selection from the universe of possible stimuli and possible responses.

Bergson's attempt to solve this problem is well known. Our mental life shows various degrees of tension which depend upon our attention to reality or, as the philosopher prefers to call it, our attention to life. What is generally believed to be a disturbance of the mental life or a disease of the personality can be explained as a relaxation of the tension of the tie that connects the psychological life with its concomitant motor activities. The central nervous system is the specific organ of the attention to life but the brain does not determine thought. The cerebral mechanism of thought has a mere pantomimic function: it imitates the life of thought, it does not create it.

The preceding paragraphs are only apparently a digression from our main topic. The link between Bergson's theory and the problem dealt with by Professor Goldstein seems to be twofold. On the one hand, Bergson based his analysis partially upon the study of language disturbances and found his assumptions verified by the researches of Pierre Marie and his school (the basic paper of Pierre Marie was published in 1906), which are also fundamental for Goldstein's investigations. On the other hand, it appears that Bergson's concepts of the varying degrees of tension of consciousness might contribute to a clarification of Goldstein's theory of concrete and abstract attitudes, a theory of particular interest to all the social sciences.

Bergson examines the classic localization theory which was dominant when he started his work at the end of the last century. He comes to the conclusion that the only mental function which could be localized in the brain is that of memory, more precisely, the memory of words. He refers to Broca's discovery that in case of certain specific brain lesions the word-memory disappears. This fact is interpreted, for the most part, to mean that impressions of the outer world – in our case, "phonograms" – subsist within certain parts of the brain like grooves on a phonograph record. If these anatomical elements are destroyed, the phonograms disappear. Yet if this theory were sound, how could we then explain the fact that the same word, articulated by different persons or even by the same person in different ways, or used in different contexts, is understood as the same word? How is it possible on this assumption that in certain cases aphasic persons cannot under emotional stress find certain words otherwise available to them? Have we not rather to assume that the brain has the function of remembering and not of preserving recollections? In case of paraphasia the patient circumscribes the word that he cannot find; he does not have the force to "put his finger on it." But does that prove that he has forgotten this word? Is it not a better explanation to assume that the patient's capacity to adjust himself to the situation (or as Goldstein would prefer to phrase it, to come to terms with his environment) has weakened, a capacity which it is the job of the cerebral mechanism to assure? Specifically weakened is the faculty to activate the recollection by projecting in advance the movements which normally would translate the remembered word into the action of speech. This explains the fact that the aphasic patient recalls verbs better than adjectives, adjectives better than nouns, nouns better than "small words." It explains also the ability of patients, incapable of spontaneous speech, to repeat words spoken by Others; moreover, it explains the occurrence of word-deafness in spite of correct sound perception and intact memory for sounds, and also the fact that patients suffering from motor aphasia are able to read silently with understanding and even to express themselves in writing. Bergson hoped that advances in the study of aphasia would corroborate his theory, and it seems to the present writer that Goldstein's investigations have fulfilled this hope to a considerable extent.

To be sure, Bergson, speaking of images, still uses the traditional language of sensualistic psychology. But he bestows upon this terminology an entirely new sense and gives it an interpretation that sheds a new light on the difference between concrete and abstract attitudes. The basic pragmatistic motive of our thinking is our possible or real action in the outer world; mind and body communicate through the medium of the experience of time, and the central nervous system regulates our attention to life and therewith the tensions of our consciousness. Abstract and concrete attitudes, in the sense of Professor Goldstein's interpretation, coulb be conceived then as two different forms of our attitude to life, two different degrees of tension of our consciousness, and this would be a perfectly satisfactory explanation for the loss of the abstract attitude in the case of brain lesion, if the brain were really the specific organ of our *attention à la vie*. This, however, is an assumption, which is intimately connected with the basic metaphysical position of Bergson's interpretation of *durée* and space, matter and mind, thought and action.

Ernst Cassirer. Another very interesting conclusion has been drawn from the study of the problem of aphasia and related diseases by Ernst Cassirer in the third volume of his *Philosophie der symbolischen Formen* (Berlin 1929). He deals with the research of Jackson, Head, Pierre Marie, Gelb and Goldstein, and others under the heading, "Pathology of the Symbolic Consciousness." Cassirer accepts the fundamental thesis of Wilhelm von Humboldt that not only does man use the medium of language in his conceptual thinking but also his general world experience and the way in which he organizes his perceptions are determined or at least codetermined by his language. The world of "perceptions" is not a mere sum total of sense data; it is organized in a threefold way. First, there are phenomena of a central character, called things and qualities; second, there is the order of these phenomena in spatial coexistence; and third, in their succession in time. The human mind, for the purpose of establishing this order, has to interrupt in some way the continuous flux of its experienced phenomena and to establish "nodes" (*ausgezeichnete Punkte*) around which the eddies of the flux coalesce into dynamic and functional entities. The single experience, then, is always "directed" experience, directed precisely toward these preorganized centers and participating in their total form and in their total movement. Language, as the expression of these experiences, shows a structurization of three levels, too. It is first mimic expression, imitation of the sensuous perception by sound, so characteristic of the language of the child and primitive man. The second level is that of analogical expression. Here the relationship between sound and designated content is not of a material nature, but that of an analogy of formal structure. Only the third level is that of symbolic expression proper.

Cassirer finds this assumption about the general structure of the world of perception corroborated by the discoveries in the realm of the pathology of language. Aphasic disturbances have to be explained as impairments of symbolic formulation and expression and they were characterized as such by Henry Head, whereas Jackson interpreted them as the loss of power to "propositionalize." But if it is true that the structure of our perception itself depends upon language, then we must expect that aphasic disturbances will never be isolated phenomena, but will be accompanied by a change in the patient's basic attitude to the world.

This thesis seems to be supported by Goldstein's findings. Not only are aphasia, agnosia, and apraxia closely connected with one another, but also in each of these disturbances impairment of the so-called categorial attitude can be observed. The concrete situation is not conceived by the patient as representing a particular case of a "species": he lives *in* his instantaneous impressions without any feeling of their significative functions. Any normal perception, however, necessarily includes a symbolic element and this fact alone makes the symbolic system of language possible. The word just makes explicit the representative content implied in perception itself. On the basis of this theory any merely individual and singular experience – and sensualism and skepticism presuppose every experience to be of this nature – is a pathological phenomenon; it occurs whenever perception loses its hold on the support of language. As Goldstein has observed, certain patients become unable to understand analogies and metaphors, others lose their bearing in time and space, still others are unable to grasp the meaning of numbers or to repeat sentences the sense of which is in contradiction to the concrete situation. All these forms of disturbances are interpreted by Cassirer as an impairment of symbolic behavior. From this point of view, symbolic behavior and abstract attitude are one and the same. Cassirer agrees with Gelb and Goldstein that the concrete attitude is nearer to life and its practical requirements. Any kind of knowledge of the world (and also any attempt to act upon it in accordance with preconceived projects) requires the establishing of a certain distance between the self and the world, a distance of which the animal is not aware because it simply lives within its world, without placing itself over against it presentationally.

Maurice Merleau-Ponty. Cassirer's theory has been criticized by Maurice Merleau-Ponty in his remarkable book, *Phénoménologie de la perception* (Paris 1945), which also deals at length with the work of Goldstein. According to this author (pp. 142ff.) it is impossible to reduce the distinction between the concrete and the abstract attitudes to the distinction between physiological and psychological phenomena, between body and mind. Any attempt at a physiological explanation must necessarily end in a universal mechanistic physiology, any attempt at a psychological explanation in a universal intellectualistic psychology. The distinction can be maintained only if there are for the body several ways of being a body and for the consciousness several ways of being consciousness. To be sure, the symbolic function can be found in all our bodily movements, but it is the fallacy of the intellectualistic psychology to detach by way of an artificial abstraction this function from the underlying substratum in which it materializes itself and to assume an originary presence of the world without distance. Taking such an assumption as the point of departure means reducing everything that separates us from the true world – error, disease, and the like – to a mere appearance. Attempting to analyze consciousness as separated from being means disregarding the empirical variety of consciousness – for example, the diseased consciousness, the consciousness of the primitive man, of the child, of the fellow-man – and reducing all of them to the pure essence of consciousness as such.

An analysis of certain of Goldstein's case studies shows that the patient's difficulties do not originate in his incapacity to conceive the concrete fact as a special application of a general principle or to subsume it under categories; on the contrary, the patient cannot connect the two without an explicit subsumption. According to Merleau-Ponty, the thinking of the normal mind does not consist in subsuming experiences under categories. The category imposes upon the terms which it unites a significance which is exterior to them. This synthesis originates in the vivid present, that is, in the pre-predicative evidence of the unique world to which all our experiences refer. This primordial world is structurized by a system of significations, that is, of correspondences, relations, participations, which the concrete subject spreads around himself, living in them and through them and using them not by an explicit conceptual procedure but merely by his being within the world. From there the higher structurizations of our conscious life are built up by reactivating our sedimented experiences and amalgamating them with the actual vivid thought. But, whereas the normal mind performs all this spontaneously, arranging its perceptual field and its significative structure in the vivid process of familiarity and communication with the object, the aphasic or apractic patient is incapable of doing the same. The world is to him without physiognomical aspect; like the scientist he has to start from a hypothesis to be verified by supervening experiences. That is why he is incapable of finding, as the normal man does, his perceptions imbued with linguistic significance. The words uttered by the fellow-man are to the normal man a transparent envelope of a sense in which he could live; to the aphasic patient, however, they are signs which he has to decipher piecemeal, one after the other, a mere occasion for a methodical interpretation and not a motive for grasping the fellow-man's thought. The normal life of consciousness connects by an "intentional arc" our past, our future, our human environment, our physical, ideological, moral situation with the vivid present. This intentional arc unifies our senses with one another, our senses with our intelligence, our sensibility with our motor mechanism. It makes us aware of the fact that all these relations place us in a particular situation. It is the unity created by this intentional arc that breaks asunder in pathological cases. From this Merleau-Ponty concludes that only an existential analysis can overcome the dilemma created by the classic theories of empiricism and intellectualism. The further development of this theory, however, interesting as it is, has no bearing on our topic.

As we have seen, the difference between the concrete and the abstract attitudes is interpreted by Bergson as a different degree of the tension of consciousness, of attention to life; by Cassirer as the difference between perceptual and symbolic consciousness; and by Merleau-Ponty as the difference between the prepredicative spontaneous evidence of the unique primordial world and its breaking asunder into a realm of a perceptual field and a realm of significative structure. Merleau-Ponty, in going back to the pre-predicative experience of the primordial world, bases his views upon certain analyses of Edmund Husserl, and we have now to show the connection of Professor Goldstein's concepts with certain results of phenomenological analysis.

Aron Gurwitsch. Professor Gurwitsch has dedicated to Goldstein an excellent study entitled, "Gelb-Goldstein's Concept of 'Concrete' and 'Categorial' Attitude and the Phenomenology of Ideation." [3] This paper in which he restricts himself intentionally to Goldstein's study of amnesia of color names examines in a careful and lucid analysis Husserl's concepts of categorial and qualitative homogeneity, and shows convincingly that Gelb and Goldstein's findings relating to the behavior of patients suffering from aphasic disturbances, especially with respect to color names, converge toward recognizing ideation as an act *sui generis* with a specific nature of its own. Both refer to an operation of consciousness which Gurwitsch calls thematization and which he defines as "disengagement and disclosure of factors which previously to the operation in question are present to consciousness in a rather implicit form" (pp. 187–188). Perception experienced in the concrete attitude appears in itself as integrable into a wider perspective, and the perspective referred to is the possibility of the categorial attitude, thus somehow preannounced and anticipated in the very perception experienced in the concrete attitude. The normal person, by adopting the categorial attitude, imposes upon the perceptual field an organizational form which that field does not possess in its own right, an organizational form determined by the point of vantage the subject chooses to take. In the perception of the normal person there is a certain readiness to receive forms of organization imposed from without, a certain ambiguity and plasticity. But things perceived by the aphasic patient are to him mere actual data and facts of a rather rigid character. To be sure, the normal person, too, perceives actual data and facts, but in addition to their actuality these data and facts are conceived as *potential examples or exemplars* of a broader context, as potentially referring to a nonperceptual order and to possibilities beyond the actual experience – in short, *as varieties of an invariant.* It is the disengagement, disclosure, explicit apprehension, in a word, the

[3] *Philosophy and Phenomenological Research,* Vol. 10, 1949, pp. 172–196.

thematization of the invariant *eidos*, which is called ideation. Husserl analyzed its phenomenological structure in his famous investigations on the eidetic reduction and the process of "free variation," presented by Gurwitsch in an excellent and clear condensation. Gurwitsch arrives at the interpretation that Goldstein's patients with brain injuries are incapable of performing any operation of ideation because, overwhelmed by the actuality of factual experience, they are unable to conceive of possibilities, that is, incapable of imaginational operations, processes, and transformations.

Professor Gurwitsch's analysis is not only clear and revealing; it is also an important contribution to both Goldstein's concept of concrete and categorial attitudes and Husserl's theory of ideation. Yet it may be permissible to question whether the origin of the difference between the two attitudes, called (and perhaps misnamed) by Goldstein the concrete and the categorial, should be looked for on the highly complex level of ideation or in the pre-predicative sphere. Moreover, it has to be investigated whether there are indeed two attitudes in question and, if so, what the term "attitude" in such a context might possibly mean. Granted that, as Gurwitsch says, Goldstein's patients are incapable of conceiving of possibilities because they are overwhelmed by the actuality of factual experiences. How comes it about that such actual experiences overwhelm them? And even if Gurwitsch's explanation of the distinction between concrete and categorial attitudes is applicable to the behavior of certain patients described in Goldstein's earlier writings, can it be applied in the same way to the problem of concrete and abstract language?

The following remarks will attempt to show that Goldstein's findings converge with another result of Husserl's phenomenological analysis, to which Merleau-Ponty also seems to refer – namely, to his description of the pre-predicative primordial world. It might be advisable to start with a very condensed and necessarily imprecise presentation of Husserl's pertinent views, propounded especially in his book, *Erfahrung und Urteil*.

Edmund Husserl. Husserl's main problem in the book cited is the phenomenological description of our experience of the world within which we live and which is pregiven to us in the form of a passive belief in its existence. In order to penetrate to the evidence of our first experience of this pregiven primordial world of our life (the *Lebenswelt*) we have to go back to the perceptual field given to us at any moment, a perceptual field which is structurized in manifold respects, having its thematic kernel and its outer and inner horizon, but which is not experienced as the explicit substratum of logical judgments and not yet split into logical subjects and predicates. In order to reveal this primordial field of our experience we have, therefore, to eliminate all kinds of idealization and generalization involved in our logical activities. This attempt has of course its limits, for instance, the very fact that even the substrata of our primordial experience can be referred to only by their names and that every name involves a kind of idealization and also refers to a linguistic community. To be sure, even the substrata of my primordial experience have meaning not only for me but also for my fellowmen with whom I am interconnected by community of space and time. Nevertheless, we have to conduct our first investigations *as if* my experiences of my primordial world were exclusively my private experience.

Let us consider first a field of sensuous perception as it is given to us at any moment of an immanent present. The visual field for instance is as such homogeneous, but within the field certain data "stand out." By an interplay of passive synthesis (of association) they refer to other data not actually present, but which have been previously present, as being similar with them or as contrasting with them. They "stand out" as such within the homogeneous field, they "strike me" as thus outstanding, and this means that they exercise an affective tendency upon the Ego, they impose themselves upon my attention, they *interest* me. Passive attention and passive interest are, according to Husserl, nothing else but the turning of the Ego toward the intentional object. Being passive, this interest is not a particular voluntary act; on the contrary, every voluntary act, every purpose and intention is based upon this turning of the Ego to the object of its interest. Yet to say that the Ego turns to the interesting object is just an abbreviation for the very complicated process involved. The interesting object wakens expectations, both actual and potential. The awakened interest demands to be satisfied, and this means that by proceeding from perceptual phase to perceptual phase, the empty expectations will have to be fulfilled, that is, by a process within the pre-predicative sphere which corresponds on a higher level to the process of making explicit the hidden implications by a series of judgments. These expectations and their fulfillments refer in turn to previous perceptual experiences, retained or recollected. No object is perceived as an insulated object; it is from the outset perceived as "an object within its horizon," a horizon of typical familiarity and preacquaintanceship. (Even the novel experience refers to this horizon of preacquaintanceship over against which it stands out as being a novel experience.) But this horizon is continuously in flux: with each new step, that which has been anticipated in a typical way becomes more precisely determined. Thus the stock of pre-experienced material becomes a habitual possession; it is always at hand, ready to waken other actual associations. Every interest leads to an appropriation, to a retaining of the interesting object. Yet this appropriation takes place not by acts of logical judgment but according to a certain *typicalness* of the appropriated object, by reason of which it is experienced as being in relation (of overlapping, of superimposition and concealment, of similarity and dissimilarity, and so on) with other objects of the same familiar type, and by reason of which all anticipations adhering to this typical experience come to have a typical character too. With many modifications which cannot be enumerated here, the same principles prevail with respect to the relations which we experience among several objects.

This is very roughly the function of interest for the constitution of typical objects and typical relations in the prepredicative sphere. The categorial knowledge, the act of predicative judging belongs to a higher level, that of the spontaneous activity of the Ego. This level is characterized by the fact that the particular interest belonging to it is not an interest directed toward perception (as in the prepredicative sphere) but one directed toward knowledge. Knowledge is a form of spontaneous activity with the purpose not of producing objects (which would be the goal of all outer activities gearing into the world) but of becoming better and better acquainted with a pregiven object. Whereas the first level is characterized by receptive experience, the second is characterized by predicative spontaneity. Every form of predicative thinking implies generality. On the prepredicative level every object is given to the passive receptivity as an object of a somewhat foreknown type. Now the substratum to be made explicit turns, by the spontaneous activity of our conceptual thinking, into a subject, and its implications are transformed into its predicates. What was before just grasped passively in the open horizon becomes now the topic ("theme"), which is determinable under the idealization of "and so on." Under this term it has to be understood that any judgment is of the form: "S is p *and so on*" (that is, "S is *among other things* p"), "S is q *and so on*." Predication, briefly, consists in the thematization of the horizon of undetermined determinability.*

But this mechanism merely describes judgment relating to individual substrata. The judged state of affairs has still not been brought within the framework of general concepts. This performance requires the transition to a third level. It is the level of abstractive separation leading to conceptual generalizations. To be sure, in a certain sense generalization starts even at the first level, that of receptivity, since every object of such receptivity is from the outset an object of a somehow foreknown type. And there is also on the second level a general form contained in any form of predicative judgment. To determine the subject S as being of such and such a nature – for instance, predicating of this concrete perceptual objects its being red – refers to a general concept (in this case, "redness in general"), although this reference itself has not become thematic. On the second level, that of mere referring and determining predication, the reference to the general is only implicitly contained. Conceptual thinking proper – the third level – is distinguished from the second by the thematization of the relationship to the general: this is *one* red object (among many other red objects, one of the possible actualizations of Redness as such, of the *eidos* "red"). But the universal "Redness" is a result of a peculiar spontaneous production. On the second level we have a series of judgments predicating of each substratum and individual feature: S' is p', S" is p", and so on. The generality, the unity of the species, is grasped only in judgments, by which we predicate the one and

* See "Common–Sense and Scientific Interpretation of Human Action," p. 7f. (M.N.)

same p (without any prime) to all the subjects S', S", and so on. Such new, spontaneously produced objectivities can enter into judgments as general cores. S' is red, S" is red, S'" is red, is then transformed into the proposition: Redness (now main substratum, having become the new logical subject in the new synthetic form) inheres in S', S", and S'". There are degrees of generalities: empirical generalities and those of a higher level of abstraction. It is the former, the empirical ones, which interest us in connection with our present investigation.

In the article mentioned before, Professor Gurwitsch has explained the ideational process of free variation and eidetic reduction occuring on the third level. But it seems that Husserl considers the eidetic method merely a special case of the problem of generalization. This method aims at the constitution of what he calls *"pure concepts of generality,"* which are *a priori* in the sense that they are independent of the contingencies of the factual object that serves as the starting point of the process of generalization, and also of the contingencies of the empirical horizon this factual object carries along with it. *"Empirical general concepts,"* however, are not formed by the eidetical method but are guided by the types passively constituted on the first prepredicative level. Obviously, it is these empirical general concepts which are at the core of Goldstein's distinction between the concrete and categorial attitude, and it is therefore indispensable to explain in more detail the process by which, according to Husserl, the passively preconstituted types lead to the formation of these concepts.

The factual world of our experience, as has been explained before, is experienced from the outset as a typical one. Objects are experienced as trees, animals, and the like, and more specifically as oaks, firs, maples, or rattlesnakes, sparrows, dogs. This table I am now perceiving is characterized as something recognized, as something foreknown and, nevertheless, novel. What is newly experienced is already known in the sense that it recalls similar or equal things formerly perceived. But what has been grasped once in its typicality carries with it a horizon of possible experience with corresponding references to familiarity, that is, a series of typical characteristics still not actually experienced but expected to be potentially experienced. If we see a dog, that is, if we recognize an object as being an animal and more precisely as a dog, we anticipate a certain behavior on the part of this dog, a typical (not individual) way of eating, of running, of playing, of jumping, and so on. Actually we do not see his teeth, but having experienced before what a dog's teeth typically look like, we may expect that the teeth of the dog before us will show the same typical features though with individual modifications. In other words, what has been experienced in the actual perception of one object is apperceptively transferred to any other similar object, perceived merely as to its type. Actual experience will or will not confirm our anticipation of the typical conformity of these other objects. If confirmed, the content of the anticipated type will be enlarged; at the same time, the type will be split up into subtypes. On the other hand, the concrete real object will prove to have its individual characteristics which, nevertheless, have a form of typicality. Now, and this seems to be of special importance, we *may* take the typically apperceived object as an example of a general type and allow ourselves to be led to the general concept of the type, but we do not *need* by any means to think of the concrete dog thematically as an exemplar of the general concept "dog." "In general," this dog here is a dog like any other dog and will show all the characteristics which the type "dog," according to our previous experience, implies; nevertheless, this known type carries along a horizon of still unknown typical characteristics pertaining not only to this or that individual dog but to dogs in general. Every empirical idea of the general has the character of an open concept to be rectified or corroborated by supervening experience.

This holds good for both the prescientific natural apperceptions of daily life and the concepts of the empirical sciences. The latter are distinguished from the former by the fact that they use types determined by a limited number of well-defined characteristics. There is a very good chance that these scientific concepts will carry along an open horizon of typical content which is codetermined by these characteristics and which, although yet undisclosed, can be revealed by further research. Types of this kind are called by Husserl "essential types" (*wesentliche Typen*). Nonscientific empirical concepts as used in daily life are, however, not limited as to the number of their characteristics. Their formation is frequently guided by a typification which separates and distinguishes objects in accordance with characteristics which these objects have *only seemingly* in common with other objects – for example, conceiving of the whale as a fish because of his bodily shape and the fact that he lives in water. Types of this kind are called by Husserl nonessential types (*ausserwesentliche Typen*). They do not carry along an infinite open horizon of typical material, and any expectation that they may be helpful in the further progress of searching for such material will finally be disappointed. So much for Husserl.

III. RELEVANCE AND TYPIFICATION

If we seek to find a convergence between Goldstein's findings and the results of phenomenological analysis, we do not need to turn, as Gurwitsch did, to the highly complicated level of ideation, but to the constitution of empirical general types in the pre-predicative sphere. The view of Merleau-Ponty seems to corroborate this statement. And among the empirical general types, we do not have to use, for the explanation of pathological behavior, the essential types of the empirical sciences but the prescientific nonessential types so characteristic of our thinking in daily life. The thesis we wish to submit is that the selection of these nonessential types by the person with a brain injury is performed according to a principle other than that used by the normal person. But what are the principles governing such a selection? What brings it about that among all the objects within my perceptual field at any given moment this particular object, and among the manifold characteristics of this object *this* particular characteristic, appeals to me as being typical? Husserl answers, as we have seen, that it is our passive interest that makes me turn toward the object, the interesting object wakening expectations of a particular kind. This is certainly correct, but the term "interest" is simply the heading for a series of complicated problems, which for the sake of convenience shall be called the problem of *relevance*. We turn our interest to those experiences which for one reason or another seem to us to be relevant to the sum total of our situation as experienced by us in any given present. Of course, such a present is a specious present, encompassing parts of my past and of my future, and my situation includes, as Merleau-Ponty has correctly seen, not only my physical but also my human environment, my ideological and moral position. The system of relevance determines not only what belongs to the situation with which, in Goldstein's language, the individual has to come to terms, but also what has to be made a substratum of the generalizing typification, what traits have to be selected as characteristically typical, and how far we have to plunge into the open, still undisclosed horizon of typicality. If this interpretation is correct, then we may say that Goldstein's patients use a system of relevance other than that of the normal person. Then we must not call one attitude the concrete, the other the abstract. We must not speak of two attitudes, because there is no attitude at all involved, except in the metaphorical sense. We have simply in both cases different systems of relevances, which govern the process of typification and generalization. How can we characterize these differences? It seems to us that here Bergson's theory gives us valuable help.

The normal person is fully awake and this means fully attentive to life. His system of relevance is determined by the practical task before him. He pulls, so to speak, into his specious present the open possibilities of his typical expectations of typical events and occurrences, which though hidden in the open horizon, will, so he believes, materialize in conformity with his anticipation. And this belief, in turn, is founded on his preknowledge of typical occurrences and events in the past which have proved to be relevant in a similar way in similar situations. The relevance system of the person with a brain lesion is entirely different. His *attention à la vie* has diminished, the tension of his consciousness is relaxed, his specious present becomes more and more narrowed to the actual instant, and only what is within his actual reach determines the characteristics of the types which he can use for recognizing concrete objects and subsuming the novel. This small world then constitutes the environment with which the patient "has to come to terms" – terms, of course, of his own definition. That his world gets so narrow is due to the fact that the context of the present with the past has weakened, and the possible anticipations of the future are restricted to the imminent occurrence. Husserl has distinguished in his analysis of our sense of inner time with regard to our consciousness of the past between retention of the experiences just passed, on which I still have a hold, and reproduction of more remote events and correspondingly with regard to the future, between protentions and anticipations. We may use this terminology in saying that in extreme cases the specious present of Goldstein's patients includes merely actual experiences, retentions and protentions, but not reproductions and anticipations. In other words, the disturbance of their relevance system seems to be referred to a disturbance of their sense of inner time. This might corroborate one of the fundamental hypotheses of Bergson's philosophy, namely, that the brain and the central nervous system is the organ which regulates our attention to life.

But there is another point of view from which the aforementioned thesis, which refers the distinction between concrete and categorial attitudes to a difference of the underlying system of relevances, gains some weight. Let us not forget that Professor Goldstein's study is a study of language disturbances. Language as used in daily life, however, is primarily a language of named things and events. Now any name includes a typification and is, in Husserl's sense, a nonessential empirical generalization. We may interpret the prescientific human language as a treasure house of preconstituted types and characteristics, each of them carrying along an open horizon of unexplored typical contents. By naming an experienced object, we are relating it by its typicality to preexperienced things of similar typical structure, and we accept its open horizon referring to future experiences of the same type, which are therefore capable of being given the same name. To find a thing or event relevant enough to bestow a separate name upon it is again the outcome of the prevailing system of relevance. Here is an animal and this animal is a dog, but a dog of a particular kind which is unknown to me. I am, if sufficiently interested in this object, not satisfied with subsuming it under the name of "dog." The characteristics which it has in common with all other dogs are precisely those which are irrelevant to me; relevant, however, are those which lead to the building of a new subtype. I ask: What kind of dog is this? And my curiosity is satisfied if I learn that it is an Irish setter. At the same time, recognizing the animal as a dog, it is normally not relevant to me to continue the generalization: A dog is a mammal, an animal, a living thing, an object of the outer world, and so on. It is always the system of relevance that chooses from the vocabulary of my vernacular (and also from its syntactical structure) the relevant term, and that term is the typical pre-experienced generalization interesting me (or my interlocutor) in the present situation.

The situation of the aphasic patient seems not to require the continuation of typifying generalization beyond that which is immediately given and therefore relevant to him. There is no incentive for him to give the "pencil sharpener" and the "apple parer" the common name of knife, just as for the normal person there is – except in particular circumstances – no incentive to call the Irish setter an object of the outer world. On the other hand it may be that the patient cannot find certain names because these names have lost for him any typicality: they do not carry along open horizons; their horizon is closed, has shrunk to the individual concrete experience in the now irrelevant past to which it adhered. Names are no longer essential types: all have turned into nonessential ones, that is, types without infinite horizons. This explanation seems to correspond not only to Bergson's theory, but also to Cassirer's explanation of aphasic disturbances as an impairment of symbolic behavior. And it appears that this hypothesis converges with several of Goldstein's findings: his theory of concrete and abstract language, his characterization of "inner speech," his interpretation of the child's language, of paraphasia, of naming and pseudonaming.

The preceding remarks are, despite their length, merely fragmentary. They have fulfilled their purpose if they have shown the importance of Professor Goldstein's work for the clarification of certain fundamental problems of philosophy. To the social scientist, however, the findings of Goldstein and the philosophical questions implied therein are of vital concern. All social sciences have to deal in a still unclarified way with concepts such as situation and attitudes, typification and systems of relevance, symbols and communication, speech production and speech understanding. It would seem that especially Husserl's theory of typification in the prepredicative sphere might be a useful starting point for further investigation of these questions.

SYMBOL, REALITY AND SOCIETY

> Do not interpretations belong to God?
> *Genesis* 40.8

I. INTRODUCTORY REMARKS

1) Some controversial points in the present discussion of signs and symbols

Present day discussion of the problem of symbolic reference shows several bewildering features.

a) There is first a group of terms, such as "mark," "indication," "sign," "symbol," etc., which, in spite of the efforts of the best minds, seem to resist any attempt toward a precise definition. The customary distinction between natural and conventional signs makes it possible to subsume under these terms phenomena as different as the halo around the moon indicating rain, the footprint of an animal, the ringing of a buzzer, a traffic light, characters used in musical notation, gestures of approval, and so on. The term "symbol" is used for designating no less heterogeneous phenomena: names or linguistic expressions are considered as symbols, but also the lion is called the symbol of courage, the circle a symbol of eternity, the cross a Christian symbol of salvation, the flag a symbol of a nation, the letter *O* a symbol of oxygen, *Moby Dick* or Kafka's *The Trial* a symbol of the human condition. But even more: according to some authors the formation of a scientific theory, the rain-dance of the Zunis, the role of the Queen in the British Commonwealth can be denoted by the term "symbol."

b) Secondly, if there seems to be some agreement that man, in the words of Cassirer, is an *"animal symbolicum,"* there is no agreement whatsoever about where the process called symbolization starts in human thinking. Some authors, such as

A. N. Whitehead in his book on *Symbolism* [1] as well as in *Process and Reality*,[2] see the origin of symbolic reference in perception, namely, in the integration of percepta in the mode of presentational immediacy with percepta in the mode of causal efficacy in our common-sense perception. Charles Morris in his book *Signs, Language and Behavior* [3] defines a sign (and he uses this term as a more general one) as something that directs behavior with respect to something that is not at the moment a stimulus. The particular event or object, such as a sound or a mark, that functions as a sign is called the sign-vehicle; the organism, for which something is a sign, the interpreter; anything that would permit the completion of the response sequence to which the interpreter is disposed because of a sign, its denotatum; and the conditions under which the sign denotes, its significatum. If the sign is produced by its interpreter and acts as substitute for some other sign with which it is synonymous, it is called a symbol, otherwise a signal.

To C. J. Ducasse [4] a sign-relation is not independent of the mind but essentially psychological in character. Interpretation is a kind of mental event, consisting in this, that consciousness of something causes us to become conscious of something else. Interpretanda are either signs or symbols. A sign proper begets an opinion or leads us to assert a proposition, whereas a symbol merely leads the mind to think of something else without a proposition.

John Wild [5] criticizes the theories of both Morris and Ducasse for interpreting sign-relations as causes and not as objects of knowledge. Both have disregarded the fact that a natural sign (for example, "Smoke is a sign of fire") is *really* connected with its signatum irrespective of its effect on us; on the other hand,

---

[1] Alfred North Whitehead, *Symbolism, its Meaning and Effect* (Barbour Page Lectures, University of Virginia), New York, 1927, Chap. I.

[2] Alfred North Whitehead, *Process and Reality, An Essay in Cosmology* (Gifford Lectures), New York, 1929, Part II, Chap. VIII.

[3] Charles W. Morris, *Signs, Language and Behavior*, New York, 1946, pp. 345ff.

[4] C. J. Ducasse in two articles, "Symbols, Signs and Signals," *Journal of Symbolic Logic*, vol. IV, 1939, and "Some Comments on C. W. Morris' 'Foundations of the Theory of Signs,'" *Philosophy and Phenomenological Research*, Vol. III, 1942, pp. 43ff.

[5] John Wild, "Introduction to the Phenomenology of Signs," *Philosophy and Phenomenological Research*, Vol. VIII, 1947, pp. 217ff. See also Ducasse's rejoinder in the same issue.

there are certain natural signs, such as concepts and imaginative images, which are formal signs, that is, their whole nature is to signify, to specify the noetic faculty by something other than themselves. Formal signs are *nothing but* signs, whereas it is characteristic for the other natural signs, called instrumental signs, that their whole being is not exhausted in their signifying function. (Smoke is certainly more than a sign of fire.) Arbitrary signs, in contrast to natural ones, are not "really" connected with what they signify. Wild's general definition of the nature of the sign-relation is that a sign is anything capable of manifesting something other than itself as an object to the knowing faculty.

Ernst Cassirer [6] distinguishes signs (or signals), which are operators and part of the physical world of being, from symbols, which are designators and part of the human world of meaning. The former, even when understood and used as signals, have, nevertheless, a sort of physical or substantial being, whereas symbols have only functional value. Signs or signals are related to the thing to which they refer in a fixed and unique way, whereas the human symbol is not rigid and inflexible, but mobile. To Susanne K. Langer,[7] who follows Cassirer's theories to a considerable extent, a sign indicates the existence – past, present, or future – of a thing, event, or condition. Signs are proxies for their objects, which they announce to the subjects, and the sign-relation is, thus, a triadic one: subject, sign, and object. Symbols, however, are vehicles for the *conception* of objects; it is the conception and not the things that symbols directly "mean." For this reason, any symbolic function requires four terms: subject, symbol, conception, and object, it being understood that not the act of conceiving but what is conceived enters into the meaning pattern. Like Cassirer, Mrs. Langer considers the name as the simplest type of symbol for the thing named and calls this complex relationship the denotation of the symbol, whereas the more direct relationship of the symbol to the associated conceptions it conveys is called its connotation. It seems that Mrs. Langer in her book, *Feeling and Form*,[8]

---

[6] Ernst Cassirer, *An Essay on Man*, New Haven, 1944, pp. 32–35.
[7] Susanne K. Langer, *Philosophy in a New Key*, Cambridge, 1942, now also as Penguin Book, New York, 1942, chap. 2–4.
[8] Susanne K. Langer, *Feeling and Form*, New York, 1953.

has extended her definition of "symbol." A symbol is now any device whereby we are enabled to make an abstraction.[9]

The preceding summary of a few theories concerned with the problem of significative or symbolic reference, although dealing merely with some samples of proposed approaches, is bewildering enough and strongly suggests that the difficulties of finding a unified approach are not of a mere terminological nature. A brief examination of two additional groups of controversial problems reinforces this suspicion.

c) As we have seen, most of the writers deal with the (real or psychological) relationship between sign and signatum or symbol and meaning. However, it is controversial whether the relationship between the two members of the pair is reversible or not. According to Whitehead, the mere fact that a common element underlies both terms within which the symbolic reference is established does not in itself decide which shall be symbol and which meaning. There are no components of experience which are only symbols or only meanings. Symbolic reference holds between two components in a complex experience, each capable of direct recognition. The more usual symbolic reference is from the less primitive component as symbol to the more primitive one as meaning.[10] According to Mrs. Langer, if it were not for the subject or interpretant, sign and object would be interchangeable. Thunder may just as well be a sign that there has been lightning, as lightning may signify that there will be thunder. In themselves they are merely correlated. It is only where one is perceptible and the other (harder or impossible to perceive) is *interesting* that we actually have a case of *signification belonging to a term*.[11] According to Wild, we take that member of the pair as a sign which is better known to us than its signatum and, therefore, *as a sign*, dissimilar to it. The footprint of the animal is more knowable than the animal. However, the sign may really signify the signatum when neither the one nor the other is actually known. Signs are discovered, not made.[12]

Yet in spite of these authors who defend the thesis of the interchangeability of signs with their signatum (at least with

[9] *Ibid.*, p. xi.
[10] Whitehead, *Symbolism, its Meaning and Effect*, p. 10.
[11] Langer, *Philosophy in a New Key*, Penguin edition, p. 47.
[12] Wild, *loc. cit.*, pp. 227–230.

respect to "natural" signs), common-sense thinking refuses to admit that fire may be a sign for smoke, pain the sign for moaning, the physical object the sign of the concept. The dilemma becomes especially complicated as soon as language is taken into consideration. The problem was clearly stated by Aristotle in the beginning of *De Interpretatione* (16a4ff.): "Spoken words are the symbols (Aristotle uses here the term '*symbola*') of mental experience and written words are the symbols of spoken words. Just as all men do not have the same writing, so all men do not have the same speech sounds, but the mental experiences ('*pathēmata tēs psychēs*') which these directly symbolize (here Aristotle does not use as before the term '*symbolon*' but '*semeion*', that is, sign) are the same for all as also are those things of which our experiences are the images (*homoiomata*)." We have here the rather complicated relationship: physical event (sound or penstrokes on paper) denoting the thing named, connoting the conception referred to. These are most certainly irreversible relations. The same holds good for all symbolic references of a higher order.

d) Another controversial question is that of the intersubjective character of signs in the broadest sense. For the purpose of the present discussion we wish to disregard the behavioristic thesis so ingeniously defended by George H. Mead, Charles Morris, and others. We are, therefore, not concerned with the signal functions of certain signs, nor with the – otherwise eminently interesting – problem of so-called animal language. We follow Aristotle's statement that "a name is a sound significant by convention (*kata synthēkēn*)" (*De Interpretatione*, 16a19). Aristotle explains that this limitation is necessary because nothing is by nature a name, it is only so when it becomes a symbol (16a26f.). And he adds that inarticulate sounds, such as those which brutes produce, are significant, yet none of these constitutes a name (*onoma*). According to Aristotle, therefore, language and artificial signs in general are matters of conventions. But the concept of convention presupposes the existence of society and also the possibility of some communication with the help of which the "convention" can be established.

Our question is now a more general one: Does this statement hold good also for other than linguistic signs? Or for all signs other than natural ones? Or even perhaps for the latter? Or still more generally: if it is true, as it is widely believed, that any sign or symbol-relation involves at least three terms, of which one is the subject of the interpreter, is this interpreter tacitly assumed to have already established communication with his fellow-man so that the sign or symbol-relation is from the outset a public one? Or, are sign or symbol-relations possible within the private psychological or spiritual life of the lonely individual? If so, to what extent can they be shared? Are my fantasies, my dreams, and the symbolic system involved therein also capable of socialization? Does artistic creation, religious experience, philosophizing presuppose intersubjectivity? If, on the other hand, there are private and public symbols, does a particular sociocultural environment influence the structure of either or both of them and to what extent? Is it not possible that what is a sign or a symbol for one individual or one group has no significative or symbolic meaning to another? Moreover, can intersubjectivity as such, society and community as such, be experienced otherwise than by the use of a symbol? Then, is it the symbol which creates society and community, or is the symbol a creation of society imposed upon the individual? Or is this interrelationship between society and the system of symbols a process of such kind that symbols, or at least some of them, originate in society and, once established, influence in turn the structure of society itself?

2) *Plan of the following investigation*

This group of problems will be our present particular concern, although it would, of course, be futile to hope to do more than arrive at a highly incomplete catalogue of open questions. But even this modest task cannot be accomplished without some preparatory work which we propose to perform in three steps.

Our first step will be concerned with the question how it happens that in ordinary language, as well as in philosophical discussion, so many heterogeneous ideas are clustered around a set of terms (sign, symbol, mark, indication, etc.) aimed at denoting the significative or symbolic reference. If we encounter a synonymy of such extent we have, of course, the duty of determining as clearly and unequivocally as possible the meaning of each term used in the discussion. Nearly all the writers on this topic have made such an attempt, but as our introductory remarks have shown, without arriving at any consensus. Yet there is a second task involved, namely, to try to find the ground of such a state of affairs, that is, the basic features common to the various conceptualizations; moreover, if this can be done, to demonstrate (by sketching a kind of typology of their possible interpretations) that many controversial views defended by various writers result from the application of different schemes of interpretation to the same basic phenomenon which is, we believe, the phenomenon of appresentation studied by Husserl. His teachings will be connected with Bergson's theory of multiple orders. It is hoped that this discussion will help us to establish certain principles governing all kinds of sign and symbol-relations which might be helpful for the discussion of more concrete problems.

Our second step will deal with the investigation of the motives which lead a man to the use and development of significative and symbolic relations in order to obtain knowledge of the world he lives in, of his fellow-men, and of himself. In a very sketchy way we will have to deal in this section with certain basic problems of philosophical anthropology, namely, the place of man in a cosmos which transcends his existence, but within which he has to find his bearings. Signs and symbols, so we propose to show, are among the means by which man tries to come to terms with his manifold experiences of transcendency. We will have to describe how the perceptible world actually given to the individual at any moment of his biographical existence carries its open horizons of space and time which transcend the actual Here and Now; and we will have to show how the communicative common environment originates in the comprehension of fellow-men, how society transcends in still another sense the individual's actual experiences.

We submit that a specific form of appresentational relations – called marks, indications, signs – corresponds to each of these particular transcendencies. They all have in common the fact that they are experienced within the reality of everyday life. But this is not the only reality in which man lives. There are other transcendencies beyond those mentioned so far. In a third step we will, starting from a theory proposed by William James, briefly consider the multiple realities, or "subuniverses," such as the world of religion, of art, and of science, that can only be experienced in a particular form of appresentation for which we reserve the term symbol. We will study the function of the symbolic relation on some of these various levels of reality and as means for interconnecting one level with another. For we will find that the world of everyday life, the common-sense world, has a paramount position among the various provinces of reality, since only within it does communication with our fellow-men become possible. But the common-sense world is from the outset a sociocultural world, and the many questions connected with the intersubjectivity of the symbolic relations originate within it, are determined by it, and find their solution within it.

II. APPRESENTATION AS THE GENERAL FORM OF SIGNIFICATIVE AND SYMBOLIC RELATIONS

1) Husserl's concept of appresentation

If we try to find the common denominator of the various theories on significative and symbolic relations studied in the previous section, we may say that the object, fact, or event called sign or symbol refers to something other than itself. Smoke is a physical thing given to our sensory perception. It can be seen and smelled and chemically analyzed. But if we take smoke not as a mere physical object, but as an indication of fire, then we take it as manifesting something other than itself. Calling smoke the sign and the indicated fire the signatum, as some of our authors do, we may say that both form a pair.

Husserl, in the later period of his life,[13] studied the general phenomenon of pairing or coupling which is, according to him, a general feature of our consciousness. It is a form of passive

---

[13] Edmund Husserl, *Cartesianische Meditationen* (*Husserliana* I), Haag, 1950 (French Version, "*Méditations Cartésiennes*," Paris, 1931), especially V. *Méditation*, Secs. 49–54; see also *Ideen II* (*Husserliana* IV), Haag, 1952, esp. Secs. 44–47, Sec. 50 (with supplement p. 410), Sec. 51. esp. p. 198, See also Marvin Farber, *The Foundation of Phenomenology*, Cambridge, 1943, pp. 529ff., esp. p. 532.

synthesis which is commonly called association. It is beyond the scope of this discussion to embark upon a presentation of the phenomenological interpretation of association. We restrict ourselves to the discussion of that particular form of pairing or coupling, which Husserl calls "appresentation" or "analogical apperception." The most primitive case of a coupling or pairing association is characterized by the fact that two or more data are intuitively given in the unity of consciousness, which, by this very reason, constitutes two distinct phenomena as a unity, regardless of whether or not they are attended to.

Let us take as an illustration our perception of an object of the outer world. We may say that in immediate apperception the thing is perceived as this or that object, perspectively shortened and adumbrated, etc. Here it is, in copresence with us, and through acts of immediate intuition we intuit the object as a "self." Yet, strictly speaking, if we apperceive an object of the outer world, then that which we really see in our visual perception is merely the frontside of the object. But this perception of the visible frontside of the object involves an apperception by analogy of the unseen backside, an apperception which, to be sure, is a more or less empty anticipation of what we might perceive if we turned the object around or if we walked around the object. This anticipation is based on our past experiences of normal objects of this kind. From the apperception of the frontside we believe that this object is a wooden cube of red color, and we expect that the unseen backside will be of the same shape, color, and material. But it is quite possible that our anticipation will be disappointed. It may turn out that the unseen backside is deformed, of iron, and blue. Nevertheless, the unseen side will have *some* shape, *some* color, and consist of *some* material. At any rate, we may say that the frontside, which is apperceived in immediacy or given to us in presentation, appresents the unseen backside in an analogical way, which, however, does not mean by way of an *inference* by analogy. The appresenting term, that which is present in immediate apperception, is coupled or paired with the appresented term.

This is, however, just an example in order to make the problem of appresentation understandable. In his *Logical Investigation* VI (sec. 14f. and 26)[14] and in the first volume of his *Ideas* (sec. 43)[15] Husserl has shown that all significative relations are special cases of this form of analogical apperception or appresentation which is based upon the general phenomenon of pairing or coupling. To be sure, in these earlier writings Husserl's terminology was somewhat different. But he states quite clearly that if we perceive an object of the outer world as a self, no apprehension on a higher level, that is, no appresentational references are built up on the basis of this apprehending act of intuition. On the other hand, in the case of a significative relation, we have the appresenting object as perceived in the intuitive field, but we are not directed toward it, but through the medium of a secondary apprehension or a *"fundiertes Auffassen"* toward something else which is indicated or, in Husserl's later terminology, appresented by the first object. Thus, by appresentation, we experience intuitively something as indicating or depicting significantly something else.

Experience by appresentation has its particular style of confirmation: each appresentation carries along its particular appresented horizons, which refer to further fulfilling and confirming experiences, to systems of well ordered indications, including new potentially confirmable syntheses and new nonintuitive anticipations.

This is, however, only half the story. So far we have tacitly presupposed that appresentation requires copresence of the appresenting with the appresented member of the pair. This, however, is just a special case of a more general situation. In his study *Erfahrung und Urteil* (secs. 34–43),[16] Husserl has shown that a passive synthesis of pairing is also possible between an actual perception and a recollection, between a perception and a fantasm (*fictum*), and thus between actual and potential experiences, between the apprehension of facts and possibilities. The result of the passive synthesis of association here involved is that the apprehension of a present element of a previously

[14] Edmund Husserl, *Logische Untersuchungen*, Vol. II, part II, Halle, 2nd ed., 1920; see Farber, *op. cit.*, pp. 410–415, and 430f.

[15] Edmund Husserl, *Ideas*, Vol. I, translated by Boyce Gibson, New York, 1931, pp. 135ff.

[16] Edmund Husserl, *Erfahrung und Urteil*, edited by L. Landgrebe, Prague, 1939, pp. 174–223.

constituted pair "wakens" or "calls forth" the appresented element, it being immaterial whether one or the other is a perception, a recollection, a fantasm, or a fictum. All this happens, in principle, in pure passivity without any active interference of the mind. To give an example: the present percept "wakens" submerged recollections which then "start rising," whether or not we want them to do so. And, even further, according to Husserl, any active remembering takes place on the basis of an associative wakening that had occurred previously. In general, by the functioning of the passive synthesis a unity of intuition is constituted not only between perceptions and recollections, but also between perceptions and fantasms.

So far we have considered Husserl. It seems to us that Husserl's theory of appresentation covers all cases of significative and symbolic references dealt with by the various authors discussed before. In all these cases an object, fact, or event is not experienced as a "self," but as standing for another object which is not given in immediacy to the experiencing subject. The appresenting member "wakens" or "calls forth" or "evokes" the appresented one. The latter may be either a physical event, fact, or object which, however, is not perceivable to the subject in immediacy, or something spiritual or immaterial; it may be real in the sense of common-sense reality, or a fantasm; it may be simultaneous with the appresenting one or precede or follow it, or it may even be timeless. These appresentational relations may occur on various levels: an appresented object may in turn appresent another one, there are signs of signs, and symbols of symbols, etc. Moreover, the appresenting immediate experience need by no means consist in the perception of the physical object: it may be a recollection, a fantasm, a dream, etc.

2) The various orders involved in the appresentational situation

We have, however, to go a step further. So far we have directed our attention merely to the pair formed by the appresenting and the appresented object, as if neither were interconnected with other objects. There is, however, neither in immediate nor in analogical apprehension such a thing as an isolated object of which I could have an isolated experience.

Each object is an object within a field; each experience carries along its horizon; both belong to an order of a particular style. The physical object, for example, is interconnected with all the other objects of Nature, present, past, and future, by spatial, temporal, and causal relations, whose sum-total constitutes the order of physical Nature. A mathematical object, say, an equilateral triangle, refers to all the axioms and theorems by which this mathematical object is defined and to all the theorems, etc., which are based on the concepts of triangularity and equilaterality, of a regular polygon, or of a geometrical figure in general. The same holds good for any kind of object and our experiences of it. There is even an order of our fantasms and an intrinsic order of our dreams which separates them from all the other realms, and constitutes them as a finite province of meaning.

We will have to revert to this problem later on (section VI). For the time being we have to consider that in the relationship of coupling either member of the pair is merely one object within an order which includes other objects pertaining to the same realm. If the appresenting object is a physical thing of nature, then it is connected with all the other physical objects, events, and occurrences within the realm of nature. And, in a like manner, there is also an interrelationship between the appresented objects and other objects pertaining to the same order as the appresented one.

We are, consequently, led to the conclusion that in any appresentational reference a relationship between several orders is involved. This is obvious if the appresenting object is a physical thing (say, a flag), whereas the appresented object belongs to another realm (the republic for which it stands). But brief deliberation will show that there are also several orders involved if both the appresenting and the appresented objects belong to the *same* realm, say, if both are physical things of the outer world. Smoke and fire are both physical things, perceptible by our senses. But being paired with the unseen fire, that is, in its appresentational reference, the physical thing "smoke" is not interpreted as this or that perceived object in the intuitive field toward which we are directed, but as a carrier or vehicle or medium of a secondary apprehension which is directed toward something else, namely, the fire indicated by the smoke. Thus, we find in this simple relation several orders involved. But even this is not enough. In higher forms of appresentational references I may know that an object refers appresentationally to another one, but either without knowing the nature of this appresentational reference, that is, the context established by it, or (even if I know the context) without being able to establish the synthesis of pairing the appresenting objects with the particular appresented one. I find, for example, in a catalogue of a bookseller some items marked with an "*." I know that the character "*" is generally used as reference to a footnote. But there is no footnote and I am at a loss as to what this sign means. Or I may recognize certain patterns of inkstrokes on paper as Chinese ideograms or as Gregg shorthand, without being capable of reading them. Appresentational references of a higher degree also presuppose, therefore, a knowledge of the order within which the pairing itself occurs.

In general, we may state that in any appresentational situation the following four orders are involved:

a) the order of objects to which the immediately apperceived object belongs if experienced as a self, disregarding any appresentational references. We shall call this order the *"apperceptual scheme."*

b) the order of objects to which the immediately apperceived object belongs if taken not as a self but as a member of an appresentational pair, thus referring to something other than itself. We shall call this order the *"appresentational scheme."*

c) the order of objects to which the appresented member of the pair belongs which is apperceived in a merely analogical manner. We shall call this order the *"referential scheme."*

d) the order to which the particular appresentational reference itself belongs, that is, the particular type of pairing or context by which the appresenting member is connected with the appresented one, or, more generally, the relationship which prevails between the appresentational and the referential scheme. We shall call this order the *"contextual or interpretational scheme."*

Now in describing an appresentational relationship we may take any of these orders as our home base, as our starting point, as our system of reference, or, to use the term of Husserl, we may "live in" any of these orders. Of course, we may at any time substitute one system of reference for another and, in the natural attitude of daily life, we indeed continuously do so. But while we attend to one of these schemes as the basic order, the other schemes seem to be characterized by arbitrariness, contingency, or even by a want or absence of order.

3) Bergson's theory of concurring orders

Bergson has studied the problem of the absence of order in a famous section of his *Creative Evolution* entitled: *"Les deux ordres et le désordre"* ("The two orders and the disorder").[17] We are here not concerned with the particular nature of the two orders established in the system of Bergson's philosophy, namely, the spontaneous order of life *versus* the automatic order of the intellect. We are, however, much interested in his interpretation of the relationship between several coexisting orders. Bergson starts from the examination of the notion of disorder and comes to the conclusion that what we call "disorder" is merely the want or absence of a particular kind of order we expected and to which any other order appears just a contingent arrangement. This can be illustrated by the use we make in daily life of the notion of disorder. What do we mean if we enter a bedroom and say, "it is in disorder"? The position of each object can be explained by the automatic movements of the persons who inhabited this room or by the efficient causes, whatever they may be, which put each piece of furniture or clothing, etc., in its place. All this occurs strictly in accordance with the order of physical causality. But we are simply not interested in this kind of order if we expected to find a tidy room. What we expected to find is the human orderliness of appropriate, although arbitrary, arrangements of things in the room. If, on the other hand, we imagine chaos, we have in mind a state in the world of physical nature which is not subject to the laws of physics but in which events emerge and disappear in an arbitrary way. In this case we apply to the world of nature the principles of human (and this is arbitrary) order, replacing *"l'ordre automatique"* by *"l'ordre voulu."* Absence of order in the sense of absence of *any kind of*

[17] Henri Bergson, *Evolution créatrice*, Paris, Chap. III, pp. 238–244, and 252–258.

order at all is, therefore, says Bergson, a meaningless expression, and refers only to the fact that an expected *particular* kind of order is wanting. Yet, this implies that another kind of order, irreducible to the former, prevails. One order is, however, necessarily contingent with reference to the other. And Bergson comes to the conclusion that the geometrical order is merely the suppression of the spontaneous order, a suppression required by certain necessities of our practical life.

4) Application of Bergson's theory to some controversial opinions concerning signs and symbols

Let us apply Bergson's findings to our problem of the various schemes of orders involved in the appresentational reference. We stated that we may interpret the appresentational relation by taking either the apperceptual, appresentational, referential, or contextual scheme as a system of reference. In doing so the selected system of reference becomes the prototype of order. Seen from it, all the other schemes have seemingly the character of arbitrariness and mere contingency. This is important in several respects if applied to the particular appresentational forms generally referred to by the terms "signs" and "symbols." It explains also certain controversial theories proposed for the solution of the problems involved.

It is the common opinion of nearly all otherwise highly dissident authors that all sign- or symbol-relations are of at least a triadic character, involving not only the sign or symbol and the object for which it stands, but also the mind of the interpreter (or the interpretant's thought) for whom the significative or symbolic relation exists. Now it is obvious that not only the philosopher, who tries to describe the sign-symbol relation, but also the interpreter, who lives in it, has a certain, although limited, freedom to select one of the schemes as a basic system of reference for interpreting the significative or symbolic relation. This becomes of particular importance if the Bergsonian idea of the relativity of systems of orders is taken into account. It leads to the conclusion that what is sign or symbol for one individual (or, as we will later see, for one social group) might be without any significance for another.

Furthermore, we pointed out that several authors are of the opinion that the relationship between sign and signatum is largely reversible. It follows from Bergson's interpretation of the relativity of several orders that the question of which member of the pair is taken as a sign and which as a signatum depends first upon the decision of whether the appresentational or the referential scheme is taken as system of reference, and second upon the particular contextual scheme by which the appresentational scheme is related to the others.

Moreover, Bergson's theory seems to explain the customary distinction between natural and arbitrary (or conventional) signs. This distinction implies that a particular scheme was chosen as system of reference, as a prototype of the appresentational relationship. The so-called "real relation" underlying natural signs consists in the fact that both, sign and signatum, are events within the physical world of nature. The same apperceptual scheme, then, is actually applicable to the sign and potentially to the signatum. Or in other words, those authors who – and rightly – see that a triadic relationship including the interpreter has to be established, hold that in the case of natural signs the appresentational scheme coincides with the referential one, whereas the interpretational scheme is merely taken for granted. In the case of arbitrary signs, however, the interpretational scheme has to be taken as a basic system of reference.

Finally, those authors who maintain that all conceptualizations are as such already symbols or signs and those who believe that in addition imaginative images have to be considered as signs, take the referential scheme as the basic system, and interpret the paired elements belonging to the apperceptual scheme in terms of context.

The preceding all too condensed remarks are an attempt to show that the prevailing confusion in dealing with the group of phenomena designated by terms such as signs and symbols is not entirely of a terminological origin. It emanates, at least partially, from the possibility of choosing either the apperceptual or the appresentational, the referential or even the interpretational scheme involved as a basic order from which the others have to be explained. But the interpreter having once made a decision to consider one of those schemes as the archetype of order, sees the other schemes as merely contingent, arbitrary arrangements, or as wanting in all order. This is at least one of the reasons why it is generally maintained that signs and symbol-relationships are essentially ambiguous.

5) *The principles governing structural changes of appresentational relations*

Another reason for the essential ambiguity of appresentational relations consists in the fact that higher forms of appresentational references are especially subject to an internal structural change. Without entering into all the implications involved here, we want to mention three principles by which this internal structural change is governed.

a) *The principle of the relative irrelevance of the vehicle*

This principle means that an appresented object X, which was originally paired with an appresenting object A, might enter a new pairing with an object B, which will henceforth appresent X. The new vehicle B, if apprehended (remembered, fantasied) in copresence will "waken" or "call forth" in the mind of the experiencing subject the same appresented object X which formerly was paired with the original vehicle A. This principle explains several otherwise bewildering phenomena:

a) The meaning of a scientific paper is independent of whether it is printed in this or that typographical style, written in typescript or longhand, or read aloud to an audience. To the patriot the meaning of his national anthem remains unchanged whether it is sung in any particular key or played on any particular instrument.

b) The possibility of substituting one vehicle for another is one prerequisite – but only one – for translating the same appresentational content – at least to a certain extent – from one sign system to another one (London, Londres; two, *deux, duo, zwei,* etc.)[18]

c) If the pairing of the appresented object X with the new vehicle B takes place, two cases are possible:

[18] Husserl, *Logische Untersuchungen*, Vol. I, Sec. 12; Farber, *loc. cit.*, p. 229.

i) *either* the original appresenting vehicle A is preserved and continues beside the new one (B) in its appresentational functions. Then both the former (A) and the new vehicle (B) will become *"synonyms"* in the broadest, not merely linguistic, sense of this term. Both will evoke the same appresented object X (ship – vessel; leap – jump; but also 10 and ten, MDCCCCLIV and 1954, *Fer* and iron, etc.);

ii) *or* the appresented object X may become detached from the originally appresenting one (A) with which it formed a pair, in which case the original appresentational reference may become obfuscated or entirely forgotten. If this happens the former vehicle ceases to "waken" the appresented object: although it might be preserved in a more or less ritualistic way, it loses its significance. For example, many *surahs* of the Koran begin with a number of disconnected letters of the Arabic alphabet, whose significance is no longer understood.

b) The principle of variability of the appresentational meaning

The same situation prevails here as in i, but the appresentational meaning changes with the substitution of A by B although the appresented object X remains the same. Husserl [19] has shown (and Ogden and Richards [20] came to the same conclusion), that several proper names may have different meanings but name the same object. The Commander in Chief of the Allied Armies on D Day, 1944, the author of the book *Crusade in Europe*, the thirty fourth President of the United States, are all proper names denoting Dwight D. Eisenhower, but each appresentational reference is a different one. The expressions, "an equilateral triangle" and an "equiangular triangle," denote the same geometrical figure but have different appresentational meanings. The same situation refers to relations such as $A > B$ and $B < A$, and although in terms of geography and transportation, of milestones and signposts, the road which connects Paris and Chartres is identical, regardless of whether we follow it in one direction or the other, Péguy,[21] to whom Chartres is the symbol

---

[19] *Ibid.*, "The victor of Jena" and "the one who was defeated at Waterloo."
[20] C. K. Ogden and I. A. Richards, *The Meaning of Meaning*, London, 1946, p. 92: "The King of England" and "the owner of Buckingham Palace."
[21] Charles Péguy, *Note conjointe sur la philosophie Bergsonienne et la philosophie Cartésienne*, Paris, 1935, pp. 312ff.

of French Catholicism, has to deny that the road leading to Chartres can be termed identical with the road leading away from it.

c) The principle of figurative transference

This principle is the opposite of the principle of the relative irrelevance of the vehicle: an appresenting object A, originally paired with the appresented object X, enters into a new pairing with an appresented object Y, eventually also with a third object Z, etc. Again two cases are possible:

a) *either* the original appresentational reference (A-X) is preserved and continues to coexist with the new one (A-Y). One single appresenting object (A) may then appresent two or more objects (X, Y, ...). This is the origin of any form of tropes in the broadest, not merely linguistic, sense and of the figurative use of the originally appresented object. This case is of particular importance: on the one hand, it leads to the equivocal use of the appresenting term A; on the other hand it makes the construction of higher levels of appresentational relations possible;

b) *or* the original appresentational reference (A-X) is obfuscated or entirely forgotten, and merely the new one (A-Y) preserved: this is the phenomenon of the "shift of meaning," well known to all students of signs or symbols in whatever form. For example, the circle, but also the serpent rolled into a circle, becomes a symbol of eternity because, like eternity, it has no beginning and no end.

The three principles just discussed will prove to be useful if applied to more concrete problems. In order to prepare for their study we will now pass to our second step, the investigation of the motives which lead men to the use and development of symbolic relations.

III. THE WORLD WITHIN MY REACH AND ITS DIMENSIONS, MARKS, AND INDICATIONS

1) The world within my actual and potential reach and the manipulatory sphere

We start our analysis with the description of the situation in which I find myself within the world at any moment of my everyday life, intentionally disregarding at this level the existence of fellow-men and of society. Through my natural attitude I take this world for granted as my reality. I have to understand it to the extent necessary to come to terms with it, to act within it and upon it, and to carry out my projects at hand. In this sense the world is given to my experience and to my interpretation. This interpretation is based upon a stock of my previous experiences which in the form of "knowledge at hand" functions as a scheme of reference. To this knowledge at hand belongs also my knowledge that the world I live in is not a mere aggregate of colored spots, incoherent noises, centers of warm and cold, but a world of well circumscribed objects with definite qualities, objects among which I move, which resist me, and upon which I may act. From the outset these objects are experienced in their typicality:[22] as mountains and stones, trees and animals, and, more specifically, as birds and fishes and snakes.

This world as experienced through my natural attitude is the scene and also the object of my actions. I have to dominate it and change it in order to carry out my purposes. My bodily movement – kinesthetic, locomotive, operative – gear, so to speak, into the world, modifying or changing its objects and their mutual interrelationship. On the other hand, these objects offer resistance to my acts, which I have either to overcome or to which I have to yield. In this sense it may be correctly said that a pragmatic motive governs my natural attitude in daily life.

In this attitude I experience the world as organized in space and time around myself as a center. The place my body occupies at a certain moment within this world, my actual "Here," is the starting point from which I take my bearing in space. It is, so to

---

[22] See Husserl, *Erfahrung und Urteil*, Secs. 18–22; see also, "Common-sense and Scientific Interpretation of Human Action," esp. p. 7f.; also "Language, Language Disturbances, and the Texture of Consciousness," esp. pp. 277–283.

speak, the center "O" of a system of coordinates which determines certain dimensions of orientation in the surrounding field and the distances and perspectives of the objects therein: they are above or underneath, before or behind, right or left, nearer or farther. And, in a similar way, my actual "Now" is the origin of all the time-perspectives under which I organize the events within the world, such as the categories of fore and aft, past and future, simultaneity and succession, sooner or later, etc.

This sector of the world of perceived and perceptible objects at whose center I am shall be called *the world within my actual reach*, which includes, thus, the objects within the scope of my view and the range of my hearing. Inside this field within my reach there is a region of things which I can manipulate. (It is hoped that this highly sketchy characterization will be sufficient for present purposes. The problem involved is more complicated, especially at a time when, through the use of long range rockets, the manipulatory sphere may be extended beyond the world within my reach. The spreading of the manipulatory sphere is perhaps one of the outstanding characteristics of the actual state of Western civilization.)

The manipulatory sphere [23] is the region open to my immediate interference which I can modify either directly by movements of my body or with the help of artificial extensions of my body, that is, by tools and instruments in the broadest sense of this term. The manipulatory zone is that portion of the outer world upon which I can actually act. In a certain sense it might be said that the part of the world within my reach which does not belong to the manipulatory zone transcends it: it constitutes the zone of my potential manipulations or, as we prefer to call it, of my potential working acts.[24] Of course, these realms have no rigid frontiers; to each belong specific halos and open horizons, and there are even "enclaves" within "foreign territory." It is also clear that this whole system "world within my actual reach," including the manipulatory area, undergoes changes by any of

---

[23] It is the great merit of G. H. Mead to have shown that the "manipulatory area" constitutes the core of reality. See his *Philosophy of the Present*, Chicago, 1932, pp. 124ff.; *The Philosophy of the Act*, Chicago, 1938, pp. 103–106, 121ff., 151f., 190–192, 196–197, 282–284.

[24] Regarding the concept of "working," see "On Multiple Realities," esp. p. 226f.

my locomotions; by displacing my body I shift the center O of my system of coordinates to O', and this alone changes all the numbers (coordinates) pertaining to this system.

2) Marks

I experience the world within my actual reach as an element or phase of my unique biographical situation, and this involves a transcending of the Here and Now to which it belongs. To my unique biographical situation pertain, among many other things, my recollections of the world within my reach in the past but no longer within it since I moved from There to Here, and my anticipations of a world to come within my reach and which I must move from Here to another There in order to bring it into my reach. I know or assume that, disregarding technical obstacles and other limitations, such as the principal irretrievability of the past, I can bring my recollected world back into my actual reach if I return to whence I came (*world within restorable reach*); I expect also to find it substantially the same (although, perhaps, changed) as I had experienced it while it was within my actual reach; and I know or assume also that what is now within my actual reach will go out of my reach when I move away but will be, in principle, restorable if I later return.

The latter case is to me of an eminently practical interest. I expect that what is now within my actual reach will go out of my reach but will later on come into my actual reach again, and, especially, I anticipate that what is now in my manipulatory sphere will reenter it later and require my interference or will interfere with me. Therefore I have to be sure that I shall then find my bearings within it and come to terms with it as I can now while it is within my control. This presupposes that I shall be able to recognize those elements which I now find relevant in the world within my actual reach, especially within the manipulatory zone, and which (I assume by a general idealization, called the idealization of "I can do it again" by Husserl) [25] will prove relevant also when I return later on. I am, thus, *motivated* to single out and to *mark* certain objects. When I return I expect

---

[25] Edmund Husserl, *Formale und transzendentale Logik*, Halle, 1929, Sec. 74, p. 167.

these marks to be useful as "subjective reminders" or "mnemonic devices" (Wild's terms).[26] It is immaterial whether such a mnemonic device consists of the breaking of the branch of a tree or the selecting of a particular landmark to mark the trail to the waterhole. A bookmark at the page where I stopped reading or underlining certain passages of this volume or pencilstrokes on the margin are also marks or subjective reminders. What counts is merely that all these marks, themselves objects of the outer world, will from now on be intuited not as mere "selves" in the pure apperceptual scheme. They entered for me, the interpreter, into an appresentational reference. The broken branch of the tree is more than just that. It became a mark for the location of the waterhole, or, if you prefer, a signal for me to turn left. In its appresentational function, which originates in the interpretational scheme bestowed upon it by me, the broken branch is now paired with its referential meaning: "Way to the waterhole."

This mark which functions as a subjective reminder is one of the simplest forms of the appresentational relationship; it is detached from any intersubjective context. The inherently arbitrary character of my selecting certain objects as "marks" should be emphasized. The mark has "nothing to do" with what it should remind me of, both are in an interpretational context merely because such a context was established by me. According to the principle of the relative irrelevance of the vehicle, I may replace the broken branch by a stonepile, according to the principle of figurative transference, I may dedicate this stonepile to a naiad, etc.

Wild [27] sees a characteristic distinction between marks or mnemonic devices and signs in the fact that a sign might be misconstrued or misinterpreted, whereas we cannot be "misreminded" by a reminder. I cannot agree with this statement. Rereading a book I had read as a student, I find several marks on the margin whose meaning I no longer understand. Even more, I am uncertain why I found the marked passage of special interest. Why did I put a button into my pocket this morning? I tried to recall something but what it was I can no longer tell.

[26] Wild, *op. cit.*, p. 224.
[27] *Ibid.*

3) *Indications*

We mentioned before the stock of knowledge at hand as an element of my biographical situation. This stock of knowledge is by no means homogeneous. William James [28] distinguished between "knowledge about" and "knowledge of acquaintance." There are, moreover, zones of blind belief and ignorance. The structuration of my stock of knowledge at hand is determined by the fact that I am not *equally* interested in all the strata of the world within my reach. The selective function of interest organizes the world for me in strata of major and minor relevance. From the world within my actual or potential reach are selected as primarily important, those facts, objects, and events which actually are or will become possible ends or means, possible obstacles or conditions for the realization of my projects, or which are or will become dangerous or enjoyable or otherwise relevant to me.

Certain facts, objects, and events are known to me as being interrelated in a more or less typical way, but my knowledge of the particular kind of interrelatedness might be rather vague or even lack transparency. If I know that event B usually appears simultaneously or precedes or follows event A, then I take this as a manifestation of a typical and plausible relationship existing between A and B, although I know nothing of the nature of this relationship. Until further notice I simply expect or take it for granted that any future recurrence of an event of type A will be connected in typically the same way with a preceding, concomitant, or subsequent recurrence of an event of type B. I may then apprehend A not as an object, fact, or event standing for itself, but standing for something else, namely, referring to the past, present or future appearance of B. Here again we have a form of pairing by appresentation which most authors subsume under the concept of sign. We prefer to reserve the term "sign" for other purposes and to call the appresentational relationship under scrutiny *indication*.

Husserl [29] has characterized this relationship of indication (*"Anzeichen"*) as follows: an object, fact, or event (A), actually

---

[28] William James, *Principles of Psychology*, New York, 1890, Vol. I, p. 221.
[29] Husserl, *Logische Untersuchungen I*, Vol. II/I, Secs. 1-4, esp. p. 27; Farber, *op. cit.* p. 222.

perceptible to me, may be experienced as related to another past, present, or future fact or event (*B*), actually not perceptible to me, in such a way, that my conviction of the existence of the former (*A*) is experienced by me as an *opaque* motive for my conviction for, assumption of, or belief in the past, present, or future existence of the latter (*B*). This motivation constitutes for me a pairing between the indicating (*A*) and the indicated (*B*) elements. The indicating member of the pair is not only a "witness" for the indicated one, it does not only point to it, but it suggests the assumption that the other member exists, has existed, or will exist. Again, the indicating member is not perceived as a "self," that is, merely in the apperceptual scheme, but as "wakening" or "calling forth" appresentationally the indicated one. It is, however, important that the particular nature of the motivational connection remain opaque. If there is clear and sufficient insight into the nature of the connection between the two elements, we have to deal not with the referential relation of indication but with the inferential one of *proof*. The qualification contained in the last statement eliminates, therefore, the possibility of calling the footprint of a tiger (recognized as such) an indication or "sign" of his presence in the locality. But the halo around the moon indicates coming rain, the smoke fire, a certain formation of the surface oil in the subsoil, a certain pigmentation of the face Addison's disease, the position of a needle on the dial of my car an empty gas tank, etc.

The relationship of indication as described covers most of the phenomena generally subsumed under the category of "natural signs." The knowledge of indications is of eminent importance from the practical point of view, because it helps the individual transcend the world within his actual reach by relating elements within it to elements outside it. The relation of indication is again an appresentational category which does not necessarily presuppose intersubjectivity.

IV. THE INTERSUBJECTIVE WORLD AND ITS APPRESENTATIONAL RELATIONS: SIGNS

1) The world of everyday life is from the outset an intersubjective one

Marks and indications are, as we have seen, forms of appresentational relations which can be explained by the pragmatic motive governing the individual in his endeavor to come to terms with the world within his reach. These forms of appresentational references do not necessarily presuppose the existence of fellow-men and the possibility of communicating with them, although they may – and indeed do – also function within the intersubjective context. So far we have analyzed the world within my reach and its dimensions by abstaining from any reference to intersubjectivity, as if I found myself in the natural attitude alone within the world of daily life.

Yet the world of my daily life is by no means my private world but is from the outset an intersubjective one, shared with my fellow-men, experienced and interpreted by Others; in brief, it is a world common to all of us. The unique biographical situation in which I find myself within the world at any moment of my existence is only to a very small extent of my own making. I find myself always within an historically given world which, as a world of nature as well as a sociocultural world, had existed before my birth and which will continue to exist after my death. This means that this world is not only mine but also my fellow-men's environment; moreover, these fellow-men are elements of my own situation, as I am of theirs. Acting upon the Others and acted upon by them, I know of this mutual relationship, and this knowledge also implies that they, the Others, experience the common world in a way substantially similar to mine. They, too, find themselves in a unique biographical situation within a world which is, like mine, structured in terms of actual and potential reach, grouped around their actual Here and Now at the center in the same dimensions and directions of space and time, an historically given world of nature, society, and culture.

It would, of course, far surpass the purpose of the present study to enter into a detailed phenomenological analysis of the constitution of intersubjectivity. And inasmuch as we are here merely concerned with an analysis of the common-sense experience of the world in daily life, it would be sufficient to state that man takes for granted the bodily existence of fellow-men, their conscious life, the possibility of intercommunication, and the historical givenness of social organization and culture, just as he takes for granted the world of nature into which he was born.

Yet having to study the appresentational relations involved in various aspects of intersubjectivity and especially in communication, we cannot forego indicating a few implications of the topic and clarifying the notion of a social world taken for granted. This, however, can be done only step by step, and we start with some brief remarks on the foundation of the relationship between the I and the Other – or, as modern sociologists [30] call it, between ego and alter – without, in this section, taking into account the fact that the world into which I was born already contained social and political organizations of a most diversified nature and that I as well as Others are members of such organizations, having a particular role, status, and function within them. We intend, therefore, to consider first the appresentational references by which we obtain knowledge of another's mind, then the structuration of the common-sense world as shared with a fellow-man and its inherent transcendencies, before we turn to the study of comprehension, manifestation, and communication, and of the appresentational relations upon which they are founded: the signs.

2) *Our knowledge of the other mind is itself based on appresentational references*

A discussion of the age-old problem of our knowledge of other minds is not within the framework of this paper; nor can we sum up the highly controversial opinions on this subject proposed by outstanding thinkers of various philosophical schools. It seems, however, that behaviorists and existentialists, logical positivists and phenomenologists agree, if we disregard the phenomenon of telepathy, that knowledge of another's mind is possible only

---

[30] For example, Talcott Parsons and Edward A. Shils in their monograph, "Values, Motives, and Systems of Actions" in *Toward a General Theory of Action*, edited by Parsons and Shils, Cambridge, 1951, pp. 55ff.

through the intermediary of events occurring on or produced by another's body. This is, in Husserl's terminology, an outstanding case of appresentational reference. According to him,[31] the Other is from the outset given to me as both a material object with its position in space and a subject with its psychological life. His body, like all other material objects, is given to my original perception or, as Husserl says, in originary presence. His psychological life, however, is not given to me in originary presence but only in copresence; it is not presented, but appresented. By the mere continuous visual perception of the Other's body and its movements, a system of appresentations, of well ordered indications of his psychological life and his experiences is constituted, and here, says Husserl, is the origin of the various forms of the systems of signs, or expressions, and finally of language. The physical object "the Other's body," events occurring on this body, and his bodily movements are apprehended as expressing the Other's "spiritual I" toward whose motivational meaning-context I am directed. So-called "empathy" in the other person is nothing but that form of appresentational apprehension which grasps this meaning.

According to Husserl, this situation may also prevail with respect to what is generally called cultural objects. A book is an outer object, a material thing. I see it as it appears to me, here on my desk, to my right, etc.; but reading it, I am not directed toward it as an outer object but toward the meaning of what is written therein: I "live in its meaning" by comprehending it. The same holds good for a tool, a house, a theater, a temple, a machine. The spiritual meaning of all these objects is appresentationally apperceived as being founded upon the actually appearing object which is not apprehended as such but as expressing its meaning. And if we listen to somebody, we do not experience the meaning of what he says as something connected with the words in an external way. We take the words apprehensively as expressing their meaning, and we live in their meaning by comprehending what the Other means and the thought he expresses.[32] To be sure, everyone has only his own experiences

---

[31] Husserl, *Cartesianische Meditationen V*, Secs. 50ff., *Ideen II*, Secs. 43–50; see also Alfred Schutz, "Discussion of Edmund Husserl's Ideas Vol. II," *Philosophy and Phenomenological Research*, XIII, 1953, pp. 394–413, esp. 404ff.

[32] Edmund Husserl, "*Vom Ursprung der Geometrie*," edited by E. Fink, *Revue Internationale de Philosophie*, 1939, p. 210.

given in originary presence. But by the intermediary of events in the outer world, occuring on or brought about by the Other's body, especially by linguistic expressions in the broadest sense, I may comprehend the Other by appresentation; by mutual understanding and consent a *communicative common environment is thus established*, within which the subjects reciprocally motivate one another in their mental activities.

This analysis of Husserl's is modeled after one specific intersubjective relationship, namely, that which sociologists call the "face-to-face relationship." [33] In such a relationship both partners share time and space, perceiving one another. It is, moreover, supposed that the mutual appresentational comprehension of events in the Other's mind leads immediately to communication. All these assumptions, however, require some elaboration.

We begin with the characterization of the tacitly presupposed idealizations upon which the establishment of a "communicative common environment" in the face-to-face relationship is founded.

3) The general thesis of the reciprocity of perspectives [34]

a) The idealization of the interchangeability of standpoints

The sector of the world within my actual reach is centered around my Here, and the center of the world within the actual reach of my fellow-man around his, which is, seen from my Here, a There. Both sectors may partially overlap, and some of the objects, facts, and events in the outer world may be in mine as well as my fellow-man's actual reach, and even within his and my manipulatory zone. Nevertheless, such an object, fact, or event will have a different appearance as to direction, distance, perspective, adumbration, etc., seen from the center of my coordinates, called Here, than from his, called There. Now it is a basic axiom of any interpretation of the common world and its

---

[33] The term was coined by Charles H. Cooley, *Social Organization*, New York, 1909, Chaps. III–V, but used in a different sense. We designate by it merely a purely formal aspect of social relationship.

[34] This subsection 3 closely follows "Common-sense and Scientific Interpretation of Human Action," p. 10f.

objects that these various coexisting systems of coordinates can be transformed one into the other; I take it for granted, and I assume my fellow-man does the same, that I and my fellow-man would have typically the same experiences of the common world if we changed places, thus transforming my Here into his, and his – now to me a There – into mine.

b) The idealization of the congruency of the systems of relevances

Each of us, as has been stated before, finds himself in a unique biographically determined situation, and for this very reason my and my fellow-man's purpose at hand and our systems of relevances originating in such a purpose must necessarily differ. Yet, as another basic axiom, I take it for granted until counter-evidence is offered – and assume my fellow-man does the same – that the differences originating in our private systems of relevances can be disregarded for the purpose at hand and that I and he, that *"We"* interpret the actually or potentially common objects, facts, and events in an "empirically identical" manner, *i.e.*, sufficient for all practical purposes.

This general thesis of the reciprocity of perspectives which involves idealizations by which – to use Whitehead's terminology – typifying constructs of objects of thought supersede the thought objects of my and my fellow-man's private experience [35] is the presupposition for a world of common objects and therewith for communication. To give an example: we both see the "same" flying bird in spite of the difference of our spatial position, sex, age, and the fact that you want to shoot it and I just to enjoy it.

4) The transcendence of the Other's world

So far we have dealt only with the face-to-face relationship in which a sector of the world is both in my and my fellow-man's actual reach. To be precise, the world within my actual reach overlaps that within his reach but necessarily there are zones within my actual reach which are not within his, and *vice versa*. Facing another, for example, I see things unseen by him and he

---

[35] Alfred North Whitehead, *The Organization of Thought*, London, 1917, now partly republished in *The Aims of Education*, Mentor Books, New York, 1949, see p. 110 of this edition.

sees things unseen by me. The same holds good for our manipulatory spheres. This stone placed between us is within my manipulatory sphere but not within his.

In this sense, the world of another transcends mine. But it is a corollary of the idealization of the interchangeability of standpoints (above, 3a) that the world within actual reach of another is also within my attainable (potential) reach and *vice versa*. Within certain limits (to point them out would lead us too far afield) even the world within another's restorable reach and that within his anticipated one is within my potential reach (a potentiality of the second degree, so to speak) and *vice versa*.

The world of another transcends mine, however, in still another sense. In order to understand the particular form of this transcendence, we have first to consider the predominant function of the face-to-face relationship for the constitution of the social world. Only in it is another's body within my actual reach and mine within his; only in it do we experience one another in our individual uniqueness. While the face-to-face relationship lasts we are mutually involved in one another's biographical situation: we are growing older together. We have indeed a common environment and common experiences of the events within it: I and you, *We* see the flying bird. And this occurrence of the bird's flight as an event in outer (public) time is simultaneous with our perceiving it, which is an event in our inner (private) time. The two fluxes of inner time, yours and mine, become synchronous with the event in outer time (bird's flight) and therewith one with the other. This will be of special importance for our study of events in the outer world which serve as vehicles for communication, namely, significant gestures and language.

Nevertheless, another's existence transcends mine as mine does his. We have in common only a small section of our biographies. Moreover, either of us enters the relationship with only a part of his personality (Simmel) or, as some modern sociologists express it, by assuming a particular social role. And, finally, as the Other's system of relevances is founded in his unique biographical situation, it cannot be congruent with mine: it cannot be brought within my reach, although it can be understood by me.

And there is a third kind of transcendence involved, but a

transcendence which surpasses not only mine but also the Other's world: the We-relation itself, although originating in the mutual biographical involvement, transcends the existence of either of the consociates in the realm of everyday life. It belongs to a finite province of meaning other than that of the reality of everyday life and can be grasped only by symbolization. This statement anticipates a set of problems which we are not yet prepared to approach.

We have, however, to indicate that the face-to-face relationship characterized so far is only one, although the most central, dimension of the social world. If we compare it with the world within my actual reach, we can also find dimensions in the social world comparable to the various forms of the world within my potential reach. There is the world of my contemporaries, with whom I am not biographically involved in a face-to-face relationship, but with whom I have in common a sector of time which makes it possible for me to act upon them as they may act upon me within a communicative environment of mutual motivation. (In primitive societies in which the souls of the deceased are supposed to participate in the social life of the group, the dead are deemed to be contemporaries.) There is the world of my predecessors, upon whom I cannot act but whose past actions and their outcome are open to my interpretation and may influence my own actions; and there is the world of my successors of whom no experience is possible, but toward whom I may orient my actions in more or less empty anticipation. It is characteristic of all the dimensions of the social world other than the face-to-face relation that I cannot grasp my fellow-men as unique individuals but only experience their typical behavior, their typical pattern of motives and attitudes in increasing anonymity.

We cannot enter here into a detailed discussion of these various dimensions of the social world. But it is indispensable to keep the underlying problems in mind in order to analyze correctly certain issues connected with communication and the appresentational apperception of society.

5) *Comprehension, manifestation, signs, communication*

It is true that, as Husserl stated, any comprehension of the Other's thought – always disregarding telepathy – requires as vehicle, carrier, or medium the apprehension of an object, fact, or event in the outer world, which, however, is not apprehended as a self in the mere apperceptual scheme but appresentationally as expressing cogitations of a fellow-man. The term "cogitation" is here used in the broadest Cartesian sense, denoting feelings, volitions, emotions, etc. We propose, for the purpose of this paper, to use the term *"sign"* for designating objects, facts, or events in the outer world, whose apprehension appresents to an interpreter cogitations of a fellow-man. This definition needs some explanation.

a) *Comprehension*

The objects, facts, and events which are interpreted as signs must directly or indirectly refer to another's bodily existence. In the simplest case, that of a face-to-face relationship, another's body, events occurring on his body (blushing, smiling), including bodily movements (wincing, beckoning), activities performed by it (talking, walking, manipulating things) are capable of being apprehended by the interpreter as signs. If there is no face-to-face relationship, but distance in space or time, we have to keep in mind

i) that apprehension does not necessarily presuppose actual perception, but that the appresenting member of the appresentational pair may also be a recollection or even a fantasm; I remember (or: I can imagine) the facial expression of my friend when he learned (or will learn) some sad news. I can even fantasy a sad looking centaur.

ii) that the result or product of another's activity refers to the action from which it resulted and, thus, can function as a sign for his cogitations;

iii) that the principle of the relative irrelevance of the vehicle is applicable. (The printed lecture refers to the talk of the lecturer.)

b) Manifestation

That an object, fact, or event in the outer world is interpreted as a sign for a fellow-man's cogitation does not necessarily presuppose

i) that the Other meant to manifest his cogitation by this sign, even less that he did so with communicative intent. An involuntary facial expression, a furtive glance, blushing, trembling, the Other's gait, in brief, any physiognomical event can be interpreted as a sign for a fellow-man's cogitation. A certain hesitation in the Other's voice can convince me that he lies although he tries to hide that he does. The letter writer wants to convey the content of a message, but the graphologist disregards the content and takes the handwriting as such, that is, the static result of the unintentional gestures performed by the writer, as signs.

ii) If the sign was meant to function in a communicative context, the interpreter was not necessarily intended to be the addressee.

iii) It is, moreover, not necessarily presupposed that the two partners of a communicative sign-relation are known to each other (example: whoever erected this signpost wanted to show any passerby the direction).

c) Types of signs

In his excellent book, *Der Aufbau der Sprache*,[36] Bruno Snell developed a theory of three basic forms of bodily movement which, according to him, have corollaries in different kinds of sounds, words, morphological elements, the syntactical structure of Western languages, forms of literature, and even in types of philosophy. He distinguishes purposive, expressive, and mimetic movements (*Zweck-, Ausdrucks-, und Nachahmungsbewegungen*). The first category, the purposive movements, may consist in gestures, such as nodding, pointing, beckoning, but also talking; the second, the expressive movements, are exteriorizations of inner experiences, primarily without purposive intent; the spatial-temporal differentiation of movements, according to high and low, wide and narrow, fast and

[36] Bruno Snell, *Der Aufbau der Sprache*, Hamburg, 1952, Chaps. I and II.

slow, gives certain gestures their expressive meaning; the third category, the mimetic gesture, imitates or represents another being with whom the actor identifies himself. The animal and fertility dances, well known to the anthropologist,[37] are examples. Snell also points out that the pure purposive gesture reveals expressive characteristics, for example, in the pitch and speed of the voice in talking, and that all three types of gesture can be used for communicative purposes (for example, expressive ones by the actor on the stage, mimetic ones by the pantomimist). According to Snell, the purposive gesture indicates what the performer wants, the expressive gesture what he feels, and the mimetic gesture what he is or what he pretends to be.

The expressive and mimetic gestures (or, in our terminology, signs) are of particular importance as foundations of higher appresentational forms, namely, symbols. Communication as such is based foremost on purposive signs, as the communicator has at least the intention of making himself understandable to the addressee if not to induce him to react appropriately. But certain requirements have to be fulfilled to make communication possible.

d) Communication proper

i) The sign used in communication is always a sign addressed to an individual or anonymous interpreter. It originates within the actual manipulatory sphere of the communicator, and the interpreter apprehends it as an object, fact, or event in the world within his reach. However, the conditions mentioned above (under a, i iii) apply to this situation. Consequently, it is not necessary that the interpreter's world within his reach overlap spatially the manipulatory sphere of the communicator (telephone, television), nor that the production of the sign occur simultaneously with its interpretation (Egyptian papyrus, monuments), nor that the *same* physical object or event used by the communicator as carrier of the communication be apprehended by the interpreter (principle of the relative irrelevance of the vehicle). In more complicated

---

[37] There is a highly interesting discussion in Curt Sachs, *World History of the Dance*, New York, 1952, Chap. 2, pp. 49–138.

cases of communication, which cannot be studied here, any number of human beings or mechanical devices might be inserted into the communicatory process between the original communicator and the interpreter. The main point of importance for what follows is the insight that communication requires under all circumstances both events in the outer world, produced by the communicator, and events in the outer world apprehensible by the interpreter. In other words, *communication can occur only within the reality of the outer world*, and this is one of the main reasons why this world, as we will see very soon, has the character of *paramount reality*. Even the voices which the schizophrenic believes he hears are hallucinated as *voices*, and refer, therefore, to events within the outer world.

ii) The sign used in communication is always preinterpreted by the communicator in terms of its expected interpretation by the addressee. To be understood the communicator has, before producing the sign, to anticipate the apperceptual, appresentational, and referential scheme under which the interpreter will subsume it. The communicator has, therefore, as it were, to perform a rehearsal of the expected interpretation and to establish such a context between his cogitations and the communicative sign that the interpreter, guided by the appresentational scheme he will apply to the latter, will find the former an element of the related referential scheme. This context, as we have seen (section II, 2, d, of this paper), is the interpretational scheme itself. In other words, communication presupposes that the interpretational scheme which the communicator relates and that which the interpreter will relate to the communicative sign in question will *substantially* coincide.

iii) The italicized qualification is important. Strictly speaking, a full identity of both interpretational schemes, that of the communicator and that of the interpreter, is, at least in the common-sense world of everyday life, impossible. The interpretational scheme is closely determined by the biographical situation and the system of relevances originating therein. If there were no other differences between the biographical situations of the communicator and that of the interpreter, then at least the "Here" of either one is a "There" to the Other. This fact alone sets insurmountable limits for a fully successful communication in the ideal sense. But, of course, communication might be and indeed is highly successful for many good and useful purposes and may reach an optimum in highly formalized and standardized languages such as in technical terminology. These considerations, seemingly of a highly theoretical nature, have important practical consequences: successful communication is possible only between persons, social groups, nations, etc., who share a substantially similar system of relevances. The greater the differences between their system of relevances, the fewer the chances for the success of the communication. Complete disparity of the systems of relevances makes the establishment of a universe of discourse entirely impossible.

iv) To be successful, any communicative process must, therefore, involve a set of common abstractions or standardizations. We mentioned under 3)b of this section the idealization of the congruency of the system of relevances which leads to the superseding of the thought objects of private experience by typifying constructs of public objects of thought. Typification is indeed that form of abstraction which leads to the more or less standardized, yet more or less vague, conceptualization of common-sense thinking and to the necessary ambiguity of the terms of the ordinary vernacular. This is because our experience, even in what Husserl calls the prepredicative sphere, is organized from the outset under certain types. The small child who learns his mother tongue is at an early age capable of recognizing an animal as a dog or a bird or a fish, an element of his surroundings as a stone or a tree or a mountain, a piece of furniture as a table or a chair. But, as a glance in the dictionary shows, these are the terms most difficult to define in ordinary language. Most of the communicative signs are language signs, so the typification required for sufficient standardization is provided by the vocabulary and the syntactical structure of the ordinary vernacular of the mother tongue. We will revert to this problem later on.

e) *Language, pictorial, expressive, and mimetic presentation*

The structure of language as a set of signs combinable under syntactical rules, its function as a vehicle of discursive (propositional) thinking, its power not only to name things but also to express relations among them, not only to build propositions but also to formulate relations among propositions – all this has been described so carefully and extensively in recent literature that for our purpose it is unnecessary to enter into this subject.

Here we simply want to indicate that it is of the essence of language that normally any linguistic communication involves a time process; a speech is built up by sentences, a sentence by the step by step articulation of successive elements (polythetically, as Husserl [38] calls it), whereas the meaning of the sentence or the speech can be projected by the speaker and grasped by the listener in a single ray (monothetically). The stream of articulating cogitations of the speaker is thus simultaneous with the outer event of producing the sounds of the speech, and the perceiving of the latter simultaneously with the comprehending cogitations of the listener. Speech is, therefore, one of the intersubjective time-processes – others are making music together, dancing together, making love together – by which the two fluxes of inner time, that of the speaker and that of the listener, become synchronous one with the other and both with an event in outer time. The reading of a written communication establishes in the same sense a quasisimultaneity between the events within the inner time of the writer and that of the reader.

Visual presentations, however, as Mrs. Langer has correctly shown,[39] are structurally different in virtue of their nondiscursive character. They are not composed of elements having independent meanings, that is, they have no vocabulary. They cannot be defined in terms of other signs as can discursive signs. Their primary function is that of conceptualizing the flux of sensations. Mrs. Langer sees the appresentational relationship of a pictorial presentation founded in the fact that the proportion of parts, their position, and relative dimension correspond to our conception of the depicted object. That is the reason we recognize the same house in a photograph, a painting, a pencil sketch, an

---

[38] Husserl, *Ideen I*, Sec. 118, 119.
[39] Langer, *Philosophy in a New Key*, pp. 55ff. and 77ff.

architect's elevation drawing, and a builder's diagram. To Husserl,[40] the characteristic of the picture (in contradistinction to all other signs) consists in the fact that the picture is related to the depicted thing by similarity, whereas most of the other signs (disregarding, for example, onomatopoeia) have no content in common with that which is signified. (That is the reason many authors emphasize the "arbitrariness" of linguistic signs.) Nevertheless, the appresentational relationship prevails also in pictorial presentations, although sometimes in a rather complicated way of interconnected levels. Looking, for instance, at Duerer's print, "The Knight, Death, and The Devil," we distinguish first – as we would say, in the apperceptual scheme – the print as such, this thing in the portfolio; second, still in the apperceptual scheme, the black lines on paper as small colorless figures; third, these figures are *appresented* as "depicted realities" as they appear in the picture, "the knight of flesh and blood" of whom, as Husserl states, we are aware in his quasibeing, which is a "neutrality modification" of being.[41] Here Husserl stops, but we could and have to continue to follow the appresentational process further. These three figures, the knight, death, and the devil, as appresented in the neutrality modification of their quasibeing, appresent, in turn, in an appresentation of the second degree, so to speak, a meaningful context, and it is especially this meaning which Duerer wanted to convey to the beholder: the knight between death and the devil teaches us something about the condition of man between two supernatural forces. This is the *symbolic* appresentation, to which we must turn in the next section.

Communication by expressive and mimetic gestures has so far not found the attention it deserves from students of semantics. Examples of the former are gestures of greeting, paying respect, applauding, showing disapproval, gestures of surrender, of paying honor, etc. The latter combine features of the pictorial presentation, namely, similarity with the depicted object, with the time structure of speech. Even a kind of mimetic vocabulary can be developed, as, for instance, in the highly standardized use of the fan by the Japanese *Kabuki* dancer.

[40] Husserl, *Logische Untersuchungen VI*, Vol. II/2, Sec. 14; *Ideen I*, Sec. 111; see also Farber, *loc. cit.*, pp. 410–414.
[41] Husserl, *Ideen I*, Sec. 111.

6) *World within reach and world of everyday life*

It is the main thesis of this paper that appresentational references are means of coming to terms with transcendent experiences of various kinds. In an earlier part of this section we have briefly characterized the transcending character of my experiences of the Other and his world. Our analysis of the various forms of signs and communication has shown that the appresentational references characterized by these terms again have the function of overcoming a transcendent experience, namely, that of the Other and his world. Through the use of signs the communicative system permits me to become aware, to a certain extent, of another's cogitations and, under particular conditions even to bring the flux of my inner time in perfect simultaneity with his. But as we have seen, fully successful communication is, nevertheless, unattainable. There still remains an inaccessible zone of the Other's private life which transcends my possible experience.

The common-sense praxis of everyday life, however, solves this problem to such an extent that for nearly all good and useful purposes we can establish communication with our fellow-men and come to terms with them. We have already mentioned briefly that this is possible only if the communicative process is based on a set of typifications, abstractions, and standardizations, and we referred briefly to the fundamental role of the vernacular of the mother tongue in establishing this basis. A later section (VII) of the present paper will have more on this point. Here, however, we wish to clarify some basic features, simply taken for granted by common-sense thinking of everyday life, upon which the possibility of communication is founded. They are in a certain sense an amplification of the general thesis of the reciprocity of perspectives analyzed in part 3 of this section.

The term "taken for granted," used before, has perhaps to be defined. It means to accept until further notice our knowledge of certain states of affairs as unquestionably plausible. Of course, at any time that which seemed to be hitherto unquestionable might be put in question. Common-sense thinking simply takes for granted, until counterevidence appears, not only the world of physical objects but also the sociocultural world into which we are born and in which we grow up. This world of everyday life is indeed the unquestioned but always questionable matrix within which all our inquiries start and end. Dewey [42] saw this in full clarity when he described the process of inquiry as the task of transforming in a controlled or directed manner indeterminate situations encountered or emerging within this matrix into "warranted assertibility."

Reverting to our particular problem, I take for granted until counterevidence appears not only the bodily existence of my fellow-man but also the fact that his conscious life has substantially the same structure as my own and, furthermore, that to a certain extent I can apperceive analogically through appresentational references my fellow-man's cogitations (for example, the motives for his actions) as he can mine. Moreover, I take it for granted that certain objects, facts, and events within our common social environment have for him the same appresentational significances as for me, which significances transform mere things in the outer world into so-called cultural objects.

Until counterevidence is offered, I take it for granted that the various apperceptual, appresentational, referential, and contextual schemes accepted and approved as typically relevant by my social environment are also relevant for my own unique biographical situation and that of my fellow-man within the world of everyday life. This means:

a) *with respect to the apperceptual scheme* that normally our apperception of objects, facts, or events of the outer world are guided by the system of typical relevances prevailing within our social environment and that a particular motive has to originate in the personal biographical situation of each of us in order to evoke our interest in the uniqueness, in the atypicality, of a particular object, fact, or event, or in its particular aspects;

b) *with respect to the appresentational scheme* that we both, my fellow-man and I, take for granted the typical way in our sociocultural environment by which immediately apperceived objects, facts, or events in the outer world are apprehended not as "selves," but appresentationally, namely, as standing for something else, that is, as "wakening," "calling forth," or "evoking" appresentational references.

[42] John Dewey, *Logic, the Theory of Inquiry*, New York, 1938, Part I, esp. pp. 19–20, and Chap. III, *passim*.

c) *with respect to the interpretational scheme* that in the case of communication the Other (as communicator or addressee) will apply the same appresentational scheme to the appresentational references involved in the communication as I will. If, for instance, communication occurs through the medium of the vernacular of ordinary language, I take it for granted that Others who express themselves in this idiom mean by the linguistic expression they use substantially the same thing that I understand them to mean, and *vice versa*.

If the term "world of everyday life" or "reality of everyday life" does not merely designate the world of nature as experienced by me but also the sociocultural world in which I live, then it becomes clear that this world does not coincide with the world of outer objects, facts, and events. To be sure, it includes those outer objects, facts, and events which are within my actual reach and those which are within the several zones of my potential reach (comprising those within actual and potential reach of my fellow-men). It includes, however, in addition, all the appresentational functions of such objects, facts, or events which transform things into cultural objects, human bodies into fellow-men, their bodily movements into actions or significant gestures, waves of sound into speech, etc. The world of everyday life is thus permeated by appresentational references which are simply taken for granted and among which I carry on my practical activities – my working activities, as we have referred to them before [43] – in terms of common-sense thinking. But all these appresentational references still belong to the finite province of meaning, called the reality of everyday life. Nevertheless, nothing has to be changed in our thesis that all appresentational references are means of coming to terms with experiences of transcendences. This we have tried to show with respect to the appresentational references studied so far, namely, marks, indications, and signs. All the transcendences they helped to come to terms with themselves belong to what we have now characterized as the reality of everyday life. As transcendences – of my actual Here and Now, of the Other, of the Other's world, etc. – they were still immanent in the common-sense world of my everyday life, coconstituting the situation in which I find myself placed in this world.

[43] See footnote 24.

But there are experiences which transcend the finite province of meaning of the world of everyday life so that they refer to other finite provinces of meaning, to other realities, or, to use the term coined by William James,[44] to other subuniverses, such as the world of scientific theory, of arts, of religion, of politics, but also of fantasms and dreams. And there is again a group of appresentational references, called symbols, with whose help man tries to apprehend these transcendent phenomena in a way analogous to our perceptible world. We turn now to the study of these symbols and the problem of multiple realities.

V. THE TRANSCENDENCE OF NATURE AND SOCIETY: SYMBOLS

1) The experience of this transcendence

I find myself in my everyday life within a world not of my own making. I know this fact, and this knowledge itself belongs to my biographical situation. There is, first, my knowledge that Nature transcends the reality of my everyday life both in time and in space. In time, the world of Nature existed before my birth and will continue to exist after my death. It existed before man appeared on earth and will probably survive mankind. In space, the world within my actual reach carries along the open infinite horizons of my world in potential reach, but to my experiences of these horizons belongs the conviction that each world within potential reach, once transformed into actual reach, will again be surrounded by new horizons, and so on. Within the world in my reach there are, moreover, certain objects, such as the heavenly bodies, which I cannot bring within my manipulatory sphere, and there are events within my manipulatory area, such as the tides, which I cannot bring within my control.

I know, furthermore, that in a similar way the social world transcends the reality of my everyday life. I was born into a preorganized social world which will survive me, a world shared from the outset with fellow-men who are organized in groups, a

---

[44] James, *Principles of Psychology*, Vol. II, Chap. 21; also sec. VI of the present paper.

world which has its particular open horizons in time, in space, and also in what sociologists call social distance. In time, there is the infinite chain of generations which overlap one another; my clan refers to other clans, my tribe to other tribes, and they are enemies or friends, speaking the same or another language, but they are always organized in their particular social form and living their particular way of life. My actual social environment refers always to a horizon of potential social environments, and we may speak of a transcendent infinity of the social world as we speak of a transcendent infinity of the natural one.

I experience both of these transcendences, that of Nature and that of Society, as being imposed upon me in a double sense: on the one hand, I find myself at any moment of my existence as being within nature and within society; both are permanently coconstitutive elements of my biographical situation and are, therefore, experienced as inescapably belonging to it. On the other hand, they constitute the framework within which alone I have the freedom of my potentialities, and this means they prescribe the scope of all possibilities for defining my situation. In this sense, they are not elements of my situation, but determinations of it. In the first sense, I may – even more, I have to – take them for granted. In the second sense, I have to come to terms with them. But in either sense, I have to understand the natural and the social world in spite of their transcendences, in terms of an order of things and events.

From the outset I know also that any human being experiences the same imposed transcendences of Nature and of Society, although he experiences them in individual perspectives and with individual adumbrations. But the order of Nature and of Society is common to all mankind. It furnishes to everyone the setting of the cycle of his individual life, of birth, aging, death, health and sickness, hopes and fears. Each of us participates in the recurrent rhythm of nature; to each of us the movements of sun and moon and stars, the change between day and night, and the cycle of the seasons are elements of his situation. Each of us is a member of the group into which he was born or which he has joined and which continues to exist if some of its members die and others enter into it. Everywhere there will be systems of kinship, age groups and sex groups, differentiations according to occupations, and an organization of power and command which leads to the categories of social status and prestige. But in the common-sense thinking of everyday life we simply know that Nature and Society represent some kind of order; yet the essence of this order as such is unknowable to us. It reveals itself merely in images by analogical apprehending. But the images, once constituted, are taken for granted, and so are the transcendences to which they refer.

How is this possible? "The miracle of all miracles is that the genuine miracles become to us an everyday occurrence," says Lessing's Nathan. This is so because we find in our sociocultural environment itself socially approved systems offering answers for our quest for the unknowable transcendences. Devices are developed to apprehend the disquieting phenomena transcending the world of everyday life in a way analogous to the familiar phenomena within it. This is done by the creation of appresentational references of a higher order, which shall be called *symbols* in contradistinction to the terms ' marks," "indications" "signs," used so far.

2) Symbolization

a) Definition

A symbol can be defined in first approximation as an appresentational reference of a higher order in which the appresenting member of the pair is an object, fact, or event within the reality of our daily life, whereas the other appresented member of the pair refers to an idea which transcends our experience of everyday life.[45]

This definition corresponds substantially to the notion of symbol as developed by Karl Jaspers in the third volume of his *Philosophie*,[46] from which we give the following freely translated quotation, omitting certain references to Jaspers's particular philosophical position:

> We speak of meaning in the sense of sign and image, of simile, allegory, and metaphor. The main difference between meaning within the world and of metaphysical meaning consists in the criterion of whether in the

---

[45] This definition will be restated in the following Sec. VI, 3.
[46] Karl Jaspers, *Philosophie*, Berlin, 1932, Vol. 3, "*Metaphysik*," Chap. I, p. 16.

relationship between the image and that which it represents the latter itself could be apprehended as an objectivity, or whether the image is an image for something that is not accessible in any other way; that is to say, whether that which is expressed in the image could also be stated or demonstrated in a direct way, or whether it exists for us merely in so far as it exists in the image. Only in the latter case should we speak of a symbol.... The symbol cannot be interpreted except by other symbols. The understanding of a symbol does not, therefore, consist in grasping its significance in a rational way but in experiencing it existentially in the symbolic intention as this unique reference to something transcendent that vanishes at the limiting point.

b) *Genesis of the symbolic appresentation*

We have now to study the problem of the constitution of the appresentational pairing which might function as a symbol. How is it possible that an object, event, or fact within the reality of our daily life is coupled with an idea which transcends our experience of our everyday life? This problem can be approached on two different levels. There are first sets of appresentational references which are universal and can be used for symbolization because they are rooted in the human condition. It is a problem of philosophical anthropology to study these sets of appresentational references. Secondly, the particular forms of symbolic systems as developed by the various cultures in different periods might be investigated. This is the problem of cultural anthropology and of the history of ideas. We have to restrict ourselves here to fugitive remarks describing some items of the first group, illustrating them by example, belonging to the second.

As to the latter, we prefer for reasons we shall mention briefly, not to take our examples from the world of our present Western culture. The latter has developed several systems of symbols such as science, art, religion, politics, and philosophy, some of which will be characterized in the next section. We have, however, to consider that the coexistence of several symbolic systems which are merely loosely, if at all, connected one with another, is the special feature of our own historical situation and the result of our attempt to develop an interpretation of the cosmos in terms of the positive methods of the natural sciences. We take the world as defined by the mathematical natural sciences as the archetype of an ideal order of symbolic references and are inclined to explain all the other symbolic systems as derivations from it or at least as subordinated to it. Whitehead in his book *Science and the Modern World* [47] has rightly stated that Galileo's discoveries and Newton's laws of motion established the fundamental concept of the *"ideally isolated system"* which is essential to scientific theory so that science would be impossible without it. Whitehead explains that

> the isolated system is not a solipsistic system, apart from which there would be nonentity. It is isolated as within the universe. This means that there are truths respecting this system, which require reference only to the remainder of things by way of a uniform systematic scheme of relationships.

On the other hand, many investigations of modern anthropologists, sociologists, mythologists, philologists, political scientists, and historians [48] have shown that in other cultures and even in earlier periods of our own culture man experienced nature, society, and himself as equally participating in and determined by the order of the cosmos. As an illustration of this point of view, in contrast to that expressed in the quotation from Whitehead, we refer to the following passage from Ernst Cassirer's *An Essay on Man* [49] which illuminates the relationship between men, society, and nature in mythical experience and shows why any element in one of these orders may become a symbol, appresentationally referring to the corresponding element in that of the other orders:

> To mythical and religious feeling nature becomes one great society, *the society of life*. Man is not endowed with outstanding rank in this society . . . Life possesses the same religious dignity in its humblest and highest forms. Men and animals, animals and plants are all on the same level. .. . . And we find the same principle – that of the solidarity and unbroken unity of life – if we pass from space to time. It holds not only in the order of simultaneity but also in the order of succession. The generations of men form a unique and uninterrupted chain. The former stages of life are preserved by reincarnation. . . . Even totemism expresses this deep conviction of a community of all living beings – a community that must be preserved and reinforced by the constant effort of man, by the strict performance of magical rites and religious observances.

---

[47] Alfred North Whitehead, *Science and the Modern World*, New York, 1925, now also available as Pelican-Mentor Book, New York, 1949, p. 47 of the latter edition.

[48] We refer to the writings of Émile Durkheim, Lucien Lévy-Bruhl, Marcel Mauss, Marcel Granet, Bronislaw Malinowski, Ernst Cassirer, Bruno Snell, Alois Dempf, Arnold J. Toynbee, and Eric Voegelin.

[49] Cassirer, *An Essay on Man*, pp. 83–86.

And Cassirer endorses Robertson Smith's statement (*Lectures on the Religion of the Semites*):

> The indissoluble bond that unites men to their god is the same bond of blood-fellowship which in early society is the one binding link between man and man, and the one sacred principle of moral obligation.

An example of the full integration of the symbolic interrelation called by Cassirer the society of life can be found in classic Chinese thought. According to the French Sinologue Marcel Granet,[50] there is in classical Chinese literature a unity of structure between the microcosm – man – and the macrocosm – the universe – and the structure of the universe is explained by the structure of society. All these structures are dominated by two fundamental principles: first, the position of the Male and the Female, the positive and the negative, the *Yang* and the *Yin;* and second, the opposition between the chief and the vassal in the hierarchical structure of society. Based on these principles, etiquette prescribes and regulates meticulously all details of the everyday life-world.

We shall try now to show by a few examples how universal symbols originate in the general human condition. As stated before, man considers himself as a center O of a system of coordinates under which he groups the objects of his environment in terms of "above and underneath," "before and behind," "right and left." Now, for every man an element of the underneath is the earth and of the above the sky. The earth is common to men and animals; it is the procreator of vegetative life, the provider of food. The sky is the place where the celestial bodies appear and disappear, but also the place from which rain comes, without which no fertility of the earth is possible. The head, the carrier of the main sense organs and the organ of breathing and speech, is on the upper part of the human body, and the digestive organs and that of procreation in the lower part. The connection of all these phenomena makes the spatial dimension "above and below" the starting point of a set of symbolic appresentations. In Chinese thought, for example, the head symbolizes the sky (and so does the roof of the house) whereas the feet (the floor) symbolize earth. But since the sky has to send rain in order to

---

[50] Marcel Granet, *Études Sociologiques sur la Chine*, Paris, 1953, p. 268; see also Marcel Granet, *La Pensée chinoise*, Paris, 1934, *passim*.

fertilize the earth, the sky is also to Chinese thought the male principle, the positive principle, *Yang*, and earth the negative, female *Yin*. And this symbolism of higher-lower has its correlate in Chinese medicine, music, dance, social hierarchy, etiquette, all of which are correlated and can be brought into symbolic appresentational reference one with the other.[51] There is also a symbolism of the directions before-behind, things which are faced or have to be faced and are thus visible, and those which are not and therefore possibly dangerous, and also right and left.[52]

Sun, moon, and stars rise and set for all men in opposite directions which are to everyone "marks" for finding his bearings. But the four cardinal points of the compass so ascertained have also their symbolic connotations, because they are connected with the change between day and night, light and darkness, being awake and asleep, the visible and the invisible, the coming-to-be and the passing-away. The life cycle of men – birth, childhood, adolescence, manhood, old age, death – has its analogy in the cycle of the seasons and the cycle of vegetative and animal life which is equally important for farming, fishing, and animal husbandry, and is in turn correlated to the motions of the heavenly bodies. Again a set of correlations is established which permits the appresentational pairing of its elements in the form of symbols. The social organization with its hierarchies of rulers and subordinates, chiefs and vassals, has its correlate in the hierarchy of the heavenly bodies. Thus, the cosmos, the individual, and the community form a unit and are equally subject to the universal forces which govern all events. Man has to understand these forces and, because he cannot dominate them, to conjure them or to appease them. To do so is, however, not the business of the isolated individual, it is the concern of the whole community and its organization.

The symbolic forms in which the forces of the universe of nature as well as of society are appresented (*mana, orenda, manitu, Yin* and *Yang*, deities of various kinds and hierarchies, etc.) are as manifold as the symbols appresenting them (ex-

---

[51] *Ibid.*
[52] See the highly interesting article by Granet, "*La droite et la gauche en Chine*," *Études sociologiques*, pp. 261–278.

pressive, purposive, or mimetic gestures, linguistic or pictorial presentations, charms, spells, magical or religious rites, ceremonies). The symbols of myths have the particular function of justifying and vouching for the truth and validity of the order established by the other symbolic systems (Malinowski).[53]

At this level the world of the sacred and that of the profane are closely interrelated. Studying the origin of the names of deities in Greek mythology, Bruno Snell comes to the following result:

> Everything that is active is originally conceived as a deity. Many things carry the name of a deity which will later on be designated by an abstract term. Not only what is active in nature, such as the sun, the cloud, the lightning, the earth, the tree, the river, is to the primeval mind a divine being, but also everything that acts within man, within the individual (such as love, fighting spirit, prudence) as well as within the community (such as peace, war, law, fortune, injustice, and all forms of disaster).... The question whether the sun was experienced first as a thing and thereafter interpreted in the mythical way, or whether first the noun denoting the thing or the name of the deity existed, is as wrongly put as the question whether the river or the river-god existed first. The acting phenomena of nature are just divine.... It is meaningless to ask whether Eros was first a god or the emotion of love, since the emotion of love is apprehended as an intervention of the deity.[54]

As to the role of the symbol (in the sense used in this discussion) in human society and political organizations, we want finally to quote Eric Voegelin who sums up the results of his six volume study on the history of political ideas in his book, *The New Science of Politics*, as follows:

> Human society is not merely a fact, or an event, in the external world to be studied by an observer like a natural phenomenon. Though it has externality as one of its important components, it is as a whole a little world, a cosmion, illuminated with meaning from within by the human beings who continuously create and bear it as the mode and condition of their self-realization. It is illuminated through an elaborate symbolism, in various degrees of compactness and differentiation – from rite, through myth, to theory – and this symbolism illuminates it with meaning in so far as the symbols make the internal structure of such a cosmion, the relations between its members and groups of members, as well as its existence as a whole, transparent for the mystery of human existence. The self-illumination of society through symbols is an integral part of social reality, and one may even say, its essential part, for through such symbolization the members of a society experience it as more than an accident or a convenience; they experience it as of their human essence.

[53] Bronislaw Malinowski, *Magic, Science, and Religion*, New York, 1954, p. 100f.
[54] Snell, *op. cit.*, p. 160f.

And, inversely, the symbols express the experience that man is fully man by virtue of his participation in a whole which transcends his particular existence.[55]

We think that our definition of the symbol as an appresentational reference of a higher order is not only compatible with, but also corroborated by the findings of the thinkers just discussed. It might be helpful to show this in some detail.

We shall not attempt the hopeless task of outlining the manifold forms in which the experiences of the transcendences involved are appresented in the great symbolic systems of the sciences, the various branches of philosophy, the arts, mythology, religions, politics, etc. Nor do we intend to show the innumerable symbolic references to the transcendences of the real world in the life of the social group or even of the individual (for, whereas signs refer by definition to the intersubjective situation, a symbol may, and frequently does, remain outside of communication). The great themes of all symbolizations can themselves only be expressed in symbols. To outline them would require a complete encyclopedia of the philosophic sciences in the Hegelian manner. In each of these spheres – or, as we shall call them, finite provinces of meaning – the symbolic appresentations are formed according to the cognitive style characteristic of this province. Hence, we restrict ourselves to some remarks concerning the particular features of appresentational references involved in any symbol situation.

c) *The particularities of the symbolic appresentation*

First, we have to understand that symbolization is an appresentational reference of a higher order, that is, based on preformed appresentational references, such as marks, indications, signs, or even symbols. Jacob, awakened from his dream of the ladder in which God revealed Himself to him (Genesis, 28, 10–25), took the stone that he had put for his pillow and set it up for a pillar and poured oil upon the top of it, vowing that this stone shall be God's house. "Surely," he said, "the Lord is in this place; and I knew it not." The irruption of the transcendent

---

[55] Eric Voegelin, *The New Science of Politics, An Introduction* (Charles R. Walgreen Foundation Lectures), Chicago, 1952, p. 27.

experience into the world of everyday life, which transforms it and gives each element of it an appresentational significance ("the Lord is in this Place"), which it did not have before ("I knew it not"), has hardly been told in a more dramatic way. The stone becomes the pillow, the pillow a pillar, the pillar God's house. Another example can be found in Husserl's analysis of Duerer's print, "The Knight, Death, and The Devil," previously mentioned.

Second, we have to consider that on each level of a series of appresentational references the three principles pointed out in an earlier section of the present paper (II, 5) may become operative: each of the appresenting vehicles may be replaced by another, each appresentational meaning may undergo a series of variations and the principle of figurative transference pervades the whole appresentational structure. All this explains the essential ambiguity of the symbol, the vagueness of the transcendent experiences appresented by it, and the difficulty of translating their meaning into discursive terms of more or less precise denotations. This is exactly that particularity of the symbol which Jaspers has in mind when he speaks of the vanishing of the transcendent at the limiting point. To him the transcendent manifests itself in ciphers, and it is man's existential problem to decode the cryptography of the symbols.[56]

Third, we have to remember our explanations of the four orders involved in any appresentational reference, which we called the apperceptual, the appresentational, the referential, and the interpretational or contextual scheme. The complicated internal structure of the symbolic relationship implies that all of these schemes enter each of the various appresentational levels involved, and that on each of these levels one of these schemes may be selected as the archetype of the order, from which the other orders appear as merely arbitrary and contingent. But, and this point has to be emphasized, the Bergsonian problem of order refers also to the interrelationship prevailing among the various layers of appresentational references, and here the identity, or at least similarity, of the *interpretational scheme* is of the highest importance for the establishment of a universe of discourse between the interpreters. Various interpreters of a symbolic

[56] Jaspers, *op. cit.*, Vol. III, Chap. 4.

structure may accept the same referential scheme, yet apply different appresentational schemes to the apperceptual configurations. The history of sects and heresies in all religions is an example of this statement: both the *Homoiousian* and the *Homoousian* believe in the Trinity, but the former holds that the three Divine Persons are neither identical nor different in substance, but similar, whereas the latter maintains their consubstantiality. The same holds good for parties and factions in political organizations which believe equally in the basic law of the country but differ as to its interpretation.

It is, however, possible that the *appresentational* aspect is taken as a prototype of order with the consequence that various referential schemes which are frequently inconsistent are connected with the same symbolic structure. It is also possible that the *referential* scheme, once constituted, becomes, so to speak, autonomous, *i.e.*, independent of the appresentational scheme, which seems, then, merely contingent or lacking any order. In the latter case, the symbols are reinterpreted and understood without reference to the originally appresenting elements.

Finally, we have to recall that each object of our immediate or analogical apprehension is an object within a field, referring to other objects of the same experiential style. There is an intrinsic order of our perceptions of outer objects, or of so-called inner experiences, of fantasms, and even of dreams, which separates them from all other realms and constitutes them, according to our formulation, as a separate province of meaning. Here again we have within limits the freedom to select one of these realms as our system of reference, that is, to "live" in one of these orders or, to bestow upon one of them the accent of reality. We have, then, several concurrent and competing orders of reality – that of our everyday life, that of the world of our fantasy, of art, of science, etc., among which the first is paramount, because only within it is communication possible. Because of its importance for understanding symbolic structure, this problem of multiple realities deserves to be considered briefly once again.*

---

* See "On Multiple Realities" (M.N.).

VI. ON MULTIPLE REALITIES

1) William James's subuniverses; finite provinces of meaning

We have seen that in a chapter of his *Principles of Psychology* [57] William James shows that there are several, probably an infinite number of orders of realities, each with its special and separate style of existence. James calls them "subuniverses," and mentions as examples the world of senses or physical things (as the paramount reality), the world of science, the world of ideal relations, the worlds of mythology and religion, the world of "idols of the tribe," the various worlds of individual opinions, and the world of sheer madness and vagary. "Each world *whilst it is attended to* is real after its own fashion; only the reality lapses with the attention." Reality means simply relation to our emotional and active life; whatever excites and stimulates our interest is real. Our primitive impulse is to affirm immediately the reality of all that is conceived, as long as it remains uncontradicted. "... All propositions, whether attributive or existential, are believed through the very fact of being conceived, unless they clash with other propositions believed at the same time, by affirming that their terms are the same with the terms of these other propositions." [58]

Many other examples could be quoted. The play world of the little girl, as long as it is undisturbed, is her reality. She is indeed the mother, and her doll her child. Only from the point of view of the reality of the outer world is the knight in Duerer's print a pictorial presentation in the neutrality modification. In the world of art, that is, in this case, of pictorial imagination, knight, death, and devil have "real" existence as entities within the realm of artistic fantasy. While the play lasts, Hamlet is to us *really* Hamlet and not Laurence Olivier "acting the part of" or "representing" Hamlet.

The ingenious theory of William James has, of course, to be detached from its psychological setting and analyzed for its many implications. We have made such an attempt elsewhere.[59]

---

[57] James, *op. cit.*, Vol. II, Chap. 21.
[58] *Ibid.*, pp. 293, 290.
[59] *Supra*, "On Multiple Realities." Some of the following passages, esp. 4, are borrowed from this paper.

In this paper we prefer to speak of finite provinces of meaning upon which we bestow the accent of reality, instead of subuniverses as does William James. By this change of terminology we emphasize that it is the meaning of our experiences, and not the ontological structure of the objects, which constitutes reality. Each province of meaning – the paramount world of real objects and events into which we can gear by our actions, the world of imaginings and fantasms, such as the play world of the child, the world of the insane, but also the world of art, the world of dreams, the world of scientific contemplation – has its particular cognitive style. It is this particular style of a set of our experiences which constitutes them as a finite province of meaning. All experiences within each of these worlds are, with respect to this cognitive style, consistent in themselves and compatible with one another (although not compatible with the meaning of everyday life). Moreover, each of these finite provinces of meaning is, among other things, characterized by a specific tension of consciousness (from full awakeness in the reality of everyday life to sleep in the world of dreams), by a specific time-perspective, by a specific form of experiencing oneself, and, finally, by a specific form of sociality.

2) *The paramount reality*

William James rightly calls the subuniverse of senses, of physical things, the paramount reality. But we prefer to take as a paramount reality the finite province of meaning which we have called the reality of our everyday life. In an earlier section (IV, 6) we pointed out that the reality of our everyday life which our common-sense thinking takes for granted includes not only the physical objects, facts, and events within our actual and potential reach perceived as such in the mere apperceptual scheme, but also appresentational references of a lower order by which the physical objects of nature are transformed into sociocultural objects. But since these appresentations of a lower order also have objects, facts, or events of the outer world as their appresenting member, we believe that our definition is compatible with that of James. We can also agree with Santayana [60]

[60] George Santayana, *Dominations and Powers*, New York, 1951, p. 146.

that "the spirit can never possess, much less communicate, ideas without a material endowment and a material occasion":

> The tongue must move; the audible conventional word must come to the lips and reach a ready ear; the hands with tools or plans in them must intervene to carry the project out.

The outer world of everyday life is a paramount reality:

a) because we always participate in it, even during our dreams, by means of our bodies, which are themselves things in the outer world;

b) because the outer objects delimit our free possibilities of action by offering resistance which can only be overcome through effort if it can be overcome at all;

c) because it is that realm into which we can gear by our bodily activities and, hence, which we can change or transform;

d) because – and this is just a corollary to the preceding points – within this realm, and only within this realm, we can communicate with our fellow-men and thus establish a "common comprehensive environment" in the sense of Husserl.[61]

The preceding characteristics of the reality of everyday life do not mean, however, that other finite provinces of meaning are incapable of socialization. To be sure, there are certainly finite provinces of meaning which cannot be intersubjectively shared, such as my dreams or even my daydreams. There are others, such as the play world of children, which permit intersubjective participation and even interaction in terms of the shared fantasms. In the world of religious experiences there is, on the one hand, the lonely vision of the mystic or of the prophet and, on the other hand, the community service – there are lonely prayers and prayers offered by the congregation.

It is not our aim here to develop a typology of the forms of socialization in the various finite provinces of meaning. But we wish to emphasize that in all cases in which such an intersubjective participation in one of these provinces takes place, the existence of "a material occasion or a material endowment" is presupposed. In other words, communication occurs by objects, facts, or events pertaining to the paramount reality of the senses, of the outer world, which are, however, appresentationally apperceived.

---

[61] Husserl, *Ideen II*, Secs. 50 and 51.

This holds good also for symbolic appresentations, in so far as they are communicated or designed to be communicable. But there is, nevertheless, a main feature by which symbolic appresentations are distinguished from all the other appresentational relations, and a brief consideration of this situation gives us the opportunity to restate our definition of the symbol.

3) The definition of symbol restated

All appresentational references, as we have emphasized, are characterized by a specific transcendence of the appresented object in relation to the actual "Here and Now" of the interpreter. But with the exception of the symbolic appresentation, the three terms of the appresentational relation – the appresenting and the appresented members of the pair and the interpreter – pertain to the same level of reality, namely, the paramount reality of everyday life. The symbolic reference, however, is characterized by the fact that it transcends the finite province of meaning of everyday life so that only the appresenting member of the related pair pertains to it, whereas the appresented member has its reality in another finite province of meaning, or, in James's terminology, in another subuniverse. We can, therefore, redefine the symbolic relationship as an appresentational relationship between entities belonging to at least two finite provinces of meaning so that the appresenting symbol is an element of the paramount reality of everyday life. (We say "at least two" because there are many combinations such as religious art, etc., which cannot be investigated within this paper.)

4) The transition from the paramount reality to other finite provinces of meaning, experienced through a shock [62]

The world of everyday life is taken for granted by our common-sense thinking and thus receives the accent of reality as long as our practical experiences prove the unity and congruity of this world as valid. Even more, this reality seems to us to be the natural one, and we are not ready to abandon our attitude toward it without having experienced a specific shock which

[62] See footnote 57.

compels us to break through the limits of these "finite" provinces of meaning and to shift the accent of reality to another one.

To be sure, these experiences of shock befall us frequently in the midst of daily life; they themselves pertain to its reality. Within a single day or even hour I may run through several such shock experiences of various kinds. Some instances are: the inner transformation we endure if the curtain in the theater rises as a transition to the world of the stage play; the radical change in our attitude if, before a painting, we permit our visual field to be limited by what is within the frame as a passage into the pictorial world; or falling asleep as a leap into the world of dreams. But also religious experience in all its varieties – for example, Kierkegaard's experience of the "instant" as the leap into the religious sphere – is such a shock, as well as the decision of the scientist to replace all passionate participation in the affairs of "this world" by a disinterested contemplative attitude.

On the other hand, we have to emphasize that consistency and compatibility of experiences with respect to their peculiar cognitive style subsist merely within the borders of the particular province of meaning to which these experiences belong and upon which I have bestowed the accent of reality. By no means will that which is compatible within the province of meaning P be also compatible within the province of meaning Q. On the contrary, seen from P, which is supposed to be real, Q and all the experiences belonging to it would appear as merely fictitious, inconsistent, and incompatible, and *vice versa*. We have here again an application of Bergson's problem of several coexisting orders.

We want to illustrate this point by briefly discussing the "fictitiousness" of the world of everyday life as seen from the symbolic system pervading other provinces of meaning upon which the accent of reality has been bestowed. Our first example takes the world of physical theory as a system of reference, our second the world of poetry.

5) *The concept of finite provinces of meaning illustrated by symbols in science and poetry*

As to the finite province of meaning called science, we recall the statement by Whitehead that the creation of an "ideally isolated system" was the necessary prerequisite of the development of the modern natural sciences. The realm of nature with which the theory of physics deals is such an ideally isolated system, and the phenomena of nature in the common-sense experience of everyday life have been, by a process of abstractions, generalizations, and idealizations, entirely transformed into such a system. "Every physical theory," says Philipp G. Frank in his "Foundations of Physics," [63] "consists of three kinds of statements: equations between physical quantities (relations between symbols), logical rules, and semantical rules (operational definitions)." And he closes his monograph in a rather ironical vein with the statement:

> Words like "matter" and "mind" are left (namely, by the theoretical physicist) to the language of everyday life where they have their legitimate place and are understood by the famous "man in the street" unambiguously.[64]

And Hermann Weyl in his *Philosophy of Mathematics and Natural Science* sums up his criticism of Brouwer's "idealism" in mathematical thinking as follows:

> It cannot be denied that the theoretical desire, incomprehensible from the merely phenomenal point of view, is alive in us which urges us towards totality. Mathematics shows that with particular clarity; but it also teaches us that that desire can be fulfilled on one condition only, namely, that we are satisfied with the symbol and renounce the mystical error of expecting the transcendent ever to fall within the lighted circle of our intuition.[65]

And in explaining the methodological principles of physics as "the distillation of the objective world capable only of representation in symbols, from what is immediately given in intuition," Weyl gives the following illustration:

---

[63] Philipp G. Frank, "Foundations of Physics," *International Encyclopedia of Unified Sciences*, Chicago, 1946, Vol. I, No. 7, p. 73.
[64] *Ibid.*, p. 76.
[65] Hermann Weyl, *Philosophy of Mathematics and Natural Science*, Princeton, 1949, p. 60.

Whereas for Huyghens colors were "in reality" oscillations of the ether, they now appear merely as mathematical functions of periodic character depending on four variables that as coordinates represent the medium of space time. What remains is ultimately a *symbolic construction* of exactly the same kind as that which Hilbert carries through in mathematics.[66]

These statements show clearly that scientific theory is a finite province of meaning, using symbols appresenting realities within this realm and operating with them – and, of course, justly so – on the principle that their validity and usefulness are independent of any reference to the common-sense thinking of everyday life and *its* realities.

As a second illustration we turn now to a brief consideration of symbols in poetry. T. S. Eliot in his famous essay on Dante states:

> Genuine poetry can communicate before it is understood.... Words have associations, and the group of words in associations have associations, which is a kind of local self-consciousness, because they are the growth of a particular civilization.... I do not recommend, in first reading the first canto of the Inferno, worrying about the identity of the Leopard, the Lion, or the She-Wolf. It is really better at the start not to know or care what they do mean. What we should consider is not so much the meaning of the images but the reversed processes, that which leads a man having an idea to express in images.... Dante's is a visual imagination.... He lived in an age in which men still saw visions.... We have nothing but dreams and we have forgotten that seeing visions – a practice now relegated to the aberrant and uneducated – was once a more significant, interesting, and disciplined kind of dreaming.[67]

And Goethe, commenting in his *"Maerchen"* of the golden snake (*Unterhaltungen deutscher Ausgewanderter*) which combines highly symbolic elements that had already been interpreted by various writers in the most controversial way, wrote on May 27, 1796, to Wilhelm von Humboldt: "Es war freilich schwer, zugleich *bedeutend* und *deutungslos* zu sein" ("It was rather difficult to be at the same time significant [relevant, important – all the three meanings are involved in the German *"bedeutend"*] but without interpretation [or not interpretable – both meanings are involved in *"deutungslos"*]).

Both statements, that of T. S. Eliot and that of Goethe, show the poet's insight into the fact that within the finite province of meaning of the work of art the interrelationship of the symbols as

[66] *Ibid.*, p. 113.
[67] T. S. Eliot, *Selected Essays*, 1917–1932, New York, 1932, pp. 199–241, 200, 201, 204.

such is the essence of the poetic content and that it is unnecessary and may even be harmful to look for the referential scheme which the appresenting elements of the symbolic relationship would symbolize, if they were indeed objects of the world of daily life. But their connection with these objects has been cut off; the use of the appresenting elements is just a means of communication; whereas poetry communicates by using ordinary language, the ideas symbolized by this language are real entities within the finite province of poetical meaning. They have turned, to use a term of Jaspers, into "ciphers" for transcendent experiences to be understood by those who have the existential key to them. And in this sense, and only in this sense, Jaspers says: "The symbol establishes communion without communication." [68]

VII. SYMBOL AND SOCIETY

We are now prepared to answer at least two of the questions with which we started: To what extent are significative and symbolic appresentations dependent upon the sociocultural environment? How is intersubjectivity as such and how are social groups experienced by significative and symbolic appresentations?

1) The dependence of appresentational references on the social environment

The first question deals with the main problem of any sociology of knowledge that does not misunderstand its task. To answer it we start again from our experience of the reality of everyday life which, as a sociocultural world, is permeated by appresentational reference. When in section III we developed the concepts of marks and indications, we assumed for the sake of clearer presentation that a supposedly insulated individual has to "map out" the world within his reach. In truth, man finds himself from the outset in surroundings already "mapped out" for him by Others, *i.e.*, "premarked," "preindicated," "pre-

---

[68] Jaspers, *op. cit.*, Vol. III, p. 26: "*Das Symbol stiftet Gemeinschaft ohne Kommunikation.*"

signified," and even "presymbolized." Thus, his biographical situation in everyday life is always an historical one because it is constituted by the sociocultural process which had led to the actual configuration of this environment. Hence, only a small fraction of man's stock of knowledge at hand originates in his own individual experience. The greater portion of his knowledge is *socially derived*, handed down to him by his parents and teachers as his social heritage. It consists of a set of systems of relevant typifications, of typical solutions for typical practical and theoretical problems, of typical precepts for typical behavior, including the pertinent system of appresentational references. All this knowledge is taken for granted beyond question by the respective social group and is thus *"socially approved* knowledge." This concept comes very near to what Max Scheler called the *"relativ natuerliche Weltanschauung"* (relative natural conception of the world) [69] prevailing in a social group and also Sumner's [70] classical theory of the folkways of the in-group which are taken by its members as the only right, good, and efficient way of life.

Socially approved knowledge consists, thus, of a set of recipes designed to help each member of the group to define his situation in the reality of everyday life in a typical way. It is entirely irrelevant for a description of a world taken for granted by a particular society whether the socially approved and derived knowledge is indeed true knowledge. All elements of such knowledge, including appresentational references of any kind, if *believed* to be true are real components of the "definition of the situation" by the members of the group. The "definition of the situation" refers to the so-called "Thomas theorem" well known to sociologists: "If men define situations as real, they are real in their consequences." [71] Applied to our problem and translated

---

[69] Max Scheler, *Die Wissenformen und die Gesellschaft, Probleme einer Sociologie des Wissens*, Leipzig, 1926, p. 58f. Cf. Howard Becker and Helmut Dahlke, "Max Scheler's Sociology of Knowledge," *Philosophy and Phenomenological Research*, Vol. II, 1942, pp. 310–322, esp. 315.

[70] William Graham Sumner, *Folkways; A Study of the Sociological Importance of Manners, Customs, Mores, and Morals*, New York, 1906, esp. Chap. I.

[71] It was first developed by William Isaac Thomas in his book, *The Child in America: Behavior Problems and Programs*, New York, 1928, p. 572. See also W. I. Thomas, *Social Behavior and Personality*, edited by E. K. Volkart, Social Science Research Council, New York, 1951, pp. 14 and 80ff.; the term "Thomas Theorem" was coined by Robert K. Merton, *Social Theory and Social Structure*, Glencoe, 1949, 179.

into our terminology this means: if an appresentational relationship is socially approved, then the appresented object, fact, or event is believed beyond question to be in its typicality an element of the world taken for granted.

In the process of transmitting socially approved knowledge the learning of the vernacular of the mother tongue has a particularly important function. The native language can be taken as a set of references which, in accordance with the relative natural conception of the world as approved by the linguistic community, have predetermined what features of the world are worthy of being expressed, and therewith what qualities of these features and what relations among them deserve attention, and what typifications, conceptualizations, abstractions, generalizations, and idealizations are relevant for achieving typical results by typical means. Not only the vocabulary but also the morphology and the syntax of any vernacular reflects the socially approved relevance system of the linguistic group. If, for example, the Arabian language has several hundred nouns for denoting various kinds of camels but none for the general concept "camel"; if in certain North American Indian languages the simple notion, "I see a man," cannot be expressed without indicating by prefixes, suffixes, and interfixes whether this man stands or sits or walks, whether he is visible to the speaker or to the auditors; if the Greek language has developed morphological particularities such as the dual number, the optative mood, the aorist tense, and the medium voice of the verb; if the French language, so eminently suited to express philosophical thoughts, has for both "consciousness" and "conscience" a single term, namely, "*conscience*" – then all these facts reveal the relative natural conception of the world approved by the respective linguistic groups.

On the other hand, the determination of what is worthwhile and what is necessary to communicate depends on the typical, practical, and theoretical problems which have to be solved, and these will be different for men and women, for the young and for the old, for the hunter and for the fisherman, and in general, for the various social roles assumed by the members of the group. Each kind of activity has its particular relevance aspects for the performer and requires a set of particular technical terms. This is because our knowledge is *socially distributed;* each of us has precise and distinct knowledge only about that particular field in which he is an expert. Among experts a certain technical knowledge is taken for granted, but exactly this technical knowledge is inaccessible to the layman. Some things can be supposed as well known and self-explanatory and others as needing an explanation, depending upon whether I talk to a person of my sex, age, and occupation, or to somebody not sharing with me this common situation within society, or whether I talk to a member of my family, a neighbor, or to a stranger, to a partner or a nonparticipant in a particular venture, etc.

William James [72] has already observed that a language does not merely consist in the content of an ideally complete dictionary and an ideally complete and arranged grammar. The dictionary gives us only the kernel of the meaning of the words which are surrounded by "fringes." We may add that these fringes are of various kinds: those originating in a particular personal use by the speaker, others originating in the context of the speech in which the term is used, still others depending upon the addressee of my speech, or the situation in which the speech occurs, or the purpose of the communication, and, finally, upon the problem at hand to be solved. What has been stated about language holds good in general for appresentational references of all kinds. In communication or in social intercourse each appresentational reference, if socially approved, constitutes merely the kernel around which fringes of the kind described are attached.

But all this already presupposes an existing typification of social relations, of social forms of intercommunication, of social stratification taken for granted by the group, and therefore socially approved by it. This whole system of types under which any social group experiences itself has to be learned by a process of acculturation. The same holds for the various marks and indications for the position, status, role, and prestige each individual occupies or has within the stratification of the group. In order to find my bearings within the social group, I have to know the different ways of dressing and behaving, the manifold insignia, emblems, tools, etc., which are considered by the group

---

[72] James, *op. cit.*, Vol. I, p. 281f.

as indicating social status and are therefore socially approved as relevant. They indicate also the typical behavior, actions, and motives which I may expect from a chief, a medicine man, a priest, a hunter, a married woman, a young girl, etc. In a word, I have to learn the typical social roles and the typical expectations of the behavior of the incumbents of such roles, in order to assume the appropriate corresponding role and the appropriate corresponding behavior expected to be approved by the social group.[73] At the same time, I have to learn the typical distribution of knowledge prevailing in this group, and this involves knowledge of the appresentational, referential, and interpretive schemes which each of the subgroups takes for granted and applies to its respective appresentational reference. All this knowledge is in turn, of course, socially derived.

Let us focus and summarize our findings. We may say that in terms of the relevance system the following are all socially determined: first, the unquestioned matrix within which any inquiry starts;[74] second, the elements of knowledge which have to be considered as socially approved and which might, therefore, be taken for granted (here we would add that those elements which might become problematic are traced out by the social situation); third, which procedures (with respect to signs and symbols) – practical, magical, political, religious, poetical, scientific, etc. – are appropriate for dealing with the problem involved; fourth, the typical conditions under which a problem can be considered as solved and the conditions under which an inquiry may be broken off and the results incorporated into the stock of knowledge taken for granted. This is of particular importance for symbolic references to myths and to rituals. If the successful connecting of a problem at hand with a socially approved symbol is considered as its typical solution, then the appresentational relationship thus established may continue to

---

[73] Readers familiar with Parsons' and Shils' monograph quoted in footnote 30 will recognize in this statement an allusion to their theory of "role-expectancies." Although the approach of the present paper differs from these authors' in several respects, their treatment of a common system of symbols as a precondition of the reciprocity or complementarity of role expectations is compatible with the view here suggested. *Cf., f.e., op. cit.,* pp. 105, 162f., 166; see also Talcott Parsons, *The Social System,* Glencoe, 1951, esp. Chap. IX, "Expressive Symbols and the Social System." Of course, Parsons's notion of "symbol" is not the same as ours.

[74] See footnote 42.

function as an appresenting element of other and higher symbolizations which might be founded on the problem deemed typically solved.

2) *The symbolic appresentation of society*

In an earlier section (IV, 4) we described briefly the various dimensions of the social world grouped around the central face-to-face relationship between consociates. Only in the We-relation, so we stated, can consociates by their mutual biographical involvement experience one another as unique individuals. In all the other dimensions of the social world – that of contemporaries, predecessors, and successors – a fellow-man is not experienced in his individual uniqueness but in terms of his typical behavior-patterns, typical motives, and typical attitudes, and in various degrees of anonymity. In social situations of everyday life relations pertaining to all these dimensions are frequently intertwined. If in a face-to-face relationship with a friend I discuss a magazine article dealing with the attitude of the President and Congress toward the admission of China to the United Nations, I am in a relationship not only with the perhaps anonymous contemporary writer of the article but also with the contemporary individual or collective actors on the social scene designated by the terms "President," "Congress," "China," "United Nations"; and as my friend and I discussed this topic as citizens of the United States of 1954, we do so in an historical situation which is at least codetermined by the performances of our predecessors. And we have also in mind the impact which the decisions now to be taken might have on our successors, the future generations. All these notions are understandable to us as unclarified terms of common-sense thinking, because their meaning is taken for granted within our sociocultural environment. How is this possible?

We submit that in common-sense thinking we experience the social world on two levels of appresentational references:

i) We apprehend *individual* fellow-men and their cogitations as realities within the world of everyday life. They are within our actual or potential reach, and we share or could share with them through communication a common comprehensive environment.

To be sure, we can apprehend these individual fellow-men and their cogitations only analogically through the system of appresentational references already described, and in this sense the world of the Other transcends mine; but this is an "immanent transcendence" still within the reality of our daily life. Consequently, both members of the appresentational relation through which we apprehend this transcendency belong to the same finite province of meaning, the paramount reality.

ii) Social collectivities and institutionalized relations, however, are as such not entities within the province of meaning of everyday reality but constructs of common-sense thinking which have their reality in another subuniverse, perhaps that which William James called the subuniverse of ideal relations. For this very reason, we can apprehend them only symbolically; but the symbols appresenting them themselves pertain to the paramount reality and motivate our actions within it. This statement requires some comment.

We may start with the most obvious case, our experience of the social collectivity. Strictly speaking, we all are in the situation of Crainquebille, in the story by Anatole France, to whom government is just a grouchy old man behind a counter. To us government is represented by individuals: Congressmen, judges, tax collectors, soldiers, policemen, public servants, perhaps the President or the Queen or the *Fuehrer*. The political cartoonist shows us Uncle Sam conversing with John Bull and Marianne, or even the globe looking with a bewildered face at a hydrogen bomb which shows its teeth. The reason for this rude symbolism is, however, deeply rooted.

We mentioned before (IV, 4) that the We-relation as such transcends the existence of either consociate within the paramount reality and can be appresented only by symbolization. My friend is to me and I am to him an element of the reality of everyday life. But our friendship surpasses our individual situation within the finite province of meaning of the paramount reality. Since our notion of the We-relation is a purely formal one which refers to face-to-face situations of all degrees of intimacy and remoteness, the symbols by which such relations are appresented are of a great variety. Its appresenting member is always the common situation as defined by the participants, namely, that which they use, experience, enjoy, or endure together. A joint interest makes them partners, and the idea of *partnership* is perhaps the most general term for the appresented We-relation. (*We* are buddies, lovers, fellow sufferers, etc.)

The symbols become more discernible the more the social relationship is stabilized and institutionalized. The dwelling place of the family gets the appresentational meaning "home" which is protected by deities such as the *lares* and *penates*. The hearth is more than the fireplace, matrimony and wedlock are the ceremonial (or even sacramental) and legal symbols for marriage, a neighborhood is much more than an ecological concept.

All these examples refer, however, to social relations which can be brought within actual reach. This is the type of groups which Cooley [75] had in mind when he introduced the highly equivocal concept of primary group, and justifies the interest of modern sociologists in so-called small groups defined, for example, by Homans as

> a number of persons who are few enough so that every person may communicate with all the others not at second hand through other people but face-to-face.[76]

The situation is, however, different if the group is larger and a face-to-face relation cannot be established. Max Weber, who founded his theory on interpreting the social world in terms of the subjective meaning of the individual actor, is perfectly consistent in maintaining

> that it is *only* the existence of the probability that, corresponding to a certain given subjective meaning complex, a certain type of action will take place, which constitutes the "existence" of the social relationship. Thus that a "friendship" or a "state" exists or has existed means this and only this: that we, the observers, judge that there is or has been a probability that on the basis of certain kinds of known subjective attitudes of certain individuals there will result in the average sense a certain specific type of action.[77]

But this statement is itself a construct by the social scientist and, therefore, does not belong to the common-sense thinking of man within everyday life. He experiences the social and political

---

[75] See footnote 33.
[76] George C. Homans, *The Human Group*, New York, 1950, p. 1.
[77] Max Weber, *Wirtschaft und Gesellschaft*, translated as *Theory of Economic and Social Organisation* by A. M. Henderson and T. Parsons, New York, 1947, p. 119.

organization by specific appresentations which Eric Voegelin has carefully analyzed in *The New Science of Politics*. According to this author, a political society as a cosmion illuminated from within

> has its internal meaning, but this realm exists tangibly in the external world in human beings who have bodies and through their bodies participate in the organic and inorganic externality of the world.

Representation, for example, may be taken in the elemental sense of external institutions (for example, members of the legislative assembly hold their membership by virtue of popular election) or in the existential sense,[78] meaning that political societies in order to be capable of action must have such an exernal structure as will enable some of its members – the ruler, sovereign, government, prince – to find habitual obedience to the acts of command. In other words,

> a political society comes into existence when it articulates itself and produces a representative.

But that is not all. We have, in addition, to distinguish

> between the representation of society by its articulated representatives and a second relation in which *society itself becomes the representative of something beyond itself, of a transcending reality*.... All the early empires understood themselves as representatives of the cosmic order ... the great ceremonies of the empire represent the rhythms of the cosmos; festivals and sacrifices are a cosmic liturgy, a symbolic participation of the cosmion in the cosmos; and the ruler himself represents society, because on earth he represents the transcendent power which maintains cosmic order.

Voegelin's book brings abundant illustrations for this "self-interpretation" of the group which he contrasts with the interpretation of the same symbols by the theorist. We cannot enter here into this fascinating topic. We merely want to add that the symbolic appresentations by which the in-group interprets itself have their counterpart in the interpretations of the same symbols by the out-group or out-groups. However, those interpretations will be necessarily different from that of the in-group, because the system of relevances of both groups (and the respective apperceptual, appresentational, and referential schemes taken as

---

[78] See footnote 55. Voegelin, *op. cit.*, pp. 31, 34, 37, 49, 54 (italics mine).

systems of reference for interpreting the "order" so created) cannot coincide. A wide field of concrete investigations is open here for the social scientist, investigations which are important not only from the theoretical but also from the practical point of view; for the manipulating of symbols, whether for persuasion or propaganda, requires at least a clarification of their intrinsic structure.

VIII. CONCLUDING REMARKS

We have seen that man is indeed an *"animal symbolicum,"* if we understand under this term his need and also his capacity to come to terms, with the help of appresentational relations, with the various transcendences surpassing his actual Here and Now. The analysis of these transcendences – from those going beyond the limits of the world within his actual reach to those transgressing the paramount reality of everyday life – is a major task of any philosophical anthropology. At the same time, the clarification of the categories of common-sense thinking within everyday life is indispensable for the proper foundation of all the social sciences. As far as symbols in the narrower sense are concerned, the fact that they transcend the realm of the paramount reality tends not to exclude, but rather to encourage the investigations of symbolic functions and forms within the social world by the empirical social sciences in accordance with the rules governing the concept and theory formation of these sciences.[79] The philosophical problem involved, however, was stated by Goethe with unsurpassable clarity:

Das ist die wahre Symbolik, wo das Besondere das Allgemeinere repraesentiert, nicht als Traum und Schatten, sondern als lebendig-augenblickliche Offenbarung des Unerforschlichen.

(True symbolism is where the particular represents the general, not as a dream and a shadow, but as a vivid instantaneous revelation of that which cannot be explored.) [80]*

---

[79] See "Concept and Theory Formation in the Social Sciences."
[80] Johann Wolfgang von Goethe, *Aus Kunst und Altertum*, 1826.
* A comment on this paper by Professor Charles Morris together with a reply by the author appears on pp. 202–203 in the original publication in *Symbols and Society*, Fourteenth Symposium of the Conference on Science, Philosophy and Religion, ed. by L. Bryson, L. Finkelstein, H. Hoagland, and R. M. MacIver, New York and London, 1955. (M.N.)

INDEX

abstract attitude, 262, 271
abstraction, 260, 323, 349
accessibility, 134 following (hereafter abbreviated as "f.")
act, 19 f., 67, 87, 153 f., 214 f.
action, 19 f., 24, 42, 60, 67, 87, 95, 146, 200 f., 209, 214 f., 235, 246
Adler, Max, 165 footnote (hereafter abbreviated as "n")
Allport, Gordon W., 151 n, 157 n, 159 n, 171 n, 177 n
analogical apperception (see appresentation)
"and so forth", 146, 224
anonymity, 134 f., 144, 148, 225, 352
anxiety, 247, 249
aphasia, 264, 271, 275, 286
apperceptual scheme, 299, 327, 355-6
appresentation, 125, 143, 147-8, 166, 196, 293, 294 f., 325, 339, 349, 353
appresentational reference, 313 f., 326, 327, 328, 332, 335, 337, 338, 347 f., 351, 352-3
appresentational relations, 303 f., 309, 356
appresentational scheme, 299, 301, 327, 351, 355-6
Aquinas, St. Thomas, 247 n
Aristotle, 84, 112, 250-1 n, 291
associates, 15 f., 39, 134
association, 295
associative memory, 151
attention, 79, 109, 241, 278
attention à la vie, 212 f., 230, 232, 242, 246, 272, 284

Bayle, 88-9
because-motive, 22, 69 f., 72, 77 n, 95, 218, 235
Becker, Howard, 28 n, 172 n
behaviorism, 6, 51, 54, 58, 168, 209, 223, 313
being-with (*Mitsein*), 186-7
Berdyaev, Nicolas, 153 n

Bergson, Henri, 4, 57, 72, 77 n, 85 f., 91, 92, 165, 173 n, 177, 212 f., 215, 240 n, 264, 268, 269 f., 275, 284, 285, 293, 300 f., 338, 344
biographical situation, 9, 18, 39, 60, 76-7, 83, 94, 96, 293, 312, 317, 322, 348
body, 124, 143, 155, 159, 160 f., 177, 180 f., 191 f., 215, 222, 248, 269, 306, 314, 327
bracketing, 104 f.
Brentano, Franz, 102-3
Broca, 270
Bryson, L., 356 n

Cairns, Dorion, 211 n
Carnap, Rudolf, 168 n
Cassirer, Ernst, 260, 268, 272 f., 275, 286, 289 f., 333
categorial attitude, 277
center of social world, 37, 39
Chinese thought, 334-6
choosing, 84 f.
ciphers, 347
Clayton, Alfred S., 217 n
common-sense constructs, 4 f., 55 f., 58 f., 61 f., 65
communication, 321 f., 325, 347
comprehension, 319 f.
concept formation, 48 f., 356
concrete attitude, 262, 271, 277
conduct, 211
consociates, 15 f., 39, 352
constitution, 111, 115, 127, 165, 184, 239
constitutive phenomenology, 121, 123, 137, 138, 149
constructs of thought objects, 7 f., 34 f.
contemporaries, 15 f., 39, 148, 221, 318
contextual scheme, 299, 328
Cooley, Charles H., 16, 18, 315 n, 354
coupling (see appresentation)
course-of-action patterns, 40, 45, 64

Dahlke, Helmut O., 172 n
Dante, 346
defining the situation, 9 n, 83, 201, 348
deliberation, 77 f., 86
Dempf, Alois, 333 n
de Saussure, Ferdinand, 263
Descartes, 102 f.
determinism, 72, 85 f.
de Waelhens, Alphonse, 180 n, 186 n, 198
Dewey, John, 4, 30, 53, 57, 68, 78, 82, 83, 113, 169, 215, 327
disappointment, 80
Don Quixote, 236 f., 237 n
doubt, 77 f., 94, 100
dreams, 240 f., 292
Driesch, 158
Ducasse, C. J., 288
Duerer, 325, 338, 340
durée, 85 f., 91, 215 f., 222, 231, 239, 243, 252, 272
Durkheim, Émile, 144, 333 n

ego, 79 f., 85 f., 91, 103, 143, 156, 168 n, 278, 279, 313
egological sphere, 149
eidetic approach, 113 f., 132, 140, 281
eidetic reduction, 277, 281
eidos, 114, 277, 280
Eliot, T. S., 346
emotional impulse, 150
empathy, 159, 166, 196, 201, 314
empirical psychology, 157, 175, 179
enclave, 245, 307
epoché, 122, 124, 229, 230, 232, 233, 249
epoché of natural attitude, 229, 233
essence, 113 f., 132, 152
essentially actual experiences, 211, 248
essentially social acts, 158
essential types, 282
Eulenspiegel, 236
existentialism, 182, 260, 275, 313, 338
experimental psychology, 157

"face-to-face" relationship, 16, 55, 220 f., 315, 317, 318, 352, 353
familiarity, 134 f., 178, 226, 281
fancying, 72 f.
Farber, Marvin, 46 n, 101, 103 n, 118 n, 211 n, 237 n, 249 n, 252 n, 294 n, 325 n
fields (*Zentren*), 134
Fink, Eugen, 256, 314 n
formalization, 138, 146
formal logic, 112-3
France, Anatole, 353
Frank, Philipp G., 345

free variation, 277, 281
Freud, 241, 242, 243
fringe, 108, 112, 266, 350
functionalism, 61

Galileo, 333
Geisteswissenschaften, 120
Gelb, 273, 276
Generalized Other, 189
general sociology, 137
general thesis, 135, 136
genesis, 104
geometry, 127-8
Gesamtperson, 141, 161-2 n
Gestalt psychology, 109, 116, 264
Goethe, 346, 356
Goldstein, Kurt, 260 f.
Granet, Marcel, 333 n, 334, 335 n
growing older, 20, 220, 255, 317
Gurwitsch, Aron, 109 n, 169-70 n, 268, 276 f., 283

Hayek, F. A., 15 n, 35 n
Head, Henry, 263, 273
Hegel, 165, 183, 185 f., 198, 337
Heidegger, Martin, 144, 183, 186 f.
Heisenberg, 254 n
Hempel, Carl G., 48 f., 61, 63
Henderson, A. M., 354 n
"Here and Now", 133 f., 293, 307, 312, 328, 343, 356
"Here and There", 41, 76, 125 f., 135, 143, 147, 178, 196, 201 f., 225, 306, 308, 315 f., 323
Hilbert, 346
historicity, 131, 133, 147, 149
Hoagland, H., 356 n
Homans, George C., 354
"*homo-faber*-theory", 151
homunculi, 41, 47, 64, 168, 255
horizon, 46, 59, 79, 108 f., 112, 136, 148, 169, 208, 250, 279, 280, 281, 284, 285, 286, 293, 296, 298, 307, 329, 330
Husserl, Edmund, 4, 8, 20, 33 n, 46, 57 f., 59, 75, 78 f., 80 f., 88, 91, 99 f., 128 f., 140 f., 176, 183 f., 194 f., 215, 224, 236 n, 237 f., 256, 268, 277 f., 284, 293, 294 f., 308, 310, 314, 315, 323, 324, 325, 338, 342
Huyghens, 346

"I" and "Me", 216-7, 221, 253
"I-can-do-it-again", 20-21, 29, 146, 224, 308
idealism, 101, 180 f., 269
idealization, 138, 146, 349
ideal objects, 110 f.

INDEX

ideal types, 50, 61, 138
imagined objects, 114 f.
inauthenticity, 144, 187
indeterminism, 72, 85 f.
indication, 287, 310 f.
indirect communication, 233, 244, 255, 256
inference, 159
in-group, 348, 355
inquiry, 57
inner speech, 264 f., 286
"in-order-to" motive, 21 f., 69 f., 77 n, 91, 94 f., 218, 235
instant, 231, 344
instinctive life, 150
intentionality, 79, 102 f., 106, 132, 143, 195, 241, 252
intentional psychology, 137
interest, 76–77, 83, 136
interpretational scheme, 299, 328, 338 f., 351
intersubjectivity, 10 f., 112, 116, 125 f., 127, 145, 150 f., 156 f., 164, 167 f., 180 f., 257, 292, 294, 311, 312 f., 337, 342, 347 f.
intimacy, 134 f., 148, 225, 353

Jackson, 263, 264, 273
James, William, 4, 14, 55, 57, 67, 107 n, 108, 109, 113, 116, 158 n, 162 n, 169, 172, 177, 207, 216, 229, 237, 253, 294, 310, 329, 340 f., 350
Jaspers, Karl, 331–2, 338, 347

Kant, 57, 110, 152, 153 n, 165, 181
Kaufmann, Felix, 6 n, 36 n, 50, 54, 63, 250 n
Kierkegaard, 231, 232, 244, 344
knowledge at hand, 20, 208
knowledge of acquaintance & knowledge-about, 14, 55, 158, 310
Koehler, Wolfgang, 151, 160
Koffka, 160, 168 n
Kuhn, Helmut, 46 n

Landgrebe, Ludwig, 46 n
Langer, Susanne K., 289 f., 324
language disturbances, 260 f.
leap, 232, 247, 248
Lebenswelt (see Life-world)
Leibniz, 28 n, 72, 77 n, 88 f., 165, 178, 183, 213
Lessing, 331
Levy-Bruhl, Lucien, 142, 160, 333 n
Life-world, 45, 57 f., 120 f., 122 f., 127, 130 f., 133 f., 136 f., 140, 148, 149, 167, 247, 255, 278
likelihood, 33, 81, 91
Litt, Theodor, 99

Locke, 90, 132
logical empiricism, 53
look (*le regard*), 189
looking glass effect, 18
Lynd, Robert S., 13 n

Machlup, Fritz, 46 n, 118 n
MacIver, R. M., 356 n
Malinowski, Bronislaw, 333 n, 336
manifestation, 319–20
manipulatory area, 223, 307, 308, 317, 328, 329
marginal principle, 84
Marie, Pierre, 263, 270
Maritain, 154 n
mark, 287, 308 f., 335
Marx, 165
mathematical universe, 129 f., 332
mathesis universalis, 111, 130
Mauss, Marcel, 333 n
Mead, George H., 18, 19, 54, 116, 154 n, 162 n, 172, 189, 216–7, 223, 224, 225, 291, 307 n
meaning, 210
Merleau-Ponty, Maurice, 9 n, 142, 268, 274 f., 277, 283, 284
Merton, Robert K., 348 n
modalizations of judgment, 79 f., 92
model, 36, 40 f., 42, 45–46, 64 f., 255
Morris, Charles, 288, 291, 356 n
motive, 19 f., 60, 70 f., 249, 308, 311, 318
multiple realities, 207 f., 294, 329, 339 f.
mundane sphere, 104 f., 175, 201, 257

Nagel, Ernest, 48 f., 58, 61, 62, 65
Natanson, Maurice, 116 n
natural attitude, 104 f., 121, 126, 132, 136, 145, 149, 168, 208, 218, 222, 223, 227, 231, 246, 254, 255, 256, 306
naturalism, 53, 65, 131
nature, 156, 157, 329, 330, 331
negative actions, 54, 67–68
negative weight, 88 f., 93
neutrality-modification, 145
Newton, 333
noema, 107 f., 184
noesis, 107 f.
nonessential types, 283, 285
null point, 127, 133 f., 137, 147, 222, 224, 248, 306 f., 315, 334

objectivism, 131
observer, 26 f., 36 f., 95, 137, 246
occasional expression, 154
"of-course" statements, 13
open possibilities, 79 f., 81 f., 83, 87, 147

operationalism, 113
originary experience, 123
Ortega y Gasset, 142 f.
"Other", 18, 19, 25, 31 f., 55, 60, 117, 121, 123, 125 f., 133 f., 135, 141, 147, 156, 158 f., 160, 166 f., 170 f., 180 f., 194 f., 218 f., 244, 254, 258, 266, 312, 313 f., 316 f., 320, 326 f., 328, 353

pairing (see appresentation)
paradoxes, 256 f.
paramount reality, 226 f., 231, 232 n, 234, 259, 294, 322, 341 f., 356
paraphasia, 271, 286
Pareto, Vilfredo, 28 n
Parsons, Talcott, 28 n, 138 n, 313 n, 351 n
Péguy, Charles, 304
performance, 211 f., 246
person, 141, 152 f.
phantasying, 20, 30, 68, 71, 73, 85, 87, 234 f., 238 f., 252, 292, 296
phenomenological method, 101, 122
phenomenological philosophy, 115 f., 117, 120
phenomenological psychology, 113, 115 f., 117, 175, 179
phenomenological reduction, 104 f., 114, 121 f., 132, 139, 142, 167, 249 n
phenomenologist, 256 f.
phenomenology, 66, 99 f., 113, 118 f., 141, 195, 229, 277, 313
phenomenon, 106 f.
philosophical anthropology, 141, 149, 293, 332, 356
Piaget, 265
Plato, 84, 110, 113
positive weight, 88 f., 93
positivism, 52, 313
postulate of adequacy, 44
postulate of logical consistency, 43, 64
postulate of subjective interpretation, 43, 62
practicability, 74 f.
practical intelligence, 151
pragmatism, 113, 213 n, 271
predecessors, 15 f., 39, 134, 148, 221, 318
pre-predicative experience, 75, 79, 92, 112, 148, 274, 276, 279, 286, 323
principle of continuity, 65
problematic possibilities, 79 f., 81 f., 83, 85, 147
procedural rules, 6
project, 19 f., 21, 30, 42, 60, 67 f., 84 f., 93, 146, 211, 235, 249, 306

projecting, 72 f., 84, 87, 145
protention, 109, 172, 285
protocol propositions, 54
provinces of meaning, 231 f., 233, 257 f., 328, 329, 340 f., 345 f.
psychoanalysis, 241 f.
psychologism, 124
psycho-physical parallelism, 162–3
Pythagorean theorem, 111

rational action, 27 f., 29, 33, 44 f., 83, 94, 136
realism, 101, 180 f., 269
reciprocity of motives, 23
reciprocity of perspectives, 11 f., 29, 61, 147, 315 f.
recollection, 109
reduced sphere, 104 f., 135, 149
referential scheme, 299, 339, 351, 355–6
reflexes, 210 f.
relativism, 124, 149
relevance, 9, 39, 63, 69, 95, 136, 149, 202, 227 f., 247, 249, 283 f., 317, 322, 323, 348, 349, 351, 355
representation, 355
resistance, 209, 306
retention, 109, 172, 285
Runes, Dagobert D., 101 n
Russell, Bertrand, 168

Sachs, Curt, 321 n
Santayana, George, 341–2
Sartre, Jean-Paul, 169 n, 180 f.
Scheler, Max, 13 n, 99, 141 f., 150 f., 265, 348
Schutz, Alfred, 14 n, 16 n, 17 n, 107 n, 139 n, 175 n, 202 n, 210 n, 237 n, 255 n, 314 n, 356 n
scientific constructs, 5 f., 62 f.
scientific situation, 36 n, 38, 63, 96, 137, 246, 250, 344
scientific theory, 245 f.
sedimentation, 77, 128, 136, 242, 275
self, 154 f., 161, 171, 241
self-typification, 60, 148
semantics, 110
sensory observation, 54
Shils, Edward A., 313 n, 351 n
shock, 231, 343 f.
signs, 110, 148, 287 f., 301 f., 311, 313 f., 320–1
Simmel, Georg, 18, 41, 317
situation, 201, 330
Smith, Robertson, 334
Snell, Bruno, 320–1, 333 n, 336
social distribution of knowledge, 11, 14 f., 61, 350

INDEX

sociality, 230, 256, 259
socialization, 61
social origin of knowledge, 11, 13 f., 61
social reality, 53, 59
social role, 149, 216, 248, 317, 351
sociology of knowledge, 13 n, 39 n, 149, 156 n
solipsism, 121, 124, 158, 165, 168, 185, 197, 199, 203
Sophists, 84
spatialized time, 85 f.
specious present, 173, 284
Spiegelberg, Herbert, 229 n
Spinoza, 76
Stein, Edith, 140
Stern, William, 154 n, 160
stock of knowledge, 20–21, 38 f., 42, 72, 136, 146, 226, 228, 306
Stonier, A., & Bode, K., 16 n
strangeness, 134 f., 178, 225
subjective interpretation of meaning, 24–25, 34 f., 60, 138, 145, 149, 354
successors, 15, 39, 134, 148, 221, 318
Sumner, William G., 13 n, 348
symbolic appresentation, 325, 332 f., 337 f., 347 f., 352 f., 355
symbols, 110, 148, 267, 286, 287 f., 301 f., 318, 331 f., 335, 343, 354 f.
synthesis, 107

"taken for granted", 25, 37, 74 f., 94, 313, 326, 330, 348
theory formation, 51 f., 65, 356
Thomas theorem, 348
Thomas, W. I., 9 n, 54, 348
time, 68–69, 85, 172 f., 203, 214 f., 219, 230, 239, 243, 252 f., 318, 324
Toynbee, Arnold J., 333 n
transcendence, 329 f., 337 f., 353, 355
transcendental ego, 115, 166, 167, 257
transcendental intersubjectivity, 126, 149, 195 f.
transcendental phenomenology, 120 f., 122, 139, 149, 165, 175, 257
transcendental psychology, 157
transcendental reduction, 105 f., 165

transcendental sphere, 124 f., 131, 257
transcendental subjectivity, 120, 122 f., 166, 172, 184, 195 f., 197
"tuning-in" relationship, 202
types, 148, 255
typification, 7, 59 f., 73 f., 260, 279, 281 f., 283 f., 285, 323, 348, 349, 350, 352
typology, 138, 233

understanding (see *Verstehen*)
unity of sciences, 65–66

Verstehen, 56 f., 62 f., 138
Vigotsky, 265
vivid present, 174, 216, 219, 252
Voegelin, Eric, 333 n, 336–7, 355
volition, 89 f.
Volkart, E. K., 348 n
voluntative fiat, 67, 70, 88, 91, 235
von Humboldt, Wilhelm, 264, 346
von Mises, Ludwig, 35 n
von Ranke, 131

Wahl, Jean, 180 n
Walther, Gerda, 140
Weber, Max, 13 n, 24–25, 28 n, 31, 50, 57, 62 f., 138, 145, 149, 201 n, 354
Weierstrass, 100
We-relationship, 25, 32, 95, 175, 198, 240, 253, 316, 318, 352, 353
Wesensschau, 101, 113 f.
Weyl, Hermann, 345–6
Whitehead, Alfred N., 3, 4, 17, 35, 57, 288, 290, 316, 333, 345
wide-awakeness, 213
Wild, John, 288, 290, 309
Williams, Richard H., 118 n
Woodworth, R. S., 152 n
working, 212, 226 f., 233, 242, 258
world, 124, 127, 209
world within reach, 306 f., 326 f., 352–3

zero point (see null point)

GOVERNORS STATE UNIVERSITY LIBRARY

3 1611 00095 8618

Not Weeded
BCL 3
1-05 BHS

DATE DUE

114406